INTERNATIONAL UNIFORM COMMERCIAL LAW

To Geneviève, Marc-Antoine, Vincent, Félix, and Andréanne

International Uniform Commercial Law
Toward a Progressive Consciousness

LOUIS MARQUIS
University of Sherbrooke, Québec, Canada

ASHGATE

Published by
Ashgate Publishing Limited
Gower House
Croft Road
Aldershot
Hampshire GU11 3HR
England

Ashgate Publishing Company
Suite 420
101 Cherry Street
Burlington, VT 05401-4405
USA

Ashgate website: http://www.ashgate.com

British Library Cataloguing in Publication Data
Marquis, Louis
   International uniform commercial law : toward a progressive
   consciousness. - (Applied legal philosophy)
   1.Commercial law 2.International business enterprises - Law
   and legislation 3.Foreign trade regulation 4.Law -
   International unification
   I.Title
   343'.087

Library of Congress Cataloging-in-Publication Data
Marquis, Louis.
 International uniform commercial law : toward a progressive consciousness / by Louis
Marquis.
    p. cm. -- (Applied legal philosophy)
 Includes bibliographical references and index.
 ISBN 0-7546-2396-3
 1. Commercial law--Codification. 2. Law--International unification. I. Title. II. Series.

  K1005.M377 2005
  346.07--dc22

2005005531

ISBN 0 7546 2396 3

Printed and bound in Great Britain by MPG Books Ltd, Bodmin, Cornwall.

Contents

PART II: CONSERVATIVE CONSCIOUSNESS: CRITIQUE

PART III: THE REFORMULATION OF UNIFORM LAW: TOWARD A PROGRESSIVE CONSCIOUSNESS

PART IV: APPLICATIONS

Series Preface

The principal objective of this series is to encourage the publication of books which adopt a theoretical approach to the study of particular areas or aspects of law, or deal with general theories of law in a way which is directed at issues of practical, moral and political concern in specific legal contexts. The general approach is both analytical and critical and relates to the socio-political background of law reform issues.

The series includes studies of all the main areas of law, presented in a manner which relates to the concerns of specialist legal academics and practitioners. Each book makes an original contribution to an area of legal study while being comprehensible to those engaged in a wide variety of disciplines. Their legal content is principally Anglo-American, but a wide-ranging comparative approach is encouraged and authors are drawn from a variety of jurisdictions.

Tom D. Campbell
Series Editor
Centre for Applied Philosophy and Public Ethics,
Charles Sturt University, Canberra

Preamble

As a child, I was troubled by the mysteriousness of things, beginning with my own presence in the world. True, the answers I was given by family and friends, as well as those I found on my own, helped guide and reassure me. But this effect was never more than transitory: fresh questions arose with each new day. Little by little, I learned that many things are either impossible or useless to explain – for example, what we call tastes. Other things, on the other hand, seemed already to have been fully if not very deeply explained, as if by magic. Often, these things were the domain of people the encyclopedias designated as erudite, the experts. As my knowledge about my own tastes and those of others increased, and with the help of the teaching of experts, I acquired a maturity that tended to dissipate the mysteriousness of things. Paradoxically, though, it became more and more important to me to test the depths of this mystery. At the same time, the frontier between tastes and intellectual knowledge sometimes blurred. Would the questions never end?

In hindsight, I realize the troubling quality of this constant confrontation with the inexplicable was a small price to pay for what I learned from it. In fact, it catalysed everything that fascinated me most, and I now see that the question I took so much pleasure in asking in my youth is one I still ask today. 'Why are things this way?' still rings in my mind when I wonder about the best way to understand and change some aspect of the world we live in. And asking it is just as satisfying as ever. 'Why are things this way?' As P. Amselek writes, 'To ask this question is to be conscious of the arbitrariness of the world, its contingency; it is to realize that it might have been or could be otherwise and experience how singular it is.'[1]

Many things could explain how I came to choose international commercial uniform law[2] as the focal point of the reflection conducted in this book. They include affinities, tastes, opinions and certain intellectual considerations. One factor seems to me fundamental: the flourishing legal scholarship that gives the field of uniform law confidence and breadth currently makes of it an obligatory

---

1   P. Amselek, 'L'étonnement devant le droit' (1964) 13 Archives de philosophie du droit 163 at 165-166.
2   Hereafter, 'uniform law'.

reference point. Uniform law is like the realization of a global dream.[3] To cite just one example, some people view the *Vienna Convention on Contracts for the International Sale of Goods*[4] as the cornerstone for the creation of an international private law.[5] Others invoke Thomas Kuhn's concept of paradigm shift[6] and interpret the Vienna Convention as a sign of the birth of a new paradigm for international commercial transactions.[7] It has been described as the germ of a future amalgamation of all sales laws[8] and said to constitute remarkable progress.[9] The defenders of unification view the Vienna Convention as unification's most fully worked out form. It is not merely a model law that can serve to provide varying degrees of inspiration; nor is it a simple unification of the rules of conflict of laws. Rather, it is an international convention that features a full set of substantive provisions regarding sale.

Faced with a strike force of this intensity, I wished to undertake the intellectual act that will reintroduce to uniform law the mystery it has lost and has a right to, like all other things in life. And so I came to ask myself, 'Why is there uniform international commercial law rather than nothing?' This fundamental metaphysical question[10] underlies my entire reflection in this book. It expresses the intrinsic but unacknowledged strangeness of uniform law and the corresponding posture of astonishment that should be adopted before it.

---

3 See, for example, the authors' preamble in P. A. Crépeau & É. M. Charpentier, *The UNIDROIT Principles and the Civil Code of Québec: Shared Values?* (Toronto: Carswell, 1998), which declares, 'The International Institute for the Unification of Private Law (known as UNIDROIT) strives to make the dream of a *jus commune* a reality.' For a more general commentary on the idea of the dream, see R. J. Barnet & J. Cavanaugh, *Global Dreams: Imperial Corporations of the New World Order* (New York: Simon and Schuster, 1995).

4 April 11, 1980, UN Doc. A/CONF.97/18, Annex I (1980). Hereafter, 'Vienna Convention' or 'CISG'.

5 J. A. Spanogle, 'The Arrival of International Private Law' (1991) 25 Geo. Wash. J. Int'l L. & Econ. 447.

6 (Chicago: Univ. of Chicago Press, 1962).

7 K. C. Randall & J. E. Norris, 'A New Paradigm for International Business Transactions' (1993) 71 Wash. U. L. Q. 599.

8 A. Kassis, *Le nouveau droit européen des contrats internationaux* (Paris: L.G.D.J., 1993) at 559ff.

9 V. Heuzé, *La vente internationale de marchandises. Droit uniforme* (Paris: GLN Joly, 1992) at 367.

10 M. Heidegger frames the fundamental metaphysical question as 'Why are there beings rather than nothing?' (*Qu'est-ce que la métaphysique?* Paris: Gallimard, 1951, at 44.)

Introduction

In a book called *Un café pour Socrate*, M. Sautet asks the question, 'What are we aiming for?' and answers as follows:

> The fact that pessimists are wrong does not prove that optimists are right. To describe the future of our civilization as a return to barbarity could be nonsense. However, that does not at all justify the undisputed reign of market laws over the destiny of humanity.[1]

Sautet thus summarizes the contradictory feelings of disenchantment, disillusion, unconsciousness and uneasiness on the one hand and enchantment, charm, continuity and progress on the other hand that are prompted by the era we live in.[2] For Sautet, knowing what we are aiming at requires that we 'suspend judgement for an instant'[3] while we review what we have been and where we are. In short, it requires that we take the time to conduct an in-depth examination and reconsideration of our epistemology and our values. In this regard, he is in harmony with the movement that seeks to combine acknowledgement of the end of certainty with a renewed search for the right and the good and to face the challenge of making that combination work for the best.[4] This appeal for a return by thought upon itself is echoed in the juridical field constituted by the junction of law and development, the field that provides the backdrop to the present reflection. Currently, the law and development movement is responding to a foundational problematic that I would illustrate with this question: 'What, if anything, does law

---

1   (Paris: Robert Laffont, 1995) at 15.
2   See, for example, R. Aron, *Les désillusions du progrès: essai sur la dialectique de la modernité* (Paris: Calmann-Lévy, 1969); P. Collin & O. Mongin, *Un monde désenchanté? Débat avec Marcel Gauchet sur le 'Désenchantement du monde'* (Paris: Éditions du Cerf, 1998); A. Seminatore, 'De la crise des fondements au choc des civilisations' (1995) 31 Études internationales 32. For an analysis focused on the American situation, see H. Johnson, 'America and the Crisis of Change' (1996) 39 Saint Louis University Law Journal 1143.
3   Sautet, *supra*, note 1; at 15.
4   See, for example, I. Wallerstein, 'Social Sciences and the Quest for a Just Society' (1997) 102 American Journal of Sociology 1241; C. Taylor, *Sources of the Self: The Making of the Modern Identity* (Cambridge: Harvard University Press, 1989); J. Rawls, *A Theory of Justice* (Cambridge: Harvard University Press, 1971); B. de Sousa Santos, *Toward a New Common Sense: Law, Science and Politics in the Paradigmatic Transition* (New York: Routledge, 1995).

have to say to economic, sociocultural, and political development, and vice versa?'[5]

The orthodox answer to this fundamental question is based on four ideas. First, the conception of law that underlies it derives from *positivism.* This means it presumes that law must be based on real and observable facts and that any legal theoretical construct must be established by induction from ascertained facts that are empirically confirmed. More specifically, positivism assumes the jurist must observe the facts of the law, that is, its formally acknowledged sources and institutions (governments, courts, laws, regulations and so on) in order to frame reasoning that will correctly account for legal reality. Then, the orthodox answer views the law so conceived as intrinsically possessing the constituents likely to ensure development. In other words, the relationship of law to development is *unilinear,* a view that understands the law as a necessity and attribute to it a direct, if not exclusive, role in every prospect for development. Third, the notion of the *transplantation* of law unifies these statements. It takes for granted that it is possible to identify and conceptualize the juridical factors that explain a society's progress and, with certain adjustments, export them to another society. Fourth and last, orthodoxy relates both the appropriateness and the usefulness of law to its capacity to influence development effectively. It thus seeks to establish a *cause-and-effect relationship*, marked by certainty and predictability, between law and development. Overall, these precepts promote universalist perspectives on the relationship between law and development. This tendency is inherent in the approach adopted from these perspectives, one that consists of seeking to grasp reality objectively, rationalize it according to abstract legal categories, and act on it through general commandments and principles.

Another, emergent, answer to this problematic proposes both a vision and an approach that are essentially different from those underlying the orthodox response. In this emergent answer, the nature and the meaning of law are not linked to observation of facts that are foreign to thought and deemed to constitute a neutral, objective, consistent reference point. Rather, they derive from an *internal* reality, a vision Amselek designates with the phrase 'the law in minds'[6] that extends legal frontiers beyond the positive framework constituted by the State and its legislative and regulatory actions. What the law is comes to be bound up with a given context of human life, as comprised of attitudes, experiences, and hopes. As well, this internal reality turns law into a permeable and permeating entity:[7] juridical facts navigate among other kinds of facts (economical, political and so on), thereby creating reciprocal zones of contact and influence whose manifestations and results are manifold and often indeterminate. The emergent

---

5   M. O. Chibundu, 'Law in Development: On Tapping, Gourding and Serving Palm-Wine' (1997) 29 Case W. Res. J. Int'l L. 167 at 213.

6   P. Amselek, 'Le droit dans les esprits', in P. Amselek & C. Grzegorczyk, eds., *Controverses autour de l'ontologie du droit* (Paris, P.U.F., 1989) at 46.

7   J. G. Belley, *Le droit soluble: contributions québécoises à l'étude de l'internormativité* (Paris: L.G.D.J., 1996).

answer thus tackles the law-development equation from the perspective of *complexity*. Further, it replaces the idea of transplantation with the idea of *interaction*. In so doing, it manifests a twofold concern: first, to understand the way one or several aspects of the law-development relationship are diffused and transformed from one human site to another, and second, to grasp what a given human site has been able to do (in terms of innovation, consolidation and so on) with a given aspect. Finally, these concerns in turn are allied to an approach that views the law-development relationship as a web that can be disentangled through *interpretation*.[8] Hence, whereas the orthodox response has been concerned with establishing sure links with predictable repercussions, the emergent answer demonstrates willingness to emphasize the web of significations[9] linking law and development.

In my opinion the emergent answer strikes out in new directions that may help us better understand *what we are aiming for*. Put differently, 'It is these considerations [those of the emergent answer] that ought to dictate the nature and direction of future inquiries into law and development.'[10] How, then, are we to act upon this by using uniform law? The sense of transformation found at the heart of the shift that Sautet is associated with provides more than one right answer to this question. As I. Wallerstein writes, 'It must be recognized that our truths are not universal truths and if there exist universal truths they are complex, contradictory and plural.'[11] For the purposes of the present reflection, I would submit one of these right answers resides in the pursuit of two objectives. The first objective consists of putting forward and justifying the constituents of a progressive consciousness for uniform law. The premise underlying this objective is that the call to better know what we are aiming at, as manifested in the emergent answer to the problematic of law and development, constitutes a significant index of the present-day shift from modernity to postmodernity. As A. Huyssen writes:

> What appears on one level as the latest fad, advertising pitch and hollow spectacle is part of a slowly emerging cultural transformation in Western societies, a change in sensibility for which the term postmodern is actually, at least for now, wholly adequate. The nature and depth of that transformation is debatable, but transformation it is.[12]

While agreeing with Huyssen in essence, I prefer not to use the word 'postmodern' for the transformation that is under way. In my view, to speak of

---

8   D. E. Apter, *Rethinking Development: Modernization, Dependency, and Post Modern Politics* (New York: Sage, 1987).

9   C. Geertz, *Local Knowledge* (New York: Basic Books, 1983); also, *The Interpretation of Cultures* (New York: Basic Books, 1973).

10   Chibundu, *supra*, note 5; at 228.

11   I. Wallerstein, 'Social Science and Contemporary Society' (1996) 11 International Sociology 7 at 24.

12   A. Huyssen, 'Mapping the Postmodern' (1984) 33 New German Critique 5 at 8. See also N. Rouland, 'Les fondements anthropologiques des droits de l'Homme' (1994) 25 R.G.D. 5 at 7ff.

*post*modernity implies a kind of break between modernity and a new age. I believe that, though it may appear desirable for something to succeed modernity, we must privilege a vision that will allow us to keep the soundest components of the legacy of the past. I would propose this vision be called a second modernity. Although the vision of a second modernity would remain open to critiques of modernity that include those articulated by postmodernism, I conceive of it as a vision connected with the past and strongly committed to both a better present and a better future.

In a second modernity of this kind, 'it is no longer more facts that we need, it is more thought.'[13] Therefore, to work on conceiving a type of reasoning – a consciousness – that lends a progressive direction to uniform law does not consist of pure evasion or artifice. Rather, it is in the first instance a way to make uniform law congruent with an ever evolving, urgently sought after reality, that of a second modernity. As I intend to show, the present consciousness associated with uniform law does not match this reality,[14] rendering its ability 'to guide self-directed social interaction'[15] precarious. Progressive consciousness would thus be a way to make uniform law a teleological juridical phenomenon – one tending toward a goal, as opposed to a legal metaphenomenon[16] – capable of inspiring as many practical applications as necessary. This brings us to the second objective, that of developing two such applications. One will consist of an interpretive schema of uniform law and the other of a *uniformist* reading of the Quebec world.[17]

In a famous address, J. P. Sartre wrote of the writer's responsibility.[18] One must recognize that words contain attitudes and gazes; they convey ideas, 'universes of knowledge, consciousness, and culture' that run through things and beings.[19] The very fact of living begins with, or depends on, the words we assemble: 'In speaking, I know that I effect change. It is not possible for me to speak if it is not to effect change, unless I speak to say nothing; but to utter is to effect change and to be conscious that one effects change.'[20] From this perspective, to work on the design of a progressive consciousness for uniform law is an interested act which yields concrete achievements. To this end, appropriate methodology must be used.

---

13 The idea of second modernity is borrowed from J.-G. Belley, 'Une justice de la seconde modernité' (2000) 46 McGill L. J. 317; T. Todorov, *Critique de la critique: un roman d'apprentissage* (Paris: Seuil, 1984) at 15.

14 See Part I, below.

15 G. Postema, 'Implicit Law' (1994) 13 Law & Phil. 361 at 374.

16 R. A. Samek, *The Meta Phenomenon* (New York: The Philosophical Library, 1981) at 4 and 206: 'The meta-phenomenon is the human propensity to displace "primary" with "secondary" concerns, that is, concerns about ends with concerns about means. . . . The legal system is a meta system *par excellence*. In separating social problems from the human condition, and converting them into legal issues, they serve the cause of the meta-system.'

17 See Chapter 9, below.

18 J. P. Sartre, *La responsabilité de l'écrivain* (Paris: Verdier, 1998).

19 *Ibid.* at 30.

20 *Ibid.* at 32.

Methodology

My method of pursuing my two objectives consists of three distinct processes.

The first, related more specifically to the first objective, is inspired by the approach used by M. Koskenniemi in *From Apology to Utopia: The Structure of International Argument.*[21] Koskenniemi writes that he wishes to conduct 'an exposition and discussion of the assumptions which control modern discourse about international law,'[22] assumptions that derive from liberal political theory. As he writes, 'it is neither useful nor ultimately possible to work with international law in abstraction from descriptive theories about the . . . character of social life among States and on the desirable forms of such life.'[23] Koskenniemi employs a method he summarizes thus:

> The approach followed here is one of 'regressive analysis'. I shall attempt to investigate discourse about international law by arguing back to the existence of certain conditions without which this discourse could not possess the kind of self-evidence for professional lawyers which it has. In other words, I shall argue, as it were, 'backwards' from explicit arguments to their 'deep-structure', the assumptions within which the problems which modern lawyers face, either in theory or in doctrine, are constituted.[24]

According to Koskenniemi, then, it is important to unravel the explicit arguments in order to access deep structure – the assumptions – , since these determine '*the conditions of what can acceptably be said* within [the arguments], or what it is possible to think or believe [within them].'[25] This operation is combined with critical insight, because, in arriving at the essential considerations 'which control the production of particular agreements within discourse,'[26] it becomes possible to better understand why these arguments produce a given result. Similarly, 'it opens up a possibility for alternative descriptive – and simultaneously normative – characterizations of the world'[27] we live in and would like to live in. If they do not act this way, jurists will be condemned to live 'with the prevalent routine of interpretative intuitionism'[28] and thus experience difficulty 'in integrating their descriptive and normative commitments into analytical studies about the content of the law.'[29] Consequently, the process of analysis as a whole consists of a three-part sequence: unravelling (regressive analysis), critique, reformulation.

---

21 (Helsinki: Lakimiesliiton Kustannus, 1989).
22 *Ibid.* at xvi.
23 *Ibid.* at xiii.
24 *Ibid.* at xvii.
25 *Ibid.* at xxi–xxii.
26 *Ibid.* at xxii.
27 *Ibid.* at xxiii.
28 *Ibid.* at xxiv.
29 *Ibid.* at xiii.

In putting forward the constituents of a progressive consciousness, I shall adapt and condense this threefold process as follows:

- I will examine uniform law as discourse, that is, as a web incorporating various means of expression and persuasion.
- These means will be represented by arguments or concepts that, if viewed in perspective, form the surface or primary level of uniform law.
- The meaning of these arguments is bound up with a background picture of uniform law consisting of principles of thought – ways of seeing things and encompassing reality – and a normative content – values – that permit one to grasp this reality. I will be interested in the philosophical turn taken by these principles of thought and these values.
- The background of uniform law forms a whole that cannot be divided up and apportioned among various arguments in an exclusive and definitive way. This implies that the meaning of a given argument is bound up with, or depends on, that found in the other, coexisting, arguments; that it is not predetermined nor definitively granted; and that it is possible to use different arguments to arrive at the same result.[30]

Arriving at the background of uniform law through regressive analysis or unravelling will take up Part I of this reflection. It will uncover the kind of consciousness that dominates uniform law at the present time, a consciousness I will call conservative. On completion of this stage, Part II, working with the premise of a shift to a second modernity, will proceed to a critique of conservative consciousness. This will pave the way for the stage called reformulation, to be conducted in Part III, which will put forward a progressive consciousness for uniform law. The first three parts will not take the form of clause-by-clause analysis of the various sources of uniform law. Rather, they will take the form of a philosophical, conceptual and doctrinal discussion centred on various arguments. This discussion is likely to appear very distant from the usual mode of analysis of uniform law; it is likely many scholars and jurists would disapprove of it. We should not be troubled by this. For now, I wish to stress only that the method is strictly and rigorously consistent with Koskenniemi's approach. Indeed, to adopt a method such as clause-by-clause analysis would amount to misapprehending Koskenniemi's approach. It is my belief that we must follow this unorthodox course in order to address what appear to be broader issues surrounding the efforts to unify international commercial law. One of the most representative of these broader issues is globalization, a topic that is the site of lively debate about what awaits our world in the near and distant future and that, among other currents of thought and action, contributes to the climate of ambivalence described by Sautet. A notion commonly associated with the issues of globalization is that megaforces are giving birth to systems and frames of reference of unparalleled magnitude, one

---

30   J. C. Smith, 'Action Theory and Legal Reasoning' in K. Cooper-Stephensen & Elaine Gibson, eds., *Tort Theory* (North York: Captus U. P., 1993) at 56.

of those being, in fact, uniform law. This very link renders uniform law particularly well suited to the kind of fundamental analysis I propose to conduct. Further, as I mean to show, Koskenniemi's approach productively combines reflection (as exemplified in my Parts I to III) and application (Part IV).

The second process will consist of establishing a distinction, through the threefold process of unravelling, critique, and reformulation, between the *context of discovery* and the *context of justification* of the consciousness of uniform law. These two expressions were coined by the philosopher of science H. Reichenbach, who sought to distinguish between the description of the origin or genesis of an idea, proposition, or argument (the context of discovery) and the proof or demonstration of this argument (the context of justification):

> The act of discovery escapes logical analysis; there are no logical rules that could be applied to the construction of a 'discovery machine' that would assume the creative function of genius. But it is not the logician's task to explain scientific discoveries; all the logician can do is analyse the relation between the facts as given and a theory that is presented to her or him that claims to explain this relation. In other words, logic is not concerned with the context of discovery.[31]

For Reichenbach, the philosophical analysis of science and scientific theories themselves belong to the context of justification. The factors that explain why scientists have favoured certain approaches to the detriment of others, and how they have come to create a given theory, would belong to the realms of psychology and history and thus to the context of discovery. This distinction corresponds to a particular conception of science, in which the type of truth sought takes the form of universal spatio-temporal laws constituted by the observation of facts presumed to be neutral and to reside outside human thought. For its supporters, it has the advantage of giving the philosophy of science a transcendental vision, that is, one in which the justifications for an argument command universal assent.[32]

I propose to use the distinction in a different way, adapted to the discursive perspective on uniform law that I advocate throughout the reflection presented in this book. Both the context of discovery and the context of justification will be assimilated to deliberative instances allowing us to weigh the pros and cons of arguments that reflect different economic, cultural, political, and moral interests and convictions. Ideally, in this type of process the encounter among arguments should hone their precision, coherence, and reflexive character.[33] The difference between the two contexts, then, does not lie in the way the arguments are undertaken. It is found rather in the degree of significance of the motivations and criteria invoked to justify a given orientation, decision, or action. Thus only those

---

31 H. Reichenbach, *L'avènement de la philosophie scientifique* (Paris: Flammarion, 1955) at 199. See also, by the same author, *Experience and Prediction* (Chicago: The University of Chicago Press, 1938) at 6-7.

32 R. Nadeau, 'La philosophie des sciences après Kuhn' (1994) 21 Philosophiques 159.

33 P. Gérard, *Droit et démocratie. Réflexions sur la légitimité du droit dans la société démocratique* (Brussels: Facultés universitaires Saint-Louis, 1995).

arguments that play a significant or decisive role in the realm of the consciousness of uniform law will be part of the context of justification; all other arguments will be assigned to the context of discovery.

Finally, the third process will aim to view the consciousnesses – conservative as well as progressive – of uniform law as a kind of ideal type. This is a concept developed by M. Weber: for purposes of research, the ideal type emerges from an assemblage of characteristic, typical, or deliberately attributed traits of a given phenomenon, situation, or doctrine.[34] This permits the ideal type, as a structure of thought, to display a 'conceptual purity [that] cannot be found in reality.'[35] Thus constituted, it becomes a measuring device that facilitates the determination of the singularity of the object under study by indicating up to what point, in each particular case, reality diverges from what is perceived from the angle of a homogeneous and unreal mental image. It goes without saying that in the present case the analysis of the consciousness of uniform law will be as precise, detailed and clear as possible. Nevertheless, in certain ways, this consciousness cannot but be somewhat unreal, approximate, tentative, or transitory, in part by virtue of the attention I will pay to certain aspects that appear to me to be dominant, but also because of my own emphasis and approach in presenting any given argument. These will naturally confer a relative character on my presentation of the consciousness of uniform law, a relativity reinforced by the Weberian perspective according to which conceptual tools, however necessary, are continually rendered obsolete by a reality that is itself in motion.

The ideal type also serves as an instrument of applied research[36] through the hypothesis and statements it helps formulate, as well as the ideas and ideals it contains and puts forward. Here its value is determined uniquely by its efficiency and its ability to encourage various uses. And it is at this level that the two applications I will develop in Part IV – the interpretive schema of uniform law and the uniformist reading of the Quebec world – will be formulated.

Conceptualization

In general terms, uniform law refers to any intelligible set of rules intended to govern one or more aspects of commercial life. It is distinguished from national legal systems mainly by virtue of its geographic scope: by its very nature, it applies to transactions whose implementation reaches beyond the borders of a single state. In the present study, I will refer more specifically to three versions of uniform law.

---

34 M. Weber, *Basic Concepts in Sociology*, trans. H. Secher (London: Owen, 1968).
35 C. G. Hampel, *Aspects of Scientific Explanation* (New York: Free Press, 1965) at 165.
36 By analogy, see R. H. Fallon, 'The Rule of Law as a Concept in Constitutional Discourse' (1997) 97 Colum. L. Rev. 1.

The first is designated by the name *lex mercatoria*.[37] It postulates the existence of transnational rules made up of usages and principles which would constitute a true juridical order specific to the operators of international commerce. The second version of uniform law is the result of a multi-state codification of a single and unique international commercial law. This codification is destined to put an end to the phenomenon of diversity in national juridical regimes. The Vienna Convention, which contains a set of substantive provisions in the matter of the sale of goods, constitutes one of its fullest expressions. For our present purposes, this convention will embody most aspects of the second version, which I will designate State law. The third version, which I will call intermediate law, will be represented principally by the *UNIDROIT Principles of International Commercial Contracts*.[38] In the opinion of C. Kessedjan, these principles are closer to an intellectual study than to the work proper to an intergovernmental organization.[39] They serve many purposes, such as providing the contractual juridical framework for the parties, forming a juridical reference for means of interpretation in general, and acting as a model for national and international legislators.[40]

To what extent are these three versions really law? If they are not law, when can they become so? To what extent are my designations for them appropriate? To what extent is each designation distinct from the others, hermetic? This type of questioning occurs often in the juridical literature that deals with uniform law, notably so when *lex mercatoria* confronts State law. Some, like B. Goldman, argue in favour of *lex mercatoria*,[41] while A. Kassis typifies the opposition to it, maintaining that any contract must necessarily be subject to State law.[42] More specifically, criticism of *lex mercatoria* takes three forms: theoretical, ideological and practical.

The theoretical critique denies that *lex mercatoria* could constitute a real legal order equivalent to that of State legal orders. The dispersed norms covered by the

---

37 The article often considered as the foundation of the movement is B. Goldman, 'Frontières du droit et lex mercatoria' (1964) 9 Arch. de philosophie du droit 177. For a recent analysis, see F. de Ly, *International Business Law and Lex Mercatoria* (North Holland: Elsevier Science, 1992).

38 Rome, UNIDROIT, 1994. Hereafter, 'Principles'. A new edition was approved in April 2004. M. J. Bonell, 'UNIDROIT Principles 2004' (2004) Uniform L. R. 5. According to Bonell, the new edition was conceived primarily as an enlargement rather than a revision. In this book, I rely on the 1994 edition, more relevant to my analysis.

39 C. Kessedjan, 'Un exercice de rénovation des sources du droit des contrats du commerce international : les Principes proposés par l'Unidroit' (1995) 84 Rev. crit. dr. internat. privé 641.

40 See *supra*, note 38; the Preamble to the Principles.

41 B. Goldman, 'La lex mercatoria dans les contrats et l'arbitrage internationaux' (1979) 106 J.D.I. 747; E. Gaillard, 'Trente ans de lex mercatoria' 122 (1995) J.D.I. 625.

42 A. Kassis, *Théorie générale des usages du commerce* (Paris: L.G.D.J., 1984); see also G. Delaume, 'Comparative Analysis as a Basis of Law in State Contracts: The Myth of *Lex Mercatoria*' (1989) 63 Tul. L. R. 575. For a balanced account, see J. Béguin, ' Le développement de la *lex mercatoria* menace-t-il l'ordre juridique international' (1985) 30 McGill L. J. 478.

expression *lex mercatoria* do not present a sufficiently organized character to meet the specifications for a legal order identified by the Italian jurist S. Romano.[43] At this point, ideological critique takes over from theory to question the bias of *lex mercatoria*,[44] which is presented as benefiting only stronger parties and, especially in North-South relations, developed countries. In other words, according to this analysis, *lex mercatoria* essentially constitutes a doctrine of *laissez-faire*. Finally, the practical critique deals with the supposed difficulty of identifying the content of *lex mercatoria* with any degree of precision.[45] The vague and ambitious nature of its rules, its contradictions and the disappointing results yielded by years of application are all emphasized in this critique.

The adoption and coming into force of the CISG has not closed the debate. B. Audit for one argues that the CISG and *lex mercatoria* do not claim to have the status of exclusive sources of international commercial law.[46] Although the rules of the Vienna Convention have been adopted by some states, they are considered to coexist with the usages of international commerce and the principle of the autonomy of parties. The Vienna Convention is thus argued to have created a law sanctioned by states but also to recognize the validity of rules issuing from commercial practice. Others support Kassis's position by advocating a systematic vision of the CISG as a law of sales consisting of norms gathered up into a statute.[47] On this view, potential further norms would either be governed by this statute, as provided under Section 7,[48] or ignored. One of the most striking examples of an ignored potential norm is that of *lex mercatoria*. One of the reasons advanced to justify this omission is symptomatic of this systematic vision: it would simply be integrated, replaced, or eliminated by the CISG. Why should it matter? – it would not even exist any more. It is as if we had succeeded, in the manner described by H. Kelsen, in constituting a purified and self-sufficient statute in which the norms converge on the concept of the autonomy of parties.

The debate *State Law vs Lex Mercatoria* is largely fruitless, principally because it has never been convincingly argued that the two theories lead to different results. Issues are formulated in distinct ways and the reasoning exhibits

---

43   *L'ordre juridique* (Paris: Dalloz, 1975).

44   W. Wrengler, 'Les principes généraux du droit en tant que loi du contrat' (1982) 71 R. crit. d. i. p. 467; M. Mustill 'The New *Lex Mercatoria*' in M. Bos, ed., *Études Wilberforce* (New York: Oxford U.P., 1987) 149.

45   G. Delaume, 'The Proper Law of State Contracts and the *Lex Mercatoria*: A Reappraisal' (1988) ICSID Rev. 79.

46   'The Vienna Sales Convention and the *Lex Mercatoria*' in *Lex Mercatoria and Arbitration*, T. E. Carbonneau, ed. (New York: Transn. Juris, 1990) 139.

47   Norris & Randall, *supra*, Preamble, note 7; at 93.

48   '(1) In the interpretation of this Convention, regard is to be had to its international character and to the need to promote uniformity in its application and the observance of good faith in international trade; (2) Questions concerning matters governed by this Convention which are not expressly settled in it are to be settled in conformity with the general principles on which it is based, or in the absence of such principles, in conformity with the law applicable by virtue of the rules of private international law.'

distinct styles, but the conclusions are markedly similar. Moreover, *lex mercatoria*'s proponents have been able to respond to criticism by arguing that:

i)   the determination of the law applicable to the contract must not necessarily be linked to a complete legal order;
ii) the ideological bias was not inherent in *lex mercatoria*;
iii) *lex mercatoria* relied essentially upon a methodology likely to provide adequate solutions to each dispute.

The question of the delimitation of law from non-law is not of primary importance to my own study. I prefer to postulate that each version of uniform law possesses a potential for persuasive authority[49] that must be properly used according to circumstance. This perspective seems to me more fertile and respectful of the style of argumentation I wish to ascribe to this consciousness of uniform law, following Koskenniemi. By linking this conceptualization to the other structural elements provided above – prolegomenon, purpose and methodology – I will be able to show that conservative consciousness follows this logic: uniform law facilitates international trade by setting the juridical conditions favourable to it; the growth of trading activity creates greater individual and collective wealth; the wealth thus created is translated into a more fully experienced joie de vivre and happiness. Through the critique in Part II, I will relativize each of these assumptions. Specifically, I will show that:

i)   conservative consciousness is unsuited to dealing with certain significant realities of commercial life in a progressive context, such as irrationality and unpredictability;
ii) increased international trade does not automatically bring about increase in wealth, owing especially to what are called negative externalities;
iii) wealth is not synonymous with *joie de vivre* and happiness, if for no other reason than that for many, the turbulence and instability associated with cyclical economic processes are a source of frustration.

Working on the hypothesis that the contemporary world is entering a second modernity, I will preserve that portion of each assumption whose validity and relevance survive this critique, integrating it into a progressive consciousness for uniform law. The arguments used to build this consciousness, to be presented in Part III, will emphasize the need to place fulfilment and human solidarity at the heart of a uniform law concerned to produce durable contractual ties and result in spinoffs that harmonize with both the wider interest and the interest of each community involved. Part IV will complement the earlier parts by presenting two applications that illustrate the pragmatic dimensions of progressive consciousness.

---

49   H. P. Glenn, 'Persuasive Authority' (1987) 32 McGill L. J. 261.

PART I

REGRESSIVE ANALYSIS:
CONSERVATIVE CONSCIOUSNESS

Preliminary Remarks

Two series of remarks appear to be necessary in order to specify the type of regressive analysis that is the object of Part I.

An Emphasis on Legal Scholarship

One of the fundamental characteristics of uniform law is to have as its object human actions. The effect of uniform law is to assign to these actions the juridical, commercial and international dimensions that correspond to the qualifications and the field of application of this discipline. Conversely, these actions themselves act on the meaning and scope of uniform law. The evolution of the norms that it contains is not fixed or stopped in space: new forces move it, in particular, new practices and attitudes. Uniform law and human actions are thus parties to a dialogue.

In the midst of this coming and going, uniform law is called upon to manifest itself through its conceptual framework. This means that in order to delimit the practices to which it refers and to influence them, as well as to be informed by them, uniform law uses a body of notions which are more or less familiar and unequivocal: the contract, good faith, the essential breach, damages and so on. These notions constitute the identity of uniform law. They allow for both its recognition and the observation of its relations, in their formal expression, with human actions.

The conceptualization at the source of the identity of uniform law is subordinated to two operations that subject the dialogue described above to particular conditions. First of all, human actions are only retained and understood by uniform law by using a method. This is because to grasp reality is not a phenomenon prior to experience, something innate. It relies rather on a series of operations that *orient* the understanding that uniform law makes of reality. Secondly, given the complexity flowing from the variety of factual situations, uniform law is led to show a concern for concision. This implies that it will constantly tend to the modelling of human actions: only a certain number of traits judged to be pertinent and representative of these actions will be privileged. The juridical concepts at the root of uniform law can thus be viewed in a dual perspective: for example, a contract will be presented from a factual angle (an agreement between the parties, an exchange of goods), but it will have no less force as a theoretical representation for that.

But then we encounter risk: first, that the modelling will create a self-conscious and self-sufficient uniform law rather than one that exists in relation to human actions; and then that the mode of grasping reality will propose something other than effective and actual action, without really contributing to their clarification and comprehension. If these risks arise, what is to be done? In this regard, R. Boudon has formulated a proposition corresponding to the idea of background that constitutes one of the main components of the methodology of this reflection and adds to that concept's precision. Boudon proposes to analyse the reasons underlying the formation of knowledge and beliefs. We must unravel the arguments that sustain our knowledge and beliefs in order to shed light on the determining role of the implicit in our arrival at conclusions.

> Simmel has said that when, as scientists or lay people, we build a theory that tries to explain a phenomenon, we always introduce, besides the explicit propositions that we base our reasoning on, implicit propositions which do not appear directly in the field of our consciousness. Yet, he suggests, it may very well be that the structure of the theory will be modified once we succeed in explicating these propositions. It may also be the case that the conclusions we draw from a theory appear to be different as soon as its implicit propositions are made explicit.[1]

Boudon thus emphasizes the multiplicity of the indispensable *presuppositions* to all knowledge, which form a sort of subconscious. This subconscious cannot be ignored or underestimated: taking it into consideration is a way to explain the epistemological and normative situation of a discipline, as well as to avoid the risks named above or to reestablish contact with reality, as the case may be. In the Boudonian concept of knowledge, this subconscious is located primarily in the theory that serves as the foundation of every discipline. This entire process goes beyond a current epistemology which, starting from the legitimate abstraction of concepts, tends to concern itself only with the discrepancy between theories and facts as it questions the background arguments that have contributed to their development.

Insofar as these suppositions are admitted, they direct the regressive analysis toward legal scholarship on uniform law. It is legal scholarship, more than legislative provisions and case law, that assembles and synthesizes knowledge in this matter and integrates knowledge into a methodical and organized intellectual construct. Whether it be for State law, for the *lex mercatoria*, or for the intermediate law, it is legal scholarship that simultaneously crystallizes and rearranges the reasons underlying the formation of knowledge and the beliefs in this field, reasons that then take the form of principles and thoughts and values. In this present reflection, certain standard works will serve to represent legal scholarship. While this may seem unusual, I submit that the progressive orientation of this study allows me to focus on a limited number of materials to the extent that they are fully representative and that I subject them to thorough analysis.

---

1   R. Boudon, *L'idéologie* (Paris: Fayard, 1986) at 103.

A Poly-background

The second preliminary remark consists of explaining that the regressive analysis I am about to undertake tends toward a *poly*-background. This reveals, to repeat the words of C. Douzinas and R. Warrington, a 'distrust . . . of creating [a] large-scale, totalizing [background] in order to explain' uniform law.[2] In contrast, a *poly*-background calls upon 'small-scale, provisional, open stories about'[3] uniform law. The principles of thought and the values that will be brought to light will consequently be numerous as well as potentially both *compatible* and *contradictory*.

This is possible because of what P. Amselek calls the irresolute or indecisive nature of law.[4] For him, rules and juridical principles, as contents of thought and purely intelligible objects, only have their reality as mental processes. Their use occurs only through intellectual processes of reconstitution, decoding, and analysis. They are a part of the world of products of the mind. This implies that the meaning of law is not already constituted and filed away somewhere so that it would suffice to take passive cognizance of it. Rather, it should be treated as an element of depth and weight that is constituted in and distributed among the interstices of consciousness; an element open to plurality, indeed abundance and mutation. According to Amselek, the irresolution of law is due, as well, to its incompleteness. The juridical experience cannot be strictly predetermined in all circumstances, whether through narrative coherence or a process of pure and formal logic. This experience covers a number of disparate components, intermingled and patched together; it refers to commandments conceived in different periods, inspired by various and sometimes diametrically opposed considerations, and adopted by multiple authorities, always changing, extended as well as restricted. Therefore, 'there is no core component of the [law], only a shifting set of unstable references of multiple identities.'[5] This makes law an off-centre phenomenon.

In these conditions, how is a *poly*-background still capable of uncovering something perceivable? What is the kind of connection that exists among the constituting fragments of this background? In this respect, Amselek relies on an idea of flexible coherence, of simple adjustment.[6] The operation of adjustment, which consists of transforming simple eclecticism into intelligible avenues, invites subtlety, refinement, or a predisposition to understand the differences and resemblances that are inaccessible at first glance. These types of attitude are required because juridical experience is closely linked to opinion – and thus to

---

2   C. Douzinas & R. Warrington, *Postmodern Jurisprudence: The Law of the Text in the Texts of Law* (London: Routledge, 1991) at x.

3   *Ibid.*

4   P. Amselek, 'La teneur indécise du droit' (1992) 26 R. J. Thémis 1.

5   G. Minda, *Postmodern Legal Movements: Law and Jurisprudence at Century's End* (New York: New York University Press, 1995) at 241.

6   See Chapter 5, 'A History of Uniform Law', below, for more on this topic.

discussion and controversy – and not to determinate knowledge. In other words, the experience of law is based on arguments of varying degrees of persuasiveness, developed by reasoning that only contains relative convictions, which vary according to the facts in a given context and in particular according to the audience to which the reasoning is addressed; and experience that is therefore distinguished from a purely mechanical and deductive intellectual operation.[7] If there is an equilibrium, it must be found in what I. Prigogine calls the *structures of dissipated equilibrium*, that is to say, constellations permanently open to fluctuations that are both predictable and subject to chance and can divert the constellations toward new structures of equilibrium.[8]

---

7   C. Perelman & L. Olbrechts-Tyteca, *Traité de l'argumentation: la nouvelle rhétorique*, 5th ed. (Paris: P.U.F., 1988).
8   I. Prigogine & I. Stengers, *La nouvelle alliance: métaphore de la science* (Paris: Gallimard, 1979).

Chapter 1

Principles of Thought

The Context of Discovery

The context of discovery that surrounds uniform law rests on a composite of three types of thought: metaphysical, analytical and simplifying. Within each type of thought is found a discursive argument essential to the coherence of uniform law. These discursive arguments are, respectively, good faith, the autonomy of the will and juridical convergence.

A Metaphysical Form of Thought: The Argument of Good Faith

Initially, the metaphysical approach finds support in the search for a state of good faith that remains true regardless of its components. This is the search for the *identity* of good faith. Both the *lex mercatoria* and the State law express, each in its own way, a concern for this search. In the case of the *lex mercatoria*, the metaphysical element of identity is found in the idea that good faith provides for a permanent and continuous source of law and that it possesses a transcendence that renders it more important than all other categories, all other juridical principles. These characteristics are evident in particular in the remarkable synthesis of the *lex mercatoria* realized by F. Osman.[1] In the first pages of his study, Osman depicts good faith as a 'common denominator of general principles that emerge from precedent,'[2] 'the keystone of the arbitral system,'[3] 'a superior principle.'[4] He quotes R. Vouin to the effect that it is 'always identical to itself. . . . Its juridical efficiency can increase or diminish, yet it remains always the same, perfectly defined and constant,'[5] and M. Horsmans makes it 'a rule of interpretation and the guide of any action and every judgement.'[6] Osman's position implicitly incorporates the ideas or permanence, continuity and superiority. State law is also

---

1   F. Osman, *Les principes généraux de la lex mercatoria. Contribution à l'étude d'un ordre juridique anational* (Paris: L.G.D.J., 1992).
2   *Ibid.* at 18.
3   *Ibid.*
4   *Ibid.* at 19.
5   *Ibid.*
6   *Ibid.*

concerned with identity and this translates into its desire to determine good faith.[7]
Here, the question is to establish *one determinate* state of good faith from
reasoning that is founded upon considerations of compatibility, homogeneity, and
community. Thus, the identity of good faith is articulated in the guise of a concept:

i)   that can go together with the existing economic, social, political and juridical
      systems;
ii)   that should be made up of elements of the same or a similar nature; and
iii) whose viability and juridical efficiency depend on its ability to function as a
      common denominator for those who are subject to it.

This reasoning is in opposition to that which would allow an interpretation of
good faith sensitive to possible differences in the status of the contracting parties,
or which would admit the idea of variability of good faith according to culture,
rather than ignore or destroy this reality. The two strategies, permanence and
determination, both produce a generalizing effect peculiar to the element of
identity. Good faith *is*. This makes it a principle *universal in its essence* according
to the *lex mercatoria*, or a principle whose interpretation is standardized in every
respect – form, substance and results – according to State law.

This dimension of identity finds support in another dimension, which is
isolationist in character. In fact, *isolation* embodies identity by translating the fact
that a thing cannot be another thing. In other words, a thing invariably possesses
its own existence and autonomy. This leads to the compartmentalization of good
faith in a specific sphere, that of commerce, whence *lex mercatoria*'s very strong
tendency toward compartmentalization. One compartment results from the
argument that the rules and principles of the *lex mercatoria* have an institutional
origin, that they can be ascribed to a form of authority. This appears to be
necessary to supporters of the *lex mercatoria*, so that this doctrine may be qualified
as a juridical order. In the language characteristic of this version of uniform law,
the expression *community of operators of international commerce* and others of a
similar kind give a personal form to the institution and thus ensure good faith does
not evolve in a juridical vacuum. A second compartment consists of rallying the
members of this community around '[the] same end, [a] unique commercial idea:
to answer the needs of international commerce.'[8] The institutional unity of the
operators is thus assured, a unity whose universalism goes beyond the multiplicity
of objective practices and groupings. In short, the origin and the *raison d'être* of
good faith both belong to commercialism. As for State law, the isolation of good
faith is first of all simply formal in the sense that it results from a sphere of
application which is reserved for certain commercial activities. But this isolation is
potentially much deeper than that. This may be explained as follows. The

---

7   On this topic, see G. Lefebvre, 'La bonne foi dans la Convention des Nations Unies sur
     les contrats de vente internationale de marchandises' (1993) 27 R. J. Thémis 563 at
     570ff.
8   Osman, *supra*, note 1; at 409.

preamble to the Vienna Convention contains three statements of principle.[9] The first two are strongly normative. They refer to the 'general objectives written in resolutions concerning the founding of a new international economic order,' and to the fact 'that the development of international commerce on a basis of equality and mutual benefit is an important element in the promotion of amicable relations between States.' Further, the third statement stipulates 'that the adoption of uniform rules will favour the development of international trade.' In my opinion, this preamble should be understood as an invitation, not to say a constraint, to evaluate uniform law in the light of its contribution to the improvement of the quality of life in general and interpret it accordingly; that is, to transform uniform law – including, it goes without saying, good faith – into a unity open to other realities that surround it. However, and this is particularly striking in the case of good faith, the only statement that is fully accepted is the third, concerning juridical commercial uniformization. Only with difficulty or with little interest is good faith invoked regarding aspects not strictly related to trade but undoubtedly relevant, given their fundamental nature. Consequently, the universe of good faith is reduced to the ultimately technical stake in creating a uniform version of it for commercial ends.[10]

Along with identity and isolation, the idea of *non-contradiction* also characterizes good faith. Non-contradiction is founded on the internal unity of things and beings. On the level of thought, the underlying conviction of this idea is that the necessary true and precise description of things and beings requires that these be seen as free of contradictory and antinomic components. Staying in the realm of State law, the idea of non-contradiction appears first in the role of a general principle of interpretation given to good faith, around which the other norms of the Vienna Convention must be articulated. Article 7 (1) CISG, part of Chapter II entitled 'General Dispositions', actually stipulates that, 'in the interpretation of the present Convention, regard is to be had . . . to the need . . . to promote the observance of good faith in international trade.' In this respect, good faith becomes an agent of unity and convergence with respect to the norms placed under its control. Until now, this first manifestation was overshadowed in intensity by a second. In fact, what becomes more revealing about the idea of non-contradiction is the tendency to consider good faith in the light of the 'large number of substantive provisions [that] directly apply it'[11] or that are susceptible of being influenced by it. The right of the seller to remedy an imperfect delivery during an anticipated delivery, the principle of non-liability of the seller if the buyer knew or could not have been unaware of a lack of compliance at the time the contract was concluded, the rule of mitigation of damages and other provision, are thus associated with applications or specific formulations of good faith. Furthermore, late acceptance of an offer; the handing over, by the seller to the

---

9   *Supra*, Preamble, note 4.
10   See, for example, F. Enderlain & D. Maskow, *International Sales Law* (New York: Oceana, 1992) at 56.
11   Audit, *supra*, Introduction, note 46; at 49.

buyer, of documents concerning goods; and the quantity of goods delivered are all situations that enable good faith to be particularized and to be better understood. Such a decomposition of good faith shows a concern to reach a true and precise description of it, free from any contradiction.

Finally, uniform law integrates the argument of good faith into a *dualism*. This vision posits the coexistence of two orders or principles of different natures. It sanctions the idea of *the excluded third party*, which has the methodological advantage of facilitating classification. In the matter of uniform law, dualism refers to the coexistence of national and international orders (or the classification national-international), it being understood that the *lex mercatoria* and State law are defined as belonging to the international order. Therefore, in spite of its substantive borrowing from, and its subordination in certain respects to, national legal systems, the *lex mercatoria* claims an autonomy and independence in the realm of the creation and sanctioning of a law which is meant for different sectors of the international world of business. According to T. Carbonneau, 'a body of juridical principles governing international law . . . , a common law of international transactions'[12] is developed principally under the impulse of arbitration. This common law takes place beside national laws and reinforces the widespread national-international general classification. As for State law, it justifies the principle of the irreducibility of its international nature to a national nature in two ways. First of all, it falls back on the reflection of the specificity of international commercial transactions in comparison with their equivalent on the internal level. The international sphere would bring together circumstances (the distance separating the parties, the possible lack of understanding among them, etc.) that do not exist, or that present themselves differently on a national level, and these circumstances would entail the development of a specific juridical regime. Secondly, State law appeals to the necessity for uniformization. This can be seen at the present time in the widely held position that the interpretation of uniform law in the light of correspondence to national law, or following national techniques, risks compromising uniformity. To avoid running such a risk, the watchword is simply that uniform law must be viewed with an internationalist mentality.[13]

An Analytical Form of Thought: The Argument of the Autonomy of the Will

Analytical thought relies first of all on a rule of obviousness concerning the principle of the autonomy of the will. Obviousness, which presupposes certainty as a state which is accessible to thought, consists of doubting everything in order to avoid error and to arrive, through a process of elimination, at an indubitable truth. Uniform law borrows from this form of reasoning, a borrowing which is particularly striking in the case of the Vienna Convention. On the one hand, the

---

12　T. Carbonneau, 'Étude historique et comparée de l'arbitrage: vers un droit matériel de l'arbitrage commercial international fondé sur la motivation des sentences' 36 (1984) R.I.D.C. 727 at 774.

13　R. David, *Cours de droit privé comparé* (Paris: Les Cours de droit, 1968) at 60-62.

process of reflection which is open to doubt, which constitutes the first phase of obviousness, is recognized in the volume of legal scholarship devoted to the body of rules (other than the autonomy of will) that govern one aspect or another of financial international contract of sale. These rules are discussed and debated at length. They do not take effect merely by virtue of being explicitly stated in the text of the Vienna Convention. Indeed, some jurists openly voice their own views and comments on them as contributions to a discussion and debate, sometimes going as far as to identify the features of this debate. This is the case of J. Honnold, who pleads in favour of a 'continuing dialogue, spanning legal and economic backgrounds.'[14] In this context, doubt can truly be said to become a tool of knowledge. On the other hand, the doubt thus expressed goes along with a principle which is stamped with certainty, that of autonomy of the will. The components of the Vienna Convention can be accepted and considered stable to a greater or lesser extent; the fact remains that the autonomy of the will is the only element that cannot be put in doubt or contested in the formation and execution of a contract of sale. The primacy of the will of the parties, autonomy as the primary source of a contract of sale: the pervasive presence of these expressions demonstrates this certainty. But there is more: in comparison with the other principles of the juridical regime of international law, the principle of the autonomy of the will has been hardly examined at all, aside from an occasional simple statement. If one accepts the affirmation of the primary and fundamental role of the principle, only one conclusion appears to be logically acceptable: the autonomy of the will asserts itself with such vigour that it does not need any proof. It is self-evident or obvious.[15]

While the manner in which the autonomy of the will and the other components of uniform law are articulated relies upon the rule of obviousness, the observation of the manner in which they are structured attests to the second dimension of analytical thought: division. This intellectual attitude aims at decomposing, at dividing, concepts and difficulties into smaller units. This breaking down of concepts into smaller units is supposed to facilitate the study of these concepts as well as the resolution of the difficulties that they engender. In appearance, the *lex mercatoria* may seem impervious to this type of reasoning. As has been mentioned by several of its critics, the inherent generality of *lex mercatoria* even militates against a precise definition of its content. For example, these critics underline its vagueness, its lack of organization and the insufficient number of its principles.[16] Nonetheless, in considering *lex mercatoria* as it has been conceived and without prejudging its juridical validity, it appears to me to be truly engaged in

---

14 J. O. Honnold, *Uniform Law for International Sales under the 1980 United Nations Convention* (Deventer: Kluwer, 1991) at 9.

15 J. D. Feltham, 'The United Nations Convention on Contracts for the International Sale of Goods' (1981) Business Law Journal 346; D. J. Rhodes, 'The United Nations Convention on Contracts for the International Sale of Goods: Encouraging the Use of Uniform International Law' (1992) 5 The Transnational Lawyer 387.

16 G. Delaume, 'The Proper Law of State Contracts and the Lex Mercatoria: A Reappraisal' (1988) ICSID Review 79.

the process of dividing the autonomy of the will. It is important to realize, in effect, that this 'corporate system independent of States'[17] could not have seen the light of day and progress without the principle of the autonomy of the will. Therein lies an authentic basis. However, probably in order to generate 'a body of rules sufficiently accessible and certain to permit the efficient conduct of commercial transactions,'[18] *lex mercatoria* has progressively divided this basis. In reality, it has woven, in accordance with its own method, an indefinite network of rules likely to furnish juridical norms pertinent to any litigation. For its part, State law makes this division one of its principle attributes in the pursuit of the objective of making international commercial transactions a more stable and predictable milieu. Underlying a juridical regime such as that of the Vienna Convention lies the premise that the predictability and the security of transactions depend upon its degree of precision. It is with this in mind that the Vienna Convention establishes a compartmentalized juridical regime (its structure follows the hierarchy part – chapter – section – article) and is detailed on the basis of a presumed intention of the parties. It is thus enabled to consider different aspects of a contract of sale (offer, delivery, etc.) in isolation.

In addition to obviousness and division, there is the integration of the autonomy of the will into a reasoning of a causal nature. *Causality* assumes that laws exist and that they must be identified to ensure the indispensable explanation of phenomena. In the sphere of uniform law, autonomy of the will represents this fundamental explanatory reason of contract. The current crisis that, according to several authors, has been shaking up the law of contracts and contributing to a rethinking or even replacement of the autonomy of the will as an explanatory reason has thus not reached uniform law. We do not find, in uniform law, critical analyses for which contract law is one or more of the following: indeterminate, legitimating, dead, unsuitable, or irrelevant.[19] The words of Honnold on the subject of the Vienna Convention offer eloquent testimony to this situation. He writes, 'The dominant theme of the Convention is the role of the contract.'[20] This domination results from the fact that the Convention 'in two fundamental ways responds to the power of agreement.'[21] First of all, 'The Convention itself was produced by an agreement,' that is to say, 'States from all parts of the world, through collaboration . . . , reached consensus.'[22] Then, 'Consistent with these origins, the Convention does not interfere with the freedom of sellers and buyers to shape the terms of their transactions.'[23] In light of what preceded, Honnold concludes:

---

17 P. Kahn, 'La Convention de Vienne du 11 avril 1980 sur les contrats de vente internationale de marchandises' (1991) J. D. I. 951 at 961.
18 Mustill, *supra*, Introduction, note 44; at 180.
19 R. A. Hillman, 'The Crisis in Modern Contract Theory' (1988) 67 Tex. L. Rev. 103 at 103.
20 Honnold, *supra*, note 14; at 47.
21 *Ibid.* at 48.
22 *Ibid.*
23 *Ibid.*

A highly respected legal scholar in a rhetorical flourish (later modified) announced the 'Death of Contract'. At least for international sales this report (as Mark Twain said of a report that he had died) is grossly exaggerated.[24]

This point of view is largely dominant, some would say wholly dominant, in uniform law. Consequently, the best explanation for the birth, the formation and the end of a contract remains that this is what the parties wished.

Finally, the connection between uniform law and analytical thought springs from the quasi-total *exhaustiveness* of the principle of the autonomy of the will. For our present purposes, this exhaustiveness can best be demonstrated through the contribution to the legitimacy of uniform law of the principle of the autonomy of the will. Two elements are at the centre of this contribution. The first refers to the omnipresence that legal scholarship and case law grant to the autonomy of the will. P. Lalive for one affirms that 'it is a principle so generally recognized in all systems of private international law that we can hold it as an international custom or as a general principle of law recognized by civilized nations.'[25] In similar fashion, the Topco-Calasiatic award decision contains the following passage:

> All juridical systems, be they what they may, apply the principle of the autonomy of the will to international contracts. As to substantive law, all juridical systems consecrate this principle, which appears consequently to be universally admitted.[26]

The second element is founded upon confidence in a twofold capability of international merchants: to generate, by themselves, fundamental values that are in conformity with the aspirations of individuals and nations, or simply to see them integrated into their practices. This conviction is held by the merchants, of course, but also by States. According to Lalive, States 'have chosen, and judged it according to their interests, to partake in international commerce,'[27] leaving, notably, *'broad powers of self-regulation* to the international community of merchants.'[28] The importance granted to the principle extends to justifying the taking into consideration of public order 'by the nature of things [but also by] the very wishes or the legitimate expectation of the parties.'[29] Given its omnipresence and the allegiance it commands, the autonomy of the will thus becomes an exhaustive argument, because it asserts its priority, among all possible means of favouring and legitimizing the development of international commerce.

---

24 *Ibid.*
25 P. Lalive, 'Ordre public transnational (ou réellement international) et arbitrage international' (1986) Rev. arb. 329 at 351-352.
26 *Topco Calasiatic* v. *Gouvernement Libyen*, reported at (1977) J.D.I. 350.
27 Lalive, *supra*, note 25; at 370.
28 *Ibid.*
29 *Ibid.* at 371.

A Simplifying Form of Thought: The Argument of Juridical Convergence

Initially, juridical convergence is in keeping with the search for *order*, as appears from the affirmation of B. Bonnell to the effect that the unification of law answers the almost too evident need 'to assure the most orderly and secure development possible for commercial life.'[30] Order would permit the subjection of commercial activity to a body of rules that present 'the essential characteristics of practicality, simplicity and clarity, free of legal shorthand, free of complicated legal theory, and which [are] easy for the businessperson to understand.'[31] Essentially, the search for order would impose itself as the antidote to the phenomenon called 'nationalization of private international law' by R. David.[32] By virtue of this phenomenon, the juridical regime applicable to international commercial relations would be built from national instruments, that is to say from those developed by State legislators. With time, nationalization would have set itself up as an obstacle to international commerce. David for one stresses the diversity of rules of conflict of laws and of the national material rules that would put the juridical security of transactions in peril, while A. Kassis endorses the 'concert of lamentations on the deficiencies'[33] of the conflictual method. In short, it would become manifest and patent that 'national laws are the international merchants', and traders', worst enemy.'[34] The establishment of intelligible relations among what would otherwise be a disorganized and ill-assorted plurality of national laws can take one of two courses. The first, that of amalgamation, characterizes the process of development of State law. It consists of bringing together elements from various juridical cultures as well as other original elements and combining them all as carefully as possible to create a new body that cannot be reduced to its component parts. The second avenue, which underlies *lex mercatoria*, is associated with spontaneity. Here, merchants are supposed to generate, on their own initiative, a juridical regime in conformity with the requirements which naturally result from commerce. They are seen to be acting for themselves, without outside interference (especially not from States), in respect to a commercial activity which is part of the order of things.

Amalgamation and spontaneity constitute strategies of the first order for imposing on international commercial law, and thus favour juridical convergence. On another level, each is supported by another component of simplifying thought known as *linearity*. As a means of acceding to knowledge, linearity is

---

30   M. J. Bonell, 'Introduction to the Convention' in M. J. Bonell & G. M. Bianca, eds., *Commentary on the International Sales Law: The 1980 Vienna Sales Convention* (Milan: Guiffré, 1987) at 3.

31   E. P. Mendes, 'The U. N. Sales Convention and U. S. – Canada Transactions; Enticing the World's Largest Trading Bloc to Do Business under a Global Sales Law' (1988) 109 Journal of Law and Commerce 109 at 121.

32   R. David, *Le droit du commerce international: réflexions d'un comparatiste sur le droit international privé* (Paris: Économica, 1987) at 10ff.

33   A. Kassis, *supra*, Preamble, note 8; at 559.

34   Mendes, *supra*, note 31; at 112.

characterized by the search for processes, rules and principles free from ambiguity and permitting the prediction of the appearance of phenomena. In all matters, the absence of ambiguity and the capacity of prediction should lead to the acceptance of one single point of view for describing and understanding the world, things and beings. It is precisely toward these attributes and this unity that uniform law turns. On the one hand, the idea according to which 'the key objectives of stability, safety and foreseeability . . . are essential for international trade law'[35] is an intrinsic part of the conception of uniform law held by the vast majority of jurists. In many cases, this conception turns out to have priority, or perhaps exclusivity. On the other hand, the simplest solution to these imperatives is to be found in the formulation and the perfection of a form of juridical unity. Various ideological principles have served in the past as the foundation for the promotion of unity in international commercial law.[36] Idealism (the unity of the human species and planetary harmony), pragmatism (the practical value, in everyday commercial life, of working with a single regime) and historicism (the persistence or the return of *jus commune*) have each in turn served to justify it. But more recently, H. Berman has proposed a global justification which he conceptualizes under the expression of *world law*. Berman refers to all fields of activity (sports, literature, commerce, etc.), to all types of rules of conduct (laws, customs, usages, etc.) and to all facts of human life (history, humanism, society, etc.) to show that, for the first time in the history of the human race, most of the peoples of the world have been brought into more or less continual relations with each other.[37] From this, he concludes that 'the right name for the new era is "emerging world society", and the right name for the law by which it is governed is world law.'[38]

To take for granted that uniform law embodies the only point of view legitimated by linearity is one thing. However, uniform law goes even further in its integration of simplifying thought by falling back on the principles of *determinism*. The objective consists in identifying the conditions, the circumstances, or the facts that will ensure constancy and persistence in the convergence of uniformity of law. In order to do so, *lex mercatoria* relies upon a comprehensive type of determinism which is evaluated in time. Both academic studies and jurisprudence resulting from *lex mercatoria* reveal a method of reasoning founded upon the joining together and the putting in sequence of a large range of sources. And even if many facets of the sources do not always formally possess a juridical value, they acquire an authority by the self-referential practices proper to this type of reasoning. Furthermore, the collection thus created inspires a feeling of security sought after by the merchants because it is founded on a

---

35 H. G. Naon, 'The UN Convention on Contracts for the International Sale of Goods' in N. Horn, C. M. Schmitthoff (ed.), *The Transnational Law of International Commercial Ttransactions* (Deventer: Kluwer, 1982) 89 at 92.

36 J. W. Westenberg, 'The Quest for Unification' in *Forty Years On: The Evolution of Postwar Private International Law in Europe* (Deventer: Kluwer, 1990) at 195.

37 H. Berman, 'The Role of International Law in the Twenty-first Century: World Law' (1995) 18 Fordham Int'l L. J. 1617 at 1617.

38 *Ibid.* at 1618.

master orientation, a guiding thread that Osman summarizes thus: 'Uncover those rules that systematically respond to the needs of international trade.'[39] To sum up, *lex mercatoria* functions as if each decision were cumulative and bound up with, and the fruit of, the totality of all previous decisions. For its part, State law adheres to a determinism of a more scientific order, as reflected in the axiom *the same causes produce the same effects*. Thus, the drafters of the Vienna Convention wished to go further than the simple development of a uniform text. Very conscious of the risk that diversity of juridical families and political and economical systems could spill over onto the interpretation of the Vienna Convention, they undertook to identify the conditions of existence of uniformity that are objective and invariable, such that if these conditions are respected, uniformity will necessarily be achieved. The difficulty of this endeavour explains the dearth of rules provided for on this subject in CISG Article 7. But this does not prevent the determinist objective from holding firm, because, as R. Monaco declares, 'A uniform interpretation is an absolute necessity.'[40]

Finally, uniform law projects an image of simplification insofar as its connection with normality is beyond doubt. This connection is motivated by at least two types of arguments. The first, perhaps the most striking, refers to the intellectual and mental dimensions of the normality in question. It consists of referring to uniformization in such a manner that to prefer a different approach to regulating international commercial transactions would be equivalent to being incomprehensible. It is in this sense that David, in a critique of the nationalization of private international law, concludes that it is 'contrary to sane reasoning.'[41] The alternative of uniform law is there, and if it is obvious it is because 'logic and reason cannot be left aside with impunity.'[42] Kassis argues in the same vein. Emphasizing the enormous potential of the development of uniform law through international agreements, he affirms that 'it would be irrational and unfortunate [for States] not to go further along this path.'[43] Monaco is caught in the same kind of enthusiasm when he speaks of 'all [these] eminent jurists who work and devote themselves to the grand phenomenon of uniform law,'[44] which is thus viewed as essentially good. All these arguments contribute to procure for uniformization an aura of something *always-already there – given –* that is to say, whose presence is unmediated in the juridical ordering of international trade. The second type of argument refers more to the diverse circumstances that frame uniformization. Viewed in context, this analysis displays the *ineluctable* dimensions of uniformization. The following affirmation by C. Samson is a good illustration of this type of argument:

---

39   Osman, *supra*, note 1; at 403.
40   R. Monaco, 'Allocution d'ouverture' in *Le droit uniforme international dans la pratique* (Rome: Oceana, 1988) at 3.
41   David, *supra*, note 32; at 11.
42   *Ibid.*
43   Kassis, *supra*, Preamble, note 8; at 562.
44   Monaco, *supra*, note 40; at 1.

In the present context of the globalization of trade, uniformization of the applicable rules to commercial trade has become a necessity for participants in international trade.[45]

In this perspective, interdependence and globalization go together with '[the] explosive proliferation of attempts to unify and harmonize private international law.'[46] When all is said and done, the movement appears quite *simply* to be irreversible.

The Context of Justification

I have proposed above that the context of justification refers to considerations that play a superior and decisive role in the making of a given decision. When it comes to uniform law, these ultimate considerations, in whose light we come to discern the context of discovery, are conceived in terms I will refer to as those of instrumental reason as opposed to ends-based reason.

M. Horkheimer writes as follows on reason:

Reason for a long time meant the activity of understanding and assimilating the eternal ideas which were to function as goals for men. Today, on the contrary, it is not only the business but the essential work of reason to find means for the goals one adopts at any given time.[47]

The first part of the statement refers to what Horkheimer designates by the words *objective reason* (or ends-based reason). This consists of the process of reflection on the objectives, the goals and the visions that we choose and propose to reach or to realize. In other words, it concerns an exercise which is oriented toward the determination of one or many ends. According to Horkheimer, it implies the conviction that it is possible to discover 'an encompassing or fundamental structure of being'[48] and to deduce from that a human destiny founded on the ideals of the greatest good. The exercise assumes as well the recognition that persons and societies have the necessary capacities to identify, rank and revise their values, as well as to proceed to make choices on the individual and collective process of becoming that are forged from these same values. At this point, the degree of reason associated with the existence of a person or society depends on

---

45 C. Samson, 'L'harmonisation du droit de la vente: l'influence de la Convention de Vienne sur l'évolution et l'harmonisation du droit des provinces canadiennes' (1991) 32 C. de D. 1001 at 1003.

46 Spanogle, *supra*, Preamble, note 5; at 478.

47 M. Horkheimer, *Critique of Instrumental Reason: Lectures and Essays since the End of World War II* (New York: Seabury Press, 1974) at vii. See also H. Stewart, 'A Critique of Instrumental Reason in Economics' (1995) 11 Economics and Philosophy 57.

48 M. Horkheimer, *Éclipse de la raison* (Paris: Payot, 1974), trans. J. Debouzy and J. Laizé, at 14.

the degree of harmony between their lives and this *encompassing structure*. This first impulse is echoed in the second, which seeks the appropriateness of favouring such and such a view to attaining or realizing certain ends. This is subjective reason (or instrumental reason). Here, the field of analysis and application of thought is limited to the way to attain an objective. It does not apply to the objective itself. This objective is always in the end followed for some other reason, and so forth. This creates a spiral where the degree of reason corresponds to the efficiency with which an objective is attained. For instrumental reason it is useless to inquire about the ends because these cannot be weighed or judged according to reason or in relation to any existing order. Horkheimer sees in it the expression of an abstract process of thought: the reason depends on 'the faculty of classification, inference, and deduction,'[49] regardless of the substance of thought being conceived in these operations.

Is uniform law framed by a form of instrumental thought, in which the emphasis is placed on the means, or on ends-based thought, which is centred on the ends? Initial observation of the structure and content of the argumentation that I believe belongs to the context of justification reveals the presence of both components, *means* and *ends*. In fact, *to answer to the needs of international trade* and to *favour the development of international trade*, which represent the key formulae of the *lex mercatoria* and State law respectively, would appear to combine these ideas, in that uniform law fills an instrumental function in relation to a true end that is intrinsically and essentially good, namely trade. Is this to say that uniform law has succeeded in occupying an intermediate position between Horkheimer's analytic poles, one which seeks the best of each form of reason and brings them to reflect on one another? I do not think so. More detailed observations will lead to different findings.

The initial finding concerns the breadth of instrumental thought. At this level, we should note the impact of the idea according to which uniform law has been constituted with the view of *serving* trade. Legal scholarship, case law and statute law make it possible to evaluate this perspective with some acuity. What can be drawn from this is that uniform law exists to aid, help and be useful to commercial activity. This characterization applies at the same time to merchants, on the one hand, and trade, on the other. It can thus be observed in those approaches that treat uniform law as an instrument placed at the disposal of merchants, which they can use for their own profit. As well, it is evident in the viewpoints that model and frame it in light of conditions which are held to be normal for the functioning of trade. Furthermore, in many cases, uniform law is represented as the best juridical *resource* available concerning commercial activity. More specifically, the conclusions drawn from the analysis of it are that it is definitely the most efficient resource, that is to say, that which will produce the best results in commercial matters. This perspective underlies analysis of all forms, even those of a fundamental character. For example, K. C. Randall and J. E. Norris's thorough demonstration of the birth of a new juridical paradigm of international commercial

---

49   *Ibid.* at 16.

transactions, embodied notably in the Vienna Convention, takes a resolutely instrumental form.[50]   They justify this culmination of a long socio-historical process by three brief considerations: it fits perfectly with their vision of present reality, which would be that of an 'increasingly interdependent global community';[51] it facilitates an increasing volume of international trade; and it further satisfies 'the increased involvement of nation states as parties to international business.'[52]   In short, that uniform law is there in order to furnish means is a shining truth.

The presence of ends-based thought in uniform law is not at all of the same nature. Of course, as I have previously affirmed, it is trade that seems to be understood as playing the role of end. However, I would submit that in this role, trade does not assert itself in a very forceful manner.   To the glamour of instrumental thought there corresponds here something much more modest, as I hope to demonstrate.

First of all, the clearly dominant perception of trade can be reduced to a formal recognition of it. Trade exists; it is a fact. This suffices for one to embrace and understand it. In terms of analysis, factual existence prevails over content. This basic perception is particularized in different ways.   One of them could be translated as follows: while it is the *raison d'être* of uniform law, trade, in itself, remains hardly debated, whether as to its orientations or as to its effects. What is trade? Where is it going? How may one benefit from it? In the present state of affairs, these questions occupy a marginal place in the consciousness of uniform law. In short, trade is not examined in the light of, for example, the interests, the preferences and the aspirations of all who participate in it and those who are affected by its fallout. At the very limit, it takes on the look, rather, of an objective entity, that is to say, an entity independent of these considerations. Another way of particularizing consists in automatically relating trade and happiness, without substantially deepening this analysis. This automatic tie appears in the feeling of assurance associated with trade and the hopes it creates for advancement and progress in general, a feeling very prominent in uniform law. But it does not follow that the truth of these assertions has been demonstrated. In the words of G. C. J. J. van den Bergh, 'We know in fact very little about the mechanisms of legal development or the interdependence of legal and economic development.'[53] In these conditions, it becomes difficult to affirm that we really know what is good in trade and in what measure this end can become a shining horizon, capable of both reflecting on the means that must be undertaken in a given situation and creating a reliable destiny.

---

50   Randall & Norris, *supra*, Preamble, note 7.
51   *Ibid.* at 600-601.
52   *Ibid.* at 601.
53   G. C. J. J. van den Bergh, 'What Law for Whose Development?' in E. Hondius, ed., *Unification and Comparative Law in Theory and Practice: Contributions in Honour of Jean Georges Sauveplanne* (Boston: Kluwer, 1984) 29 at 41.

It sometimes happens, however, that trade tends toward such a horizon. In this case, however, the thought that results from it shows weaknesses that prevent it from being qualified as ends-based.

The most frequent weakness of this thought is that it rests upon unrefined reasoning. Thus, at the beginning of the century, L. J. Kennedy joined uniform law and trade together and situated them at the centre of a humanist vision, that of a sincere sentiment of human solidarity, which he formulated as 'the far-off fulfilment of the divine message, *On earth peace, goodwill towards men.*'[54] Uniform law and trade, on the one hand, and happiness, on the other, were indissolubly bound up. Paradoxically, this vision has not been the object of an intellectual development that corresponds to its depth and significance. It is true that on occasion, it has been clarified by references to the objectives relative to the creation of a new international economic order, to equality, mutual benefit and other fundamental principles. It has also been admitted that these are 'illuminating indications.'[55] However, such details have remained secondary in both the pure and applied theory of uniform law. It is impossible to affirm that they are at the centre of demonstrations carried out in order to seriously integrate them into the method and organization of uniform law. Integration emerges rather from a simple but strong belief in the natural communion of trade and progress in all its forms; or in a type of automatism evident in the feeling of assurance that trade has been, is and will be bound up with the needs of the international community.

Besides, when reasoning on this subject does appear to go beyond an unrefined state, it still suffers from ambiguity. A key passage of the analysis of *lex mercatoria* written by Osman offers a typical illustration of this problem. He begins this passage by affirming that the *societas mercatorum* 'develops the rules that respond to the needs of its members in an empirical manner.'[56] This would explain that law belongs to normative disciplines, in opposition to purely explanatory ones. On the basis of the premise that law accords with a value judgement, Osman posits:

> The judgement being necessarily founded on an evaluation of the objectives undertaken, these disciplines will postulate the search for an end to be discovered. Hence, the facts of life of society are part of the foundation of the rules of law produced by the *societas mercatorum*. These facts generally cover political and social, religious and moral, or simply economic factors.[57]

Osman follows this with the declaration, 'The development of an anational law rests essentially, if not exclusively, on economic considerations,'[58] a position reinforced further along with this statement:

---

54   L. J. Kennedy, 'The Unification of Law' (1909) 10 J. Soc'y Comp. Legis. 212 at 214.
55   M. J. Bonell, *supra*, note 30; at 94.
56   Osman, *supra*, note 1; at 410.
57   *Ibid.* at 411.
58   *Ibid.*

We can therefore without objection transpose to the level of *lex mercatoria* the reflection of Josserand, which recognizes the transformation of law into a *code of wealth and economic phenomena; put differently, the just has become what is in accordance with economic postulates and necessities.*[59]

In the end, according to Osman, the 'aspiration of the *mercantile* institution that will imperatively reply to the needs of international trade in its normative production'[60] is derived from this context.

In my opinion, the end Osman writes of that remains to be discovered is falsely determined. In particular, the place and real influence of *the facts of life in society* in the juridical order of the *lex mercatoria* remain obscure. These facts, it should be admitted, are extremely variable, complex and understood to a greater or lesser degree. Yet, if their place and influence are really as important as Osman affirms, in that they participate in the foundation of the *lex mercatoria*, it is difficult to conceive that they could be concentrated and synthesized in this *raison d'être* of *the needs of international trade* and continue to grow in all their possibilities. In other words, the enormous reduction operation that compresses *the facts of life in society* into this *raison d'être* risks diminishing their scope unduly, substantially stripping them of meaning and, consequently, preventing their full and complete evolution.

Moreover, to affirm that the *lex mercatoria rests essentially, if not exclusively, on economic considerations* and to subordinate its legitimacy to its conformity to the needs of international trade takes the search for ends onto shaky ground. In any event, it is important to bear in mind that identifying the needs is one thing; understanding and justifying why they must be satisfied is another. As well, comprehension and justification of this *why* cannot be exact and rigorous without opening up toward what it could be convenient to call a totality of motives and considerations. The arguments put forth by Osman tend in a different direction. Instead of opening up *lex mercatoria* toward a whole, they close it around a single subgroup, that of economics. Furthermore, this subgroup is said to be exclusive: it keeps at bay anything that is not bound up with its nature. Here there is a tendency to regression, to an opposition and separation that contrasts with the idea of the encompassing structure as defined by Horkheimer. To respond in the words of L. Josserand, written in precisely the analysis Osman refers to, this tendency is symptomatic of instrumental thought. In fact, Josserand considers that the unilateral juridical movement toward the economy is accompanied by the overshadowing of an ideal and a spiritual force in favour of an excessive materialism and of a mechanization of law.[61] For my part, I deem it sufficient to put forward the hypothesis that, in the absence of close communication between economics and that which is outside of it, *the needs of international trade* can be linked at best only very tenuously to an end.

---

59   *Ibid.*
60   *Ibid.* at 412.
61   L. Josserand, 'Vers un ordre juridique nouveau' (1937) 6 Dalloz ch. 43.

Chapter 2

Values

The Context of Discovery

The context of discovery in relation to the values of uniform law reveal four primary norms: liberty, wealth, utility and justice. They occur, in the reasoning on the context of discovery, in many arguments centred respectively on the concrete intention (the real choice) of the parties, growth, maximization of interests, and equality and cooperation between parties.

In contrast to the type of demonstration I undertook relating to the context of discovery of the principles of thought, I will here proceed in two steps. I will first develop several propositions characteristic of the way each argument is presented in the discourse of uniform law. This synthesis – placed in italics – will enable us to eventually attain a plausible anticipation of the sense and the scope of the corresponding value.[1]

The Value of 'Liberty': The Argument of the Concrete Intention (Real Choice) of the Parties

'[I]n order to define the rules of the contracting game, we must first identify the values CISG seeks to further by enforcing contractual promises in the first place.'[2] For M. P. Van Alstine, the resolution of this problematic results from taking consciousness of the respect given to the real choice of the parties by the Vienna Convention. This respect, which is in a sense supreme, makes the argument of concrete intention the Gründnorm of the Vienna Convention, crystallized specifically at Article 6.[3] In addition to the following consequence that it 'should . . . be abundantly clear [that] the agreement of the parties stands at the very top of the Convention's hierarchy norms,'[4] Van Alstine deduces from the argument different effects with respect to the formation of the sales contract:

---

1   I am relying on E. Bloch's comments on 'La conscience anticipante', in E. Bloch, ed., *Le Principe Espérance* (Paris: Gallimard, 1976) at 61ff.

2   M. P. Van Alstine, 'Consensus, Dissensus, and Contractual Obligation Through the Prism of Uniform International Sales Law' (1996) 37 Va. J. Int'l L. 1 at 37.

3   'The parties may exclude the application of this Convention or, subject to Article 12, derogate from or vary the effect of any of its provisions.'

4   Van Alstine, *supra*, note 2; at 83.

i)   *the determination of the obligational content fundamentally depends on an analysis of the intention of the parties;*

ii)   *as a corollary, a quasi-unlimited flexibility prevails as to the manner in which proof of this intention can be provided;*

iii) *the fact that the approach of State law is 'highly particularized'[5] reveals, for its part, an ambivalence, if not a mistrust, toward other modes of analysis founded on objective or normative criteria;*

iv)   *the interpretation and the application of State law must avoid being rigid or prescriptive to the point of interfering with the manifestation of the real choice of the parties.*

Behind the argument of the concrete intention of the parties is found the attachment of uniform law to the value of liberty.[6] In a general way, this attachment refers to liberty as the exercise of rational action.[7] This conception of liberty relies upon a distinction between intentions bound up with individual actions and the cognitive capacities of individuals. Action follows from the intentions particular to the individuals, while knowledge can be constituted as a common end that imposes itself on every one. It is so because knowledge is presumed to be developed on the basis of facts that are exterior to thought and that are not dependent upon it. This permits one to *judge* the conformity of belief to facts. It is otherwise for action: subject to desires, passions, it depends on a variety of characteristics and situations, with the result that individuals do not share the same tastes and interests. From this distinction is derived the duality of ends and means. Ends are dependent on subjective impressions tied up with the tastes of individuals and cannot as such be reduced to an external unity. As for the means, they could be numerous, of a comparable pertinence in relation to the desired effect, or subjected to subjective preferences. Nonetheless, because they are the object of knowledge, they remain objectively available and therefore capable of founding an intersubjective unity. Human action is thus understood. We do not discuss the tastes of individuals, which are essentially divergent. However, in judging their efficiency, or in other words their rationality, we are interested in the means they use to satisfy these ends.

How, in this perspective, do we envisage the role given to society? The basic postulate consists of admitting that any action is undertaken in order to assure the greatest benefit with the least hardship, independently of the objectives that are

5   *Ibid.* at 67.

6   D. P. Chattopadhyaya, *Knowledge, Freedom, and Language: An Interwoven Fabric of Man, Time, and World* (Delhi: Motilal Banarsidass Publishers, 1989).

7   M. M. Carrilho, *Rationalités: les avatars de la raison dans la philosophie contemporaine* (Paris: Hatier, 1997); P. Moessinger, *Irrationalité individuelle et ordre social* (Geneva: Droz, 1996); D. P. Gauthier & R. Sugden, *Rationality, Justice and the Social Contract: Themes from Morals by Agreement* (Ann Arbor: University of Michigan Press, 1993).

chosen. Everyone seeks good and wants to avoid evil.[8] Human action is strictly indissociable from this union of two opposite poles: satisfaction and dissatisfaction. This stems from the fact that human beings have desires and needs, that is to say, they are faced with the possibility of lacking something, but also with the possibility of satisfying this lack by action, in a manner which is nonetheless always incomplete and without ever being able to hope for its absolute fulfilment. Desire and needs thus have scarcity as a corollary. And scarcity is a potential source of conflict. In fact, it is not certain that attempts to go beyond needs will be realized on the basis of an agreement between the individuals concerned. On the contrary, whether because of the competition entered into to obtain a scarce resource, or because of difference in taste, individuals may not agree upon the nature of the distributions to be made. Yet, because of the instability, the insecurity and the discouragement that it produces, conflict itself increases scarcity. Thus, the role of society will be to lessen tensions and reduce scarcity in assuring the effective use of rights, the transfer of rights by consent and the fulfilment of promises. Given their interest in society's adequately filling this role, individuals will be induced to adopt a certain type of altruistic attitude. They will know that a healthy reciprocity among them will help create a peace favourable to overcoming scarcity.

Accordingly, the pacification of society, an objective intended to ensure prosperity, presupposes a general agreement on the rules concerning the enjoyment of rights, of their free transfer and of the guarantee of promises.[9] More specifically, these rules are declaratory of individual liberty in two respects: first of all, in the enjoyment of the product of one's activities and, secondly, in the transfer of goods according to the convenience of each person, which is the opposite of constraint and permits the satisfaction of personal interests. In the realm of prosperity, this liberty is understood as follows: each person chooses to work or to produce, knowing that the fruits of her/his labour or her/his production will not be taken away from her/him; and each person, in the absence of unanimity, is not inclined to work or to produce freely for others. Overall, such a society based on the liberty of exchange will be a place of prosperity, not only because of the free choice of activities, but also because of the complementarity that permits the practice of exchanges.

If it is admitted that a society is composed of individuals who go about their business according to their interests, and that the activities of these individuals can be complementary, then there arises the problem of the connection between the different activities. Transfer by agreement permits exchange, which ensures complementarity on the basis of the respect of rights. However, given the fact that society is the playing field where different needs are expressed or different capacities that are not known to everyone are brought to light, there may be a lack of information about what must be done. In the absence of a complete and integral

8   R. Chappuis, *Les relations humaines: la relation à soi et aux autres* (Paris: Vigot, 1994).

9   A. P. Hamlin, *Ethics, Economics and the State* (New York: St. Martin's Press, 1986).

agreement, there is no assurance that the goods produced will be useful to certain people. Furthermore, no one is assured of finding what she/he wishes to obtain. Again, complementarity can imply a loss of autonomy and thus a dependence upon certain goods produced by other people. How can we render these various activities coherent, when the general rules do not describe nor prescribe the content of individual actions that are to be undertaken? It is up to economic activity as such to fulfil this informational role, and consequently the role of connecting the activities in general into a common and operational plan.[10] In what way can it act as a substitute for the absence of planning and organization in society and become a means of communication capable of provoking the necessary adjustments, as the case may be? Economic activity solves the problem of liaison by permeating itself with a guiding thread that is to be considered dominant and of universal import: the search for wealth.

The Value of 'Wealth': The Argument of Growth

'The commercial policy of fostering free international trade is the raison d'être for harmonizing contract law.'[11] Uniform law is not an end in itself. Its legitimacy lies in various bases for justification. The most important of them, according to H. Honka, resides in the growth in volume of economic activities that result from the process of uniformization. The argument of growth is therefore intrinsically bound up with uniform law. As such, the association between the development of trade and the existence of a unique juridical regime is not without historic precedent. The lex mercatoria *of medieval Europe partook of this spirit: the full and entire exercise of liberty in commerce implied, there too, the creation of an identical juridical space exempt from barriers to commercial activity. However, the present situation is distinguished by the magnitude of the phenomenon and a greater insistence on the efficiency of uniformization in the economic field. On the one hand, the idea that the Vienna Convention (for example) brings together most of the world's commercial partners, in spite of their social, economic and juridical differences, is a leitmotiv of current uniform law. Adherence to uniform law, whether explicit or implicit, benefits from a snowball effect: we adhere to it, notably, because others did so before us.[12] On the other hand, uniformization has become a many-sided reality.[13] It occurs under various guises, which is testimony to its versatility and its likelihood of ensuring growth, whether it intervenes at the level of public law or private law, in the matter of economic integration or simply on an individual basis.*

---

10   J. M. Buchanan, *The Economics and the Ethics of Constitutional Order* (Ann Arbor: University of Michigan Press, 1991).

11   H. Honka, 'Harmonization of Contract Law through International Trade: A Nordic perspective' (1996) 11 Tul. Eur. & Civ. L. F. 111 at 116.

12   K. Sono, 'UNCITRAL and the Vienna Sales Convention' (1984) 18 Int'l Law. 7 at 14.

13   H. P. Glenn, 'Harmonization of Private Law Rules Between Civil and Common Law Jurisdictions' in *Contemporary Law: Canadian Reports to the 1994 International Congress of Comparative Law* (Cowansville: Éditions Yvon Blais, 1995) at 79.

The argument of growth permits uniform law to promote wealth as one of its values.[14] This second value intervenes on the basis of reasoning that unfolds thus: if in society we constantly had to arrive at a unanimous agreement concerning which activities to undertake and which needs to satisfy, nothing or practically nothing would ever be accomplished. Possibly unanimity does not exist because there are irreducible differences as to what to do, or because of the practical obstacles that would prevent us from defining agreements on everything that is to be done, or for some other reason. Nonetheless, the absence of a determination regarding all activities and needs and the inability to obtain full information about them do not lead to chaos. What is important is to permit the repeated exercise of these complementarities through exchange, which reveals a partial agreement each time. And the sum of the partial agreements points to a functional system because it is animated by a *modus vivendi*: the individual and the collective both seek an improvement in status, translated mainly into the search for increased wealth.

How can we come to identify and to take for granted this *modus vivendi*, this 'interest that all peoples have, particularly those of developing countries, in broad development of international trade?'[15] The answer can be found in a postulate of an epistemological nature: the understanding of a phenomenon is made easier by the existence of causes that are more important than others, which renders secondary or negligible the study of less powerful factors. Furthermore, the separate examination of the more important causes permits their grading and thus the determination of the predominant cause in relation to a phenomenon or a social field. It thus becomes possible to act as if, in this field, this single cause intervenes, even if some of the details are false. Abstraction permits one to accede to a truth as a whole, not in detail.[16] Put differently, from the body of phenomena that it considers, abstraction will affect reality, even if this is not so from the point of view of the particular. To abstraction in this method is added deduction: thus, by separating out a typical cause, we can observe the consequences this cause will have on subsequent facts and manifestations in which it may intervene. The method that results is imperfectly predictive, because of its inability to grasp the totality of particular phenomena,[17] but it remains indicative of the trends that express the constancy of the predominant cause across variations in detail. In the instance under study here, if the motivations for action are viewed as a play of forces in competition and opposition, the value of wealth then represents the most frequent human force, whatever the contrary influences. Wealth, because of disturbances, cannot explain all situations, only most of them, and even then only as a predominant force in comparison with other existing values, which remain

14   A. K. Sen, *Choice, Welfare, and Measurement* (Cambridge: MIT Press, 1982); R. O'Donnell, *Adam Smith's Theory of Value and Distribution: A Reappraisal* (New York: St. Martin's Press, 1990).

15   United Nations, *Loi type de la CNUDCI sur le commerce électronique et Guide pour son incorporation 1996* (New York: United Nations, 1997) at 1.

16   A. Quinton, *The Nature of Things* (London: Routledge, 1973).

17   J. Vuillemin, *La logique et le monde sensible: étude sur les théories contemporaines de l'abstraction* (Paris: Flammarion, 1971).

present.[18] Thus, in the presence of many buyers and sellers for a given good, we could imagine that there will be a plurality of prices, according to the interests of each person. However, the existence of the value of wealth imposes unification. In fact, it enables one to predict that the seller, wishing to obtain the highest possible price for a good, will only sell it to the person who offers the most. Reciprocally, the buyer, wishing to pay the cheapest price, will turn to the person who is capable of offering her/him this price. So, from the interplay of supply and demand comes a tendency to establish a single price, which, for the sellers, will be the highest price possible. As for the buyers, none will find a lower price and none will be interested in offering more than this price. The egoism at the heart of these exchanges can be called normal: it is simply a psychological disposition that pushes everyone to follow her/his own interests when they are not directly harmful to others, from lack of unanimity in the planning of activities and the division of needs. The unifying capacity of wealth is therefore quite considerable. It succeeds in combining a diversity of interests in a measure which is recognizable by all and acceptable for all.

The general equilibrium to which wealth contributes, with the help of other values, is characterized by its dynamism.[19] In fact, the search for the best equivalence between the ends and the means necessarily opens up different combinations. Now, innovation has a dual character which is in complete opposition to immobility. It is marked first of all by discontinuity. By definition, innovation cannot come from some objective method; it is therefore not subjected to regularity in the periodicity of its manifestations. It also possesses the faculty of eliminating old forms and processes: the *new* competes with the *old* until it replaces it. Discontinuity and elimination are liable to create an unequal rhythm of social evolution, a rhythm made up of growth and depression, profit and loss. The potential or actual instability that risks appearing as a result is nonetheless viewed positively. It gives birth, among those who suffer from it or who fear suffering from it, as well as among those who sympathize with the problems of others, to a renewed wish for stability and a return to equilibrium and wealth. In short, new combinations, in spite of their negative repercussions, are ultimately beneficial. They are part of a continuing effort to create wealth in the most satisfying manner possible, and they are valued for the *utility* that they represent in this respect.

---

18 R. M. Starr, *General Equilibrium Models of Monetary Economics: Studies in the Static Foundations of Monetary Theory* (Boston: Academic Press, 1989); A. Lapidus, *Le détour de valeur* (Paris: Économica, 1986).

19 E. R. Weintraub, *General Equilibrium Analysis: Studies in Appraisal* (Cambridge: Cambridge University Press, 1985); A. K. Dixit & V. D. Norman, *Theory of International Trade: A Dual, General Equilibrium Approach* (Welwyn: J. Nisbet, 1980).

The Value of 'Utility': The Argument of the Maximization of Interests

'[C]ontract practice is the key to understanding the economic properties of contracting that are necessary to work out sensible uniform laws for commercial purposes.'[20] At the outset, this postulate emerges, according to R. Amissah, within the framework of surrounding globalization. If it is true that 'globalization is unstoppable,'[21] it remains to determine how to optimize the repercussions of this phenomenon. For Amissah, it is commercial contractual practice, because of its capacity to innovate, that is the most instructive. Law only intervenes afterwards, in order to support the practice.[22] More specifically, under the phrase 'autonomous contract', Amissah conceptualizes the relationship between commercial reality and uniform law that is likely to obtain maximization of sought for interests. This concept is laid out along three axes, as follows:

i)   The 'autonomous' contract as an expression of the will that 'governs' international commerce.
ii) The 'autonomous contract' as seeking the means to transcend national boundaries.
iii) The 'autonomous contract' designed to be virtually self-contained and 'self-governing'.[23]

These axes trace what it would be convenient to call the prospective of uniform law, a prospective that is not to be evaluated on a technical level alone. In fact, it is ideologically supported by an international normative consensus founded principally on liberalism. According to J. Wiener, it contains a common set of principles that lay 'the foundation for the harmonization and unification activities, which, in turn, is a symptom of the larger, globalizing force of capital.'[24]

Uniform law, through the argument of the maximization of interests, reveals its approval of the value of utility. At the same time, it finds itself adopting a

---

20   R. Amissah, 'The Autonomous Contract', online: University of Tromso <http://ananse.irv.uit.no/trade_law...s.Contract.03.10.1997.Amissah.html>.
21   M. L. Cattaui, 'The global economy: An opportunity to be seized', online: Business World <http://www.iccwbo.org/html/globalec.htm>.
22   R. Coase, 'Industrial Organization: A Proposal for Research' in P. Coase, ed., *The Firm, The Market and The Law* (Chicago: University of Chicago Press, 1988) at 57.
23   Amissah, *supra*, note 20.
24   J. Wiener, 'The Transnational Political Economy: A Framework for Analysis', online: University of Tromso <http://ananse.irv.uit.no/trade_law or Analysis.Jarrod.Wiener.UKC.html>.
     See also Commentary 1 on Article 1.1 of the Unidroit Principles, *supra*, Introduction, note 38: 'The principle of freedom of contract is of paramount importance in the context of international trade. The right of business people to decide freely to whom they will offer their goods and services and by whom they wish to be supplied, as well as the possibility for them freely to agree on the terms of individual transactions, are the cornerstones of an open, market-oriented and competitive international economic order.'

consequentialist position:[25] the justification of actions taken directly or indirectly, according to uniform law, resides in their consequences, that is to say in the state of things produced by these actions. In other words, we will judge the virtuousness or the badness of an action from the good or bad nature of its consequences. And this justification, or this good or bad quality, will be associated with the idea of the maximization of happiness or the welfare of humanity, which can be reduced to a few hypotheses and deductions: no one, outside of coercion or trickery, may increase wealth other than by satisfying interests; the search for the maximization of wealth urges producers to try to satisfy the most remunerative interests, that is to say those which users want the most, and thus to maximize their satisfaction; furthermore, users obtain the goods that they desire at the lowest prices among those that are offered; thus there is a harmony of interests and, *consequently*, an optimization of collective happiness.[26]

As for wealth, this form of utility plays an essential role in the linking and coherence of activities that take place in a society.[27] These activities not only bind the interests of two isolated partners, who are part of a world that knows nothing whatever about their actions. On the contrary, even if it happens that these interests have no effect on those of third parties, it also happens that transactions, without any formal relation between them, can influence one another. These are externalities. These may be positive, or favourable to the interests of some or all people. In this respect, they do not cause any particular difficulties and they are part of the good side of life. On the other hand, negative externalities create a considerable potential problem. In fact, in accordance with liberty and wealth, a transaction presupposes:

i)   the common initiative of contractants who assert their will and come to agreement after negotiation;
ii) the precise and unequivocal definition of the object of the transaction; and
iii) a common evaluation of the object of the transaction.

Yet the externalities are not the result of a voluntary common approach; they are *endured*. Furthermore, their limits are not defined with precision, as it would be practically impossible to take a census of everybody affected by externalities. Finally, insofar as these externalities are unilaterally endured, they cannot be the object of a common evaluation by the contractants. In this context, could it be that negative externalities create such a distortion that they push society from the

---

25   D. R. Mapel & T. Nardin, 'Convergence and Divergence in International Ethics' in T. Nardin & D. R. Mapel, eds., *Traditions of International Ethics* (Cambridge: Cambridge University Press, 1992) at 297.

26   J. Riley, *Liberal Utilitarianism: Social Choice Theory and J. S. Mill's Philosophy* (Cambridge: Cambridge University Press, 1988).

27   J. Elster & J. E. Roemer, *Interpersonal Comparisons of Well-Being* (Cambridge: Cambridge University Press, 1991); R. E. Sartorius, *Individual Conduct and Social Norms: A Utilitarian Account of Social Union and the Rule of Law* (Encino: Dickenson Pub., 1975).

pacific field of exchange to the field of conflict and risk of coercion? It is precisely utility that is called upon to undertake the task of eliminating this risk by tracing a twofold path. The first consists of properly grasping the meaning and scope of utility in relation to the abovementioned question. Utility corresponds to that which is chosen or preferred. It does not designate a quality associated with a good or a service, but the attraction that this good or service may represent for a person. The attraction depends upon a satisfaction that this person may derive from it (whatever the degree of this satisfaction), which makes up the ingredient that is the basis of happiness. The second path introduces the market, which possesses the virtue of permitting the convergence of all factors – including negative externalities – in a quantified measure that takes the form of an exchange price. Certain factors probably look undesirable in view of the necessity of maintaining social harmony and peace. However, they are ironed out in view of the evidence of a common interest for a quantum, money, which thus represents the medium of unification of all the variants of utility.

The conception of society which is conveyed by utility can be further developed by stating that its ultimate locus of value is the individual.[28] The reason is simple: it is individuals, not communities, who can feel happiness or pain, see their hopes satisfied or unsatisfied and so on. It is possible to think of a community as wishing something, but this can always be brought back to, and broken down in light of, the individuals who are part of this community. Such a conception does not mean that communities are useless. It is obvious that the welfare or happiness of the individual depends, in varying degrees and following diverse modalities, on her/his relations with the community of which she/he is a member. It remains that the value of a community does not represent more than the sum of the respective values of the individuals that compose it. From this, the primary function of the community, if there is one, consists of protecting and supporting, in one manner or another, the individual, a legitimate function because it constitutes the most efficient manner of promoting general welfare. But what happens if we judge that the protection and help offered by a community do not adequately take into account its mission to offer the most efficient promotion possible of the general welfare? This problematic is concretely evident in the insurmountable tension that prevails between two modes of interpretation: the utility of the act and the utility of the rule. The first mode puts the emphasis on the act itself. The justification of an act depends entirely on circumstances: it will be correct if it maximizes utility, regardless of whether or not it conforms to otherwise pertinent rules. The second mode interprets utility on the basis of norms and principles established by the community. It takes for granted that the maximization of utility comes from the generalized observation of these norms and principles. The correct act is thus that which respects these norms and principles, even if, in a particular case, it does not

---

28   J. J. C. Smart & B. Williams, *Utilitarisme: le pour et le contre*, trans. H. Poltier (Geneva: Labor, 1997); D. H. Hodgson, *Consequences of Utilitarianism: A Study in Normative Ethics and Legal Theory* (Oxford: Clarendon, 1967).

attain the objective of maximization.[29] But no matter how this tension is displayed, uniform law adds a fundamental modality to the search for general happiness: it wishes to maximize happiness on the condition that this is done in an *equitable* manner.

The Value of 'Justice': The Argument of Equality and Cooperation between the Parties

'Justice and equity can and should be considered as the essential nuclei of a community's juridical and economic life, especially in light of the dynamic developments occurring in the modern commercial world.'[30] In asserting this principle in a study of the principles of UNIDROIT, H. Veytia reiterates uniform law's concern to ensure an equilibrium of forces and benefits between parties, and ensure also that they collaborate. Discarding a certain image whereby the international sphere is the exclusive domain of experienced professionals in business relations, who have access to adequate resources and are experienced in the rules of good conduct, uniform law here recognizes the inevitable existence of unequal situations.[31] It expresses its concern with this subject, underlined in terms of the search for a contractual justice, in the following elements:

i)   *Public order: certain rules, provided for by uniform law itself or by national laws, have an imperative character susceptible of remediating certain forms of contractual injustice.[32]*
ii) *Good faith: charged with meaning, it deploys its possible interventions in many areas. For example, concerning the formation of contracts, good faith is a cornerstone of the duties of confidentiality[33] and loyalty,[34] just as much as it justifies an exception to the principle of the revocability of an offer.[35]*

---

29   D. Regan, *Utilitarianism and Co-operation* (New York: Clarendon, 1980).

30   H. Veytia, 'The Requirement of Justice and Equity in Contracts' (1995) 69 Tul. L. Rev. 1191 at 1206.

31   M. J. Bonell, *An International Restatement of Contract Law: The Unidroit Principles of International Contracts Law* (Irvington: Transnational Juris Publications, 1994) at 90.

32   See, for example, Art. 1.7 of the Principles: '(1) Each party must act in accordance with good faith and fair dealing in international trade; (2) The parties may not exclude or limit this duty.'

33   See Principles, Art. 2.16: 'Where information is given as confidential by one party in the course of negotiations, the other party is under a duty not to disclose that information or to use it improperly for its own purposes, whether or not a contract is subsequently concluded. Where appropriate, the remedy for breach of that duty may include compensation based on the benefit received by the other party.'

34   See Principles, Art. 2.15 (2): 'However, the party who negotiates or breaks off in bad faith is liable for the losses caused to the other party.'

35   See Principles, Art. 2.4 (2) (b): 'However, an offer cannot be revoked, if it was reasonable for the offeree to rely on the offer as being irrevocable and the offeree has acted in reliance on the offer.'

iii) A just contractual equilibrium, which is an objective that the rules governing excessive benefit, hardship, the abusive clause and the exonerating clause contribute to.[36]

iv) The promotion of the reasonable: contractual justice requires, as well, the satisfaction of the normal and predictable expectations of the parties.[37]

The argument of equilibrium and cooperation accounts for the presence of the just in the context of discovery of uniform law's own values. What interpretation can we draw from this presence? This creates a considerable challenge, because justice always resists ready made solutions, if only because of the diversity and contradiction of its many images. In the same manner, it would be risky to claim that uniform law clearly establishes a mature and proven conception of justice. The exercise is nonetheless still valuable if we imagine it as the development of a map. A map furnishes an imperfect sketch of the reality that it projects, but the information it provides is of value nonetheless. We must simply avoid looking to it for information that it does not possess and that it does not claim to possess. The map that enables a definition of the justice of uniform law should be viewed this way.

The first kind of information it can yield concerns the *raison d'être* of justice. Why must we fear injustice and, correlatively, promote justice?[38] Two reasons, one cognitive and the other normative, can be adduced. First of all, injustice perturbs predictable models of relations that individuals create in order to harmonize their relations and make them functional; it thus menaces the whole logic of their behaviour. In fact, this logic relies upon the possibility of predicting the fulfilment and consequences of actions. Furthermore, injustice reveals a disdain or a low esteem for others. But this threatens their identity, which is an essential element of their development.

The second kind of information relates to the definition and the content of justice, which bring us back to needs, equality and merit. However, this apparent simplicity hides a tangled set of rules.[39] Equality may be subdivided into equality of opportunity (to be re-subdivided between simple expectations and effective means of obtaining something), satisfaction and treatment. Merit is sometimes linked to effort, sometimes to productivity or talent. Needs oscillate between subjectivity and objectivity. These rules are often combined and mixed together in a single judgement. Furthermore, they are often contradictory: the equality of satisfaction presupposes a lesser significance being assigned to equality of

---

36 See, for example, Principles, Art. 7.1.6: 'A clause which limits or excludes one party for non-performance or which permits one party to render performance substantially different from what the other party reasonably expected may not be invoked if it would be grossly unfair to do so, having regard to the purpose of the contract.'

37 See Principles, notably Art. 4.1 (1): 'A contract shall be interpreted according to the common intention of the parties.'

38 P. Ricoeur, *Le Juste* (Paris: Éditions Esprit, 1995).

39 W. B. Griffith, 'Equality and Egalitarianism: Framing the Contemporary Debate' (1994) 12 C.J.L.J. 5; D. Rae, *Equalities* (Cambridge: Harvard University Press, 1981).

opportunity; to ensure the fulfilment of this last element may require that we set aside equality of treatment. Added to this is the delicate determination of who are the parties concerned: is this a relationship between individuals of one particular population, or between different groups, communities or entities?

Nonetheless, at least three conceptions of a just contract with respect to uniform law may be deduced from these considerations. Each articulates differently the inherent dimensions of a contractual relationship: contractual liberty, the validity of the contract, the responsibilities of the parties and the impact of prescription.[40] Among these conceptions we find voluntarism, which equates justice with the expression of the will of the parties. Once this will has been expressed, the contract dictates its law to the parties. As to validity, this means there is no unilateral right of rescission. It also means the responsibilities are those the parties have defined and damages will not vary according to the means of the party at fault. Finally, the impact of prescription is of little consequence: the passage of time does not suppress nor create obligations outside of the common will of the parties. In opposition to voluntarism we find providentialism. It rests upon a central idea that a person bound by a contract who is judged to be weaker or less well informed must be protected in all circumstances. This objective transcends both the force of the contracted obligations and the principle of the pre-established division of the responsibilities. Rights are born and disappear without being bound to the initial intentions expressed by the parties. Thus the validity of the contract remains subject to a more systematic right of rescission. Symmetrically, it is taken for granted that the individual should be protected against the consequences of her/his acts and that the compensation for the real value of the prejudice is necessary even if this is contrary to the explicit agreement of the parties. In addition, prescription plays an important role: prolonged usage creates a right, in spite of the absence of agreement on this subject. Finally, the conception called finalism leads the analysis to the consequences of the execution of the contract incurred by the parties. More than the will of the parties, it is the welfare of the contractants, the intrinsic values of things and the evaluation of the ultimate interests of society that serve as criteria for a just contract. As a result, without recognizing a systematic right to rescission, the onerous character of the execution of a contract for a party might justify that this party be relieved of her/his obligations. When a contract directly affects many people in the family circle of a contracting party, these should be authorized to give their assent or impose their veto: one's concern for the consequences of an engagement must win out over the right of each person to make transactions as she/he pleases. The same type of concern prevails in the sphere of responsibility, such that the guarantee attached to an object must be made according to the value of this object. Extinctive prescription is not easily given: a debt is a debt, and unless the debtor finds

---

40 R. E. Barnett, 'Conflicting Visions: A Critique of Ian Macneil's Relational Theory of Contract' (1992) 78 Va. L. Rev. 1175; I. R. Macneil, 'Relational Contract: What We Do and Do Not Know' 55 (1985) Wis. L. Rev. 483.; J. M. Feinman, 'Critical Approaches of Contract Law' (1983) 30 UCLA L. Rev. 829.

her/himself in a very awkward situation, she/he has to pay it. On the other hand, acquisitive prescription is tolerated if it corresponds to a major interest. Thus, this conception cannot be reduced to a simple question of protection. Rather, it falls back upon the defense and the improvement of the welfare of the greatest number by weighing the interests at hand, including those of the society as a whole. Furthermore, the degree of cooperation between the parties will oscillate in the following way. In a rigid contractual view, associated with voluntarism, the degree of cooperation will be lesser, because the obligations tend to be limited to the precise object of the contract. The optimal degree will be reached under the flexible contractual perspective of finalism, where the parties define their obligations by attempting to anticipate the future.

The Context of Justification

In liberty, wealth, utility and justice, uniform law recognizes values likely to underpin its legitimacy. But what principles and what arithmetic are appropriate to determine the relative weight of each, and the type of articulation likely, both in individual cases and overall, to effectively attain this objective of legitimacy? By what frame of reference are we able to evaluate the degree with which the objective of legitimacy is attained? This is the role that devolves upon the context of justification, which corresponds to a sort of *Rule of Law* of uniform law. It presents itself as a norm possessing the greatest influence within uniform law, a norm that exercises a form of primacy over all others. As regards values, the context of justification presents two distinct 'tableaux'. The first presents the formal content of the context of justification, while the second presents the procedure for the determination of its constitutive values. This dichotomy calls for some comment.

Tableau 1 assembles certain values presented by uniform law as acting as *ultima ratio*. Clearly this presentation is potentially enlightening in itself. That is why it is important to stop and look at it. However, concretely, this first tableau is more of a sketch than a completed work. This is explained in part by the prominence of instrumental reasoning and the weak presence of ends-based reasoning revealed in the analysis of the context of justification of the principles of thought. As has been shown, this apportionment of relative prominence to these two kinds of reasoning has a distinct significance for the role of values: it renders them subordinate, secondary.[41] On the other hand, the incomplete state of Tableau 1 may also be accounted for by the specific procedure for determining values (see Tableau 2). Nothing guarantees the reliability of this procedure: it can thus constitute an additional factor in understanding the paleness of Tableau 1. This is in itself a sufficient reason, without being the exclusive one, to take an interest in Tableau 2. This tableau is also of interest because of the fact that, in some views, procedure directly influences the degree of acceptability of values in general, a

---

41 See Chapter 1, above.

consideration that is also important as regards the values that may be used as a 'Rule of Law' of uniform law. Procedure thus assumes fundamental importance. It becomes a value in itself; from this moment on, we should turn our attention to it rather than to its content. In fact, uniform law, particularly in its State and intermediate versions, assigns considerable importance to the conditions of the formation of values in establishing its own legitimacy. Whatever the reason why this is not reflected in the tableau presenting the content of values, it becomes necessary to examine the parameters and boundaries of procedure. Furthermore, an emphasis on procedure permits us to go beyond the inherent immobility of the formal presentation of values that are taken for granted, by showing how uniform law is capable of making them evolve.

Tableau 1: Content

Depending on the version of uniform law that is considered, the definition of content in the ultimate frame of reference will vary. One of the most developed contents belongs to State law and it is to State law that I would like to turn my attention. This is because its origins, as prepared by the United Nations Commission on International Trade Law (UNCITRAL), frame a very great body of orientations and measures that have been put forward for a number of years by various agencies and constituent bodies of the United Nations. This body of orientations forms a reservoir of superior and decisive considerations in the light of which the legitimacy of uniform law may be evaluated, whether from up close or far away. Going from the general to the particular, we observe this in Tableau 1.

First of all, analysing the underlying values of the matters covered and the vocabulary used by the Vienna Convention, A. H. Kastely writes as follows: 'Perhaps the most fundamental of these is the conception of actors under the Convention as different in background and circumstances, yet entitled to equal treatment and respect.'[42] In the opinion of Kastely, this preeminent value of equality provides, together with others, a coherence which is indispensable to the language of the Vienna Convention.

Secondly, it is interesting to bring to the surface the basic considerations which prevailed at the time of the creation of UNCITRAL, which is at the origin of the Vienna Convention and other instruments of uniformization. Initially, they stressed the importance of international commerce and the conditions of its realization in the quest for global harmony. The Romanian delegate spoke as follows during the discussion concerning the proposal to create UNCITRAL, sounding the call of a destiny to which the world had been summoned:

> The development of international trade, therefore, would meet real needs of the international community; it would be an essential contribution to the efforts to create

---

42   A. H. Kastely, 'Unification and Community: A Rhetorical Analysis of the United Nations Sales Convention' (1988) 8 Northwestern Journal of International Law and Business 574 at 594.

... conditions of stability and well-being, which were necessary for peaceful and friendly relations among nations based on respect for the principle of equal rights and self-determination of peoples. Accordingly, it was necessary to establish rules that would facilitate commercial transactions on the basis of respect for sovereignty and national independence, non-intervention in the domestic affairs of States and mutual benefit.[43]

At the same time, it had become clear that the uniformization of law could strengthen interdependent developments in international commerce and world harmony. In order to do so, it was necessary that uniform rules be impregnated with, and tend toward, the abovementioned values and ideal. But uniformization was also by its very nature a necessity, given its inherent capacity to eliminate national juridical divergences perceived as obstacles to the necessary growth of commercial exchange. In addition, it became clear both at that time and thereafter that the United Nations and its agencies, including UNCITRAL, became an appropriate forum in which to ensure there was a junction of uniformization and general welfare, as well as being the forum for the activation of programmes and actions required under the circumstances.

Finally, what followed these events led notably to the establishment of a direct link between the Vienna Convention and *the general objectives written in the resolutions concerning the creation of a New International Economic Order that the General Assembly of the United Nations adopted at its sixth extraordinary session.*[44] The frame of reference of uniform law thus became more specific than it had been at the time of the creation of UNCITRAL. It appears, however, that the New International Economic Order (NIEO) must itself be re-situated in light of a more recent reflection and a dynamic that culminated, according to J. C. N. Paul, in an international law of development (known as ILD).[45] The ILD confirms the preponderant role of juridical instruments with respect to development.[46] According to Paul, the ILD subordinates the legitimacy of actions undertaken in this perspective to the promotion, direct or indirect, of a development founded on the following principles:

- people-centred animation, that is, development designed to promote human dignity, capacities, security and welfare;
- participation: enabling and empowering people to initiate self-reliant and self-managed development efforts in all spheres relevant to well-being;
- respect and protection of rights and liberties of the person;
- elimination of forms of discrimination founded on sex or ethnic background;
- protection of the environment and a favourable bias toward avenues of sustainable development;

---

43 (1970) 1 Y. B. U. N. Comm'n on Int'l Trade L., U. N. Doc. a/CN.9/SER.A/1970 at 54.
44 See the Preamble of the Vienna Convention, *supra*, Preamble, note 4.
45 J. C. N. Paul, 'The United Nations and the Creation of an International Law of Development' (1995) 36 Harv. Int'l L. J. 307.
46 *Ibid.* at 307-309.

- respect and protection of cultural diversity;
- a favourable bias toward the emergence and consolidation of democratic modes of representation;
- accessibility of the means necessary for the full efficiency of the abovementioned principles.

Tableau 2: Procedure

I submit that uniform law conceives its procedure for the determination of values as a communicative process. This emerges in particular from the functions and attributes that the General Assembly gave to UNCITRAL at the time of its creation. In accordance with the report of the Secretary-General entitled 'Progressive Development of the Law of International Trade',[47] the General Assembly articulated the mandate of UNCITRAL along various axes emerging from one or another of three basic elements of communication.[48] First of all, the leadership and the credibility of UNCITRAL were dependent upon its capacity to *make known* to the greatest number the various types of information relevant to its mission.[49] This element of dissemination was followed up, secondly, by another element, *broad-mindedness.*[50] On the institutional level, UNCITRAL had to be transparent and active with respect to cooperation; on the normative level, it had to encourage participation and sharing in the development of uniform law. Dissemination and broad-mindedness worked together toward the creation of the third element of communication, which consists of *rendering common.*[51] The idea of community, in fact, was omnipresent in the mandate of UNCITRAL. Subsequent developments would reaffirm this orientation of uniform law toward a paradigm of communication. In her remarkable analysis, Kastely shows to what extent the Vienna Convention 'is deeply political, *fundamentally rhetorical,* in its aspirations.'[52] This turns out to be necessary for the attainment of an international community, without which the goal of uniformization would remain a pure abstraction.[53] The dissemination of information, deliberations, 'sense of shared interest,'[54] the utilization of discourse and so on, are all examples of the modes and provisions belonging to communication that can be drawn from the Vienna Convention and that support the emergence and flourishing of the sought-for community. As Kastely affirms,

---

47 *Progressive Development of the Law of International Trade: Report of the Secretary-General,* 21 U.N. GAOR, U.N. Doc. A/6396 (1966).
48 G.A. Res. 2205 (XXI), U.N. Doc. A/6396 (1966).
49 *Ibid.* at par. 8(e), (f), (g).
50 *Ibid.* at par. (a), (b).
51 *Ibid.* at par. 8(c), (d).
52 Kastely, *supra,* note 42; at 577 [emphasis added].
53 'There must be an international community of people who perceive themselves as bound together and governed by a common legal system and who have some way to deliberate together over matters of continuing verification and development.' *Ibid.*
54 *Ibid.*

The text of the Convention seeks to establish . . . a rhetorical community in which its readers first assent to the language and values of the text itself, and then use the language and values to inform their relations with one another.[55]

Having formulated and backed up this initial proposition, let us now examine the communicative procedure characteristic of uniform law in greater depth.

The basis of the determination and the articulation of values depends upon the relationship between procedure and the phenomenon called the antinomy of truth. This is how A. Wellmer presents this phenomenon in the perspective of a communicative paradigm:

When we communicate, present or write something, we inevitably make claims to truth, or rather . . . claims to truth of different orders. Thus, if I do it in a serious manner, I expect that others, whoever they may be, have good reason to agree with what I have affirmed, on the condition that they understand what I said and possess sufficient information, competence, and judgement, etc. In this sense, I presuppose that my claim to validity lends itself perfectly to intersubjective agreement founded on good reasons. But if it happens that someone opposes what I affirm with the help of solid arguments, than I have to take back my claim to validity or at least admit that doubt is justified. All of this may seem quite trivial, but we know that it is often such trivialities that are at the heart of some of the most interesting philosophical controversies. If we undertake to reflect on what makes a good argument or an irrefutable proof, we easily lose our footing; especially when we realize how difficult it may be to reach agreement in this field. Given the fact that there are irreducible disagreements among the members of various linguistic, scientific, or cultural communities concerning the possibility of justifying truth claims about the existence of schemes of argumentation or the inherent persuasive force of empirical proof, it may be appropriate to ask whether we can even believe that adequate schemes and persuasion, that is, an objective truth that would be acceptable for the problems in question, exist – somewhere. Or else should we rather admit that truth is always 'relative' to cultures, languages, societies, even individuals? If the latter solution – relativism – seems inconsistent, the first – the 'absolutism' of truth – seems necessarily to entail metaphysical presuppositions. This is what I call the 'antinomy of truth.'[56]

What is the position of uniform law in relation to the antinomy of truth? One way of looking at this is to affirm that it is enclosed in it. Thus, its values would be determined and weighed among themselves through avenues and forces tending, sometimes toward absolutism, sometimes toward relativism. In support of absolutism, it would be possible to invoke arguments that vigorously refute any form of ethnocentrism or pluralism in the interpretation of uniform law, or those that hold to a hard and fast objective of uniform interpretation.[57] On the other hand,

---

55   *Ibid.*

56   A. Wellmer, 'Vérité, contingence et modernité', in J. Poulain, ed., *De la vérité: pragmatisme, historicisme et relativisme* (Paris: Albin Michel, 1996) at 177-178.

57   For example, see V. S. Cook, 'The U.N. Convention for the International Sale of Goods: A Mandate to Abandon Legal Ethnocentricity' (1997) 16 J. L. & Com. 49.

essentially sceptical arguments of the idea of uniformization,[58] or those that hesitate to recognize the simply functional character of uniform law in the present circumstances, could serve to illustrate support for relativism.[59] Nonetheless, I believe it more proper to affirm, on the basis of the interpretation of two sections of Kastely's analysis, that uniform law more often uses strategies to escape the antinomy of truth. What are they? And are they well founded?

The first section may be illustrated with this quotation:

> The community created and promoted by the Convention is . . . thoroughly consensual and artificial. This approach is quite different from the view that human communities are natural, organic, or inevitable . . . . The Sales Convention, in contrast, begins with the assumption that a community may be created by choice and agreement.[60]

In strategic terms, a serious interpretation of this statement would consist of the following: The members of this *consensual and artificial* community are endowed with various social, economic and juridical systems, as recognized in the preamble to the Vienna Convention.[61] This differential element may be interpreted as signifying that there is not, overall, an obvious unanimity of values or of the hierarchy of values. Thus, the challenge consists in asking what general principles could the members of the international community agree upon, whatever their differences of views and of interests, seeing in such general principles the prerequisites of a just society. Uniform law must then search for principles everyone can subscribe to, without, for all that, one's having to renounce one's right to put forward one's convictions or orientations. If it were possible to develop principles that offer to each and every person the greatest latitude to express their preferences and to fulfil their ends without limiting the expression of preferences and the fulfilment of the ends of others, then there would not be any reason such a system could not bring about a consensus. To do so one must still ensure that the members agree, at least implicitly, on certain cardinal values, such as liberty, wealth, utility and justice. How are these values to be evaluated? How are they tied up with other values? How can we attest to the superiority of judgement that is attained thanks to these values, generally and in each particular case? It is here that

---

58   See the comments of J. Honnold about the legal realists in 'The Sales Convention in Action – Uniform International Words: Uniform Application?' (1988) 8 J. L. & Com. 207; also, F. M. Bannes, 'L'impact de l'adoption des *Principes* Unidroit 1994 sur l'unification du droit commercial international: réalité ou utopie?' (1996) 21 R.R.J. 933.

59   See the comments of A. Rosett in 'Critical Reflections on the United Nations Convention on Contracts for the International Sale of Goods' (1984) 45 Ohio State Law Journal 265.

60   Kastely, *supra*, note 42; at 588.

61   The following analysis relies on an analogy with the argumentation of J.-M. Ferry, *Philosophie de la communication, 2: Justice politique et démocratie procédurale* (Paris: Éditions du Cerf, 1994). See, for a similar approach, C. Kukathas & P. Pettit, *Rawls: A Theory of Justice and its Critics* (Stanford: Stanford University Press, 1990).

both individualism born of consensualism and abstraction born of artifice find their true meaning. They invite one to imagine any party (a contractant, a State, a decider, etc.) interested in uniform law as being capable of placing her/himself in a position of impartiality. In order to answer the questions above, this party would not have any vision of her/his actual and contextual situation, nor that of others. She/he would be led, by prudence and following her/his interest rightly understood, to imagine every possible situation and to mentally place her/himself, in good faith, in these situations. It is this 'decentring' of the interested party which would permit her/him to choose the *best possible* values.

From a communicative point of view, this strategy has one important drawback: by its marked insistence of the 'self', it comes back, finally, to a form of monologue or, at best, to a dialogue by an interested party, but with her/himself. In fact, it is important to realize that the *best possible* is obtained as the result of a cost/benefit calculation of interests aimed at attaining the best for oneself, in opposition to mutual welfare. Of course, that this calculation should integrate, and deeply integrate, the values of uniform law is not excluded a priori. But in essence, it can only translate a gentle form of egoism purged of concrete empirical interests. Thus it is not required, in all logic, that the interested party actively inform her/himself or be informed of the experience of others in order to arouse at least minimal discussion. At the same time, the abstraction of the interested party from the position that she/he occupies in society does not necessarily lead to the recognition of the other. It is limited to constraining the interested party to imagine her/himself as the other, which remains different from forcing her/him to put her/himself concretely in the place of the other. In these circumstances, it is not surprising that Kastely concludes the first of the passages referred to above by pointing out that 'the Convention suggests that the principal motive for joining [the] community will be self-interest.'[62]

Is it possible to mitigate the communicative inadequacies of this strategy? Further on in her analysis, Kastely examines common language, the bearer of many values, established by the Vienna Convention, and the 'occasions for discussions and deliberations'[63] offered by it. Her words open the door to another strategy synthesized in the following passage:

> What is called for, in essence, is the development of a jurisprudence of international *trade*. This is the heart of the rhetorical aspiration [of the Convention]. Its success . . . directly depends on the achievement of this goal.[64]

I interpret this statement as follows. Contrary to the first argument, founded on abstract calculation, this one tends toward an ideal speech situation.[65] Here, the attainment of the *best possible*, as well as the mastery of the differential element,

---

62 *Ibid.*
63 Kastely, *supra*, note 42; at 600.
64 *Ibid.* at 600-601 [emphasis added].
65 See J. Habermas, *De l'éthique de la discussion*, trans. M. Hunyadi (Paris: Éditions du Cerf, 1992) at 17ff.

are credited to the community that can best realize the conditions of an equal participation in discussion and in deliberation. The whole should facilitate, given the diversity of points of view and exchanges, a constant questioning of the existing order at a given moment, and is thus more conducive to progress than the first strategy.

What is it really, still viewing it from the angle of communication? Everything depends on the effective power for reception, animation and dissemination of the main tool of communication of uniform law that is established by this juris-prudence of international commerce. By power, we must understand a real capacity to create an ideal speech situation, which I will outline theoretically. First of all, circumstances of interest must be made known to the community in the terms in which they are experienced, interpreted and evaluated by the interested parties. Each needs the others' stories in order to understand how they live: this is the pri-mary source of true and mutual understanding. It follows, then, that any interested party may present her/his arguments her/himself. These cannot be left to the ima-gination of others and become in any manner a prejudice. Finally, because basic sensibilities are not identical for all, the stories and arguments will take on quite different orientations that only full and open types of discussion could reconcile.[66]

At the present time, the general doctrinal trend is to translate the evaluation of the power of the case law of international trade in terms of challenges.[67] The novelty of State law, combined with the attention drawn, and the challenges uncovered, by its interpretive dimension, clearly show that nothing has been won yet.[68] A similar situation prevails in intermediate law.[69] As for *lex mercatoria*, its renewal in today's conditions and those of tomorrow forces us to admit that it is also in the process of revising its optic of communication.[70] In short, the second strategy put forward by uniform law to escape the antinomy of truth is filled with precariousness and uncertainty. However, I feel that it is now time to reinforce this finding by stating a hypothesis, to be confirmed further on, that the case law of international commerce, even when viewed in the light of what is most dynamic

---

66 A. A. Moles & E. Rohmer, *Théorie structurale de la communication et société* (Paris: Masson, 1986); R. A. Adler & L. B. Rosenfeld, *Interplay: The Process of Interpersonal Communication* (New York: Holt, Rinehart, and Winston, 1983).

67 P. B. Stephan, 'The Futility of Unification and Harmonization in International Commercial Law' (1999) 39 Va. J. Int'l L. 743.

68 See Part IV, Preliminary Remarks, below. Also, F. Ferrari, 'CISG Case Law: A New Challenge for Interpreters' (1998) 17 J. L. & Com. 245; J. O. Honnold, 'The Sales Convention: From Idea to Practice' (1998) 17 J. L. & Com. 181.

69 A. M. Garro, 'The Contribution of the UNIDROIT Principles to the Advancement of International Commercial Arbitration' (1995) 3 Tul. J. Int'l & Comp. L. 93; M. J. Bonell, 'The Unidroit Principles in Practice: The Experience of the First Two Years' (1997) 1 R.D.U. 30.

70 T. E. Carbonneau, ed., *Lex Mercatoria and Arbitration: A Discussion of the New Law Merchant* (New York: Juris Publishing, 1998).

and innovative in its present impact, will not be able to possess the power required to create an ideal speech situation.[71]

---

71 See Chapter 6, below.

Final Remarks

In this first part, I have explored the background of uniform law. This exploration was necessary because of the methodological premise laid out in the Introduction, according to which the sense of the explicit arguments used in the discourse of uniform law depends on a 'deep structure' – that is to say a reservoir of assumptions, a background – which has to be exposed to view. In doing this, I have brought to light a series of little stories, of philosophic terms, divided into two chapters. The first is devoted to the principles of thought. It shows that arguments of good faith, the autonomy of the will and juridical convergence (the context of discovery) testify to a uniform law which is subordinate to metaphysical, analytical and simplifying thoughts. It shows, also, that these thoughts interact according to instrumental reason (the context of justification). Chapter 2 describes values. Four arguments are analysed: those of the concrete intention of the parties, of growth, of the maximization of interests and of equality and cooperation among parties. They reflect respectively the values of liberty, wealth, utility and justice (the context of discovery). These values remain subject to a context of justification based on the norms of an international law of development (ILD) and a communicative paradigm.

These little stories can be read independently or somehow tied in with one another. Does their reading 'ring false'? If such is the case, it is not abnormal. In fact, we must not forget that, even once extracted from legal scholarship, they form a *poly*-background, that is to say a background which is open to dissonance as well as consonance. What is important is that they be sufficiently insightful and sensible to give the right tone and clearly set themselves apart from the intuitionist route discredited by M. Koskenniemi.

The unravelling operation that we have carried out and the background we have arrived at permit us to be thoroughly conversant with what I have called the conservative consciousness of uniform law. Having taken this step, it is now possible to proceed with an examination of the strengths and defects of uniform law, that is to say with its substantive criticism.

PART II

CONSERVATIVE CONSCIOUSNESS: CRITIQUE

Preliminary Remarks

Following the procedural method outlined in Part I, I will now take a moment to formulate some preliminary remarks in order to properly situate the ins and outs of the critical analysis of the conservative consciousness of uniform law.

This critique corresponds to the intermediate phase of the Koskenniemi triptych as adapted for the purposes of this reflection. It forms the link between the unravelling and the reformulation which complete the tri-dimensional analysis proposed by the author. As a methodological element, the importance of the critique could be perhaps assumed, without any further evidence in its favour. As well, I could also limit myself to a basic level conception of the critique and nonetheless permit myself to question several areas of conservative consciousness, as well as determine its overall value. Many might consider this approach a dangerous one: critique merits a more in-depth analysis and a deeper examination than that which is proposed by this approach. While instinctively in agreement with them, I am of the opinion that this reproach does not, in itself, offer any guarantee of a constructive analysis. At the very limit, it may be considered a cliche, an easy position to ascertain, or even a moralizing one. There is thus a great deal of groundwork to cover and to defend in order to avoid these pitfalls, a task that commands a more direct and particular attention, as it can be stated 'that we are beings whose dignity derives from the persuasive role of critical reasoning in our social lives.'[1] In this perspective, the critical vision that I propose is one that exists within the confines of the imagination. It is in fact a natural development of the element of astonishment that underlies this reflection.[2] After having fully explained the nature of this perspective, I will present what I hope to demonstrate as a result.

Critique as Legal Imagination

I will begin with a brief reminder. In the Introduction, I situated the impulse at the source of this project in the desire to suggest a *right* answer to the question, *why is there an international commercial uniform law rather than nothing?*, which little by little transformed itself into an invitation to follow the emergent route of law and development. This is the case because I am probably persuaded and stimulated by the call of many – M. Sautet among them – to attempt this exercise or naturally attracted to the necessity to undertake it. I have also given several revealing hints

---

1   M. C. Nussbaum, 'Response: Still Worthy of Praise' (1998) 111 Harv. L. Rev. 1776 at 1795.

2   See Preamble, above.

as to the magnitude of this entire activity, and the imperative needs for originality and innovation associated with it. But to what point can we hope to satisfy these imperative needs, to see answers overflowing with originality and innovation? In my opinion, this question is pertinent because I am not at all convinced of the existence of an innate faculty within the researcher and the individual in general, to overcome the tragedy that, according to Hegel, consists of being enclosed upon oneself.[3] This tragedy has many shapes, and is felt differently from one person to another. It nonetheless obeys a particular logic: it tends to restrain and slow the momentum of the new, this vast horizon where the wealth of novelty is at its realm. S. Kokis, for one, admirably described this enclosure that is constitutive of the personal ethos. It arises, on one hand, from a notion that I would qualify as internal representation. This tenet symbolizes that in the quest for meaning, 'everything gets organized around us, not as an objective and abstract reality, but as a personal world, following semantic parameters which we share in a truncated manner with the reality and our fellow creatures.'[4] More specifically, internal representation is the fruit of ongoing exchanges between the personal world and what surrounds it: the human mind does not cease to structure and reformulate the information that comes upon it. This perpetual exercise of accommodation and synthesis define what every person lives, what every person is, a definition that can be perhaps better conceived 'as a narrative rather than isolated moments.'[5] In the words of Kokis, the narrative of every individual takes this shape:

> The internal experiences retain a certain substantial permanency, for with the assistance of linguistic syntax, the often heterogeneous elements of memory are organized in a sort of unitary fashion that evolves as a narrative. . . . We must therefore continually correct the elements of our history – even the most unusual facts – by adding logical yet often reinforced ties. . . . We silence the great contradictions, we alter the meaning of our worst defeats, we embellish it all, and this is how we regain the image that we are indeed masters of our universe. The false reasonings, the open ellipses, the over-whelming analogies and all sorts of mythical discourses are abundant in the inner narrative tissue that we term personal identity. The necessity for a coherent together-ness and the obligations of syntax are so powerful that even the best of memories is weakened in order to soften the corners and enhance the coherence of the narrative.[6]

In this context, creation consists of 'freeing thought from the ties of concrete feeling, [which takes place by means of a] process of remoulding facts of human experience.'[7] In other terms, creation resembles acts of decentring, of rearrangement of what is real, which necessarily implies a certain destabilization, a fracture, an uprooting of the self, all of which is done to substantiate the new. In my opinion, this is a key passage, but one that remains preliminary and insufficient

---

3   C. Taylor, *Hegel* (New York: Cambridge University Press, 1975).

4   S. Kokis, *Les langages de la création* (Montreal: Nuit blanche, 1996) at 18.

5   *Ibid.* at 33.

6   *Ibid.* at 33-34.

7   *Ibid.* at 26.

on its own, within the confines of the path of creation. If it is true that we have to learn to move the pieces of the jigsaw of life,[8] as we may understand it to be at any given moment in time, and risk the unknown for the purposes of discovery, I highly doubt that the level of novelty is maximized when this exercise is limited to a sort of *defamiliarization*, in the words of Sousa Santos.[9] I deem it preferable to see, in this passage, an opportunity to develop one's own strength and confidence[10] in exploring the unknown and a springboard toward something even more creative. Yet what exactly are we looking to find?

In my humble opinion, this goal is incarnated through the simple yet nonetheless effective maxim of I. Prigogine, who states that 'the possible is richer than the real.'[11] The bearing of this maxim is timeless and universal. For now, it can be safely presented as follows:

> The possible is richer than the real. Who should know this better than social scientists? Why are we so afraid of discussing the possible, or exploring the possible? We must move not utopias, but utopistics, to the centre of social science. Utopistics is the analysis of possible utopias, their limitations, and the constraints on achieving them. *It is the analytic study of real historical alternatives in the present.* It is the reconciliation of the search for truth and the search for goodness.
>
> Utopistics represents a continuing responsibility for social scientists. But it represents a particularly urgent task when the range of choice is greatest. When is this? Precisely when the historical social system of which we are part is furthest from equilibrium, when the fluctuations are greatest, when the bifurcations are nearest, when small input has great output. This is the moment in which we are now living and shall be living for the next 25-50 years.[12]

In comparison with the process of defamiliarization, the notion of utopia supposes a greater detachment, indeed a complete separation between the spirit and experienced reality. It allows for an abandonment toward mental exponential variations, unknown up until now.[13] And instead of beginning with facts of

---

8   I am drawing, here, an analogy with N. Goodman's celebrated metaphor *Ways of Worldmaking* (Indianapolis: Hackett Pub., 1978) at 31.

9   Sousa Santos, *supra*, Introduction, note 4; at x.

10 On the importance of confidence in general and in particular as a ferment of the social fabric, see B. A. Misztal, *Trust in Modern Societies: The Search for the Bases of Social Order* (Cambridge: Polity, 1996). Also, B. Barber, *The Logic and Limits of Trust* (New Brunswick: Rutgers University Press, 1983).

11 I. Prigogine, *La fin des certitudes* (Paris: Odile Jacob,1996) at 230.

12 Wallerstein, *supra*, Introduction, note 4; at 1254-1255.

13 J. Fourastier, *Les conditions de l'esprit scientifique* (Paris: Gallimard, 1996) at 54; K. Mannheim, *Ideology and Utopia* (New York: Harcourt, Brace, 1959).

immediate experience and their remodelling, utopian thought 'leaps upon the final result, the ends that one is meant to discover.'[14]

It is thus this particular vision of the criticism – defamiliarization, followed by utopia – that I will apply to the core of my analysis of conservative consciousness. What remains is to describe the nature and sequence of the demonstration that this vision will serve to realize.

What Demonstration?

I will once again mention comments I made in the Introduction, namely the premise that the contemporary world is currently passing from an age of modernity to that of a second modernity and the ascription of conservatism to the consciousness that presently dominates over uniform law. Until now, this premise and this characteristic were assumed to be true, without the need for further analysis. However, the ongoing search for a progressive consciousness requires that they be specified before going any further. In the case of the premise, this is imposed in order to determine exactly what the contemporary world is likely to leave behind, to conserve and seek out, as a result of current transformations. In the case of the characteristic, it is important to justify its selection by explaining where conservative consciousness comes from and to what it is attached.

I propose that the link between the preceding paragraph and critique as legal imagination entails a thorough demonstration distributed over three chapters. I will first show that conservative consciousness reflects the principles and values of modernity and modern law. Assuming that the inherent relationship or the *correlation* at the heart of Chapter 3 is indeed true, it will become possible to proceed with the stage of defamiliarization, presented in Chapter 4. I will then present the rupturing factors in conservative consciousness that arise from the crisis of modernity and modern law, as well as some progressive paths of reorientation in which one can recognize the emerging route of law and development. This should be considered as the pre-reformulation phase of uniform law. Chapter 5 will proceed with a utopian perspective: it will represent the middle reformulation of uniform law. In this chapter, I will present, as a logical response to the progressive reorientation, three utopian variations on the theme of uniform law. On the whole, Part II will allow me to attain the final phase of the Koskenniemi triptych. I will then have to join together all the information deriving from the regressive and critical analyses within a full reformulation of uniform law, which will be constitutive of the progressive consciousness of uniform law (Part III).

---

14 On this point, H. Bergson adds that 'we must admit that the whole self is presented in the form of a schema and that the work of invention consists precisely in converting the schema into an image,' in *Dictionnaire encyclopédique universel*, vol. 5 (Paris: Quillet & Grolier, 1962) at 3013.

Chapter 3

Conservative Consciousness, Modernity, and Modern Law

Modernity[1] and modern law[2] refer to a particular socio-historical context. They reflect the mode of social construction that has been prevalent throughout the Western world. They did not appear spontaneously, fully developed and readily accepted by all. Rather, they were the product of a lengthy intellectual process, of an accumulation of a series of mutations of ancient occidental culture. The spirit of this process pervades conservative consciousness, a link which must be further examined here. In order to render this link visible and as sound as possible, I will begin by examining the relationship between conservative consciousness and modernity, followed by its relationship to modern law.

The Correlation with Modernity

Main Features of Modernity

From a general point of view, modernity is based on two major premises, reason and individualism, and is positioned as a dynamic model.[3]

Historically, the premise of reason marks a rupture from submission to the laws of nature. Belief in the virtues of reason will entail a general process of rationalization.[4] This process will result in a technical, economic and political organization and will be further developed through industrialization, capitalism and the construction of a State whose authority is founded on a legal-rational legitimacy, exercised following pre-established guidelines and fully supported by a professional and disciplined bureaucracy. This domination of reason is

---

1 J. M. Domenach, *Approches de la modernité* (Paris: Ellipses, 1995); J. Habermas, *The Philosophical Discourse of Modernity*, trans. F. Lawrence (Cambridge: MIT Press, 1987); A. MacIntyre, *After Virtue: A Study in Moral Theory*, 2nd ed. (Notre Dame: University of Notre Dame Press, 1984).

2 H. J. Berman, *Law and Revolution: The Formation of the Western Legal Tradition* (Cambridge: Harvard University Press, 1983).

3 These main features are identified by J. Chevalier, 'Vers un droit post-moderne? Les transformations de la régulation juridique' (1998) Revue du droit public 659; see, also, R. Tarnas, *The Passion of the Western Mind* (New York: Ballantine, 1991).

4 M. Weber, *Économie et société*, trans. J. Freund (Paris: Pocket, 1995).

complemented by a series of other beliefs, ones that constitute the many myths that are inherent in modernity: belief in the virtues of science, endowing the human being with the power to dominate the forces of nature; faith in progress, through the progressive improvement of material conditions; the idea that history makes sense and that reason must progressively impose its discourse; finally, a conviction in the universalism of the paradigms constructed in the Occident, called to serve, as the very expression of reason, as models of reference.[5]

Modernity also relies on another premise, individualism, which places the individual at the core of society. Individualism affirms the uniqueness of every individual. Similarly, individualism allows every individual a certain margin of autonomy and liberty so that she/he may live in conformity with her/his own uniqueness. Individualism also implies a certain relaxation of community ties in order to provide for the construction of an individual-based social and political organization. As a result, the individual is the cornerstone of everything. The individual metaphor transcends the private sphere, where the individual is displayed as a human being, as well as the public sphere, where she/he is presented as citizen. Civil society is based on the free association of individuals, the State being the mere result of their common interests and the expression of their common will.

Different factors are at the source of the *dynamism of modernity*, an expression that evokes a great diffusion from an Occident-born model. A. Giddens,[6] for one, attributes this dynamism to the following characteristics of modernity:

i) *the dissociation of time and space*, which allows for a rationalized organization of social relations and a unification of spacial-temporal frameworks;
ii) *the delocalization of social systems*, made possible by the creation of universal exchange instruments and the bringing into play of professional know-how, all relying on confidence;
iii) *institutionalized reflexiveness*, which entails a constant examination and revision of social practices in the light of new information.

More specifically, I would emphasize the significance of three aspects born of modernity.

First aspect: Modernity, knowledge and progress[7] This first aspect pays tribute to the crossbreeding and evolution of certain Greek and Hebrew roots of modernity,

---

5   P. A. Schouls, *Descartes and the Enlightenment* (Kingston: McGill-Queen's University Press, 1989).
6   A. Giddens, *Les conséquences de la modernité* (Paris: L'Harmattan, 1994).
7   This first aspect appears as a resume of J. Wojciechowski, 'La modernité et le progrès du savoir' (1995) 3 Agora 19; R. S. Westfall, *Never at Rest: A Biography of Isaac Newton* (Cambridge: Cambridge University Press, 1980); A. Hayli, *Newton* (Paris: Seghers, 1970).

of which the ultimate goal was to place the individual at the centre of a universe that was continually at her/his service. There exists, on one hand, an abstract way to formulate the concepts that led to the Cartesian ideal of clear and distinct ideas. There is also, on the other hand, a linear approach to time that has engendered an optimistic outlook toward life and a rejection of destiny as a dominant force. If the preoccupation with precision dates back to Greek civilization and to the philosophy of logic heralded by Aristotle and the Stoics, the notion of a time where every instant is unique, non-repetitive, derives from the Old Testament. With regard to knowledge and progress, the features of modernity, these origins and their gradual evolution have followed a shaky and irregular path.

In the beginning, the religious notion of time as linear phenomenon is charged with supernatural significance. It seeks to express each and every aspect of human history, from the Expulsion from Paradise to the Last Judgement. It is a period that is confined, bordered, one that has a definitive beginning and ending. The religious version of linear time will eventually be caught in the ideology of progress. But in order to play a significant role in the development of knowledge, it will have to undergo a substantial change, as demonstrated by its integration to abstract mathematics. Within his definitions of time and space, Newton retained the linear nature of time and its unidirectional character, yet transforms it into one of infinite and thoroughly homogeneous duration. Due to its homogeneity, time becomes divisible into equal parts, and becomes therefore measurable and quantifiable. With space, which is also infinite, homogeneous and quantifiable, Newton creates his system of mechanical explanation. In this perspective, physical events are calculable, readily predictable, and by the same token understandable. It is thus that the world becomes scientifically explainable and the human being becomes more and more efficient.

The growth of efficiency and of human power goes hand in hand with the ideology of progress. This power aims in particular to further the progressive Baconian precept according to which nature is there to be utilized rather than contemplated.[8] It is a task entrusted to knowledge at the peak of its development, which allows one to confidently envision radical improvement in the human condition. Nonetheless, if the significance of the growth of knowledge for the ideology of progress appears indisputable, the contribution of Judeo-Christian religion remains irrefutable as well. First, the belief in the superiority of the human being over nature deriving from the Old Testament consolidates progress. Then, the temporal perspective in which progress is inscribed corresponds fundamentally to the religious version of linear time. It is a qualitative time, fixated upon a definitive goal, which justifies and gives significance to each of its moments. And this goal is nothing other than the realization of a kind of Garden of Eden. In this perspective, the relevance of linear scientific time is limited to being a tool in the pursuit of this end.

---

8   F. Bacon, *Du progrès et de la promotion des savoirs*, trans. M. Le Doeuff (Paris: Gallimard, 1991); J. J. Epstein, *Francis Bacon: A Political Biography* (Athens: Ohio University Press, 1977).

What results from this entanglement is a process of positive feedback: knowledge procures progress which, in return, fosters the surpassing of the frontiers of knowledge.

Second aspect: Modernity and the dichotomous point of view　This aspect maintains that the general idea of division transcends a variety of notions, values and methods characteristic of modernity. By separating individuals from other individuals, fact from value, reason from belief and emotion, religion from the State and so on, modernity undertakes a specific vision of human existence and truth. What is termed the dichotomous point of view is recognized and further distinguished within certain sub-concepts.

The sub-concept of *individuation* pushes individual differentiation to the point of separating human beings from social relationships. In the words of D. Cornell, 'The Enlightenment includes the principle that we might call the expressive ideal, suggesting that the self can be defined as an entity free from its containment within social roles.'[9] Seen from the initial modernist perspective, individuation is associated with the large scale ideas of purity, progress and freedom: it serves to liberate the human being from the weight of tradition, outside expectations and hierarchical arbitrariness, to the advantage of self-determination and personal self-suggestion. Another sub-concept, one of *detachment*, finds a striking illustration in the Cartesian formulation of *cogito ergo sum*, this being the famous rift between the thinking abilities of the human being and the rest of her/his universe. It delineates a separation of the subjective mind from the objective material world, of the subject from the object. As well, it implicitly favours reason over experience, that is to say, the product of reason over the product of the senses in determining what is true. Reason seeks to impose its frame of thought upon the outside world and to allow for the attainment of precision and certainty. This is contrary to the seizure and interpretation of reality by the senses, a process which proves to be highly variable and unstable. The separation of the object and the subject becomes the cornerstone of the autonomous human will. This being a purified and superior milieu, the human will dispose of faculties that render the physical person apt to bear judgement all the while being conversely responsible for her/his actions. Judgement and responsibility are aligned to form a strong humanist image, one of a profound sense of existence. The sub-concept of *segmentation* complements the preceding ones. It gives even more significance to reason by separating from its context the life of individuals and objects that then appear more pure, comprehensible and coherent with the rest of modern thought. The latter, as is emphasized by M. C. Regan, 'demands abstraction of individuals from their particular social settings and attachments in an effort to ascertain which propositions would have appeal to persons solely in their capacity as rational

---

9　D. Cornell, 'Toward a Modern/Postmodern Reconstruction of Ethics' (1985) U. Pa. L. 9 Rev. 291 at 323.

agents.'[10] This contextual extraction follows a reducible strategy: history is divided into independent *tableaux*, the different facets of a person's life are considered separately. The combination of disconnection and reduction opens the door toward objectivity and systematization that, in turn, tend toward universalization.

Third aspect: Modern knowledge, economics and opulence This aspect underlines, for one, the influence of modern knowledge upon human desire. The precept upon which this influence lies derives from the Latin maxim *nihil volitum nisi praecognitum*, which means that nothing is desired without being known or, at the very least, suspected to exist. From this, modernity extrapolates the following principles: knowledge puts forward certain desirable objects to the human being; the universe of desirable objects is proportional to knowledge; and knowledge, through its gradual evolution, awakens these desires by continually presenting a growing number of desirable things.

On an economic level, these principles, together with other characteristics of modern thought, confirm a vision of opulence.[11] By definition, opulence assimilates the development of society to a process of economic growth. In the analysis, this is demonstrated by the taking into consideration of various factors and indicators such as heightened production, peaking productivity and increase in per capita income. Besides, it is an analysis which is oriented by three tendencies. First, a tendency to adhere to a linear and mechanized vision of evolution. A linear vision that is such that societies are called to journey across identical steps toward the desired level of economic growth. It is also a mechanized one, which gives to these steps a quantitative nature enabling one to measure, calculate and predict them. Secondly, a tendency that gives a unidirectional dimension to those methods that guarantee economic growth. This single direction for each society consists of privileging the methods advocated by the most advanced among them. Lastly, a tendency that gives a utilitarian role to values. The questioning of these values is as follows: do they favour or infringe upon the economy? The values are thus mainly instruments to be utilized or to be avoided, and not elements that are intrinsically assessed and valorized.

Opulence is reinforced, qualitatively, by other considerations issued from the modernist corpus. One of these considerations is a generalized and deterministic reason where economic interests are perceived as being an indispensable antidote against violence and dogmatism. If every individual pursues his or her own personal interest, it is all of society that benefits and achieves maximum well-being. All of this occurs as if harmonious and efficient leadership operates in such a way so that the sum of individual interests, founded on utility – that is to say, use is or can be advantageous, can satisfy a given need – is equal to the general interest. This leadership accomplishes its mission of convergence in a specific

---

10   M. C. Regan Jr., 'Reason, Tradition, and Family Law: A Comment on Social Constructionism' (1993) 79 Va L. Rev. 1515 at 1518.

11   J. K. Galbraith, *L'ère de l'opulence*, trans. G. Coffin (Paris: Calmann-Lévy, 1970); M. Lauesen, *Le temps de l'opulence* (Paris: Stock, 1943).

institutionalized context, namely the competitive market. And it is comforted by the powerful paradigm of rational anticipations. This paradigm postulates that every active economic policy is thwarted by the predictions of economic agents that incorporate the effects of these policies into their own models. In other words, every collectivist mechanism proves inefficient because it will eventually be incorporated into the predictions of these agents. The latter will use all of their knowledge to overcome the effects of the policies. This then serves to favour and legitimize pan-economic discourse.

The Correlation

To what do we attribute the correlation between modernity and conservative consciousness? First, the correlation emerges from the fact that the two major premises of modernity, reason and individualism, are deeply rooted in conservative consciousness. This is reflected in particular in the first strategy advanced by conservative consciousness in order to escape the antinomy of truth. This strategy consists, as mentioned above, of a junction between individuality and abstraction that allows access to the best possible values. The individual is thus envisioned as being able to overcome her/his contextual situation and place her/himself in an impartial position. This elevation remains essentially monologist and translates a soft egoism that does not necessarily imply the recognition of others. The values of liberty and utility, considered from the points of view, respectively, of rational actions and the individual as privileged interpreter of happiness, each reinforce the overall link between modernity and conservative consciousness. These values recognize that the individual represents the ideal frame of reference to interpret the social organization as well as the element most conducive to its evolution. The fact that we speak of a nation (or a country) instead of the individual does not significantly alter this way of reasoning, since any notion of a collectivity can be reduced, at the very limit, to individualist considerations. The factors that are inherent in the dynamism of modernity are also observable within conservative consciousness. The latter is not inert, amorphous, nor discarded. It is altered and reworked in order to allow the greatest possible audience for uniform law and attach an indubitable character of normality to it. In this regard, we are forced to recognize the contribution of the phenomenon of professionalization: following the example of modernity, uniform law is spreading under the effect of the models and typologies advanced by members of the legal profession[12] and public[13] and private

---

12   Y. Dezalay, B. G. Garth & P. Bourdieu, *Dealing in Virtue: International Commercial Arbitration and the Construction of a Transnational Legal Order* (Chicago: Chicago University Press, 1998).

13   See, for example, the activities and the work carried out by UNCITRAL and mentioned in the *UNCITRAL Yearbook* (New York: United Nations).

administration.[14] In so doing, uniform law becomes more user friendly, thus readily exportable from one place to another.

Secondly, the context of justification of the principles of thought involves the integration of the unique hybrid aspect I have called 'modernity, knowledge and progress'. The linear nature of time, in its scientific version, is readily self-observable in the emphasis placed by conservative consciousness on instrumental thought. As can be understood, Newtonian linear time represents the ideal tool available to the human being, that is to say the most efficient, in order to understand and dominate the surrounding world. It is no more nor less than an abstract knowledge, yet clear and precise all the while. In allowing one to know exactly what one can expect, in proceeding with certain predictions, it is indissociable from the march of progress. Conservative consciousness fully undertakes this role. Moulded by obviousness, division, causality and exhaustiveness, it acquires certainty, precision and omnipotence. It is a reassuring consciousness that rebounds onto uniform law by allowing it to personify a perfect or ideal knowledge. As a result, uniform law readily positions itself as a high calibre juridical resource in the mastering of a surrounding world that, apparently, is becoming more and more globalized. But conservative consciousness goes further than simply integrating linear scientific time. It also serves to integrate the religious counterpart of the latter. What emerged from the analysis of the context of justification is the presence of a modest ends-based thought, founded on commerce, in the midst of conservative consciousness. This affirmation relies on different elements: a formal understanding of trade, a commercial end left in the rough, unexplored and closed in upon itself. All of this serves to benefit an enchanted vision of commerce, one that evokes the search for the Garden of Eden that is characteristic of the idea of progress. A profound belief in the virtues of commerce and its benefits is at the root of this level of *faith*. Responding to the needs of international commerce or favouring the development of international trade do not lead us nowhere: they lead us toward the realization of a truly humanist vision that is within arm's reach.

In addition, the dichotomous point of view that transcends modernity is found in conservative consciousness. The latter separates the means from the ends, as appears from the value of liberty. The tastes (ends) of individuals are not discussed because of their insurmountable diversities. Nevertheless, the identified strategies (means), the very root of reason, are clearly relevant. In addition, conservative consciousness, on the basis of its autonomy, specificity and distinctive character, defines uniform law as being an integral part of the international order rather than the national one. Finally, it isolates good faith, in order to fully differentiate between the good faith of uniform international commercial law and all other types of good faith. More specifically, individuation, by the power of self-determination and self-suggestion that it attributes to every individual, underlies the dynamism of

---

14 The ICC (International Chamber of Commerce) is an example of a private organization very active in the field of international uniform commercial law. See 'About ICC', online: <http://www.iccwbo.org/home/intro_icc/introducing_icc.asp>.

the value of wealth. Innovation, new combinations and the sometimes obligatory passage through various hardships would not be better accomplished without recourse to an individual capable of overcoming any constraints inherent in any aspect of the social fabric. In a similar way, the unifying capacity of the value of wealth would be much less important were it not under the influence of the separation of subject and object carried out through the element of detachment. I am here referring to autonomous human will, and not to human will that is dependent upon feelings and experience, that personalizes the individual as central player between supply and demand. This individual, driven by the desire for wealth, will adopt behaviours and make judgements accordingly, following all other individuals. The overall result is a mechanism giving credibility to the principle of a uniform market price for a good or service. Finally, the combined effects of disconnection and reduction associated with segmentation permeates the epistemological postulate underlying the value of wealth. Through disconnection and reduction, it is indeed possible to accede to this comprehensive truth that is represented by the pursuit of wealth and to make of it a method of analysis as well as a means of predicting future behaviours.

The vision of opulence completes the correlation between modernity and conservative consciousness. Straightaway, the very high quality of uniform law as knowledge is a perfect complement to the *always more* premise that is at the root of opulence. This top-level knowledge is moulded and understood as being definitely in a position to give effect to the desire to possess material goods. And the more uniform legal knowledge succeeds in doing this, the more it becomes susceptible of being improved by those who possess material goods. Furthermore, the value of utility is especially linked to the vision of opulence. If conservative consciousness can serve to maximize and harmonize personal interests and, consequently, optimize collective happiness, it is because it conforms to the complexities of this vision. On the one hand, opulence and utility share a common medium, namely money. The latter serves as a conduit to the economic growth which characterizes opulence. Money is apprehended in the form of an analytical tool, that is to say a measuring, calculation and prediction device. Hence, money allows one to coordinate and organize hierarchically the elements necessary to the linear and mechanical march toward the economic *always more*. Utility draws inspiration from money, in an identical fashion. Money serves to assure a peaceful liaison between different social activities, by equalizing and confounding the externalities. Reinforced by the attributes attached to the efficiency of instrumental thought, utility can seriously claim that it leads to maximal satisfaction for individuals. On the other hand, the shape of utility according to which the individual is the key to everything is inherently linked to other considerations of the vision of opulence that the analysis has established. The individual, and not the community, is able to feel happiness; the community is no more than the sum of the individuals of which it is composed; the community serves above all to protect the individual; in sum, when utility is expressed in these terms and furthermore falls back upon the virtues of convergence deployed by the market, it draws from an opulence that also holds a great deal of confidence in the individual and competitive market context.

The Correlation with Modern Law

Main Features of Modern Law

Law and modernity are very closely related.[15] On the one hand, the values and the methodological foundations of modernity permeate every aspect of law, which entails a particular juridical representation. On the other hand, law serves as an important catalyst in the rationalization of social and political organization, upon which it projects its attributes of objectivity and necessity. Law therefore serves both as expression and vector of modernity. This reciprocity constitutes a key element in the exact understanding of the four main features of modern law.

Modern law and individuation The notion of the individual is one of the pillars of modern law. Its aspect is twofold. From a fundamental point of view, the individual precedes social organization; moreover, she/he is the bearer of subjective rights.

The individuation at the heart of modern law has its theoretical roots in the doctrine of natural law.[16] This doctrine is founded upon the notion that the individual comes before the State. The latter is merely the result of a social contract, concluded in the interests, and for the utility, of every individual. On the mere basis of her/his human nature, the individual naturally bears certain rights. The State, moreover, is expected to guarantee the provision of these rights. This train of thought is reformulated and adapted by the modernists. The latter define the rights that are held by the human being as such. These rights are then given priority over society. And the modernists establish that the individual cannot renounce these rights through her/his entering into society. The protection of these natural rights, rights that are both permanent and inalienable, becomes the responsibility of the political and social organization. The same mode of thought is prevalent with respect to the idea of a nation, considered to be the logical extension of the individual. The nation, that is to say the grouping together of individuals, constitutes a collective subject that is also a bearer of rights. It exercises its rights

---

15 These main features are identified by J. Chevalier, *supra*, note 3; 'The law is the ideal form of active discourse, able, by its own merit, to produce effects. It is not excessive to say that it creates the social world, but under the condition of not forgetting that it is created by it': P. Bourdieu, 'La force du droit. Éléments pour une sociologie du champ juridique' (1986) 64 Actes de la recherche en sciences sociales 3 at 13.

16 A. Sériaux, *Le droit naturel* (Paris: Presses Universitaires de France, 1993); Y. Simon & V. Kuic, *The Tradition of Natural Law: A Philosophe's Reflections* (New York: Fordham University Press, 1992); J. Finnis, *Natural Law and Natural Rights* (New York: Clarendon Press, 1980).

due to its sovereignty over a number of matters, rights that it may exercise through the support of the State.

Liberatory and protective, law also becomes synonymous with benevolence and charity. It preserves the equality of individuals in their mutual relations, and it establishes measures that serve to uphold human dignity. For example, based on specific criteria for hygiene, security, moral integrity and physical capacity, these measures can favour decent working conditions. Or they can redistribute the wealth collectively produced, or serve to guarantee to everyone equal access to essential goods and resources. Quite simply, law fosters an ideal of justice.

Modern law and reason Modernity transforms law as it was previously known, and confers upon it a number of new attributes.

The creation of an autonomous legal field and the unification of law are important aspects of the transformations that issue from modernity.[17] The autonomy of law, for one, derives from a movement of secularization. Contrary to previous law, whose authority and legitimacy are founded on divine will, modern law is self-defined as a specific normative device, governed by its own logic. The autonomy of law means that it is able to find its underpinnings within itself, internally rather than relying on some external support. The other transformation, unification, is the work of the State. The latter transforms the multiplicity, juxtaposition and entanglement that are characteristic of the juridical sources and instances that had been known until then. Henceforth, the State imposes itself as being the exclusive source of law. It replaces the pre-existing juridical orders, thereby becoming the unique legal frame of reference for the entire collectivity. It confers upon specialized institutions, with carefully defined jurisdictions, the role of producer of the law. It also delegates to various entities its constraining power in order to suppress violations of its rules. In short, the omnipresent State fosters the transition from a pluralistic conception of the law to a monistic one.

In a parallel analysis, the rationalized law acquires a new profile, which in turn demonstrates its many attributes. Thus, the configuration of law corresponds to that of an *ongoing logic* on the part of its constituents. The legal norms are all integrated, completely and harmoniously. The law is presented through the perspective of a coherent and unified whole, which gives it a sense of simplicity, certainty and clarity. And even then, the law *generalizes*: it reads reality with the help of abstract concepts and masters it through the assembling of neutral rules of great stature. Finally, the law is an agent of *stability*. Through the projection of an objective point of view upon the particular situations and by formalizing its rules into models, the law serves as a constant link between past and present. The legal future is in fact a reflection of the legal past, that is to say, the changes are coloured by what has previously occurred. This way, every individual can determine the consequences of her/his actions in advance and can plan accordingly. As a vector of modernity, the law is placed under the realm of reason and consequently

17 W. J. Waluchow, *Inclusive Legal Positivism* (Oxford: Clarendon Press, 1994); C. Grzegorczyk, *Le positivisme juridique* (Brussels: E. Story-Scientia, 1992).

provides the guarantee for an organized, peaceful and unified society. It transmits the message to every individual that she/he evolves in an intelligible totality.

The law thus acquires a 'universalist posture',[18] strengthened by the 'force of the form',[19] a phenomenon that Bourdieu describes as follows:

> If the rule of law assumes that there is a junction between an adhesion to common values . . . and the existence of rules and explicit sanctions and regularized procedures, it is certain that the latter factor, which cannot be separated from the written, plays a decisive role: with the written appears the possibility of universal commentary, one that determines the rules and especially the universal principles, of the objective and generalized transmission (through a given method of learning), above the spatial (between the territories) and temporal (within the generations). . . . Written law favours the autonomization of the text, which we criticize, and which serves as a link between the commentators and reality; what then becomes possible . . . is a form of scientific knowledge, with its own norms and its own logic, able to produce all the exterior effects of coherent rationality.[20]

A transcendental perspective can be added to this universalist one. In truth, the law is embedded within all social realities: on one hand, it expresses all its breadth under the authority of the impersonal subject we call the State. On the other hand, it acts as a lens in allowing all individuals to recognize one another and judge one another. This transcendence of the law is even clearer, since it can rely upon the tangible support of the legal profession.[21]

Modern law and contract Following the reassuring approach of modern thought, the contract *fixes obligations*. This dimension can be demonstrated in three ways.

First, on a temporal level, fixedness symbolizes that the contract is reputed to be localized in a single and unique moment: before and after this moment, no obligation is deemed to exist. The various possible times of the contract are brought together and confounded into one, at the actual present moment. This faculty of 'presentation'[22] appears to be plausible because of the stability and the continuity which characterize the parties' environment. Past and future conditions being supposed to remain similar, it becomes conceivable that the parties could sufficiently remember the past and anticipate the future to define completely, at a given moment, their commitments. Secondly, the insistence on the contract's compulsory character is explained by an immanent dualism which leads to considering the parties as separate and diametrically opposed entities. In this spirit, the dualistic analysis limits the spectrum of motivations of each contracting party to mainly pursuing her/his own ends, which is synonymous with both antagonism

---

18 Bourdieu, *supra*, note 15; at 5.
19 *Ibid.* at 14.
20 *Ibid.* at 15.
21 *Ibid.* at 5.
22 I. R. Macneil, 'Contracts: Adjustment of Long-Term Economic Relations under Classical, Neoclassical, and Relational Contract Law' (1978) 72 NW. U. L. Rev. 854 at 863.

and egocentric maximization of interests. In view of these contradictory motivations, the dimension of fixation of the obligations would allow the parties to control and stabilize them and to avoid seeing them unexpectedly modified.[23]

And thirdly, the fixation of the obligations is justified by the fact that it flows from a rational choice made by the parties. What is a rational choice? This concept is based on a twofold premise. On the one hand, choice is at the centre of human activity. The human being can grasp the reality that surrounds her/him and be in a position to see the entire spectrum of possibilities open to her/him. This contact permits her/him to express her/his preferences toward such or such a possibility, that is to say to appraise the relative value of one or another option. On the other hand, the choice is rational from the moment when the human being makes choices which are consonant with her/his preferences. As such, this is not particularly problematic. As a matter of fact, a human being is a stable person, consistent with her/himself, reasonable and capable of making the right choice. Given one's aptitudes, one is allowed to be uninterested in the nature and in the content of one's preferences, to be neutral in this regard. So conceived, rational choice becomes the modern tool for both describing and understanding human action. It also becomes something that it is important to protect and sanction. The concept of the contract shares this point of view. The principle according to which the obligations of a party simply reflect the consequences of her/his choices flows from the joining of the concept of rational choice to the contract. Rational choice is sufficiently representative of everyone's behaviour to explain that the situation is such. Thinking differently would amount to both discrediting and hampering the full use of each person's capacity.

Modern law as strong law Because of its dependence on reason, justice and security, law naturally becomes the most convenient mode of structuring and regulating social relations in modern society. It shows the way to social evolution and coordinates the action of the constituting elements of society. Social rationality and legal rationality become perfectly symmetrical. Given the premise that legal norms are rational, everything that conforms to legal norms is rational. Hence, modern society places its complete trust in the law, and this leads to considering the rule as sacred. The legal norm is mistaken for reality itself. It is seen as truly having the capacity to realize what it comprises and what it promises. This vision of law as rational mechanism is clearly linked to an idealized conception of law which cannot be found in the concrete reality of everyday life. The idea of a legal order based on a rigorous sequence of normative propositions and governed by the laws of formal logic is but a product of reason and is equivalent to a kind of belief. This idea nonetheless represents a determining element of the power of law, of strong law.[24]

---

23 C. Fried, *Contract as Promise: A Theory of Contractual Obligation* (Cambridge: Harvard U.P., 1981).

24 This expression is derived from the title of P. Bouretz, ed., *La force du droit: panorama des débats contemporains* (Paris: Éditions Esprit, 1991).

The Correlation

At its very basis, the correlation between modern law and conservative consciousness centres on individuation. Modern law is shaped by the idea of the legal pre-existence of the individual in relation to the State. And this idea is rooted in the background of the argument of the autonomy of the will. First, it is a self-evident argument: its existence is absolute and natural. Secondly, the autonomy of the will, and not the State, represents the causal law which explains the genesis, execution and end of the contract. Finally, due to its apparent ability to be invoked in conformity with individual, national and State aspirations, the argument of the autonomy of the will legitimates the slogan advocating the development of international commerce. Besides, the States expressly rely on this argument to satisfy their interests and expectations. Both the argument of the concrete intention of the parties as the *Grundnorm* of the Vienna Convention, and that of the maximization of interests based on the autonomous contract concept, consolidate as well the idea that, in conservative consciousness, the will of the parties precedes the State. As a matter of fact, the State here plays a role which corresponds to that of the State in modern law, that is, to guarantee individual rights. As demonstrated, the value of freedom, which characterizes the argument of the concrete intention of the parties, is, for that matter, unequivocal: it confers on the State the task of securing the enjoyment of individual rights, their free transfer and the guarantee of promises, all of which are indispensable ingredients of the creation of prosperity. From the idea that the individual precedes the State, we go to the benevolent and beneficent State, be it in conservative consciousness or modern law. The State in uniform law is preoccupied with the just, is spite of the difficulties arising from its contradictions, its complexity and the diversity of its conceptions. Even more, it can do it in distributing equitably the fruit of wealth.

Pushing the correlation further, the overlapping of modern law and reason with the background of the argument of juridical convergence is striking. First, the transformations of law derived from modernity partake of monism. Due to the centripetal force of the State, law becomes one. It crystallizes into an organized whole, with clearly definite contours. Its functioning obeys clear rules, which endows it with an ability for self-determination. The search for order underlying the argument of juridical convergence perfectly corresponds to the monist perspective of modern law. In this regard, conservative consciousness demonstrates, too, its concern for clarity and simplicity. And it can answer these requirements by merging national laws or by allowing business people to spontaneously establish *one* legal regime suitable to their needs. The result is, as for modern law, a juridical unity said to be intelligible. Secondly, the logical sequence, the generalizing power and the stabilizing capacity shaping so called rational law are also present in the linearity and the determinism which influence the simplifying thought of conservative consciousness. As regards linearity, it leads to the recognition of a unique point of view to describe and understand reality and constitutes a kind of generalization equivalent to that which is found in modern law. As regards determinism, it takes up the attributes of modern law relating to the complete and harmonious integration of its norms, and to its stability. As a matter of fact, by definition, determinism ensures constancy in the reaching of expected results. And if it is capable of doing so, it is because it knows how to establish the relevant links among its constituting parts or to systematize them. Thirdly, the universalizing and transcendental perspectives of modern law agree with the undoubted character of normality of uniform law. Viewed as the flip side of irrationality, and as inescapable, uniform law cannot but exist through time, space and spirit.

As for the idea of fixation of obligations which is at the heart of modern contract, it spreads throughout conservative consciousness. In its temporal dimension, this idea partly explains the form taken by the argument of good faith. For instance, the continuity which stamps the environment of the contracting parties is equally present in the argument of good faith as understood by *lex mercatoria*: under the guise of the quest for identity, good faith displays constancy and permanency. Moreover, the phenomenon of *presentiation*, that is to say the synthesis of the various possible times of the contract into *one* unique time, is assimilated to the good faith of State law which, under the guise of non-contradiction, constitutes an element of *unity* as regards the other peripheral norms. Besides, the fixation of the obligations that is aimed at controlling antagonisms and excessive egoism and, consequently, at avoiding seeing the obligations unexpectedly modified, is clearly reflected in the role conferred on society through the value of freedom. At that level, it is important to recall that human nature and human action constantly oscillate between satisfaction and dissatisfaction. And that this pendulum has, as a corollary, rarity, whose overcoming can be the source of conflict. Hence, the role of society accounts for the role of contract: it consists in deciding between interests and in stabilizing mutual relationships. Finally, rational choice expresses the faith and confidence demonstrated by modern law toward the individual endowed with reason, able to determine what is good for her/him and to assume the consequences of her/his actions. Rational choice also demonstrates the neutrality of modern law toward individual preferences. Through its principles of thought and its values, conservative consciousness firmly adheres to this vision of things. All of its elements – stability, precision, simplicity, freedom, utility, etc. – ensure that this is so. The intellectual guides of the contract are first and foremost the contracting parties themselves. Admittedly, they can make mistakes or blunders and they will be, if the case arises, answerable for their actions. However, this does not put into question the fact that what they think is very likely to be legitimate for the community.

The correlation is completed by the borrowing of the image of modern law as strong law by conservative consciousness. The transfer is visible at several levels. For example, the attributes of modern law form the basic frame of reference chosen to trace and coordinate the social evolutionary cycle. As well, these attributes are such that they render the law subject to absolute respect: it is the basis of the optimism that everyone feels toward life. Thus, this *sacred* legal structure is put in evidence in the instrumental thought process of conservative consciousness. The result is that uniform law is automatically tied to the joy of living. It is assumed that it will generate the overall advancement of all plans, for all. The firmness of this conviction leads to an idealization of uniform law. Like its modern counterpart, uniform law comes to represent reality. The 'tableau' relative to the content of the context of justification of values can clearly attest to this. We have in fact already witnessed to what point conservative consciousness fits closely the notions of equality, world harmony, well-being and other elements that are actualized within the international law of development. And everything indicates that we can see there a durable union, due to the perspective according to which it is 'particularly through the development of legal instruments that the world community of nations attempts to provide for the basic conditions for social progress.'[25] Moreover, this idealized image of uniform law also allows for it to be reconciled with the providentialist and finalistic conceptions of the value of justice: benevolent, it derives occasionally inspiration from this providentialism and finalism, even though these notions of justice may appear somewhat removed from reason and individuation. At the end of the line, it appears that the symbol of modern law as strong law has acquired its proper position within the scope of uniform law. This could be illustrated by the transformation of *modern law as strong law* into one of *uniform law as strong law*.

The demonstration of this correlation of conservative consciousness with modernity and modern law having been undertaken, it appears necessary to discuss at present the critical process of defamiliarization, or the pre-reformulation of uniform law.

---

25 *World Summit for Social Development: An Overview Report of the Secretary-General*, U. N. Doc. A/Conf. 166/PC/6 (1994) at par. 172.

Chapter 4

Defamiliarization, or the
Pre-reformulation of Uniform Law

As stated, the step of defamiliarization can be divided into an analysis of the factors conducive to the rupture of the conservative consciousness of uniform law and the paths of progressive reorientation that are thereby entailed.

The Rupture in Conservative Consciousness

The conservative consciousness of uniform law substantially integrates the principles of thought and the values of modernity and modern law. Thus, it appears that the legacy of modernity is currently the object of intense scrutiny. Terms such as crisis, shock and others are there as a tribute to the underpinnings, landmarks and solutions that are distanced from their original mission, or that are entirely brought back into question, stimulating and opening the pathway toward new progressive avenues.

Taking for granted, as I have previously stated, the idea of a changeover of the contemporary world from the realm of modernity to that of a second modernity is one thing; to understand the reality of this phenomenon is another. Of course, the exacerbated eclecticism of the descriptions, analyses and appreciations of the changeover in question creates a palpitating zone of observation. However, as a result, the equivocal, the interference and the dispersal that cover this zone can rapidly disconcert the observer. Nonetheless, I will present, within the confines of this text, three series of considerations that will support, in their own way, the hypothesis of the changeover. The first series involves a discussion of extra-juridical elements, while the second deals more specifically with the arguments relative to the law in general. The third presents the alternative developed by B. de Sousa Santos,[1] whose interest resides in the lineage he shows to exist between law and 'non-law' and in the transnational dimension of his analysis. Put together, this may seem somewhat eclectic, thereby reflecting the general allure of current thought.

---

1   *Supra*, Introduction, note 4.

Some Extra-legal Elements of Rupture

An interpretation of the changeover presents it as a form of a challenge, one that is largely up to the modernist quest to overcome. C. Taylor incarnates this appeal to rediscover the profound sense of modernity, to redefine its authenticity in order to heal the many malaises that it has itself engendered.[2] In effect, according to him, the cardinal points of modernity often point in the wrong direction.[3] The advancement of individualism has favoured a too great withdrawal into the self. The instrumental thought has unduly contributed to a rupture of the bonds of collective allegiance due to a marked concern for efficiency on an individual level. And the liberating hope of modernity has been greatly attenuated before the hegemonic forces of the market and of the State. In order to correct this fault, Taylor proposes 'a renewed understanding of modernity'[4] on the basis of a conviction that is imperative to his argument: 'Understanding modernity aright is an exercise in retrieval.'[5] For Taylor, the confusing idea that we have of ourselves at the present time, and the worries that it in turn creates, are due in great part to the lack of knowledge we possess with regard to the fundamental dimensions of modernity. To discover the image of these unarticulated[6] dimensions of modern identity should produce a twofold effect: 'first, how much we are all caught up in it, for all our attempts to repudiate it; and second, how shallow and partial are the one-sided judgements we bandy around about it.'[7] According to Taylor, the reformulation of the genesis of modernity must indeed spark

i)   the complexity and the richness of modern inwardness, that is to say the sentiment of interior depth that every individual feels as 'I';
ii)   the affirmation of ordinary life, be it the family and the workplace; and
iii) the expressivist notion of nature 'as an inner moral source.'[8]

Other approaches concur with the Taylorian strategy of reaffirming modernity and opposing its rejection.[9] However, still others can be found at the opposing end, placing modernity squarely in the dock. Here, the changeover receives a different interpretation: it 'announces or implies that a rupture has occurred, an irreparable break with the past, and that nothing can ever be the same again.'[10] P. M. Roseneau

---

2   Taylor, *supra*, Introduction, note 4.
3   C. Taylor, *Grandeurs et misères de la modernité*, trans. C. Melançon (Montreal: Bellarmin, 1992).
4   Taylor, *supra*, Introduction, note 4; at ix.
5   *Ibid.* at xi.
6   *Ibid.*
7   *Ibid.* at x.
8   *Ibid.*
9   Giddens, *supra*, Chapter 3, note 6. A. Touraine, *Critique de la modernité* (Paris: Fayard, 1992).
10   D. Lehman, *Signs of the Time: Deconstruction and the Fall of Paul DeMan* (New York: Poseidon Press, 1992) at 41.

offers a gripping portrait of a variant of this interpretation that she terms the sceptical post-modernism:

> The sceptical post-modernist (or merely sceptic), offering a pessimistic, negative, gloomy assessment, argue that the post-modern age is one of fragmentation, disintegration, malaise, meaninglessness, a vagueness or even absence of moral parameters and societal chaos. Inspired by Continental European philosophies, especially Heidegger and Nietzsche, this is the dark side of post-modernism, the post-modernism of despair, the post-modernism that speaks of the immediacy of death, the demise of the subject, the end of the author, the impossibility of truth, and the abrogation of the Order of Representation. Post-modernists of this orientation adopt a blasé attitude, as if 'they have seen it all' and concluded that nothing really new is possible. They argue that the destructive character of modernity makes the post-modern age one of 'radical, unsurpassable uncertainty, characterized by all that is grim, cruel, alienating, tired, and ambiguous.'[11]

For Roseneau, sceptical post-modernism can be compared with an affirmative variant, more inclined toward optimism. Between these two there are several key facets of the changes characterized as a reaction against modernity, the following being a brief overview of these:

- From a postmodern point of view, the importance given to the search for what is called the author's intent is greatly reduced as compared with its role within modernity. One favours the text itself and its reader. On the one hand, the text is seen as having no predetermined objective meaning. On the other hand, its interpretation is entirely left to the reader's imagination. This accords with the idea that there is no object or element of reference (therefore no author) from which we may derive unity and consistency.
- The concepts of theory and truth are no longer linked to neutrality and objectivity. The consequences of this sudden change are variously appreciated, but they call, at the very least, for intellectual humility and tolerance. These feelings are justified by the fact that truth and theory cannot lead to systematization and homogenization. Relativism is set against universalism.
- Finally, in the field of epistemology and methodology, post-modernism favours a multitude of approaches, which go from pure deconstruction, all the way to a kind of interpretation based on intuition. In the first case, any perception of reality is understood as a pure illusion: uncertainty impregnates each and every personal view. In the second case, recourse to a kind of rationality in order to understand and explain, is not totally excluded, but is melted into an approach which emphasizes immediate knowledge and human experience more than reasoning.

---

11 P. M. Roseneau, *Post-Modernism and the Social Sciences: Insights, Inroads, and Intrusions* (Princeton: Princeton University Press, 1992) at 15 [references omitted].

Some Legal Elements of Rupture

In law as in other fields, the critique of the project of modernity and the tracing of a pathway toward a second modernity share a sinuous discourse. Many efforts at synthesis have procured, in spite of their approximations, an elaborate and enlightening view of this undertaking. Nonetheless, it appears even more instructive and useful to direct my analysis toward two particular currents perfectly resumed by P. Issalys: the ideological critique of law and juridical feminism.[12]

Ideological critique   As mentioned by Issalys, ideological critique usually begins with Marxism.[13] Marxism's main contribution can be found in its analysis of pre-socialist societies, notably the *bourgeoisie*. Legislation is dependent on the *bourgeoisie*'s superstructure, for the same reason as is law as a whole. It is an instrument for managing the interests of the ruling class. But its fundamental role is at the ideological level. By resorting to universalism, legislative discourse tends to validate the fiction of a society constituted of purely individual, free and equal persons. Marxist critique therefore highlights the formal, abstract and unreal character of legislation when it claims that society is organized by individual reason. This critique emerges from a practice whose aim is to expose the true nature of law and the contradictions that it encloses and to question it as a social organizing process. So far as Marxism is concerned, the legality of the *bourgeoisie* flows from a moral forfeiture and an economic necessity. On the one hand, this legality diverts citizens' free adherence to the society for the benefit of a structure of domination. On the other hand, sovereign law, static and impersonal, meets the needs of the capitalist economy, based on a hierarchical, formalistic and abstract pattern of power and social relations.

In the English-speaking world, Issalys writes that the trend of Critical Legal Studies revitalizes and updates some Marxist theses, emphasizing both legislation and case law.[14] These are seen as devices being submitted to a purely political rhetoric. The latter tries to produce a mystifying and legitimizing effect in order to protect an unjustified power's hegemony. As far as legislation is more specifically concerned, the school of Critical Legal Studies suggests that its new contents, such as open norms and appreciation standards, modify the idea of classical legality. The abstract formulation of new universal rules permits the transference of a

---

12   P. Issalys, 'La loi dans le droit' (1992) 33 C. de D. 665; see, also, the introduction by G. Minda in *Postmodern Legal Movement: Law and Jurisprudence at Century's End* (New York: New York University Press, 1995); T. D. Burton, 'Troublesome Connections: The Law and Post-Enlightenment Culture' (1998) 47 Emory L. J. 163.

13   A. Hunt, 'Marxism, Law, Legal Theory, and Jurisprudence' in P. Fitzpatrick, ed., *Dangerous Supplements: Resistance and Renewal in Jurisprudence* (Duke: Duke University Press, 1991); C. Stoyanovitch, *Marxisme et droit* (Paris: L.G.D.J., 1964).

14   A. Altman, *Critical Legal Studies: A Liberal Critique* (Princeton: Princeton University Press, 1990); M. Kelman, *A Guide to Critical Legal Studies* (Cambridge: Harvard University Press, 1987).

political and economic debate in the legal text itself. The law and the authorities charged with its application have become more than ever before both the arena of social conflicts and the stakes involved in it.

Pursuing his analysis, Issalys indicates that J. Habermas revives Marx's critique in the context of the contemporary State of law.[15] He describes how the latter was constituted through an increasing influence of the legal phenomenon over the social one. The regulation of social relations by the State has produced the notion of social rights, whose benefits must not mask the fact that they sanction and cement into law power relations which are connected to the class structure. This process is prompted by the ambition of an ever-increasing rationalization of social life. This rationalization contributes to the legalization of human relations, following a formalism which states that each individual is capable of exercising a real free will. It also implies the deployment of a tremendous State apparatus, intended to bring into operation the compromises included in the law. From this emerges an intense bureaucratization of the social order. This reason proper to the modern State has replaced that of the more idealistic and utopian Enlightenment philosophy.

Habermas shows however that the moderate action of the legislative power countervails the power of money. Both powers are certainly opposed in many ways, but nonetheless display a common acceptance of the principle that labour is the cornerstone of social organization and industrial economic growth. Just like the idea of a relatively authoritarian system of laws based on the legitimacy of the majority, this principle is not fundamentally questioned in the modern State. That is why some individuals are excluded, and interests and dimensions of the reality are kept in the background, despite the place given to participation, consensus and tolerance.

In these conditions, how can we explain the rise of diverse trends whose characteristic is to bring to light a kind of State legitimacy problem? These trends would essentially flow from a reaction of actual human experience against its subjection to both the economy and State political power. Through the free spaces left open, the discourse of the excluded individuals would take advantage of a certain platform or find enough soil to take root. However, the real impact of this discourse would remain considerably variable.

In conclusion, Issalys states that ideological critique denounces a fictitious reason within the State and its apparatus, a reason which tends to legitimize individual relations of power. It induces one to consider whether, since the transformation of social relations by the State is nothing but an illusion, the accomplishment of reason and justice perhaps lies more in a collective process. It is in this regard that Habermas has developed his proposition of communicational sovereignty. This project is aimed at the revival and emergence of a spontaneous mutual spirit at all levels of society. This would be made feasible by favouring the individual and collective autonomy of the participants, together with the means of

---

15   See, among other works by Habermas, Chapter 3, *supra*; note 1.

communication and of exchange between them. This living interaction, necessarily enlightening, would become a State inspiration.

Feminism   For Issalys, feminism is currently centred on three approaches: semantic, methodological and epistemological.[16]

The semantic critique of legislation through feminism addresses the legal text itself, the language it uses. By emphasizing the gendered character of this language, semantic critique takes advantage of the Marxist critique of the purely formal universality of the law. It exposes a conscious or unconscious bias toward exclusion of, or discrimination against, women, concealed behind an assumed neutral vocabulary. Methodological critique then takes over from semantics to question, according to the author, the validity of the very content of legislation. This critique consists in showing that, even in democratic States, the setting of both political life and legislative process do not guarantee the accurate reflection of the feminist perspective of reality in law. And even when this perspective is taken into account, it can hardly be actually effective. Indeed, the whole management of the law is mainly based on an authoritarian arbitration between cooperative values and interests. This arbitration usually traces its origin to abstract and impersonal criteria, supposedly conveying an objective justice. All this does not match the characteristics of a strictly feminist legal methodology: to take into account the profound point of view of each of the parties concerned; to search for the solution which best concretely reconciles all the interests of all the parties; and to favour subjective expression and exchanges of points of view in the search for solutions. Finally, Issalys shows that epistemological critique notably leads to questioning the very notion of law as expressing acts of individual will. It attacks the concept of law as an act of command and of constraint, to which are related the ideas of hierarchy, deliberate organization and the objectivization of reality. To begin with, law, far from presenting itself as neutral with regard to social reality, would express an essentially masculine perspective. By not taking into consideration the social division of both sexes, State rationality would be necessarily deviant. In addition, feminist critique sets against the masculine perspective of reality, an approach which is based on unity with the world, acceptance of reality, plenitude and harmony, integration of subject and object, etc. It ultimately results in the search for forms of social life other than that which is extraneously structured by the State.

---

16   C. A. MacKinnon, *Toward a Feminist Theory of the State* (Cambridge: Harvard University Press, 1989); C. Smart, *Feminism and the Power of Law* (London: Routledge, 1989); J. Williams, 'Is Law an Art or a Science?: Comments on Objectivity, Feminism, and Power' (1998) 7 Am. U. J. Gender Soc. Pol'y & L. 373; A. Scales, 'Disappearing Medusa: The Fate of Feminist Legal Theory?' (1997) 20 Harv. Women's L. J. 34.

The Comprehensive Critic and Alternative of Sousa Santos

The title and subtitle of Sousa Santos' book[17] evoke the principal message underlying his reflection, which is to the effect that we are currently passing through a transitory period of history, at the end of which we will have passed from occidental modernity to a multi-faceted and multi-anchored post-modernism. Enthusiastic and willing to be considered 'socially effective',[18] Sousa Santos proposes a new common sense approach that embraces the many shapes of law, power and knowledge. The author takes the time to further note that this plurality, 'far from chaotic or infinite, is structured and relational,'[19] and that its recognition, 'far from colliding with the idea of the centrality of state law, state power and scientific knowledge in contemporary societies, confirms and relativizes it at the same time by integrating these hegemonic forms in new and broader constellations of laws, powers and knowledges.'[20]

More specifically, the paradigmatic transition derives from an abnormal relationship between two central pillars of modernity, the pillar of regulation and the pillar of emancipation. According to Sousa Santos, each pillar was constituted, in the beginning, of three principles or logics. The pillar of regulation was composed of the principle of the State, based on vertical obligations between citizens and institutions; the principle of the market, based on horizontal self-interests among contracting partners; and the principle of the community based on horizontal solidarities between community members and associations. The second central pillar, that of emancipation, was composed of the three logics of rationality identified by M. Weber: aesthetic-expressive (the arts); cognitive-instrumental (science and technology); and moral-practical rationalities (ethics and law). Some transformations then managed to destabilize the internal structure of the two pillars as well as their reciprocity. On the one hand, industrialization, the expansion of capitalism and consumer-based trends conferred upon the pillar of regulation a market-oriented nature. On the other hand, the cognitive-instrumental rationality of science and technology stood out, to the detriment of the other principles of the pillar of emancipation. For Sousa Santos, these reductionist movements, 'fuelled by the conversion of science into the primordial productive force, are the determinant conditions of the historical process by which modern emancipation has collapsed into modern regulation.'[21] This collapse dragged the law down with it, the law being at the heart of the process of the scientificization of society. It also signalled

the syndrome of exhaustion and of global blockage of modernity: the proliferation of the mirrors of regulation allows for ever-more contingent and conventional social

---

17   *Supra*, Introduction, note 4.
18   *Ibid.* at 92.
19   *Ibid.* at 403-404.
20   *Ibid.* at 404.
21   *Ibid.* at 8.

practices, but such contingency and conventionality coexist with an ever-higher degree of rigidity and inflexibility at the global level. Everything seems possible in arts and science, in religion and in ethics, but, on the other hand, nothing new seems to be possible at the level of the society as a whole.[22]

The paradigmatic transition provoked by all of this has several dimensions.[23] For the purposes of his argument, Sousa Santos takes an interest in the epistemological and the societal dimensions of the transition. He interprets the social dimension as the changeover from the capitalist world system and interstate system to six forms of (in the language of Fourier) 'vibrations ascendantes'[24] or, rather, emancipations, ones that correspond to many forms of social regulation, which he names as follows: cooperative domestic communities, eco-socialist production; human needs and ethical consumerism; amoeba-communities; socialism-is-democracy-without-end; and democratic sustainability and dispersed sovereignties. The dynamic nature that animates every vibration comes from a dialogical rhetoric, which subverts the conventional speaker-audience dichotomy by creating a zone of interchange, reciprocity and multi-directional argumentation. The State's role, in this regard, is highly crucial, and consists of guaranteeing 'the conditions of experimentation of alternative sociabilities.'[25] As for the epistemological dimension, closely linked to the preceding one, the author views it as a changeover from the paradigm of modern science to the paradigm of a prudent knowledge for a decent life, represented by the concept of subjectivity. This is, in fact, a kind of attitude or a tool capable of understanding and desiring the current transition, whose nature Sousa Santos determines using three topoi: the frontier (a privileged form of sociability), the baroque (a kind of inspiring lack of proportions) and the South (a kind of circle of reciprocity much vaster than that proposed by modernity).

Conclusion

As it is presented, conservative consciousness poses a serious problem as to the future of uniform law. This problem can be summarized as follows. To begin with, conservative consciousness is a faithful reflection of modernity and modern law. The correlation that I have established between the three facets which constitute modernity and the four main features of modern law, and the traits revealed by the regressive analysis carried out in Part I clearly demonstrate this. It is also worth mentioning that modernity and modern law are presently being shaken up. The reader may not be convinced by the claims made by Taylor, Habermas, Sousa Santos and feminist writers and sceptics. It is nevertheless reasonable to conclude from these claims that modernity and modern law are being subjected to an intense

---

22   *Ibid.* at 9.
23   *Ibid.* at 482ff.
24   *Ibid.* at 481.
25   *Ibid.* at 483.

process of renewal. The strong attributes and characteristics of logic, generality and stability are less powerful than formerly, faced with a reality which produces numerous exceptions, changes of direction and unexpected results. The abstract becomes ever less efficient and satisfying in the face of the number of cases and situations that require a more contextualized approach. Rationality is no longer self-evident, so that the justice and progress often associated with the law are more than ever subject to the challenge of justification.[26] In short, the reliability of law is not granted in advance. Finally, regardless of any individual's approval or disapproval of what has just been discussed, no one can deny the transformation of the contemporary world, noted by A. Huyssen, currently taking place under our very eyes.[27]

As conservative consciousness becomes more fragile, the future of uniform law becomes more murky. If the many faces of modernity (modernity, knowledge and progress; modernity and the dichotomous point of view; modern knowledge, economics and opulence) and the features of modern law (modern law and individuation; modern law and reason; modern law and contract; modern law as strong law) must be revised and modified, then, given their firm rootedness in the conservative consciousness of uniform law, uniform law too must be revised and modified. In order to fully participate in what is ahead, uniform law must, on all fronts, remain alert to the realities of tomorrow and undertake any necessary redefinitions. This is necessary for its survival and its calibre as an avant-garde body of thought and action. By opposition, a resigned or *laissez-faire* attitude would make it increasingly difficult to believe in uniform law, to consider it valuable, and to invest it with our enthusiasm.

The Progressive Reorientation of Uniform Law

If one can admit that conservative consciousness is subject to the hardships of the crisis of modernity and of modern law and that, as a result, it must be *reformulated*, the question becomes one that asks, *on which bases?* The preceding analysis revealed several key elements, concepts and models that are representative of these bases. In particular, a few of the lessons of the previous section should be retained for the remainder of the critique of conservative consciousness.

Initially, it is important to realize that to change the imagination or consciousness, in the circumstances of the moment, is not a simple task. Not only is it an important step, but it entails accepting several important, profound and difficult consequences, because, as H. Jonas claims, 'no previous ethic had to take

---

26 R. Sève, 'Avant-Propos. La philosophie du droit aujourd'hui' (1988) 33 Archives de philosophie du droit 19 at 21.

27 *Supra*, Introduction, note 12. See also A. Carty, *Post-Modern Law: Enlightenment, Revolution, and the Death of Man* (Edinburgh: Edinburgh University Press, 1990); J. Flax, *Thinking Fragments: Psychoanalysis, Feminism, and Postmodernism in the Contemporary West* (Berkeley: University of California Press, 1990).

into consideration the overall condition of human life and . . . the existence of the species itself.'[28] In the optic of modernity, the human being was at the centre of a world which was at her/his service. This attitude produced several undesirable effects. Willy-nilly, she/he is obliged to re-evaluate her/himself and to descend from the pedestal upon which she/he was placed. In this sense, J. Wojciechowski affirms that

> what emerges from modernity is also that the human being does not know only by her/himself, nor does she/he conclusively and definitely know what is her/his place in the world. This knowledge is not born in her/him. Rather, the human being must shape it, using what is previously known to her/him. This means that her/his place depends on her/his knowledge, and is always based on it. Would she/he then be capable, in the immediate future, to form a new image of her/his place in the universe and to understand her/himself in another light? The second modernity proposes as follows: that the individual cannot survive without a vision of the world that shows her/his place in the order of things and provides an ideal for her/him to live by, a frame of reference that justifies her/his efforts and losses. The more she/he knows, the more she/he must self-legitimize, and she/he becomes responsible for her/his own survival and that of her/his species. The quest for the imagination on the basis of her/his knowledge, which progresses at a more and more rapid pace, becomes a more and more urgent task. In order to be adequate, the imagination must include an array of sensible findings and the ever complex vision of science. The pursuit of the imagination on the basis of her/his knowledge engages the individual in profoundly transforming her/his behaviour, her/his attitudes, her/his vision of the world, in short, in continuous self-reinvention. She/he must place her/himself within a system that is more vast than her/himself. Not only will the human being be obliged to respect nature, but as well, because of the growing interdependence of all of humanity and the forces of destruction that are also becoming greater and greater, she/he will be obliged to respect her/his peers. The message of wisdom becomes one of solidarity among humans and between human beings and nature.[29]

At this stage of the critique, it is important to comprehend what has just been stated in order to identify paths suggestive of a progressive reorientation inspired by the second modernity. In terms of the consolidation carried out by A. J. Arnaud, one can see the second modernity as

> constituted by a state of mind, a belief in a particular mode of knowledge of the world, a vision, a Weltanschauung, as the Germanists might say. It has a paradigmatic value, to the extent that it is presented in the following manner:

---

28 H. Jonas, *Le principe responsabilité. Une éthique pour la civilisation technologique* (Paris: Éditions du Cerf, 1995) at 26.

29 J. Wojciechowski, *supra*, Chapter 3, note 7; at 22; see, also, É. Le Roy, N. Rouland, & D. J. Anton, *Diversity, Globalization and the Ways of Nature* (Ottawa: International Development Research Centre, 1995); L. Ferry, *The New Ecological Order*, trans. C. Volk (Chicago: University of Chicago Press, 1995); R. Zoll, *Nouvel individualisme et solidarité quotidienne* (Paris: Kimé, 1992).

1) It replaces a paradigm, that of modernity, and presents itself as a rational and systematic paradigm. It puts into question the comprehensive vision of the social order, of the 'legality' of legal positivism, and the mechanistic determinism that presides over the modern juridical order.

2) It relies upon a multitude of concepts of which the product (and the product alone) assures the paradigmatic conjunction: pragmatism, relativity, the decentering of the subject, the plurality of the rationalities, polycentricity, exploding logic, complexity.

3) It suggests a generalization of the dialectic of thought and action. It suggests the undertaking of juridical policies negotiated to replace the imposed juridical order.

4) It considers as provisional, hypothetical and purely instrumental the established categories of knowledge and those that arise from the disciplinary undertakings of a portion of this knowledge. It transgresses these spaces on the path toward interdisciplinarity.

5) It recognizes the implication of the subject in knowledge of the object, and, conscious of the inescapable reciprocal transformation that operates necessarily during the course of the analysis, adopts a perspective that is decidedly teleological.[30]

The discussion that follows presents the degree to which the principles of thought and the values of conservative consciousness differ from the progressive approach, as well as the different paths that can assist in its revision. I will utilize, for the purposes of this presentation, two categories of images, those of oppositions and metaphors.

The Oppositions

First opposition The first opposition highlights the stability, the infinite and the certainty that are characteristic of the metaphysical thought that is embedded in conservative consciousness. By posing a number of immutable principles, a dualistic choice and definitive categorizations, metaphysical thought is essentially a reassuring measure. It denotes a state of mind destined to create a sentiment or a climate of confidence and of tranquillity.

Dialectical progressive thought, on the other hand, in a way comes to surpass it.[31] Initially, this passing over comes from a *change* that goes over and above the identitarian element of metaphysical thought. The change supposes a future that is continuously under construction. This construction is fed by a number of experiences, both past and present, in order to better attach oneself to a future that is synonymous with other mutations. Past, present and future form a block of time, at the helm of which a principle of *reciprocal influence* acts between objects and beings. All of their facets are, a priori, open to the effects of this principle that ensures a mutual deepening – every part can enter into the knowledge and the

30   A. J. Arnaud, *Entre modernité et mondialisation. Cinq leçons d'histoire de la philosophie du droit et de l'État* (Paris: L.G.D.J., 1998) at 168.

31   T. Adorno, *Dialectique négative*, trans. G. Coffin (Paris: Payot, 1978); also B. Puchalska-Tych & M. Salter, 'Comparing legal cultures of Eastern Europe: The need for a dialectical analysis' (1996) 16 Legal Studies 157.

comprehension of another, and reciprocally – and a complementarity – various components can be perfected, enriching themselves through their joint ventures. As well, the relational dimension that is inherent in reciprocal influence is marked by a *contradiction* and an ambivalence. It leaves behind the binary logic characteristic of the metaphysical type that refutes any opposition: a thing is either good or bad, pretty or homely. For the dialectical type, the coexistence of opposites is a normal fact, in the same way as the fact of wanting and needing to solve contradictions constitutes an attitude that is at the basis of the formulation of sense.[32] Finally, these factors are inscribed in a method of *evolution by stages*. This means that reality is not always modified at the same rhythm. Its evolution is a function of phases, of periods of time whose succession will depend on the intensity of change and the contradictions to overcome.

The legal scholarship to which I referred in Part I does not attach much importance to dialectical thought. As demonstrated through the argument of good faith, legal scholarship puts the emphasis on the conditions capable of stabilizing uniform law. Unfortunately, this emphasis does not fit with the second modernity. The latter does not urge us to search for stabilization. Rather, it invites us to model uniform law in conformity with a reality in motion. Consequently, uniform law must be linked with a flexible and interactive type of thought, such as dialectical thought. In my opinion, dialectical thought is likely to be especially useful on the level of contractual relationships. Without anticipating too much what will be proposed in the phase of reformulation (Part III), I submit that contractual relationships are usually much more subject to unexpected circumstances and opportunities than what is assumed by conservative consciousness. The intervention of dialectical thought is consequently more susceptible of showing them in their true light.

Second opposition The second opposition refers to the analytical type of approach, which is driven by the need to omit nothing, and which therefore consists in dissecting reality as finely as possible in order to analyse its constitutive elements in detail. This method, which characterizes conservative consciousness, is legitimized by the idea that every element can be considered independently from that which surrounds it; in other words, a global reality would result, but from the accumulation of these independent elements.

Systemic progressive thought proceeds in a different way.[33] To begin with, it brings forth the principle of *organization*. It implies that reality must be questioned according to what it contains, but also in relation to the way in which it is organized. This leads one to observe the links that unite the various components of reality and their function, as well as the components themselves. The principle of

---

32   J. Jacobs, *Systèmes de survie. Dialogue sur les fondements moraux du commerce et de la politique*, trans. C. Teasdale (Montreal: Boréal, 1995).

33   L. von Bertalanffy, *Théorie générale des systèmes*, trans. J. Chabrol (Paris: Dunod, 1973); also, P. Valentin, 'Jurisprudence et philosophie du droit' (1993) 4 Revue de la recherche. Droit prospectif 1265.

association supports this first finding. It postulates that, on the one hand, the ties and the functioning of the aforesaid components form a whole. By definition, the whole symbolizes more than the mere conjunction of its parts: it is not so readily reducible. On the other hand, the parts and the whole are associated according to the transformation they have undergone. The whole is reflected upon the parts, encouraging them to modify themselves, and vice versa. Furthermore, the organization and association open upon a *totality*. They are receptive to the slightest movement, dimension and effects connected with the parts as well as the whole. This sensitivity defines the originality and the richness of a system in which the parts and the whole can be found. Through the intervention of these methodological premises, it becomes possible to develop an overall vision unique to the principle of *holism*. A holistic vision is useful on two separate levels. First, it corresponds to the idea that a mobilization of knowledge must be attempted for solving every particular problem. And, secondly, it allows one to take a step back from the system, to take into consideration the phenomenon of uncertainty linked to the principle of totality and to bring the necessary adjustments, if need be.

In my opinion, the immediate result of systemic thought is to place uniform law in connection with the other components of social life. And as soon as uniform law forms part of a system, it loses its independence to gain interdependence. Consequently, it can no longer appear as dominant as it is in conservative consciousness. More specifically, legal scholarship cannot attach a kind of pre-eminence to an argument such as the autonomy of the will within uniform law. This pre-eminence must be relativized in accordance with other considerations which will be deemed relevant by progressive consciousness. At first sight, the relevance of these considerations may not be obvious. But it will be for progressive consciousness to explain clearly why they are relevant and, especially, which methodology can allow for their integration within uniform law.

Third opposition The third opposition begins with the following belief that is pivotal to simplifying thought: universal and permanent laws exist; they are founded upon, or can be reduced to, a few principles; and the organization of these principles can be marked by a cleanness that, excluding misapprehension and ambiguity, can be readily compared to formalism. Simplifying thought causes the human being to believe that she/he controls everything because of her/his capacity to be all-knowing.

When contrasted to these qualities of conservative consciousness, progressive complex thought appears full of nuances. By basing its behaviour upon the tenets of G. Bachelard to the effect that *there is nothing simple in nature, nature is merely simplified,*[34] it shows its orientation toward the density of reality. In so doing, complex thought is reduced to three main principles. The first is the *dialogical* principle,[35] which seeks to bring closer, to unite, the many facets of reality that

---

34   G. Bachelard, *Le nouvel esprit scientifique*, 4th ed. (Paris: P.U.F., 1991).
35   M. Bakhtin, *The Dialogical Imagination*, trans. C. Emerson and M. Holquist (Austin: University of Texas Press, 1981).

appear to be complementary and antagonistic at the same time. For instance, order and disorder can be seen from a dialogical angle. At times, order and disorder are seen as enemies: one necessarily suppresses the other. But, in other circumstances, they are capable of collaborating in order to produce a new form of organization. The dialogical principle thus refers to the propensity to look for connections among diverse elements, as opposed to cut-offs between their differences. It is backed by the principle of *recursiveness*, that is understood as a process whereby products and effects are at the same time the causes and originators of what produces them. E. Morin[36] illustrates this principle using the individual, the species and the process of reproduction as an example: individuals are the product of a process of reproduction, which exists previous to them; but once they are produced, they become the producers of the process that pursues its path. This principle is also useful sociologically speaking: society is produced by the interactions between individuals; but once it is produced, society provides feedback to individuals – it produces them. Recursiveness is thus disengaged from the linear principle of cause/effect, of product/producer, since all that is produced influence what or who produces it. The principles of dialogicalism and recursiveness are supplemented by a third principle termed *multi-dimensionality*. The latter invites us to recognize that over and above the purity of each and every phenomenon there hides a composite nature. Or, rather, that behind the charm and beauty that transcends the whole of whatever it may be, there always hide the infinite, complicated, misunderstood and unknown dimensions. The factor that is conducive to the reality of a thing or a being cannot, therefore, be illustrated by a straight line. Rather, it bears the shape of a spiral or a bow.[37]

To a certain extent, complex thought warns uniform law against any temptation to fall into an easy and over-simple universalism. This criticism can be levelled at the argument of legal convergence. Legal convergence neglects a huge quantity of data, in order to avoid putting into question a globalizing process whose necessity is taken for granted. Without denying the fact that a global society is currently emerging, complex thought recalls that the components of this society nevertheless keep some autonomy and identity. For instance, when a State becomes part of uniform law in one way or another, this does not imply the annihilation of its juridical culture. The latter can remain full of vitality and very instructive for the observer. In short, complex thought tries to *bring back to life* many components of human existence that are ignored by simplifying thought.

Fourth opposition The last opposition confronts the instrumental thought that is a characteristic of conservative consciousness with the teleological dimension of the second modernity, which seeks to attain the best possible solution to the question, *what are we aiming for?*. In this sense, the establishment of a model of individual

---

36 E. Morin, *Introduction à la pensée complexe* (Paris: ESF Éditeur, 1990).
37 A. Rocque, 'Non-Linear Phenomena' (1988) 28 Int'l Phil. Q. 247.

and social life or, modestly, the construction of a human destiny, must be attempted.[38]

I would consider that this best possible solution could orient development in the following way:

i)   As a dynamic model, development is never fully achieved. It is an undertaking involving a number of players, motivated by a particular vision, the goals of which are never fully reached.

ii) It does not correspond to a unique model, given the diversity of contexts; thus, it supposes the existence of different strategies.

iii) It comprises a number of dimensions, both individual and collective, and assumes that the advancement of some is not to be achieved to the absolute detriment of others.

iv) It is defined with respect to particular territories and it values local potentialities and resources.

v)   It privileges self-centred undertakings on the local level, without disregarding the necessary articulations with external factors.

vi) It is critical with regard to dominant models, putting the accent on qualitative aspects and on the search for alternatives.

vii) It is respectful of the time and the rhythm of the different actors concerned.

To these axes of development, teleological progressive thought adds certain principles. The first is that of otherness – other people, which translates as the acknowledgement of others. No one can be deified, and no one can have his or her existence denied, abandoned to absolute exclusion and left without a grasp on reality. These two interdicts constitute the beginnings of more human development, which contrasts sharply with instrumental thought. By the mutual recognition of differences (origin, culture, belonging, status), each one exists in the face of others, without being preoccupied with assimilation. This necessitates a desire to understand the internal logic of each single and collective actor. This also requires communication, that is to say recognition of the value of the other as much as one's own, with his or her style of thought and of living. In entering into a relationship of otherness, more than things, it is a part of themselves that individuals and social groups exchange. The second principle is that of reciprocity, which is manifested in the idea of shared responsibility. Exchanging experiences, identifying the values at work through actions, being more open to other persons and groups: these are all requirements of the second modernity. It invokes the responsibility of everyone before his or her own convictions. It conceives that identity is forged in the debate which knots relationships and that identity is a source of understanding, of synergy and of integration. The last principle, that of co-administration, refers to undertakings that can truly be described as concrete. This means that the undertakings are visible and tangible: economic practices

---

38 See, in general, M. A. Max-Neef, *Human Scale Development: Conception, Applications and Further Reflections* (New York: Apex, 1991).

which do not generate exclusions, mobilizing actions for integration, experimentation of various life-styles which favour sociability, educational practices enabling actors to build their relationship with others and their future, scientific measures which take into account both social demands and the analysis of social effects, etc. Through projects to be promoted, the progressive option seeks to increase the opportunities for choice and decision-making possibilities. It is there to answer to new aspirations, in a changing environment, while remaining conscious that releasing the space of autonomy and the diversification of their expression proves to be both a formidable and imposing task.

The Metaphors

The oppositions just discussed are another type of invitation to de-familiarize one's self from conservative consciousness. To complete this step, it would be opportune to connect this to a quadrature which borrows from the metaphors of the multiple, of consensus, of the flexible and of the relative.

The metaphor of the multiple Conservative consciousness refers to many unitarist symbols of modern reason. The identitary and isolationalist dimensions of the good faith argument, as well as the causality and the exhaustiveness which characterize the argument of the autonomy of the will, adhere to this 'this and only this' logic. Taken alone, the argument of juridical convergence acts as a powerful force of integration toward unicity. With order, linearity, determinism and indubitable normality, conservative consciousness provides support for a monist and purist view of reality; the disturbing elements are eliminated in favour of a single point of view, whose conditions of recurrence are known and tested, and which constitute an element of normality. These various unitarist facets are normatively reinforced and circumscribed by the centripetal forces of the value of wealth, the workings of which are regulated by a market which guarantees coherence and healthy coordination.

The metaphor of the multiple offers a new perspective for uniform law. Its premise is the principle of the multiplicity of the sources and belongings of uniform law. This effects a change in direction in the understanding that which can be made of uniform law. The tendency toward separation (between the national and international orders), toward distinction (is the *lex mercatoria* law or not) and toward exclusivity (the original source of uniform law remains commercial practice) no longer prevail. According to the principle of multiplicity, each source, no matter what its origin, is potentially pertinent. On a prefatory basis, each source is thus considered, no matter what its origin (the State, *societas mercatorum*, professional association, NGO, civil society etc.). Then, it is evaluated on its merits, that is to say in light of its contribution to the rigour and the legitimacy of a process of reasoning. The emphasis is placed less on the defining of frontiers between sources or conceptualization than on the intrinsic value of each element able to provide some information or data. In this sense, the metaphor of the (multiple) 'is akin to a comparative approach which simply consists in drawing up the best possible solution in each case without rejecting any legal source at the outset.'[39] Correlatively, the spatio-temporal framework passes from the universal and the infinite – as it is for conservative consciousness – to another defined at the dawn of a plural and fragmented identity.[40] Instead of being confined to . . ., uniform law becomes open to . . ., and integrated in . . . . Its action becomes able to spread from the local to the global and inversely, in something other than only economics, and so forth. Its existence is no longer independent of external influences, or even self-sufficient: it is composed of imbrications – it depends on overlapping, on connections; it is a subset of a greater whole.[41] As a result, more than to the hierarchy, attention turns toward modes of exchange and articulation between the norms of uniform law and of others.[42]

The metaphor of consensus　As it appears from conservative consciousness, uniform law possesses a nearly innate power. As strong law, its contribution to the general well-being and world harmony are taken for granted. In a word, it inspires enduring confidence. As quid pro quo, we afford it unshakable respect. Likewise, it is just and necessary that one submit to it because of the inseparable ties it maintains with progress. Whether it be as expert knowledge (because it is certain, precise and omnipotent) or supernatural knowledge (because it is at the source of the enchanting vision of commerce), uniform law traces the way toward desired living conditions. At this point, its critique becomes a more unusual rather than usual process, being effected superficially rather than in depth, in a discontinuous rather than permanent manner.

The metaphor of consensus relativizes this legitimacy inherent in uniform law. Henceforth, the validity of uniform law is subordinated to the quality and the extent of the consensus of which it is the object. This change may be explained in particular by the fact that the reality to which uniform law is joined is no longer that of an ordered, unified and stable society. There is a disappearance of the notion that juridical bench-marks and others allow each one to find his or her place in a determined fashion in relation to others, and that the legitimacy of social relations proceeds from a transcendental foundation having a scientific or religious connotation. On the contrary, uniform law is instead invited to abandon the limpidity and simplicity characteristic of a pre-programmed evolution, in order to

---

39　H. P. Glenn, 'Le droit comparé et la Cour suprême du Canada', in *Mélanges Louis-Philippe Pigeon* (Ottawa: Collection Bleue, 1989) 198 at 199; by the same writer, 'Unification of Law, Harmonization of Law and Private International Law' in *Liber Memorialis François Laurent* (Brussels: E. Story-Scientia, 1989) at 783.

40　Sousa Santos speaks of a map containing 'many juridical spaces which act simultaneously on different scales', in 'Droit: une carte de lecture déformée. Pour une conception post-moderne du droit' (1988) 10 Droit et société 373.

41　G. Teubner, 'Breaking Frames: The Global Interplay of Legal and Social Systems' (1997) 45 Am. J. Comp. L. 149.

42　D. Tallon, 'L'inexécution du contrat: pour une autre représentation' 93 (1994) R.T.D.C. 287.

constantly test uncertainty, fallibility and constant resistance to dogmatism. In other words, it establishes itself as a place of debate and dispute, and as a place of discussion on the legitimacy of that which is and of that which should be. Moreover, insofar as it does not perceive itself as proceeding from an external or divine force, it leaves to the greatest number possible the incessant task of revising and redefining its norms. In sum, the representative character of uniform law constitutes an essential element of its progress toward the second modernity. This representativeness can be appreciated at more than one level. First, that which spontaneously asserts itself is the institutional plan: here, the figure of consensus implies the meeting of spokespersons truly representative of the diverse social interests in the process of elaboration and revision of uniform law. It also implies a form of assiduous diligence with regard to the degree of openness of institutions of all kinds devoted to the promotion of uniform law. The aim is to avoid a case like that of UNCITRAL, wherein jurists, typifying the intellectual class observed by A. Gramsci, could become but one entity used to legitimize a discourse symbolizing unity, whereas behind appearances, one particular ideology exercises a determining influence.[43] In addition, the metaphor of consensus brings to the forefront the plan of civil society. In one way or another, *the citizens*, with their preoccupations and aspirations, become a fundamental variable in the progressive representation of uniform law. Here, uniform law would be perceived, not so much as the result of the efforts of a specialized entity, but as the fruit of permanent negotiation between experts and other groups – the common people, those with practical experience, those who live in the field, etc.

The metaphor of the flexible Conservative consciousness utilizes a simple enough strategy in terms of emergence and evaluation of values. In effect, the first segment of this strategy is strongly monologist. It does not exclude that the cost/interest calculation to which it leads may take into account fundamental values, but it does not go beyond an abstractly conceived mild egoism. As for the second segment, it remains too rudimentary to infer anything substantial. Indeed, priority is attributed, amongst other things, to the constancy and precision of the rules. These attributes confer on uniform law a capacity to fulfil its function of fixing contractual obligations, or, expressed in more general terms, its mission of ensuring juridical security.

The metaphor of the flexible orients uniform law in another manner. It is mindful, in a constantly evolving world, of that which S. Salbu calls *the preservation of colloquy in emerging global communities*.[44] For Salbu, globalization is far from a *fait accompli*. On the contrary, the development of a society divided between the local and the global is an on-going phenomenon. That signifies that this development is an occasion for conflict, of calling into question

43   D. Grisoni & R. Maggiori, *Lire Gramsci* (Paris: Éditions Universitaires, 1973).
44   S. Salbu, 'True Codes versus Voluntary Codes of Ethics in International Markets: Towards the Preservation of Colloquy in Emerging Global Comunities' (1994) 15 U. Pa. J. Int'l Bus. L. 327.

and other adjustments. Thus under these circumstances, 'the interests of speed and certainty [are] outweighed by the interests of open discussion and persuasion.'[45] It serves no purpose, and perhaps it is harmful 'to fix expectations and understandings'[46] before minimal social and cultural cohesion has been attained. Salbu's premise is as follows: 'externally imposed moral positions which lack internal cultural support will be less effective than changes which reflect a substantive alteration of the culture itself.'[47] The author's reasoning entails two consequences: first, that the goal of legal clarity is a misguided one and, secondly, that it is important to render general norms and principles as luminous and inspiring as possible. A minority doctrinal position seems to want to tilt uniform law in this general direction. Starting with CISG Article 7, M. P. Van Alstine declares:

> At its heart, the interpretive paradigm of CISG article 7 reflects a single unifying aspiration: to initiate a process for the development of a truly independent, international body of law. If a specific convention's express provisions are the corporal frame, then its 'general principles' represent the moral values that will guide this new entity's growth to maturity.[48]

The metaphor of the flexible thus places the act of interpretation at the heart of the evolution of uniform law. Consequently, the role expected from the latter is no longer to prescribe precise and obligatory rules of conduct: it is rather to constitute a reservoir of meaning within which each and everyone can recognize him or her self, enter into relationships and grow. Moreover, the metaphor of the flexible modifies the manner of comprehending uniform law. Instead of considering it a rude fact of nature, this metaphor favours a hermeneutic interpretation of uniform law.[49] This distinction signifies that the nature of uniform law is not constituted by real, observable, neutral and constant facts which are external to thought. In reality, it is located in the mind: that means that the comprehension of uniform law proceeds from decoding a series of codes and mental fragments, actions and conduct, in addition to material and formal tools constituted by legislative, jurisprudential, doctrinal and other texts.

The metaphor of the relative   Uniform law, as outlined in conservative consciousness, represents superior knowledge which is perfectly suited for the search for opulence. In effect, it concentrates on economic growth, conforms well to a linear and mechanical vision of evolution and forges values in the light of its

---

45   *Ibid.* at 340.
46   *Ibid.* at 345.
47   *Ibid.* at 354.
48   M. P. Van Alstine, 'Dynamic Treaty Interpretation' (1998) 146 U. Pa. L. Rev. 687 at 761. But see Chapter 8 below for more on this topic.
49   R. Hollinger, *Hermeneutics and Praxis* (Notre Dame: University of Notre Dame Press, 1985); P. Dubouchet, 'Herméneutique et théorie normative du droit' (1994) 3 Revue de la recherche juridique. Droit prospectif 735.

instrumental reason. These are actions which contribute to the attainment of a state of opulence. At the same time, uniform law possesses a large capacity for structuring the social order while ensuring innovation, thanks notably to a very large scope of action granted to commercial practices; it is practically self-sufficient and legitimate ab initio, all the while remaining dynamic.

The metaphor of the relative clothes the status and ambition of uniform law with a bit more humility. First, it takes away from uniform law any attribute of exclusivity and unilaterality. By analogy with one of the guiding principles of the orthodox conception of law and development, the relation of uniform law with the development or any other type of deployment of action cannot be unilinear: uniform law is less than an absolute necessity and cannot alone undertake the realization of projected actions, insofar as they have a general application. Henceforth more modest, uniform law must contemplate its action in light of a combination or a co-ordination with other norms and means. Party to greater, more complex and urgent *problematics* which go beyond the strict domain of commerciality and which presupposes having recourse to a variety of modalities and interventions, uniform law has no other choice than to act in concert with ethical, political, and technical norms and, consequently, to fuse with them. Secondly, the metaphor of the relative forces uniform law to take sides with difference and diversity. It wants to induce uniform law to react, more particularly, against a determining current of commercial scholarship reflected in the following words of the jurist K. Yelpaala: 'In [the] new world economy, resources and markets have ceased to have the indelible national identity of the past. . . . To the more visionary global enterprises, the world is but a borderless environment with homogeneous consumers . . . .'[50] These affirmations do not in any way correspond to the principle advanced by N. Frye, according to which 'a society enriches itself by what it includes: it defines itself by what it excludes.'[51] Implicit in this principle is the notion that difference and diversity, properly understood and imagined, constitute sources of socially indispensable vitality and self-fulfilment. As stated by A. Posner, 'a comprehensive polycentric culture consisting of many relatively independent member cultures which are in close contact with one another is in many respects superior to a homogenous unified culture which is oriented only towards one centre.'[52] On the one hand, the principles proposed by Frye and Posner constitute a warning to uniform law to avoid the insipidity of a homogenized and homogenizing 'McWorld',[53] set out by Yelpaala. On the other hand, they

---

50   K. Yelpaala, 'Strategy and Planning in Global Product Distribution – Beyond the Distribution Contract' (1993) 25 Law and Pol'y Int'l Bus. at 23.

51   N. Frye, *The Critical Path: An Essay on the Social Context of Literary Criticism* (Bloomington: Indiana University Press, 1973) at 71.

52   A. Posner, 'Society, Civilization, Mentality: Prolegomena to a Language Policy for Europe', in Coulmas, ed., *A Language Policy for the European Community* (Berlin: de Gruyter, 1991) 124 at 124-125.

53   The expression is borrowed from Benjamin Barber, *Jihad vs. McWorld* (New York: Times Books, 1995).

encourage conceiving uniformization as a transformational process composed of resistance and of the birth of new particularities, that is to say, of making it a question of living with heterogeneity and of developing creative means of assuming, not destroying it.

Chapter 5

Utopia, or the Middle Reformulation of Uniform Law

The simultaneous goals of defamiliarization were to remodel uniform law and to take it out of the limitations of the personal ethos described by S. Kokis. The combined effect of these actions had to establish the confidence necessary for pursuing the exercise of *critique as legal imagination* within the boundaries of utopia. The trajectory of thought compared to what it was under the step of defamiliarization is thus inverted. Instead of starting with uniform law and arranging it according to new avenues of evolution, the thought process immediately attains the final combination sought after. Then, it specifies and develops this final combination by using a mixture of new, already existing and restored elements.[1]

The number of final combinations related to a given subject is indefinite. It is proper to utopia to open the door to every variation one can think of. In this endless universe, I have thought advisable to select and support three variations. The first consists in elaborating what I call a transitory conception of law and development. In my opinion, this first variation represents an essential step in any effort of re-definition of uniform law in a progressive perspective. As the starting point of the analysis, I have chosen to use A. K. Sen's definition of the notion of development: this constitutes a 'process that enhances the effective freedom of the people involved to pursue whatever they have reason to value.'[2] The second variation deduces certain implications from the first, as well as the stage of de-familiariza-tion, in presenting them in the form of an outline of a new discourse underlying uniform law. The structure of this variation is in line with the methodology laid out in the Introduction. In addition, it anticipates the form and content of the progressive consciousness which will be dealt with in Part III. The final and third variation centres on the theme of the history of uniform law. Its goal is to demonstrate that the manner of exposing and explaining the history of a discipline has a great influence on the intellectual process which underlies it, and vice versa.

---

1   For a similar approach, see M. M. Kleinhans & R. A. Macdonald, 'What is *Critical Legal Pluralism?*' (1997) 12 Canadian Journal of Law and Society 25 at 25-27.

2   A. K. Sen, 'Culture, Economics and Development', contribution to the work of the Commission mondiale de la culture et du développement, UNESCO, 1995 at 1.

The Transitory Conception

Keeping in mind its definition, the elements closely or more distantly linked to the changeover of modernity toward a second modernity and other elements, I believe that the transitory conception can be identified as follows.

As an introduction, it is important to underline that within the perspective of the transitory conception, it remains pertinent to question everything generally, be it in light of the four-sided question established by I. Kant (What can I know? What should I do? What can I hope for? What is Man?) or of other types of question. The reason for this questioning is to find a *modus vivendi* capable of satisfying the innate need of purpose in life.[3]

In the perspective of giving meaning to human action, the transitory conception comprises a normative and double-sided cornerstone: self-fulfilment and solidarity. The first facet adopts a sequential perspective on life and applies to people in both their individual and collective states. In this respect, life is considered as a series of actions and gestures or as projects or views which are integrated in a totality of individual or community achievements. More specifically, self-fulfilment refers to the extent of possibilities which an individual or a community can achieve: it is the formula of *what one can do or be* from which moral economy has developed the concept of *expansion of human capability*.[4] This theory does not totally exclude criteria and indicators specific to the vision of opulence (for example, income per person) or other theories such as utilitarianism (for example, happiness). However, they become relative and are analysed in accordance with the capacity they give to an individual or a society to choose and satisfy its aspirations.

The second facet, solidarity, seeks to permeate the different activities devoted to self-fulfilment with a sense of responsibility and of community of interest. It implies that the vitality of the *modus vivendi* invoked above requires more than a simple call to self-fulfilment. Moreover, self-fulfilment must be achieved with respect to what R. Petrella has called the principles of existence of the other and of coexistence.[5] He believes that these principles are at the base of a material and immaterial common good which he places at the heart of a world social contract. For Petrella, the common good rests on the contract of possession, aimed at eliminating inequalities; on the cultural contract, promoting tolerance and dialogue between cultures; on the democratic contract, which guarantees civil and political liberties; and on the contract of the earth, oriented toward sustainable development. Insofar as living together involves a meaning in itself, extending beyond the simple

---

3   E. Morin & S. Naïr, *Une politique de civilisation* (Paris: Arléa, 1997); P. Engelhard, *L'homme mondial. Les sociétés humaines peuvent-elles survivre?* (Paris: Arléa, 1996).

4   A. K. Sen is one of the authors who has most analysed this notion. See *Commodities and Capabilities* (Amsterdam: North Holland, 1985); also M. Nussbaum & A. K. Sen, *The Quality of Life* (Oxford: Clarendon, 1993) and K. Griffon & J. Knight, *Human Development and the International Development Strategy for the 1990s* (London: Macmillan, 1990).

5   R. Petrella, *Le bien commun. Éloge de la solidarité* (Brussels: Labor, 1996).

whole of personal and social aspirations, solidarity thus appears as a necessary complement to self-fulfilment.[6]

This normative cornerstone is next shaped in accordance with a proposal of N. Goodman: reality does not exist in the form of a single world waiting to be discovered, but rather of several already constructed worlds.[7] Here, the conception of opulence, which reduced the good to a single aspect, yields to a vision conditioned by at least three components of culture: historical character, which situates the good in time and gives it different priorities; spatial character, which situates the good in a given territory and attributes different perceptions to it; and ethical character, which situates the good in specific value systems and gives it different aspirations. The good is thus constructed by reference to a context. On this level, culture plays a determinative role. The elements to which the world intrinsically attaches value will be grasped and understood from the conditioning which culture operates toward the good. However, not all notions of culture are capable of filling this role. For example, a fairly widespread type of such a notion consists simply of listing the recurrent outputs of social action. This type of notion envisages culture as a totality of knowledge, beliefs, art, morality, customs and other acquired habits and abilities. Such a list has the advantage of a comprehensive approach. However, it goes no further and omits to explain how these elements are linked. This coherence is more apparent in notions of culture of an historical type, conceived as a mixture of behaviours transmitted from one generation to the next, or in notions of culture of an idealistic or normative type defining culture as the way to live together shared by individuals of a society. Nonetheless, these notions are marked with immobilism – in that the actor of culture performs acts of reproduction, ignoring change, adaptation and innovation – and essentialism,[8] in that there is no connection between the cultural whole and other cultures. In fact, the notion of culture of a semiotic type developed by C. Geertz conforms better to the search for meaning, characteristic of the transitory conception.[9] Geertz refuses to confuse culture with cults and customs. Instead, he assimilates culture to *structures of understanding* through which the human being gives direction and values to her/his existence. Conceived in this way, culture involves the existence of a code, a system of understandings through which individuals communicate, perpetuate and develop knowledge and attitudes in relation to their lives.

This last notion is connected to the transitory conception in three important ways. Firstly, it links the presence of a given world to the existence of a code. This allows for a minimal cohesion without which members of this world could not

---

6   For a more detailed analysis of the notion of solidarity, see J. Habermas, *Autonomy and Solidarity* (London: Verso, 1986).

7   Goodman, *supra*, Part II, Preliminary Remarks, note 8.

8   Note, 'Aspiration and Control: International Legal Rhetoric and the Essentialization of Culture' (1993) 106 Harv. L. R. 723.

9   C. Geertz, *Local Knowledge* (New York: Basic Books, 1983); see also, by the same author, *The Interpretation of Cultures, supra*, Introduction, note 9.

share meanings. Secondly, the code is compatible with a social dynamism and the changes which this generates. In essence, constraints exercised by meanings are limited to social organization. Nothing prevents the diversification of this action, proceeding with a choice between several different orientations. Moreover, every action sprouts from the heart of the previous action and represents in itself a source of enrichment for the future. Thirdly, the code, as a system of perception of the other by members of a world, constantly changes relative to the worlds that surround it: it is open and interactive. This way of seeing *sense* replaces the homogenizing comprehensive approach underlying K. Yelpaala's analysis with a representation of reality in which different worlds here and there maintain relations which simultaneously nourish their similarities and their differences.[10] Within these relationships, multiple constructions of meaning rest on ambiguity, resistance and correction. Meaning is thus not purely and simply exchanged, as such, between one world and another. Moreover, the shapes it may take are not fixed in time or space. The circulation of meaning between worlds is a fluid process without pre-determined limits,[11] which creates 'particular constellations of historical relations articulated at a particular locus.'[12] All this movement is far removed from notions of homogeneity: in law in particular, we should see it as supporting the appearance of what R. Coombe calls 'new legalities and juridical sensibilities.'[13]

Finally, the transitory conception incorporates the economic reality in the living.[14] This integration implies the recognition of the existence of at least three spheres.[15] The first sphere groups economic activities, the second embraces the rest of human concerns and relationships, and the third envisages the biosphere. These spheres are interdependent: this means that the reproduction and destiny of each is connected to those of the others. At the same time, each sphere is not reducible to the other two: thus, human concerns and relationships cannot all be linked to the economic reality. Inversely, the economic aspect has certain special characteristics which cannot be explained by recourse to considerations which are exterior to it. In so doing, the transitory conception takes the opposite view, in several ways, of the vision of opulence. Firstly, it refutes the idea of general and determinist laws in the economic sphere. The dependence of the economic aspect on the other spheres shows that it cannot resolve alone all the situations where interests and aspirations

---

10   G. Robinson & J. Rundell (eds.), *Rethinking Imagination: Culture and Creativity* (London: Routledge, 1994).

11   J. N. Pieterse, 'Globalisation as Hybridisation' (1994) 9 International Sociology 161 at 161-162.

12   R. J. Coombe, 'The Cultural Life of Things: Anthropological Approaches to Law and Society in Conditions of Globalization' (1995) 10 Am. U. J. Int. L. and Pol. 791 at 827.

13   *Ibid.* at 796.

14   B. Arnold, 'Challenges Facing Economists in the 21st Century' (1993) 48 Review of Social Economy 48.

15   R. Passet, *L'économique et le vivant* (Paris: Économica, 1996); H. Bartoli, *L'économie multidimensionnelle* (Paris: Économica, 1991).

of all sorts are at stake.[16] The invisible hand, or simple freedom, is not sufficient. It must be enriched by other elements stemming from coordination and cooperation. Furthermore, it refuses to dissolve the *worlds* in the economic aspect. Therefore, it cannot base itself uniquely on the game of individual rationalities and on the institutional context of the market where they evolve. On the contrary, all the aspects which are constituents of a world become pertinent in understanding its forms and its orientations. In fact, the association between the economic and the living modifies the variables of analysis: explanations and solutions framed in terms of effectiveness and wealth are integrated into questions and propositions which are much more complicated (because they relate to the her/history, morality, sociology and so forth, of a world), but also infinitely more comprehensive, inspiring and revealing. This is why, for example, the economic reality of a world could be better explained by a combination of a desire to succeed and an entrepreneurial spirit, reinforced by a moral security stemming from a cultural consistency.

The Outline of a New Discourse

Up to now, the analysis has showed many considerations likely to form part of a new discourse in connection with uniform law. Insofar as their validity is accepted, how would they be integrated within the web of means of expression and persuasion proper to a progressive consciousness of uniform law? This is the web which I propose.

The Relational Argument

The relational argument[17] views contractual relations as a network based on adaptation and flexibility, and in which the normative dimension of any exchange is a fundamental concern.[18] More specifically, the relational argument puts the contracting parties in a dialectic environment, that is, one which is sensitive to change and evolution in stages. This environment, affected by the presence of

---

16 I would add that any idea of *construction* of meaning is opposed to a strong determinism. On this subject, see the interesting ideas of S. J. Gould in *Réflexion sur l'histoire naturelle*, trans. M. Blanc (Paris: Seuil, 1996).

17 For a number of years, I. R. Macneil has been developing a theory of 'relational contract' which is rich and promising as it bears on the relational argument which I intend to develop in more depth in the future. I refer the reader to only one of his fundamental texts: *The New Social Contract: An Inquiry into Modern Contractual Relations* (New Haven: Yale University Press, 1980).

18 In a context which is different but important for further understanding, S. Salbu completed a fascinating study on the relational approach: 'The Decline of Contract as a Relational Management Form' (1995) 47 Rutgers L. Rev. See also, by the same author, 'Parental Coordination and Conflict in International Joint Venture: The Use of Contract to Address Legal, Linguistic and Cultural Concerns' (1993) 43 Case W. Res. 221.

movement, diversity, stability and instability, is perceived temporally in two complementary ways: long term and day to day. The contract is thus not a fixed point, frozen in time, but instead a moving linkage or, as Macneil has described it, *an on going operation.*[19] There is no *single* magic moment at which time the contractual obligations of the parties are determined. Since the contract evolves over time, in the long term as well as the short term, several moments or circumstances other than its formal conclusion will serve to bind the parties. Moreover, in terms of values, the linkage opens the door to a different general view of the contract. Antagonism and the self-interested maximization of interests amount to a normative range which I would describe as narrow. From the metaphysical point of view, this narrowness is appropriate since the potential of the contract is conceived as decided in advance. All the parties have to do is to apportion it in accordance with the rules of the zero sum game, in that each advantage gained by one party is a disadvantage for the other. In comparison, the relational argument situates the potential of the contract as a bundle of possibilities of advancement, in quality, for each of the contracting parties. Consequently, an enrichment and diversification of the values at work in every contract is necessary to extend these possibilities as much as possible. It must tend toward a broad normative range, comprising elements related to cooperation, confidence, coordination and so forth.[20]

The Argument of the Common Good

The transitory conception of the good can only have meaning if there exists something representing more than the simple sum of the interests of the contracting parties. On one hand, taking a cue from K. J. Arrow's impossibility theorem, it can be established that no procedure for grouping together the individual preferences manifested in contracts will allow for determining collective preferences at all times. Arrow's social choice theory, then, is not absolute. In particular, it interacts with J. N. Buchanan's. The latter relativizes and complements the former, by emphasizing positivism, individual rationality and, more generally, a subjectivist and contractualist frame of reference. Buchanan thus denies collective rationality, proposing rather that collective norms and new social states are constituted by individuals. On the other hand, the theory of cooperative games indicates that simple freedom at the base of the vision of opulence is not sufficient. It instead seems that the gain of the contracting parties is greater, in the presence of limited common resources, when they maximize their respective goals *in taking into*

---

19   I. R. Macneil, 'The Many Futures of Contracts' (1974) 47 S. Cal. L. R. 691.
20   C. Vadcar, 'Relations Nord-Sud: vers un droit international du partenariat?' (1995) 122 J.D.I. 599.

account the community. This 'something extra' translates into the argument of the common good.[21]

The argument of the common good marks a break with technocracy which culminates in the advent of a totally administered society. M. Weber saw in this a source of disillusion: there is a political, social and cultural vacuum, public debate is of little interest because it is a waste of time, and the length, the global perspective and the complexity are not a concern. The common good fills this vacuum of disillusion. It does so by becoming the arbiter or regulator of interests which are contradictory or simply different. This involves thinking simultaneously of the micro and the macro as well as responding both to short term, immediate needs and to the long term view of her/history. In short, this involves *establishing links while distinguishing, instead of constantly separating and reducing.*[22] In this context, the common good calls for a constant reflection not only on the constraints which prevent well-being, but also on the factors leading to the origin of the constraints.

The argument also contradicts the primacy of economism. The latter is at the source of an expert knowledge which gives substance to the inclination to think that the economic is always right. On this point, the common good both relativizes and fragments. To take the words of P. Ricoeur, it is essential to remember that, with regard to fundamental issues, 'the experts do not know more than every one of us.'[23] Thus the common good rehabilitates the value of political, social and cultural facts in elaborating the *modus vivendi* previously evoked. Only an ethical and cultural project gives meaning to economic activity, as it also does to political decision-making, community life, social combats and technical means. Meaning has the dual sense of direction of action and of deep understanding, giving its *raison d'être* and its goal to the *modus vivendi.* It determines its lasting orientations and stamps its rhythm on the life of human societies. As opposed to the single and reducing vision of the primacy of economism, the common good suggests a more differentiated representation of development. The notion cannot be used without recourse to a multiplicity of qualifying factors: human, long-lasting, endogenous, self-centred, ascending, cultural . . . . This transformation is positive in that it takes into account all the elements of the human condition: the economic, societal, cultural, a sense of values . . . . It also corresponds to attempts to be more precise in our definitions and seeks to propose alternative models which are more respectful of culture and nature.

---

21 K. J. Arrow, *Social Choice and Individual Values* (New Haven: Yale University Press, 1963); J. M. Buchanan, 'Individual Choice in Voting and the Market' (1954) 62 Journal of Political Economy 334.

22 See E. Morin, 'Pour une réforme de la pensée' in *Le Courrier de l'UNESCO*, February 1996, 10.

23 Quoted in J. M. Denis, 'L'ère du mépris', Le Monde, 9 December 1995.

The World-based Argument

In addition to insisting on relationalism and the common good, the discourse on uniform law must allow every given world to speak, to discuss the content of its existential context.[24] The possibility of being heard is today very limited: in simplifying thought, a formalist universalism, which is both abstract and reducing, tends to impose itself. This silences all those human sites in which uniform law is summoned to be present or already exists. In light of the transitory conception, this silence is not acceptable because the worlds play a fundamental role in the shared efforts of constructing the good they advocate. Each world must present its own argument. How? Complex thought, as I have conceptualized it, seeks to develop the mental platform of uniform law in each of these worlds. The four principles of complexity are essentially paths to clear a way to understand the *meaning* of uniform law, in the broadest sense of the term, in a given world. This is the fabric of the meanings which form part of the argument under discussion.

At the outset, the transition of an argument of legal convergence to another, based on a different sense of adherence, requires a special vision of the substance of uniform law. This substance is essentially interactionist.[25] As to its foundation, it forms, transforms and matures; in time, it is divided into continuities and discontinuities. Its interdependence with the substantive whole is general; all legal phenomena depend, to some extent, on other social and natural phenomena. It is thus not possible to simplify the reality of uniform law without observing the nature of its life in society. To the contrary, every observation in this sense finds meaning in time and place. In effect, even those phenomena which appear to be inactive or to have little in common will often contribute to the genesis – still imperceptible – of new elements inside uniform law. Complex thought thus implies working with fragmented rather than hermetic elements.

At least three elements should appear across the fabric of meanings which structure the argument of a world. The first concerns innovation: it is necessary to determine how uniform law leads or can lead a world to changing routine or tradition, or instead to consolidate them even more. The second element stems from diffusion. To emphasize it, the observation should centre on the transfer of meanings of uniform law from one world to another, but also on the use which is made of that transfer and the deformations which occur as a result. In parallel, the diffusion should demonstrate how the processes slow down, speed up or amplify the effects of the innovation. As for the final element, it tends toward the social goal sought by the world and in which uniform law, either directly or indirectly, participates. This goal could be one of well-being or comprise an ideal of modernization . . . . According to the trilogy, the understanding of a world could certainly be more within reach than it presently is.

---

24   E. R. Carraso, 'Law, Hierarchy, and Vulnerable Groups in Latin America: Towards a Communal Mode of Development in a Neoliberal World' (1994) 30 Stan. J. Int'l. L. 221, is an excellent example of what I am illustrating here.

25   V. Gessner, 'Global Legal Interaction and Legal Cultures' (1994) 7 Ratio Juris. 132.

The Argument Based on Self-fulfilment and Solidarity

In the context of the discovery and the justification of uniform law, *the needs of international trade* and *the development of international trade* can no longer assume the most important role. The teleological thought required by the second modernity invites us to seek at a higher level the elements which will truly allow uniform law to spread in conformity with the pluralist *modus vivendi* of the transitory conception. This spreading out appears necessary since – in a teleological perspective – the validity of commercialism at the heart of uniform law becomes linked to the consolidation which it brings to the normative cornerstone based on self-fulfilment and solidarity. Faced by the dual modern tendency which rips apart the social fabric, a comprehensive strategy of development founded on self-fulfilment and solidarity and constructed around territories permits the maximum number of actors to establish an identity, since it does not partition the economic, social and cultural. This strategy rests on one conviction: the advantage which the confidence in its own individual and collective potential represents. It calls for the desire to collaborate and to establish networks. The result is a feeling of belonging and ties of solidarity which help the members of a given world to control their future and achieve a specific destiny.

How is it possible for the different visions of the world and its development to co-exist and interact? This would be possible by the application of what J. Rawls describes as the overlapping consensus, whose interactions are capable of establishing the means and rules of indispensable cooperation.[26] In this case, the viability of co-existence does not depend on everyone's deep moral, philosophical or cultural commitment. The Rawlsian model is modest in this respect. Nevertheless, at bottom it appeals to a principle of fairness that, in accordance with Rawls's thinking, all can and must share. Fairness corresponds to a dynamic frame of mind which supposes being conscious of a necessary and intentional limitation of one's happiness and self-interest. More specifically, this characterizes people who do not seek to maximize their immediate advantages but also are able to place their interest and those of others in perspective. This necessitates respecting another's freedom, because each person's interests are best assured in this logic of reciprocity. Thus the freedom of partners goes hand in hand with their equality. Again, the logic of reciprocity means that it is to the advantage of each person to treat others as her/his equal, and that all have claim to the same rights.

Overall, self-fulfilment, solidarity and overlapping consensus translate into an optimistic view of the world, a vision where enchantment is still plausible due to the new possibilities of social relations.[27] It is through this relationship with this

---

26 J. Rawls, 'The Idea of an Overlapping Consensus' (1987) 7 Oxford Journal of Legal Studies 1.

27 The optimistic nature of this view is close to that developed in the philosophy of J. Habermas. See, in particular, *Moral Consciousness and Communicative Action,* trans. C. Lehnhardt of *Moralbewusstsein und Kommunikativeshandeln* (Cambridge: MIT Press, 1990).

type of constructive normative universe that uniform law could be justified on moral, social, political, and other levels. In other words, this is how it could establish and maintain its legitimacy.

A History of Uniform Law

The first contact with a discipline frequently occurs through its historical presentation. Uniform law is not an exception to this rule. And any first contact must be taken seriously. History recounts the facts of the past which deserve to be remembered. History conditions the spirit of someone who desires to know and understand a discipline by drawing attention to some elements and not to others and presenting them in one way rather than another. In brief, the retrospective is not indifferent to the notion of both a perspective and a prospective. It thus seems worthwhile to give an historical overview of uniform law in connection with the transitory conception. But, how do we present this history? I have chosen to present it in the form of an imaginary exchange, more precisely an interview, between two people. Turning persuasive discourse into speaking persons,[28] as well as the use of a language embellished with imagery, represent original interpretive techniques. They correspond to the proposition put forward by P. Pitcher, which consists in asserting that 'pseudo-scientific language is no more "objective" than poetic language.'[29] In view of this proposition, one is justified, according to Pitcher, in using a passionate and committed tone to present one's explanations. What follows is the text of this interview.

– For the purposes of this interview, can you make a contrast between the modern and progressive conception of uniform law?

Certainly. I shall situate them right away. The modern concept presents a history of uniform law where the protagonists are celebrities scattered in time and space. These celebrities discover undreamed of facts of uniform law, then induce general theories from them, and they seem to be isolated from the contingencies of reality. In the progressive concept, on the other hand, legal scholars develop their theories, whose richness they test, to give meaning to and control the world which surrounds us. The theories are based on a number of presuppositions. Over time, the authors have to re-examine the world in light of new theories as these presuppositions evolve. Social, political, economic and institutional factors condition the proceedings and the conclusions of the authors. Moreover, these researchers are part of a special community in society, and their work serves to transform and legitimate certain movements.

– You summarized the first concept very rapidly. Could you elaborate?

---

28   M. Bakhtin, *The Dialogical Imagination, supra*, Chapter 4, note 35; at 348.

29   P. Pitcher, *Artistes, artisans et technocrates dans nos organisations*, trans. J. P. Fournier (Montreal: Québec-Amérique, 1997) at 35.

Of course. According to the modern concept, the history of uniform law seems to be the fruit of a small number of initiatives. From one text to another, from one book to the next, you see the same names and institutions, often spoken highly of and admired. For example, we see Ernst Rabel, René David, Unidroit, The Hague Conference, UNCITRAL, and others, through their remarkable work and contribution.[30] *So the whole great adventure of uniform law is limited to a few personalities, organizations and anecdotes. Instead of dealing with a whole community of men and women who have developed a contradictory web of ideas from their different projects, we are restricted to a few superior individuals who are alone capable of unmasking the reality of uniform law.*

– I understand, but doesn't this have the advantage of facilitating the understanding of uniform law: our attention is centred on the important *facts*. We don't have to remember everything, and uniform law is held in high regard because famous people have developed it?

Before I deal with the question of this advantage, let me deal with the issue of our attention being drawn to the facts. This is interesting, because if we see the history of uniform law in this way, we risk doing the same with the discipline itself. On an epistemological level, this would be the same as submitting the legitimacy, truth or cogency of uniform law to a justification by correspondence.[31]

– Whoa! You've lost me there.

But it's not complicated. Justification by way of correspondence is based on a logical connection between a spoken word or an action and a reality that is foreign to thought. Therefore, it implies the existence of an observable reality, constituted by independent facts. And words and actions prove themselves to be valid when they correspond to these independent facts. Applied to uniform law, justification by correspondence implies that:

i)   *uniform law is a real fact that has meaning by itself;*

ii) *the belonging of uniform law to an external reality compels one to consider only its directly observable manifestations, such as legislation and case law;*

iii) *the meaning of uniform law is contained in these observable manifestations, and most often represented by what is called legislative intent;*

iv) *and an interpretation will be valid to the extent to which it corresponds to the meaning (legislative intent) contained within the facts (legislation, case law, . . .) by virtue of which it must be justified.*

---

30 See, for example, B. Bonell, *An International Restatement of Contract Law: The UNIDROIT Principles of International Commercial Contracts* (Irvington: Transnational Juris, 1994) at 1-25.

31 T. J. Reiss, *The Uncertainty of Analysis: Problems in Truth, Meaning, and Culture* (Ithaca, Cornell University Press, 1988); H. Putnam, *Raison, vérité et histoire*, trans. A. Gerschenfeld (Paris: Éditions du Minuit, 1984); R. M. Martin, *Pragmatics, Truth, and Language* (Boston: D. Reidel, 1979).

– I see. And what about my previous question on the advantage of centring history on important facts?

If we go with this approach, the risk is that history will only retain what interests us today. It will carefully choose the aspects of past research which are susceptible of supporting the positions we hold today and ignore all other interpretations. If we choose to attribute the discovery or development of uniform law, in its present state, to a few geniuses, we reduce it to an accumulation of facts. The development of uniform law is instead the gradual accumulation of different elements to comprise a whole which is more and more elaborate.

– But isn't the density of knowledge a richness?

Yes, but only on condition that we don't ignore the uncertainties, choices and theoretical decisions of researchers to accept only a dominant reading of an expert knowledge. If this happens, the discourse on uniform law automatically acquires a sacred character, because the choices and projects at its base are hidden.

– But how would a progressive perspective be any different?

The history of uniform law should be one of inventions and initiatives, instead of the discovery and accumulation of different concepts.[32] *This other history recentres the debate on the process of theoretical inventions and initiatives which impregnates them, motivates them and gives birth to them. Even if the researchers of the past had different ideas from our own, we have to understand why they asked questions as they did. Therefore, we have to understand the sense of these initiatives and ideas which form the basis of uniform law as we know it today. This type of history (re)situates the thought process of researchers in their context and acknowledges that economic, social and political factors influence how researchers ask questions and condition their historical developments.*

– Could you put what you have just said in the context of justification by correspondence which we discussed earlier?

Yes. In terms of uniform law as an intellectual discipline, this would mean that we should pass to a justification where an act or word is valid if it is in accordance with the totality of the beliefs that we hold to be true at a given moment. The justification becomes internal to human thought and puts all of our beliefs in relation and interdependence. In uniform law, this would mean that legal facts are no longer viewed as real objective entities which possess a sense of their own. The meaning of legal facts would be the fruit of a construction based on the whole of our beliefs, which themselves are relevant. It is in that sense that Vittorio Villa affirms that:

> *[i]f we wholeheartedly accept that reality, as the reference point of scientific theories, is never 'pure' and 'mind-independent', but linguistically interpreted and theoretically*

---

32   I. Wallerstein, *Impenser la science sociale : pour sortir du XIXe siècle*, trans. A. E. Demartini and X. Papaïs (Paris: P.U.F., 1995).

reconstructed by the research tradition, then we cannot help calling it a reality 'internal', in some sense of the word, to that tradition.[33]

Why? Villa adds:

The reason is that empirical facts, in their theoretical interpretation, are part of the framework, located as they are, at the lowest point of the theoretical system. Thus, the test of truth ... [consists] in a check on the 'internal fitness' of the propositions which are part of the framework. .... In Goodman's words, knowledge is, first of all, 'finding a fit' among a system of beliefs.[34]

– Another question comes to mind. Doesn't history, by definition, have a beginning and an end? How would you situate these two elements in your thinking?

I believe that the feeling of continuity inherent in history is always present in progressive thinking. However it is not continuity in the sense of an accumulation of facts, but a continuity which stems from a progressive development in how we ask questions. History would be the result of a series of incremental changes, rather than theoretical earthquakes. When researchers decide to re-read the world, they incorporate in their thought process a portion of the materials of the past. This portion is variable, and it is important to have a thorough knowledge of it.

– It would be exciting if you could extend your reflections to explain how the progressive concept of history could have an impact on the teaching of uniform law. Could you give us some ideas in a few words?

Certainly. First of all, I believe that the teaching of uniform law must increasingly be connected to societal goals. Secondly, it's also very clear that this teaching may be conceived in accordance with a number of different models, ranging from simple instruction to formal rules and on to more anthropological models, which invite students to learn theories which underlie uniform law and how society functions in what is essentially a human enterprise. Thirdly, the teaching of uniform law should acknowledge that these possible models convey visions of the world and of society and influence students and may confer on them both abilities and deficiencies.

– So there would be a debate on the content of courses on uniform law?

Yes, and it should deal with the following issues. Should we only teach the rules? Do we want to teach students how to use uniform law in making enlightened decisions in everyday life? Do we wish to enable individuals to reflect on how uniform law fashions our societies, understand that questions of values and ideological choices form the basis of uniform law, and have a critical sense of expert knowledge? Do we want students to understand that uniform law is a

---

33 V. Villa, 'Normative Coherence and Epistemological Presuppositions of Justification' in P. Nerhot, ed., *Law, Interpretation, and Reality: Essays in Hermeneutics and Jurisprudence* (Boston, Kluwer, 1990) at 444-445.

34 *Ibid.* at 445.

constructed human enterprise, with its strengths and weaknesses, or do we want them to believe that it is heaven sent and value-free? If such questions are important, it is essential that teachers take a position toward them if they want to teach students properly.

– I like these ideas of human invention in the writing of uniform law. I think that this helps subordinate the economic aspect to human interests, in a spirit of common good. It also helps us understand the interest and the limits of uniform law in individual and collective life, and to evaluate whether it can help us develop our desires, our projects, our hopes – in short, all those things which make us human beings. Unfortunately, we've run out of time. We'll come back to this issue another time. Thank you very much.

Final Remarks

The goal of Part II was to develop a critique of conservative consciousness. In order to optimize the rigour of this undertaking and to ally it to the propositions and premises mentioned in the Introduction, I developed a vision of critique as legal imagination, which I elaborated in three steps corresponding to the key words correlation, defamiliarization and utopia.

At the stage of correlation, I laid out the community of views between, on the one hand, conservative consciousness and modernity and, on the other, between conservative consciousness and modern law. As for the first relationship, I firstly explained the general framework of modernity. This framework is based on reason, individualism and an infinite diffusion in time and space. Three specific aspects warranted closer attention:

i)   modernity, knowledge and progress;
ii) modernity and the dichotomous point of view; and
iii) modern knowledge, economics and opulence.

In each case, thanks to the principles of thought and the values arising from regressive analysis, I established how conservative consciousness and modernity are seen as a whole. As for the second relationship, I established that it comes from the links between modern law and individuation, reason, contract and the idea of power. Here, I showed the correlation between conservative consciousness and modern law. On the basis of this first step, I embarked upon that of defamiliarization. This second step revealed the factors stimulating the changeover of modernity toward a second modernity and likely to break down conservative consciousness. It also paved the way for a re-orientation of conservative consciousness. This re-orientation emphasizes the principles of thought and the values of a dialectic, systemic, complex and teleological nature in addition to multiple, consensual, flexible and relative metaphors. Finally, the step dealing with utopia had a triple goal:

i)   elaborate a transitory conception of development translating the needs, expectations and hopes created by the second modernity;
ii) trace the main features of a progressive consciousness bringing together the relational argument, the argument of the common good, the argument of the world and the argument of self-fulfilment and solidarity; and
iii) contrast the modern and progressive versions of a history of uniform law.

We now have to integrate the repercussions of the critique of conservative consciousness within the phase of reformulation (Part III), which will lead to a progressive consciousness in uniform law.

PART III

THE REFORMULATION OF UNIFORM LAW: TOWARD A PROGRESSIVE CONSCIOUSNESS

Preliminary Remarks

The following preliminary remarks are aimed at better understanding the direction and substance of this third part, which is spread over two chapters.

The correlation, defamiliarization and utopia which form the critique developed in the previous section set the stage for the third and final phase of Koskenniemi's triptych. This phase is called *reformulation*. It corresponds to what Koskenniemi refers to as *the alternative descriptive and normative characterizations of our world*. In accordance with the main goal and methodological orientations laid out in the Introduction, the alternative characterization under discussion here takes the form of a progressive consciousness of uniform law. It unites the key arguments of a discursive web laid out in the contexts of discovery and justification. This progressive consciousness must simultaneously satisfy two imperatives: first, integrate, consolidate and synthesize as faithfully as possible the ideas developed in the critique of conservative consciousness and, secondly, portray an inspiring and revealing unity. In accordance with these two imperatives, I shall now develop the new arguments sketched out in Part II. These focused on the relational argument, the argument of the common good and the world-based argument, components of the context of discovery, and on the argument based on self-fulfilment and solidarity, located at the heart of the context of justification. To set the tone for each argument, a short introduction will precede the presentation of its structure and content, and this presentation will be developed from a number of questions. I also underline that the general perspective of each argument will be clearly pragmatic. My emphasis will be on action – the practical value of each argument and its repercussions on everyday life. That being said, I draw the reader's attention to two particular elements.

The first element concerns the degree of potential and effective overlap between progressive and conservative consciousness. My critique of the latter has made possible the moving of conservative consciousness toward a progressive version. If we wish to preserve the logic of intellectual progression to this point, it goes without saying that this progressive version should effectively be that which symbolizes henceforth the primary foundation of uniform law and to which one refers as a priority in theory and practice. However, up to what point is it possible to conceive a rupture between the two consciousnesses? Or, from another angle, up to what point can the elements of conservative consciousness survive, expressly or implicitly, in progressive consciousness? Of course, it can seem normal that the construction of a progressive consciousness provides the occasion to emphasize the principles of thought and the values of uniform law which have remained in the shadow of conservative consciousness, or have even been completely ignored, because they seemed inferior and secondary. It remains that the mechanical or automatic response to these questions is that progressive consciousness *necessarily* integrates, one way or another, the elements present in conservative consciousness. While the form of integration does not appear to be of great importance, we must understand why it exists and the implications which derive therefrom.

I should say right away that critique as legal imagination is not inconsistent with the mechanical or automatic response that has just been stated. In the case of defamiliarization, it seems easy enough to understand. The central element of this kind of critique is immediate reality. Even if it is transformed to the point where it is rendered completely novel, it is normal that this reality, in light of its importance, should leave traces of its existence in the new entity. In the case of utopia, the principle of necessary integration can seem less obvious. Here I would simply recall, as I have already explained,[1] that utopian reasoning originates in particular in present as well as past representations. Therefore, there is every reason to believe that utopia does not prevent the existence of a link between the *new and the old*. By analogy, it is thus conceivable that progressive consciousness integrates, up to a certain point, conservative consciousness. In this respect, however, I believe that another explanation may be even more powerful than that developed by the nature of the critique realized in Part II.

This explanation stems from the phenomenon of sedimentation. Viewed in its relationship with the legal sphere, this phenomenon refers to the idea, expressed forcefully by C. Atias, that

> the more they are used, the more the terms which judges and the legislator are using, in addition to jurists and anyone else for that matter, when they talk about law, become full of sense. Each new application, each new influence add something to past meanings.[2]

In law, this means that it is more appropriate to admit that the new is combined with the old, instead of being substituted for it. This is why, adds Atias,

> jurists go the wrong way and are mistaken when they believe that they are controlling their vocabulary or constructing for themselves a new language, purified of any presuppositions which they would not have otherwise accepted.[3]

When taking place, the phenomenon of sedimentation is accompanied by an increase in the number of opinions on law, whose meaning is not self-evident. At any time, any person can develop arguments and establish proof in keeping with his own beliefs and concerns and by starting from whatever she/he needs, in the sense of sources and concepts scattered here and there. Therefore, sedimentation makes it useless to attempt to explain or summarize law, wholly or in part, by means of a single line of thought. Law is the locus of too many influences to arrive

---

1   See Part II, Preliminary Remarks, 'Critique as Legal Imagination'.
2   C. Atias, *Savoir des juges et savoir des juristes. Mes premiers regards sur la culture juridique québécoise* (Montreal: McGill Legal Studies, 1990) at 108.
3   *Ibid.*

at such a result. For Atias, the sedimentation of law goes hand in hand with its indeterminacy and the controversy surrounding it, and he believes that such a combination is essential to constant improvement in legal knowledge. Right law can only be obtained by systematically weighing up the pros and cons:

> The varied and often opposed positions can certainly not be classified in a hierarchy based on the institutional power of every intervenant, they can only be compared. The hope is that the quality of justifications will be, in the short, medium and long term, the determining criteria for final success.[4]

The explanation drawn from the phenomenon of sedimentation is convincing and, furthermore, it is consistent with the position that I have so far advanced in this study. It renders inevitable, normal and, indeed, desirable that I, knowingly or not, draw on conservative consciousness in the construction of progressive consciousness. Moreover, this explanation ensures that conservative consciousness will enjoy an undisputed importance in terms of the future development of progressive consciousness. One can always act as a point of reference for the other, to find the germ of an idea, to put a statement into perspective, to enrich and clarify an argument and so on. What stems from Atias' analysis is that it is important to arrive at a better argument than that which has prevailed up to this point. In this way, even the principles of thought and the values which have apparently become untimely or outmoded following the critique in Part II can enjoy an unexpected renaissance within progressive consciousness. M. Emirbayer provides a particularly eloquent example of this kind of resurgence.[5] While drawn from sociological analysis, the example is still extremely useful in the present context since it addresses two concepts which I have dealt with and shall deal with: relationalism and freedom. Pleading for what he calls relational sociology, Emirbayer shows how freedom can be re-examined under this new paradigm and continue to enjoy a central role:

> [T]he notion of freedom is also open to far-reaching formulation in relational terms. A very common way of thinking about freedom (or liberty) is in substantialist fashion, as a possession, a 'legal status represented in laws', and as contrasted with the essentialist status of slavery. But, as Arthur Stinchcombe indicates, freedom is best described pragmatically as a set of 'liberties ... in fact enjoy[ed], whether or not they are defended in the law.' Drawing upon John R. Commons, who cautioned that ideas such as liberty refer not to the 'thing itself but [to] the expected uses of the thing, that is [to] various activities regarding the thing,' Stinchcombe regards freedom not as a fixed, pregiven attribute, but rather as *what we can do* under given circumstances. ... Freedom, in other words, means nothing apart from the concrete transactions in which individuals engage, within cultural, social structural and social psychological contexts of action; it derives its significance entirely from the ongoing interplay (akin to a game) of decision, consequence and reaction.[6]

---

4   *Ibid.* at 110.
5   M. Emirbayer, 'Manifesto for a Relational Sociology' (1997) 103 A.J.S. 281.
6   *Ibid.* at 293.

In conclusion, and without prejudging the content of progressive consciousness, one can expect to rediscover in it some characteristic facets of conservative consciousness.

The second issue I wish to emphasize concerns the way of presenting the principles of thought and the values at the heart of progressive consciousness. While it seemed preferable, from a purely methodological and formal point of view, to address them separately in the phase of regressive analysis, I believe that they should at this phase of reformulation be seen as related. This change is consistent with the second modernity, which refutes the notion of division: principles of thought, that is to say the ways of glimpsing and capturing reality, are not indifferent to the values which allow for the appreciation of this reality, and vice versa. There is a certain merging between the two, which R. Sattler illustrated by saying 'what I am doing in science goes in the same direction as my own life.'[7] In keeping with this position and to clarify my point of view at this point, I would simply add that I am not among those who deny the contribution of neutral and objective forms of knowledge in life in general: it is very useful to be able to distinguish between poisonous and edible mushrooms! But truth also comes to pass through different forms of human experiences, ranging from everyday happiness to spirituality. In short, the greatest division at the heart of progressive consciousness rests on the already known dichotomy between the context of discovery and the context of justification. I shall deal with these issues in chapters 6 and 7 respectively.

---

7   A. Cuerrier, 'Le nouvel esprit scientifique' (1997) 18(6) Interface 16 at 20.

Chapter 6

The Context of Discovery

As I have mentioned above, the context of discovery of progressive consciousness is made up of the relational argument, the argument of the common good and the world-based argument.

The Relational Argument

Prelude

The relational argument deals with the juridical relationship commonly called contract, which I define as the linkage of expectations and interests to the source of rights and obligations existing between the parties. The basic function of this linkage is to allow the realization of a project, that is to say all that by which a human being tends to change the world and/or him- or herself, in a certain direction.

In order to better appreciate the specificity of the relational argument, let us return briefly to the representation of contract which flows from conservative consciousness. The latter is dominated by the image of an exchange of free and informed consent between the parties. It definitely places emphasis on the quest and respect for that which the parties desired at a particular moment. The argument of autonomy of will is that which best explains the attachment of conservative consciousness to this representation. According to the manner in which the argument is constructed, autonomy of the will is a fact which asserts itself by its mere presence, it being so evident. The birth, execution and extinction of the contract are based on it. In addition to its deciding role in these three phases of contract, autonomy of the will is assigned a fundamental qualitative mission which consists in favouring and legitimizing international trade. The *conservative contract* is the tool which ensures a faithful and complete expression of the will of the parties at the same time as its durability. Thanks to the perfect agreement that it makes it possible to establish between wills dominated by passions and parameters reputedly few in number and identical, it makes possible a common mastery of the future. And by defining what the future will be, it affords the parties indispensable security. In order to avoid any of the turbulence likely to diminish the security which it must provide the parties, the contract is assimilated to a type of self-sufficient microcosm, stable and self-enclosed.

The relational aspect, inspired by the second modernity, offers a different vision of this juridical relationship called contract. This vision rests on the two key concepts mentioned before, those of linkage and of project. *Linkage* breaks with hermeticism and the reductionist effect of the microcosm. It opens rather on the idea of a somewhat sensitive and porous, organic,[1] juridical relationship. Probably a less sterile, and thus less stable, relationship results from this. But more subject to having to react and transform itself, it thus becomes more in keeping with the evolving character inherent in all the *projects* it allows to be realized. Also, it places itself in a position of *osmosis* with other norms and rules.

Relationship as linkage   In referring to expectations and interests, linkage demonstrates that it does not underestimate the active roles played by the parties in the definition and execution of the project they intend to carry out. The choice of the parties remains an important factor in the determination of their rights and obligations. It is not however possible, in my opinion, to state that these rights and obligations are only based upon the fact, and not the content, of choice. If that were the case, and in conformity with the typology mentioned by T. Dare, the linkage would be '*internalist*, meaning it looks to the agreement itself to determine contractual obligations, and *content-independent*, meaning that it eschews appeal to contractual content to determine such obligation.'[2] Conversely, I believe it is incorrect to affirm that linkage is only based upon the content and not upon the fact of choice, in which case it would be externalist and content-dependent: 'What matters here is not whether parties have agreed, consented or promised, but whether the agreement in substance meets a standard of fairness, justice, of efficiency.'[3] The progressive approach, through the medium of dialectical thought, allows one to assert that rights and obligations resulting from linkage depend as much on internal as external considerations. It is not necessary to choose between the two, even if they appear to be in opposition in light of Dare's typology. On the contrary, dialectical thought invites borrowing from each one, even if the analysis and appreciation of linkage in order to determine rights and obligations become more complicated exercises.

In effect, linkage corresponds to a representation of the contract more complex than that issuing from conservative consciousness. In this case, moreover, the contract derives one of its main strengths from its simplicity. Once created, the contract is imperative for the parties, the judge, and the arbitrator, as well as the legislator. And the contract remains as it has been conceived: it is afforded the power necessary to resist everything, apart from the extreme limit of public order. The contract is detached from the ascendancy of the various interested parties and it appears intangible. The life of the contract thus unfolds following a course of

---

1   S. Macaulay, 'Organic Transactions: Contract, Frank Lloyd Wright and the Johnson Building' (1996) 21 Wis. L. Rev. 75.
2   T. Dare, 'Kronman On Contract: A Study in the Relation Between Substance and Procedure in Normative and Legal Theory' (1994) 7 C.J.L.J. 331 at 332.
3   *Ibid.*

quite simple steps, recurring from one contract to another. These characteristics are recalled with vigour by certain statements in arbitral case law. The CCI 6281 award,[4] for one, clearly rejects the possibility of the mutability of contract when events external to the contract create an imbalance between the obligations assumed by the parties. Such a result would have the effect of 'exposing to uncertainty ... each commercial transaction [and would render it] totally impossible each time the mutual agreements were not executed at the same moment when the contract was concluded.'[5] Beyond the imperatives of security and certainty, the intangibility and the hermeticism of contract are solely explained by the will of the parties. In certain situations, the explanation rests upon a presumed will, such as may be found in the CCI 2708 sentence which insists that 'fluctuating circumstances constitute a major incitement to the conclusion of contracts, each party anticipating a benefit from the changes in price, while implicitly accepting the risk that such a change will be unfavourable to him.'[6] Otherwise, it is the absence of an express will which justifies maintaining the contract as it is, the 'more so since they are international transactions where, in general, the parties are aware of the risks that may occur and are thus able to formulate it in a precise manner.'[7]

In spite of its attractiveness, simplicity finally results in an impoverishment of the contract. For example, in reducing the nature of the contract to an exchange of consent, which is usually conveyed in the process of offer and acceptance, simplicity conceals a series of information which could be very useful in justifying a readjustment, perfection or improvement of the obligations. It disregards the information derived from the affective relation which supports the communication between the parties, preferring to rely on the more technical channels of emission (offer) and reception (acceptance) of information. It postulates that communication is always at the same level and that it constantly moves forward, whereas it could go in circles and confine itself in rituals because of the stakes and advantages sought by the parties. Finally, it supposes that the information is mature and complete from the outset; yet the sense of a message may emerge from the exchange and the action, or even from a setting in context. Without this enriched information, it becomes difficult for an interested party to seriously and efficiently argue in favour of making changes to the contract.[8]

In moving closer to complexity, linkage is apt to become the trigger of a representation and an existence of the contract which is distinguished by its richness and dynamism. Added to the aspects explained in the sketch of the relational argument, these distinct characteristics transform the nature of the contract; from that point, as stated by R. Gordon, 'the object of contracting is not

---

4   Reported at (1989) J.D.I. at 1114-1120.
5   *Ibid.* at 1117.
6   Sentence CCI 2708, reported at (1977) J.D.I. 943 at 943.
7   Sentence CCI 2404, reported at (1976) J.D.I. 995 at 995.
8   See, in general, A. Mucchielli & J. A. Corbalan, *Théorie des processus de la communication* (Paris: Armand-Colin, 1998).

to allocate risks, but to signify a commitment to cooperate . . . ."[9] The affirmation is in keeping with the theory of *relational contract* advanced by I. R. Macneil.[10] In his opinion, three norms fill an essential function in the formation and performance of contracts, especially in long-term contractual relations: respect for the partners' respective roles, the preservation of the relation, and the harmonization of the internal norms of the relation with those of the social environment. For his part, S. Macaulay commented on Macneil's theory by saying that it:

> sees relationships as involving overarching obligations of good faith, solidarity, role integrity, and mutuality. Solidarity demands that the parties preserve the continuing relationship within which transactions take place. We assume that others will stay in role. A partner cannot suddenly become a self-interested hard bargainer. There also must be mutuality: the parties must divide the exchange surplus properly so that each gains appropriate, but not necessarily equal returns.[11]

By adopting this rich and dynamic perspective, the contract passes from the abstract and fixative framework of the meeting of minds (the rationality of which may be measured by its ability to satisfy a dominant passion for wealth) to the concrete one of an overlapping of convergent aspirations to collaborate. An unavoidable qualitative dimension (a broad normative range that one could illustrate by the values already mentioned) is associated with this passage; it serves to support the contract and to justify its inclination in unforeseen, but ultimately desirable and profitable directions for the parties and their social environment.

Relationalism as project   Linkage has as its purpose the realization of projects. Like the parties who directly and indirectly participate in it as well as its environment, every project evolves. By analogy with the notion of self-fulfilment that I used in Part II, it is fitting to admit that a project is never static. It is subject to pitfalls as well as to new opportunities. Consequently, the parameters which orient it are in constant need of revision. In a word, its path is sinuous. The intrinsic evolution which characterizes the project thus contributes, like linkage, to contemplating the contract otherwise than from the angle of a completely intangible and secure entity. In this regard however, it is important to consider, in addition to the evolving nature of any project, the world that is opened to it.

When a project is born, the universe in which it is automatically immersed is not blank and inert. It is already made up of activities and projects already in motion. These activities and projects are linked, or at the least they influence each other. And the developing project overlaps, loosely here, tightly there, those alliances which create what one may qualify as networks.[12] The configuration of

---

9   R. Gordon, 'Macaulay, Macneil, and the Discovery of Solidarity and Power in Contract Law' (1985) Wisc. L. Rev. 565 at 569.

10 Macneil, *supra*, Chapter 5, note 17; also, by the same author, 'Values in Contract: Internal and External' (1983) 78 Northwestern Univ. L. Rev. 340.

11 *Supra*, note 1; at 110-111.

12 See, for an application, Chapter 9, 'Diffusion', below.

the network and the type of activities which are carried out in it are not pertinent for the purposes of this analysis; it suffices to recall that the network has something in common with the 'constellations of agreements.'[13] However, it must be realized that the viability and the dependability of the network rely on the confidence and flexibility present, and that these two imperatives require an interpretation of the contract as an instrument having versatility and flexibility.

The imperatives of confidence and flexibility may assume different forms which come together in the idea of a consensus (a cement) concerning certain values and principles. Paradoxically, consensus is also a fragmented, mobile and occasionally volatile entity. This is why I disagree with F. Osman when he associates his concept of *societas mercatorum* to an institution of profound stability.[14] Approving the comments of B. Goldman, he proposes that

> corporate groups, more and more powerful and united by bonds of solidarity going beyond state boundaries, have been forged from usage and are aware 'that by transgressing them they come into conflict not only with the good (as in the case of a moral rule), but also with the organization, the structures and the functioning of this collectivity'.[15]

I do not believe that the consensus that Osman depicts in the community of international commercial operators is marked by permanence and it draws its strength from its punitive (Benthamite) spirit. The value of a consensus will only be according to the transparency of the exchanges having led to its elaboration as well as from its representativeness. And like new data and information constantly grafting itself on the consensus already reached, this consensus must constantly be revised.

This being said, the usefulness of a consensus derives from its contribution to the definition and redefinition of the contract. In the face of lacunae or a contractual incident, rather than fall back on formalism and on arguments destined to punish or merely control the other party, consensus invites the parties to develop an open and constructive contractual attitude. In this regard, it constitutes a standard of reciprocal immunity and benevolence: each party owes the other respect and openness. If confidence and flexibility at the origin of consensus are generally advantageous, it is because they favour a feeling of security for the parties. It is less a formal security, guaranteed by sanctions (negative), but rather a positive security to the effect that a valid solution to any problem is likely. This conforms to the views of M. Dodgson, for whom confidence is the source of mutual experience, and the best assurance of the effectiveness and longevity of the

---

13   T. M. Jorde & D. J. Teece, 'Innovation, Cooperation, and Antitrust' in T. M. Jorde & D. J. Teece, eds., *Antitrust, Innovation, and Competitiveness* (New York: Oxford University Press, 1992) 47 at 55.

14   Osman, *supra*, Chapter 1, note 1; at 409.

15   *Ibid.* at 411.

contractual relationship. On the contrary, a sanction ordinarily constitutes a weak incentive whose impact remains temporary, except in truly insoluble situations.[16]

Viewed in the context of contractual flexibility which is derived from the evolving nature of any project and the network-like world that surrounds it, good faith offers a shape different from that prevailing in conservative consciousness. There, it is imbued with metaphysical traits which confer upon it a stabilizing function on a contractual level. Here, good faith can better highlight its contributions to the transformation of the contract, assuming a somewhat innovative function. The duty to renegotiate in order to maintain equilibrium between obligations well illustrates how good faith can certainly fulfil an interventionist yet ultimately beneficial role for the contract. Occasionally assimilated to a type of contractual loyalty, this innovative good faith forces the contracting parties to 'be perfectly aware that only a loyal, total and constant collaboration will permit them to resolve, beyond difficulties inherent in the execution of all contracts, the numerous problems resulting from the extreme complexity in the formulation of undertakings.'[17] So when, on the basis 'of general principles of law and equity',[18] all contracts are supposedly 'based on the balancing of reciprocal obligations',[19] good faith assumes the upper hand over contractual security and legitimizes the demands of one party which rest on this premise. From a presumption of contractual intangibility, one is thus led to a presumption of flexibility of the contract, which is even stronger when dealing with a long-term project. According to M. Sornarajah, the justification for such an inference is given by policy reasons. The promotion of an atmosphere in which the objectives of the contract can be achieved is necessary. The inference of the 'dynamic' clauses in international contracts in which they do not exist promotes this atmosphere and such a norm is already being developed in international practice.[20]

The crystallization of the rights and obligations of the parties, logical from the point of view of a confrontation of interests and mastery of the future, reinforced moreover by comforting good faith, then becomes an obsolete image. The image to be preferred consists of a combination of expectation and interests, defined according to a certain general direction, and stimulated by good faith.

The impetus derived by the project, added to that of linkage, to an enriched and dynamic representation of the contract, would not have as much impact without the assistance of other facets derived from the environment in general. In fact, osmosis plays an equally crucial role on this subject.

---

16   M. Dodgson, 'Learning, Trust, and Technological Collaboration' (1993) 46 Hum. Rel. 77.

17   Sentence CCI 2443, reported by Y. Derains in his observations on sentence CCI 2291 at (1976) J.D.I. 991.

18   Sentence CCI 2291, reported at (1976) J.D.I. 989 at 989.

19   *Ibid.*

20   M. Sornarajah, 'Supremacy of the Renegotiation Clause in International Contracts' (1988) 5 J. Int'l Arb. 97 at 109.

Relationalism as osmosis From the viewpoint of conservative consciousness, the parties to a contract are subject to minimal external interference and intervention. Their tranquillity is assured because, under the effect of uniform law, their agreement enjoys the status of the best juridical resource available in the context, described by H. Honka, of free international trade.[21] Their peace of mind is that much greater in that this status is automatically conceded to the contract, or proceeds from an unshakeable sentiment toward the contract. Also, the values of liberty, of richness and of usefulness in turn reinforce the notion that the contract is self-sufficient and that it dominates all the rest.[22]

The relationalist argument relativizes the status of the contractual relation as understood. On the one hand, it denies that a contract may be abstracted from a greater whole: it inevitably forms part of it. The line of thought that it proposes consists of recognizing that the unfurling of a contract must submit to diverse constraints and requirements emanating from other spheres of human and natural activity. For example, in order to properly express the integration of economics to the living effected by the transitory conception, the contract loses insensitivity and imperviousness and becomes sensitive and porous. Accordingly, the global order, which devolves from systemic thought, is capable of acting on all phases of evolution of the contract and influencing its content. The relationalist argument utilizes, on the other hand, this vision of contract in a state of subordination in order to expand its magnitude and to diversify its scale of operation. Here, the rights and obligations of a contract are no longer strictly defined only by the parties, and dedicated to a human destiny founded on the creation of *homo oeconomicus*. The determination of these rights and obligations is loosened, in order to place the contract in harmony with, notably, the ultimate progressive objectives of self-fulfilment and solidarity.

My assertions are in perfect opposition to those of M. Van Alstine on the subject of the argument of real choice of the parties, which represents, in my opinion, an attachment of conservative consciousness to the liberty value. Analysing that which he calls the formation values of the Vienna Convention, Van Alstine declares that 'one ... set of values that is not implicated in the Convention's scheme is a purely normative approach to the definition of contractual obligation (whether on the basis of idealized norms or in the form of extant societal norms).'[23] According to him, the real intention of the parties constitutes the exclusive driving force of the whole process of interpretation of the formation of the contract. In this regard, the role which he reserves for usages and practices is particularly illustrative of the power of the argument of the real choice in the juridical framework of conservative consciousness. Despite the opening of article 8 to an objective appreciation of the impact of usages and practices on the formation of contract, Van Alstine only sees there a by-product of what the parties really wanted. The point of departure and the finish line always remain the same:

---

21   Honka, *supra*, Chapter 2, note 11 and accompanying text.
22   See Chapter 2, above.
23   Van Alstine, *supra*, Chapter 2, note 2; at 52.

'. . . the analysis of the understanding of a reasonable person must proceed on the basis of the specific circumstances actually experienced by the addressee.'[24]

In my opinion, this type of demonstration is at once too elementary and too utopian. Too elementary because again, everything must be conceived and explained by way of a single conduit represented by the will of the parties, an untenable position from the progressive perspective; and also utopian because it is unlikely that the will of the parties may be loaded with so many responsibilities and remain comprehensible as Van Alstine would want. Rather I submit that that which the parties have thought, imagined and desired and the different components and movements of the environment to which they belong always constitute two facets to be taken into consideration; and that their relative importance defies all attempts to set out an a priori determination. Each facet has its pertinence, somewhere in the analysis. It may thus influence the other facet but not to the point of eliminating it. In order to illustrate this phenomenon in his attempt to reconstruct the law of contracts, A. Brudner speaks of a 'reciprocal deference of the collectivity and the individual.'[25] He more fully describes the phenomenon as follows:

> [The] experience taught us that neither the individual self nor the common good is an absolute end to the exclusion of the other, for each needs the other to be fully the end or good of the individual if it annihilates his or her distinctive identity; rather, it is the good only in being validated as such through the individual's free deference to community as to the basis of his or her independent worth. Thus the end-status of community presupposes that of the discrete self, whose spontaneous recognition it needs. But secondly, the community is the basis of the individual's distinctive reality (and so the end of the individual) only insofar as it reciprocally defers to the end-status of the discrete self, making room for a sphere of individual self-realization wherein its own primacy is held in abeyance. Thus, just as the end-status of community presupposes that of the individual, so does the end-status of the individual presuppose community, for the latter requires the individual's freedom for its own validation. And because each needs the independence of the other, each must recognize that independence for the sake of its own confirmation as an end.[26]

The relative importance of the two facets mentioned above can only be appreciated under all circumstances in light of the degree of general attainment of the *modus vivendi* founded on self-fulfilment and solidarity typical of the second modernity. That which the parties want to do will be so much more meritorious, honourable and worthy of total respect that the repercussions of their projects would continue to favourably influence an already strong *modus vivendi*. But external pressure on the contract will be felt so long as the *modus vivendi* has not reached maturity, for example, while it is gathering strength or when it is only half completed. This does not necessarily signify that the parties will see their liberty

---

24   *Ibid.* at 59.
25   A. Brudner, 'Reconstructing Contracts' (1993) 43 U.T.L.J. 1 at 10.
26   *Ibid.* at 9.

violated. On the contrary, their imagination and their creativity could be more than ever needed to permit the *modus vivendi* to attain its full potential. The determinant effect of reciprocal deference is not to favour one facet or the other. It consists of simply forcing the contract, as an entity, to constantly justify itself, beyond itself, whereas from the perspective of conservative consciousness, it is self-justified.

Structure and Content

In light of this Prelude, the advantages of life in society result in part, one may think, from possibilities available to all to cooperate, to act in concert in order to realize projects which remain inaccessible to individuals, to collectivities or to isolated entities. Without doubt, aside from these opportunities to cooperate, social existence provides other sources of satisfaction and other valid reasons to live together. But it remains undeniable that cooperation between diverse actors constitutes an important, if not essential, force of attraction which impels them to meet and to join together to lead a collective existence. Under these conditions, I submit that the relationalist argument unfolds according to three questions which pertain to concepts of linkage, of project and of osmosis. These questions are the following: How can cooperation be established between the parties? Which parameters are most likely to favour and maintain the cooperation, and consequently encourage the realization of the project in question? How can cooperation between the parties go hand in hand with cooperation between the parties and the environment?

Establishment of cooperation (or linkage)   If cooperation has a meaning, it may, first and foremost, be found in the confidence that it provides to a party to attain a better state by depending, rather than by not counting, on a partner. A certain form of value added is thus connected to cooperation. Without it, it is difficult to conceive that a party may be interested in devoting time and energy to collaboration with others. But what general principle can explain the establishment of cooperation and motivate a party to cooperate as much as possible? What kinds of psychological factors does it call upon?[27] The synthesizing formula of this principle – expressed in terms of a slogan – could be *cooperate so that the other party cooperates*. As stated, the principle does not therefore correspond to a conditional undertaking of the type *cooperate if the other party cooperates*. To reduce the initiatives taken by the parties to a conditional perspective risks reducing the vitality of the cooperation by placing each party in a state of expectation as to what the other will do before performing a concrete act. It is preferable to proceed with a principle which indicates to the partners that there has to be an initiator of the exchange, that someone must start by offering her/his obligation while assuming a potential risk of loss. Or in other words, one party

---

27   See, in general, R. Axelrod, *The Evolution of Cooperation* (New York: Basic Books, 1984); by the same author, 'The Emergence of Cooperation Among Egoists' (1981) 75 American Political Review 306.

cannot condition her/his action upon that of another and one must attempt something. Cooperation, in some fashion, calls upon the leadership of each party and her/his eagerness to serve as an example. It presupposes that a sense of initiative remains the best means of optimizing the results of a project. By taking the initiative, one party does not find her/himself at the mercy of a partner, or in a position of relative weakness. This is why the principle implies that each one enjoys, in offering to cooperate, by proposing something, the power to influence the response of her/his partner, even if one cannot be assured of the efficacy of this power. In effect, in order to optimize cooperation, it does not suffice that each party be in a certain sense the first to act and take the chance of being the only one to cooperate. It is also necessary that each one has the power or the possibility of partially determining, by the mere fact of cooperating, the choice and the orientations of the partner. This represents a form of reward to the benefit of the party who took the initiative with regard to one aspect or another of the contract.

Generally speaking, the postulates according to which the initiative of a party is indispensable and each party disposes of the power to influence the behaviour of the other are an invitation to take into consideration the fact that they are directly joined, fundamentally, by a social bond. Before even formalizing a linkage and a project, the parties are already in a relationship. It is a relationship of another order, and which may seem extremely distant. Nevertheless, the acknowledgment of its existence is important because it underlies a reason different from that present in the conservative consciousness of uniform law. According to conservative consciousness, human action consists of employing means of attaining goals. As such, the ends are not discussed because they are too divergent one from another; on the other hand, the means are subject to an appreciation realized on the basis of the criterion of efficiency, which opens the door to a quantitative evaluation of reason. From the admission of a social bond which preexists, linkage derives a rationality which is expressed, on the level of the most profound motivations, as the only manner of revealing itself to others, of making its 'appearance in the human world.'[28] A hidden action would make no sense and an action for one's own self would lose its interest without the real or supposed attention of an audience. Here, invoking the social bond is equivalent to admitting that a party always acts for another party. Not in an altruistic sense but because an action represents little if it is not intended for the appreciation of others. Under these conditions, to be rational is for one party to act in such a way that her/his actions are understood and received by her/his partner. Reason is no longer synonymous with calculation: it 'is said to be the intelligence of an actor when he or she conforms to a law and places him or her self before a spectator.'[29] In other words, the requirement which weighs on a party is to call to the attention of her/his partner the various elements by which it may explain her/his behaviour. From this point of view, the maxims,

---

28 H. Arendt, *Condition de l'homme moderne*, trans. G. Coffin (Paris: Calmann-Lévy, 1983) at 236.

29 A. Berthout, 'Remarques sur la rationalité instrumentale' (1994) 24-25 Cahier d'économie politique 105 at 110.

norms and principles of uniform law become the means by which one party can communicate her/his action. One finds there a good portion of the teachings characteristic of the metaphor of the flexible. By proposing a reason based on communication, cooperation is better defined by means of persuasion and cohesion rather than by rigidity and precision.

Thus, at the heart of the relational argument, the requirement of being rational exists because individuals are bound to render their acts comprehensible, under penalty of rendering them insignificant. This requirement does not obey a particular form of determinism, nor any mysterious force which impels it to conformism. It is there to account for the precept according to which progressive uniform law is a mental construct reposing on relations between individual and collective actors. Moreover, the requirement of reason in the sense of making oneself understood includes the idea that the actions or behaviour of a party must be pertinent in relation to the situation in question. Here, uniform law and social ties impose on the parties an imperative of justification in the sense that they must find a justifiable way of acting which rings correct. As affirmed by L. Boltanski and L. Thévenot:

> Persons are confronted by the necessity of having to justify their actions, that is to say, not by inventing after the fact false reasons for disguising secret motives, as when one finds an alibi, but to accomplish them so that they will be in harmony with a principle which is adequate in the situation.[30]

Consequently, there must be a link between the action of one party and the specified general norms suitable to direct it. In this regard, equality, equilibrium and collaboration which are at the heart of principles stimulating cooperation are susceptible of playing a key role in the evaluation of the validity of an action.[31] However, they do not stand alone. The phenomenon of osmosis, which forms part of the structure and content of the relational argument, as demonstrated in the Prelude to this discussion, expose the linkage and the project to the influence of other considerations; these are also potentially pertinent to the evaluation in question.[32]

In a certain way, the party having to justify her/his action on the basis of such or such a norm becomes the author of it. In acting on the authority of a norm, the party actualizes it by concretely illustrating it through her/his actions. Two effects result from this actualization, both to the benefit of the norm. On the one hand, there is an effect of perpetuation. The fact that the norm is taken as an example may incite others to do likewise. On the other hand, there is an innovative effect, by the fact that the action of a party may add a new particularity or nuance to the norm.

---

30 L. Boltanski & L. Thévenot, 'Les économies de la grandeur' in *Cahiers du centre d'études de l'emploi* (Paris: P.U.F., 1987) at 14.
31 See 'The principles stimulating cooperation', below.
32 See 'Cooperation between the parties and their environment', below.

The principles stimulating cooperation (or the realization of the project)   Three principles are susceptible of favouring and maintaining cooperation between the parties and, thus, have a positive effect on the realization of the project intended by them. They are the principles of equality, of equilibrium and of collaboration. All three tend to instil greater flexibility in the contract and permit its adjustment to the needs of the parties and to the circumstances as they evolve.

The principle of equality concerns the parties.[33] It is founded on the absence of natural, abstract and automatic equality between the parties. Correlatively, its objective consists in establishing an equality in fact, so that the party in a position of technical or economic inferiority may contract and execute with full knowledge, and that her/his partner not be able to abuse her/his position of strength.[34] If need be, it permits the sanctioning of inequality or of restoring between the parties equality in the formation and execution of the contract. At the formation of contract level, the principle requires in particular that the consent of the parties be similarly free and informed. In a relational perspective on the contract, where cooperation is omnipresent, the most direct consequence of the principle of equality is the establishment of a general obligation to speak, to inform and to advise. More specifically, and as a preventive measure, this general rule should incite the stronger party to take the initiative, to be careful to adequately inform her/his partner, rather than leave her/him to her/his own devices to get information and to ask questions. This is revealing of a vision of things where the equality sought does not rest on the premise of natural equality between the parties. Renouncing this abstract premise, the equality sought after is an objective to be actually and concretely attained. Otherwise, inequality in the quality of consents could be compensated by several devices. One of them, in itself quite modest, consists solely of adequately informing the party in a situation of inferiority. That could suffice, according to circumstances, if only to providing the weaker party a minimum of dignity. Another form of compensation, of greater severity, consists of permitting the party in a position of inferiority to reflect on the opportunity of concluding the contract, of granting him or her a certain delay for this purpose; if by chance the contract was already concluded, the equivalent would be to afford him or her a period of reflection on the expediency of maintaining the contract. In any event, a last form of compensation, less severe than the preceding one and more likely to favour the realization of the project and increase the sense of responsibility of the dominant party in the future, would be to interpret and modify the contract in favour of the party in a position of inferiority. By so doing, in establishing an equality which was imperfect at the formation of the contract, the linkage may proceed. And one can only hope that the stronger party has learned a lesson.

---

33   Griffith, *supra*, Chapter 2, note 39; Rae, *supra*, Chapter 2, note 39.
34   For an interesting account of the notion of equality in relation with the market, see C. L. Macleod, 'The Market, Preferences, and Equality' (1994) 7 C.J.L.J. 97.

As for the principle of equilibrium, it relates less to the partners themselves than to the content of the project.[35] It postulates that the project must, in its formation and execution, respect a reasonable balance between the obligations assumed and the advantages derived by each partner. The equilibrium sought after is not an absolute: it plays the role of a standard which refuses to accommodate significant disparities. In relation to disparities which arise at the formation of the contract, one may hesitate in deducing that there would be a possibility of revision and of modification of the project, or even the annulment of it. In effect, this opening seems contrary to nature or inconsistent: from the mere fact that it was desired, a contract is necessarily balanced. To interfere with it would constitute a type of effrontery or paternalism toward the parties. Here the watchword consists simply of remembering that the parties could not have contemplated that an unbalanced contract would be in their favour. There is less hesitation regarding imbalances which occur after the formation of the contract, especially if it is only a question of modifying the project and not of cancelling it. Obviously here also, the immutability of the contract resulting from a rule such as *pacta sunt servanda* may seem a nearly insurmountable obstacle to allowing revision of the contract following, for instance, a change of circumstances. Still, the interpretation given to this rule by scholars of the legal canon relativizes the importance afforded to the immutability of the terms of the contract and to the fact that once a project is adopted, a third party (judge, arbitrator, . . .) can only apply it as such and in some sense impose it upon the partners. Under this interpretation, the effect of the *pacta sunt servanda* rule would appear, in effect, sufficiently nuanced and qualified to admit that a party is not breaking her/his word if she/he does not fulfil an undertaking assumed under circumstances no longer the same. For the canonists, a partner 'is not unfaithful by not fulfilling a promise because the conditions have changed.'[36] Respect for a promise must be appreciated in light of the circumstances which existed at the time the contract was concluded. If these circumstances change to the point of distorting or of taking out of context the initial aims of the partners, then there is no reason to maintain the project as such.

The third principle is that of contractual collaboration.[37] It requires each partner to go beyond her/his own self-interest, and to be mindful of and have concern for the interest of the project and of the other party. The principle of collaboration must incite each partner to place herself/himself at the service of the project and of the other party, to accept certain sacrifices with the view of optimizing the chances of concluding it, executing it and of recognizing fully a contract conceived as a community of interests. This principle avails for all parties,

---

35 J. Gordley, 'Equality in Exchange' (1981) 69 Cal. L. Rev. 1587.

36 Affirmation made by St. Thomas Aquinas and cited by P. Stoffel-Munck, *Regards sur la théorie de l'imprévision: vers une souplesse contractuelle en droit privé français contemporain* (Aix-en-Provence: Presses universitaires d'Aix-Marseille, 1994) at par. 8.

37 See, for an example, J. Mestre, 'Obligations et contrats spéciaux' (1986) 85 R.T.D. Civ. 98 at 100ff.

and it can turn out to be particularly demanding for the partner in a position of superiority. Collaboration may correspond to a measure by which one party informs the other in order to help her/him in the elaboration and then in the realization of the project. Such a measure would preserve its validity and would remain justified, in spite of the fact that it would force one party, first, to inform her/himself in order to then inform the other. Moreover, the principle of collaboration may support a duty of counsel, which would manifest itself in the guidance provided to the other party regarding the appropriateness of contracting under such or such conditions. At the limit, collaboration would, apparently or in reality, go contrary to the personal interests of one party. However, fulfilling one's own obligations in best serving the interests of one's partner is to take into account a type of *affectio contractus* which favours the perenniality of the project. Manifestations flowing from this *affectio contractus* are varied. For one party to seek and serve the interest of the other and of the contract may signify conduct, a gesture or a measure which helps one's partner to execute the contract (by granting her/him a period of grace), which eases her/his pecuniary obligations (by granting her/him a reduction in interest rate), which adapts the contract to her/his needs (by supplying all logistical support necessary in the case of technological projects), etc. These manifestations are at the root of a new idea that one could have of the force of a contract associated with its mutability. Certainly, to admit their legitimacy requires favouring a complex analysis of contract, in contradiction to a simplistic one. But this is probably the price to pay for entertaining a more general view of contract, a vision which is capable of putting it in perspective. As an open and interactive universe, a contract thus becomes a living and sensitive instrument, characteristics which confer upon it, within an even larger world in a constant state of flux, a force greater than that of immobilism.

Cooperation between the parties and their environment (or osmosis) In the portion of the Prelude devoted to osmosis, I emphasized certain elements of the definition as well as certain facets relating to its operation. Under the circumstances, it would be expedient to supplement the Prelude by first of all explaining all the obstacles which could prevent the phenomenon from occurring fully. To do so, it is important to deal with the analysis in general terms, assuming that its spirit is fully relevant to the relational argument such as I defined it initially. The obstacles that come to mind are strongly linked to the conservative consciousness of uniform law, and consequently to modernity and modern law. Because of the importance they possess in these schemas of thought, and considering the phenomenon of sedimentation discussed at the beginning of this part, I believe that they are always potentially very influential. One must therefore accurately identify the sources of this influence in order to limit its scope.

The first source derives from the accumulation of the following facets of conservative consciousness. The environment to which it refers is characterized by the relative scarcity of property available, and the society within which it is immersed is made up of persons whose altruism is moderate and whose strengths are relatively equal. In these conditions, it is prudent and reasonable that each person limit her/his liberty as a quid pro quo for physical and material security. To state this in concrete terms, two types of contract are proposed: a greater contract in order to found a political society and lesser contracts for guaranteeing and expanding property. In each case and in all circumstances, each must discover the proper reasons for not harming those who, because they are practically equal to her/him, could represent a threat. The result is that only reciprocal obligations, accepted by each person directly concerned, are justified. Persons and other sensitive elements found outside the confined circle of each specific juridical relationship do not enjoy an actual capacity to influence. In short, it is difficult to establish duties in favour of any entity remote in time (future generations) and space (the South versus the North) on the basis of these precepts.[38] In addition, the procedure for determining the values extolled by conservative consciousness accentuates this difficulty. In effect, the first strategy utilized to escape the antinomy of truth concerns contemporaries who agree on some principles conceived to their mutual benefit. As for the second strategy, it presents two important potential lacunae: the first is that the discussion which it implies does not seem to accommodate persons, entities or other elements of reality which are not represented in one way or another; the second is that its range of action seems limited to that which is immediately foreseeable, setting aside a whole series of distant consequences which may in fact be very troubling.

The second source of undesirable influence on the phenomenon of osmosis derives from the idea that history always commences at the conclusion of the contract. All takes place as though the parties, desirous of escaping a recurrent natural state, wrote history and set up society from zero on every occasion. As such, there is no living link between the past and the future. Any reference to tradition is seen negatively, and every project for the future is likened to a dream. This situation undermines the idea that the present generation has been affected by past generations and that it will affect future generations. When each generation recreates itself, when each epoch, each instant depends only on itself, which claims and which obligations will the present generation have in relation to those of the past and of the future? When the welfare of each generation, the happiness it may expect, is considered from the perspective of the present, it will have little to expect of the others. Conversely, it would not be held to any duty concerning them. Accordingly, each generation could easily be tempted to exploit its advantage without any thought to the future, or else to carry over onto future generations the harmful consequences of decisions taken today. This attitude is not free of certain tensions because it contradicts an unavoidable reality which resides in the coexistence of at least three generations: children, adults and seniors. The needs

---

38 D. Birnbacher, *La responsabilité envers les générations futures* (Paris: Armand Colin, 1995); P. Laslett & J. S. Fiskin, *Justice between Age Groups and Generations* (New Haven: Yale University Press, 1992); B. Barry, 'Justice between Generations' in P. Hacker, ed., *Law, Morality and Societies: Essays in Honor of H. L. A. Hart* (Oxford: Oxford University Press, 1979) at 272; R. I. Sikora & B. Barry, *Obligations to Future Generations* (Philadelphia: Temple University Press, 1978).

and the aspirations of these three generations are at least partly intertwined, which should constitute a minimal incentive to favour measures of diffusion and interpenetration between concepts, things and people.

Moreover, it is in this manner that the two sources of the negative influence just discussed can be attenuated. To evoke means of diffusion and interpenetration is equivalent, to some extent, to expanding the scope of reflection and of action of the various categories of elements (parties, contract, time, space, . . .) pertinent to the relational argument. How may one attain this? The solution rests, in my opinion, in resisting the temptation to view the principles of equality, of equilibrium and of collaboration – which stimulate cooperation – deprived of their significance or otherwise completely destabilized, from the moment they no longer exclusively concern close and contemporary partners.[39] These principles, inasmuch as one at least recognizes their flexibility and their relativity, are capable of generating and of justifying duties deferred in time, or which affect third parties who, at first glance, appear extraneous to the narrow relationship between the parties immediately concerned. They do not have to be set at any fixed point or limited to a circumscribed number of considerations in order to satisfy the criteria of efficacy, justice and so on. In other words, they may be subjected to a reflexive analysis, that is to say, which reverberates in multiple directions, gathering as it progresses data and information at the outset unavailable to understanding. A good example of the result to which this type of analysis may lead, in connection with the generational question raised before, is proposed by P. van Parijs.[40] Seeking to set out a criterion of justice susceptible of transiting through time and of unifying generations, Parijs enunciates a three-pronged rule centred on inheritance, transfer and support: one, the criterion of rightful inheritance is that the 'productive potential bequeathed by the present generation is at least equal to that bequeathed by the preceding generation';[41] two, the criterion of rightful transfer is evident in the duty, assumed by the present adult generation, of bestowing on its children the equivalent of what it had itself received from the previous adult generation; three, the criterion of rightful support of older persons is that which they themselves had provided for their own seniors.[42] This example, irrespective of the validity of its assertions, illustrates the likelihood and the feasibility of conferring upon fundamental principles an orientation which integrates a sense of retrospection, of perspective and of prospection. Properly assumed, the resistance just mentioned imparts normalcy and opportunity to the phenomenon of osmosis so typical of the relational argument. It situates a linkage and a given project within a generalized process of uninterrupted transmissions between things and human beings. In fact, transmission, as a process, is the foundation of the osmotic phenomenon. It constantly requires that a specific contract be re-situated within a series of events

---

39 For an interesting application, see I. H. Rowlands, 'International Fairness and Justice in Addressing Global Climate Change' (1997) 6 Environmental Politics 1.

40 P. van Parijs, 'La justice entre générations' (1995) 41 Wallonie 7.

41 *Ibid.* at 9.

42 *Ibid.* at 9-10.

and considerations and be viewed in connection with an environment which surpasses it, that is to say a more inclusive discourse, which is open to arguments of the common good, of the world, of self-fulfilment and of solidarity.

The Common Good Argument

Prelude

Outlining the common good argument has provided some definitional elements of this *something more* which must be added to the specific expectations and interests of the parties involved in a contract. It aims at satisfying the collective well-being by re-emphasizing, in the progressive consciousness of uniform law, the political, social, cultural and ethical spheres which, otherwise, are under-utilized in conservative consciousness. One of the most evident repercussions of this re-emphasis is the place assumed by questions of relationship between human beings and nature within progressive consciousness. Thus, at the threshold of the progressive reorientation of uniform law mentioned previously in the critical phase, I indicated that it was essential that human beings participate in a system which, up to a certain point, surpasses them.[43] The new presence of nature had once again asserted itself during the description of the transitory conception. Relying on R. Petrella's notion of common good, I mentioned that it included a *contract of the earth*, synonymous with a reconciliation between human beings and nature, rather than the domination of the first over the second.[44] Always within the framework of the transitory conception, I explained that the insertion of economics within the living led to a systemic vision connecting three components including the biosphere.[45] Consequently, it is not surprising that the outline of the common good argument ended with a statement to the effect that future models of development include nature as an essential variable.

The common good does not only concern nature or the environment. However, I feel it opportune to formally limit its structure and its content to this dimension. Two reasons explain this orientation. First, the aspects which, while going beyond the environment, could devolve from the common good remain present in the progressive consciousness of uniform law. The fact that they are not expressly developed does not deprive them of anything, and especially does not prevent them from manifesting themselves through other arguments which constitute progressive consciousness. Secondly, the emphasis placed on the environment simply conveys the fact that uniform law is quite remote from the matter. Much has to be done, and the soul-searching will be extensive, before the progressive consciousness of

---

43   See Chapter 4, above.
44   See text accompanying note 5, Chapter 5, above.
45   See text accompanying note 15, Chapter 5, above.

uniform law is ready for this. The structure and the content which follow reveal the immenseness of the task inherent in the common good argument.[46]

Structure and Content

The common good argument, as set out, raises three major questions.[47] First, one must determine more precisely the significance and the effect of any aim protective of nature which may be pursued by uniform law. If, in some circumstances, a consensus may be easily reached concerning that which the parties to a contract must preserve from an environmental point of view, in other circumstances, the controversy is definitely more likely to occur. In brief, one must set out, on the basis of the critique of conservative consciousness, what one means by uniform law which protects the environment. Next, one must determine if, in light of the so called deep ecology movement, whether uniform law protecting the environment goes far enough. And finally, it is important to verify to what point the response to the first question is or is not an obstacle to the functional nature of the common good argument. Together, the second and third queries will provide the opportunity for further outlining the response to the first question.

Nature: what does uniform law protect? A progressive consciousness protective of nature can take on at least three meanings in relation to uniform law.[48] First, uniform law can vest itself with a mission to preserve nature consisting in avoiding any kind of pollution. Secondly, uniform law can be interested in keeping nature as it is, that is to say in its original condition.[49] And, thirdly, uniform law can look at the protection of nature understood as a vital source of diversity.[50] In its process of maturation toward a progressive consciousness – represented here by the argument of the common good – uniform law will constantly have to juggle these meanings

---

46   See, in general, R. Attfield, *The Ethics of Environmental Concern* (Athens: University of Georgia Press, 1991); by the same author, 'Global Warming and International Equity' in J. Parker, ed., *The European Moral Community* (Aldershot: Avebury, 1997) 142; F. de Roose & P. van Parijs, *La pensée écologiste. Essai d'inventaire à l'usage de ceux qui la pratiquent comme de ceux qui la craignent* (Brussels: De Boeck, 1991); J. B. Callicott, *Defense of Land Ethics: Essays in Environmental Philosophy* (Albany: State University of New York Press, 1986).

47   C. Larrère, *Les philosophies de l'environnement* (Paris: P.U.F., 1997); F. Yamin, 'Biodiversity, Ethics and International Law' (1995) 71 Int'l Affairs 529.

48   W. M. Adams, *Future Nature: A Vision for Conservation* (London: Earthscan, 1996); D. A. Kealey, *Revisioning Environmental Ethics* (Albany: State University of New York Press, 1990).

49   T. Sprigge, 'Are there Intrinsic Values in Nature?' in B. Almond & D. Hill, eds., *Applied Philosophy: Morals and Metaphysics in Contemporary Debate* (London: Sage, 1991) at 37.

50   B. Norton, *Why Preserve Natural Variety?* (Princeton: Princeton University Press, 1987).

and to estimate their respective importance. In my opinion, it will do it in two ways:

i)   by envisaging the meanings in isolation, one from the other, or
ii) in interdependence.[51]

The way involving putting the emphasis on interdependence (ii) will rapidly show that the three meanings do not perfectly overlap and that one can act to the detriment of the other. Preserving nature (first meaning) does not always coincide with its conservation (second meaning); safeguarding natural diversity (third meaning) implies at times more than watching over a strict preservation (first meaning) and conservation of nature (second meaning). In sum, protecting nature means that uniform law makes choices from which flow certain consequences. If uniform law favours, for example, nature free of pollution, it does not necessarily favour a nature rich and diversified. The fact of not using chemical fertilizers would be attractive from the viewpoint of protecting nature. On the other hand, the use of fertilizers could increase the potential of certain ecosystems by fostering the implantation of certain animal and vegetable species. The concern to avoid pollution of natural space may be detrimental for biodiversity. Thus, the production of clean energy such as hydroelectricity may occasion the loss of some animal and vegetable species.[52] In the same line of thought, conservation of nature as is, does not guarantee that nature will be full of diversity. Certain ecosystems are, in fact, poor in biological terms, in that they possess few species or constituents, even if they are present in great quantity. In fact, a nature rich and diversified often depends on some form of human intervention. In this type of situation, the conservation of nature in its original state is not as such restricted; at most, it is contemplated from an active and not a passive viewpoint.

Insofar as uniform law views the three significations of progressive consciousness in isolation one from the other, as in (i) above, I submit that the easiest to develop and justify is the first, concerning the avoidance of pollution. This may be explained by the fact that from the perspective of progressive consciousness, avoiding pollution constitutes a preliminary step to establishing a respectful relationship between uniform law and nature.[53] Any further initiative would be doomed to failure, or at least to mitigated success if, beforehand, there was a failure to establish a mutual uniform law/nature relationship that is sound rather than not. Obviously, the concept of pollution lends itself to controversy: at which point do human actions constitute an assault upon the natural environment? Are the means used by humans in their interaction with nature pertinent to

---

51   D. Birnbacher, 'Ethical Principles versus Guiding Principles in Environmental Ethics' (1987) 39 Philosophica 59.

52   L. Sax, 'Le petit poisson contre le grand barrage' (1978) 5 Rev. Jur. Env. 368.

53   Y. Veyret, *L'homme et l'environnement* (Paris: P.U.F., 1993); E. Bonnefous, *Réconcilier l'homme et la nature* (Paris: P.U.F., 1990); I. G. Gordon, *Changing the Face of the Earth: Culture, Environment, History* (New York: Blackwell, 1989).

determining whether or not there is pollution? These questions form part of the reflection that progressive consciousness must undertake, in conjunction with other disciplines, in order to allow nature to occupy its rightful place by virtue of the transitory conception. No matter what answers will be given, it is possible to discern from that which has been heretofore presented one guiding principle: uniform law has the responsibility of ensuring that the contributions of the major environmental axes (water, land, air) are not irremediably compromised as a result of its action. This principle could be made more specific by precisely enunciating the types of natural contribution that would be worth protecting. However, at this point, it is especially important to recall the general message contained in the principle. It affords human activity generated directly or indirectly by uniform law significant latitude so as to not excessively restrict innovation and creation. Yet the limit that it sets remains difficult to respect and it presupposes the pursuit of two objectives: On the one hand, that polluting human activity not be undertaken without forethought as to its effects on the environment. Notably, this means that there should be a strong incentive, if not a constraint, for polluting activity to include research intended to replace it with non-polluting activities, or to counter its effects, in each case as soon as practicable. On the other hand, that nature's still intact potential not be undermined without making any effort to measure the consequences of undertaking an activity before polluting.[54]

In comparison with the first meaning, the two others appear more precarious and consequently less likely to evolve. In effect, avoiding pollution inherently benefits from a presumption of favour. Polluting will always remain primarily an evil per se, something that must be repressed. In the face of this, uniform law, to a certain extent, is in a position of weakness: it must attempt to impart to this signification its full effect. The protection of nature and of biodiversity do not benefit from the same status, if only because they seem less able to adapt, from the outset, to the dynamism inherent in uniform law. This dynamism supposes that nature is there to serve and that it can be transformed by the direct and indirect actions of uniform law. Yet service and transformation may be strongly antinomical to ideas of maintaining nature as it is and of protecting nature as an essential source of diversity.[55] In the context of conservative consciousness, an antinomy of this nature did not exist. In effect, conservative consciousness imbued itself with the modernist vision of the human being/nature relationship, a vision placing the knowledge and the power of human beings face to face with nature. This confrontation was provoked by the Cartesian split between the faculty of thought enjoyed by human beings and the rest of the universe. The immediate and main consequence of this split was to permit human beings to first withdraw from the natural system and then appropriate its contents. By assuming the authority of this vision, conservative consciousness no longer had to be preoccupied with the

---

54   J. Lepart, 'La crise environnementale et les théories de l'équilibre en écologie' in C. Larrère, ed., *La crise environnementale* (Paris: I.N.R.A., 1997) at 131.
55   D. Pearce & D. Moran, *The Economic Value of Biodiversity* (London: Earthscan, 1994).

environment. What about progressive consciousness? In my opinion, one of the most interesting avenues is progressive consciousness to adjust the relationship between uniform law and the two significations presently under discussion by drawing inspiration from a reality already experienced on an internal level by nature, that of disturbance.[56] When closely examined, natural reality effectively reveals many phases of instability, of slower cycles followed by more rapid ones, and so forth, from which is derived more benefit than detriment. Integrated into progressive consciousness, the reality of disturbances legitimizes the action of uniform law, which affects the integrity and diversity of nature, as long as a general condition is satisfied: the creation of a value added measurable in terms of self-fulfilment and human solidarity.

Does uniform law go far enough? From the perspective of the call to common good just outlined, progressive consciousness takes nature into account because its existence and its protection are necessary or at least very useful to the survival and for quality of life of human beings.[57] For these reasons, progressive consciousness may be qualified as pro-environment. Meanwhile, those adhering to deep ecology, while pleased by this care for nature, would probably consider that the common good argument implied by this consciousness is ill founded and does not go far enough.[58] Essentially, they would reproach it for relating everything, in the final analysis, to human welfare (to its self-fulfilment and solidarity), thus becoming anthropocentric.[59] Would it not be better, they say, to consider as valid in itself the existence of diverse living beings and that of rich natural sites, no matter what the advantages of any order that human beings could derive therefrom, either now or in the future? Would it not be better if uniform law respected nature for its own sake, independently of human beings? To this, progressive consciousness would answer that it does not, in principle, deny the sacred character of nature. It could reply, for example, that the satisfaction for humans derived from nature is often connected to the acknowledgement of the intrinsic value, either aesthetically or biologically, of living creatures or of other natural sites. In other terms, it is from the intrinsic value of species, from the fascination that it provokes, that their protection is seen as a priority and that human beings derive satisfaction from the fact that this species still exists. However, beyond this principle, progressive consciousness would argue on a pragmatic basis that the importance of nature must be measured in terms of human satisfaction. Would this type of response convince the defenders of deep ecology? Probably not. They would only perceive such an answer as a simple form of rhetoric, a way for uniform law to appease its

---

56   C. Larrère & R. Larrère, *Du bon usage de la nature. Pour une philosophie de l'environnement* (Paris: La Découverte, 1997).

57   F. Ost, *La nature hors la loi. L'écologie à l'épreuve du droit* (Paris: La Découverte, 1995).

58   A. Naess, *Ecology, Community and Lifestyle: Outline of an Ecosophy* (Cambridge: Harvard University Press, 1989).

59   B. Devall, 'The Deep Ecology Movement' (1980) 20 Natural Resources Journal 299.

consciousness! Fundamentally, this position would be equivalent to lip service acknowledging the necessity of changing attitudes toward nature, but refusing to go any further. In response, progressive consciousness would state that deep ecology falls short of critical sense and exaggerates by mythologizing or having a blind belief in nature.

In spite of these differences, progressive consciousness and deep ecology may be mutually enriching. A basis of dialogue and understanding between the two can be set out by describing the various premises on which the deep ecology movement is founded.[60] These premises are as follows:

i) *The full development of human and non-human living entities has intrinsic merit. The intrinsic value of non-human living entities is independent of their usefulness for human beings in the pursuit of their goals.*

ii) *The richness and diversity of forms of life on earth, including forms of human culture, have an intrinsic value.*

iii) *Human beings have no right to diminish this richness and diversity except to satisfy vital needs.*

iv) *The full development of human cultures and life may be attained with a much smaller human population.*

v) *Present human interference in the non-human world is excessive and the situation is becoming worse.*

vi) *The preceding points indicate the necessity of bringing about changes to the manner in which human beings act in their relationship with nature. These changes concern all structures and spheres surrounding the lives of human beings (political, social, technological, economic, ideological).*

vii) *Ideological change in rich worlds depends on an increased appreciation of the quality of life, as opposed to the search for a higher standard of living in the material sense, in order to pave the way to sustainable development.*

viii) *Those who subscribe to the preceding points have the duty to try, directly or indirectly, to provoke the necessary changes by non-violent means.*

An examination of this list would lead one to think that progressive consciousness would generally be in agreement with premises iv) to viii). It could thus draw inspiration from them in presenting the common good argument. Yet it would not totally accept premises i) to iii). It would prefer expressing the principle that the richness and diversity of life forms must be valued by uniform law because they are *good* for human beings. In this sense, richness and diversity would be endowed with value, in the eyes of uniform law, insofar as they facilitate the attainment of a society full of vitality.

Is this an indirect means of conceding to uniform law a power over nature? That which is good for human beings can be understood in many ways, and

---

60　I rely on the description included in D. Rothenberg, *Is it Painful to Think? Conversations With Arne Naess* (Minneapolis: University of Minnesota Press, 1993), at pp. 127-128.

presupposes an exploitation and a transformation of nature on a broad scale. In order to avoid a drift leading to this type of domination, the Kantian concept of humanity becomes a most valuable aid.[61] Its content truly conveys the message advanced by the common good argument. For Kant, human beings are worthy of respect to the extent that they are autonomous, that is to say both subject and object of moral law. Such is their humanity which corresponds to that which is specifically human within them, to their faculty of self-determination and of autonomy. The highest imperative, reiterated in the second version of the categorical imperative, consists precisely in unconditionally respecting this humanity: Act such that you treat humanity, whether in your own person or in that of any other, never simply as a means but always also as an end.[62] It is important to note that for Kant, this notion of humanity is not limited to the autonomous subject so that she/he becomes autarchic. It does not seek to compartmentalize and limit the scope of action and of reflection of the autonomous subject. On the contrary, it opens up to a larger humanity, in other words, to all of humanity. According to this point of view, the humanity of a human being is defined by the project which she/he assumes, whether it is in an individual or a collective perspective. And it is precisely this project which represents the primary frame of reference, that which comes before all others and which, under the circumstances, must also direct uniform law. However, Kantian humanity and the ongoing improvement that it presupposes do not have any sense unless they are projected over the long term. The present moment and the short term remain inadequate for founding Kantian humanity because it remains an ongoing enterprise always susceptible of improvement. It is only with time that it can be appreciated. It is only the extended duration which, in fact, permits one to judge the errors of the past and fully anticipate the future, generally by way of the present. Therefore, this implies that uniform law cannot dominate nature because it is only through its assistance and its collaboration, renewed over time that it may realize a humanist contribution.

The common good argument: functional or not? Brought to a more general level, the response to the first question – uniform law protects what? – supposes that the common good argument includes two concrete steps: first, imagine the possibilities available to human beings and their consequences, and then evaluate these consequences in relation to the collective well-being that they offer. In many cases, this reasoning does not pose serious difficulty. For his part, D. Hume says that the judgements of individuals in everyday life rely on this type of reasoning, even if they do not constantly have these criteria in mind.[63] This is also J. Bentham's

---

61 I. Kant, *Métaphysique des moeurs*, trans. V. Deltos (Paris: Vrin, 1971).

62 *Ibid.* at 50.

63 For further analysis, see N. K. Smith, *The Philosophy of David Hume* (New York: Garland Pub., 1983); J. Harrison, *Hume's Moral Epistemology* (Oxford: Clarendon, 1976).

position, which holds that these evaluations are often done in secret.[64] Indeed, one can imagine the possibilities and the consequences, then evaluate their relative merit in light of the common good in the space of a nanosecond, without even being aware of it. Thus, unless there are very particular circumstances, a person who knows how to swim would not reflect for very long before jumping in the water in order to save a child from drowning, with all the positive consequences that this gesture entails on both a collective and an individual level. It is however evident that in other situations and with regard to other types of questions, one must seriously reflect at length in order to imagine the possibilities and consequences and properly assess them. For example, one would not satisfy the requirements of the common good argument if one reflected for no more than a second on the relative merit of building a hydroelectric dam in territory claimed by the First Nations. The two steps of the reasoning prescribed by the common good argument can thus be covered in the blink of an eye, without taking time to think about them, but they could otherwise command attention. What should one do in these difficult cases? What type of mental mediation should be called upon to resolve them? Certainly the metaphor of the multiple, by decompartmentalizing uniform law, by broadening its horizons, is able to enrich and improve the evaluation which progressive consciousness must undertake by virtue of the common good argument. Yet one must acknowledge that the contribution of any field of knowledge – the sciences, the humanities – will have its limits. For instance, science allows us to recognize that certain human activities are dangerous: the use of gas and fuels which have a destructive effect on the ozone layer readily comes to mind. Nevertheless, science is not always able to clearly determine the long term consequences of various options open to human beings, any more than they can provide magical solutions to all present and future problems arising from an inadequate relationship between uniform law and nature.

Consequently, the problematic inherent in difficult cases comes into sharp focus. R. Pannikar has devoted some thought to it and the solution he advances seems particularly illuminating. It is the result of an intermixing of systemic, complex and dialectical thought specific to the second modernity, and it reserves a central role for human beings and the worlds within which they evolve. The starting point of the solution includes the realization that human beings and nature are united by a common destiny:

> As long as man and the world remain estranged, as long as we insist in relating them only as master to slave – following the metaphor used by Hegel and Marx – as long as their relation is not seen to constitute both world and man, no lasting remedy will ever be found. For this reason, I submit that no dualistic solution can endure.[65]

---

64   For further analysis, see J. R. Dinwiddy, *Bentham* (Oxford: Oxford University Press, 1989).

65   R. Pannikar, 'The New Innocence' (1977) 27 Cross Currents 1 at 7.

On an analytical level, Pannikar's solution contrives to divide history into three *kairological moments* of human consciousness: pre-historical, historical and transhistorical.[66] These moments must not be understood as merely representing periods of time. Rather, they define the attitudes that predominate during certain periods. During the first kairological moment, pre-historical,

> Man lives mainly in space. . . . The World of pre-historical Man, his environment, is the *theocosmos* or *theocosm*, the divinized universe. It is not a World of Man, but it is also not the World of the Gods as a separate and superior realm hovering over the human. . . . In the pre-historical mentality, it is the World that is divinized (to use historical language). The divine permeates the cosmos. The forces of nature are all divine. Nature is supernatural. Or rather, nature is that which is 'nature', born from the divine. Pre-historical Man's milieu is a cosmotheological one. Harmony is the supreme principle – which does not mean that it has been achieved.[67]

The second kairological moment, that of historical conscience, is thus explained by Pannikar:

> Nature has been tamed and subjugated. It has been demythicized and there is nothing mysterious about it. Historical Man has overcome the fear of nature. His backdrop is cosmological. The meaning of life is not to be found in the cosmic cycles, but in the human sphere, the society. Justice is the supreme principle – which does not mean that it has been achieved.[68]

These two attitudes remain present and influential on the eve of the second modernity. However, specifies Pannikar, 'A third degree of consciousness is coming more and more to the fore':[69] it is the one founded on the transhistorical moment. Pannikar deals with it as follows:

> Pre-historical Man has fate. He is part and parcel of the universe. Historical Man has destiny. He predestines where he stands. He arranges his own life. Transhistorical Man has his lot. He is involved in the total adventure of reality. . . . We are all in the same boat, which is not just this planet Earth, but the whole mystery of Life, Consciousness, Existence. Love is the supreme principle – which, again, does not mean that it has been achieved.[70]

The comprehensive solution proposed by Pannikar in order to resolve difficult cases does not proceed exclusively from one or the other of the three attitudes described: it instead integrates them in a 'consciousness lived neither naively nor

---

66 R. Pannikar, 'Is History the Measure of Man? Three Kairological Moments of Human Consciousness' 16 The Teilhard Review at 39.

67 *Ibid.*

68 *Ibid.* at 41.

69 *Ibid.* at 42.

70 *Ibid.* at 45.

by rational projection into the future.'[71] The centre of this consciousness is 'neither in God, nor in the cosmos, nor even in man. It is a moving centre which is only to be found in the intersections of the three.'[72]

As such, Pannikar's solution does not eliminate difficult cases but it permits their contemplation with greater confidence and security. It imposes a moment of reflection before taking action, a suspension of our judgement for an instant, to paraphrase M. Sautet.[73] It is not purely idealistic or fraught with short-term pragmatism. In my view, it is more an invitation to trace a middle road between two extremes. How? Uniform law might incorporate the middle road proposed by Pannikar into the common good argument by sanctioning past faults. Responsibility, in the classic sense of imputing past faults to one party, continues to be pertinent, even if its actual implementation remains delicate. However, it would probably be more profitable over the long term if it adopted a preventive attitude, inspired by prudence. In so doing, it could impose on the parties who transact under its authority an *obligation to seek to know*. In practical terms, this could occur, in particular, through the completion of studies destined to measure the short-, middle- and long-term effects of a contractual project upon the environment. In the same way, this obligation should not be devoid of effect insofar as the scientific appraisal ends in a question mark. If the case arises, the parties should continue to support the duty of protecting human nature, in order to avoid uncertainty as to the consequences of one option becoming a pretext for failing to act. At a more general level, the middle road traced by Pannikar necessarily refers to all types of arbitration experienced by the different worlds, both internally and externally, in their daily practices. From a progressive point of view, these arbitrations constitute an opportunity for the citizens of these worlds to assume a sense of responsibility. Difficult cases may thus be dealt with by properly arranging citizen participation, along with that of associations, enterprises, public authorities, in any decision making, all of which implies an acknowledgment of the right to information and to co-ordination.

The World-based Argument

Prelude

While setting out the world-based argument, I mentioned that it had to serve to explore the mental foundation of uniform law in each given world. More specifically, I mentioned the elements of innovation, diffusion and aspiration that uniform law may contribute to in relation to a given world, and that such an argument should bring to light. From that moment, the question becomes one of knowing how to attain, read and comprehend this mental foundation and highlight

---

71   Pannikar, *supra*, note 65; at 13.
72   *Ibid.* at 14.
73   See text accompanying note 1, Introduction.

the different elements mentioned. On what should one's attention be set, while asking oneself what type of question? This is not self-evident. A world, as presented by the transitory conception, reposes above all on a cultural and symbolic mechanism. Many of its components are concealed by others or appear irrelevant at first glance. That means that the logic of a world is not directly perceptible.[74] It is therefore easy to miss the facets essential to the comprehension of a world and to misapprehend it as a result. In an effort to develop an approach and a conceptualization which would avoid these pitfalls and which conform to the objective of constituting a progressive consciousness of uniform law, I submit that a *world* may be read and understood on the basis of what I would call the concept of holistic action.

The concept of holistic action is sufficiently flexible to adapt to nearly all situations. In this case, its presentation is made in order that it may fulfil a double goal. To begin with, it directs observation toward a body of information and of variables susceptible of accurately translating one or more realities of a world, realities deemed pertinent for purposes of analysis in relation to uniform law. Thus, should it be a question of analysing the relationship between uniform law and a reality characteristic of a world, global action would provide a set of reference points, of indicators for doing so. Then, the concept may serve as a plan or a reference in the preparation and the execution of a project supported by a world. In this case, it will be perceived more as offering leads for reflection and action.[75]

Structure and Content

The structure and content of the world-based argument will be articulated from the following questions: what significance should be attributed to the concept of holistic action? How does this mode of expression of a world start working? And on what dynamics does it rely?

What does holistic action mean? To better interpret the elements of innovation, of diffusion and aspiration previously mentioned, holistic action takes an interest, in an equivalent manner, in the behaviour of actors, in activities realized or in the process of realization, and in articulations between actors and actions. It gives preference to the expression of persons and groups concerned, in the goal of rendering their general living conditions as visible as possible. More specifically, it is characterized by the fact that it:

---

74 See, for example, the comments of K. Mischel in relation to economic activity in 'Webs of Significance: Understanding Economic Activity in Its Cultural Context' (1997) 54 Review of Social Economy 67.

75 See, in general, O. Fillieule & C. Péchin, *Lutter ensemble. Les théories de l'action collective* (Paris: L'Harmattan, 1993); J. D. Reynaud, *Les règles du jeu. L'action collective et la régulation sociale* (Paris: Armand-Colin, 1989).

i)   manifests itself at a micro-social level (between persons only, in everyday life) and at a macro-social level (within institutions);
ii)   goes beyond mere actions of actors, while admitting that collective movements are possible (in spite of mechanisms of domination and of exclusion) and viable (despite the presence of individual actors);
iii) constitutes a dynamic composed of orientations and objectives.

Holistic action supposes that each component (actors, actions, articulations) contains a series of variables in constant tension in the steps taken within a world. That signifies that holistic action is constructed through the interplay of contradictory forces and that it is never totally fixed, predetermined and thus foreseeable. On a methodological level, it presents itself according to a lesser or greater range of considerations among which one may find the following.

In relation to the component *actors*,[76] one must first ponder the level (individual or collective) of the actors present, by posing the two following questions: For what reasons does a group of persons, not necessarily sharing the same aspirations or interests, undertake a holistic action? And why does a certain individual join in this form of action, what relationship can one establish between individual motivation and a collective project? Then, it is important to identify the sources of tension between actors, in order to determine to what point these tensions contribute to imparting dynamism to holistic action or curbing it. Finally, the value represented by holistic action for a given actor merits attention, whether it be positive or negative. Here, it is a question of seeing what judgement an actor makes on the realization and the effects of a holistic action, by verifying, for example, how she/he profits from its success or failure, the lessons learned in each case, etc.

For its part, the component *actions* serves to determine that which is done, undertaken. It places the actor, her/his logic and her/his *raison d'être* in the background in order to concentrate on that which an actor does to materialize an intention or an impulse.[77] Initially, this component sees the action according to whether it is practised on an internal or external level. This distinction is important because it enables determining to what point an actor is autonomous, dependent upon other actors, or again desirous of becoming free from other actors or of joining forces with them. The vital question arising therefrom could be formulated in this manner: what is the respective importance attributed by an actor to goals or internal activities in comparison with those that set her/him in an antagonistic or cooperative relationship with other actors (groups, organizations or institutions)? Then the component turns its attention to the educational and/or political orientation of the action. These orientations sometimes appear mutually exclusive. On the one hand, certain actors place emphasis on the pedagogical nature of their

---

76   A. Touraine, *Le retour de l'acteur* (Paris: Fayard, 1984).
77   B. Ollivier, *L'acteur et le sujet: vers un nouvel acteur économique* (Paris: Desclée de Brouwer, 1995); P. Bourdieu, *Raisons pratiques: sur la théorie de l'action* (Paris: Seuil, 1994).

initiatives, according to the postulate holding that awareness and consciousness precede any action. Stated in other terms, education or simply the transmission or the demonstration of something constitutes a prerequisite to initiating action. In sum, it is a question here of changing mentalities, seen as a necessary transition toward learning and adopting new global conducts. On the other hand, certain actors will express themselves in terms of a need for change: this is the political orientation. As it is, the action will be perceived as a form of adaptation or adjustment to a mobile reality. To achieve this type of action, political orientation will consider ethical questions on the freedom to choose and associate with others, including the values and structures which ensure social integration. It will turn its attention to collective achievements and benefits obtained. In so doing, it will favour the role of actors and their actions insofar as they represent instruments of change. Finally, the component 'actions' is interested in the offensive and defensive nature of the actions contemplated. Here, emphasis is placed on the external relationships of an actor. Offensive action can take the form of a simple initiative, or it may quite clearly constitute an aggressive intervention, even an attack. Inversely, a defensive action may correspond to a desire to protect oneself, to preserve something or even to react to an action. Like other variables, offensive and defensive actions are susceptible of intermingling. The constant tension between the two, between actions and reactions, adds to the characteristic dynamic of holistic action.

As already mentioned, holistic action is not limited only to the behaviour of the actors and the activities realized. It also includes the modes of articulation between these actors and activities, modes which it presumes indispensable to the comprehension of that which a world has been, is, and desires to be.[78] In my opinion, the component *articulations* may be analysed and described in terms of three sets of variables. The first puts in tension classic rational factors as opposed to post-classic ones. The classic rational factors enable the analysis of holistic action in terms of efficiency, that is to say in terms of the results, of the benefits attained. The ideal relationship of actor/action will be that which has proven itself or that we can anticipate will prove itself. In contradistinction, the post-classic factors will specifically place the accent on human relationships, on socio-affective indicators, on individual and collective mentalities. Here, holistic action appeals to complementarity by taking into account these two types of factors on the basis of the following question: what is the respective importance of each in the sought-after ends, the strategy applied and the effects desired? The second set of variables includes the content of an action and its underlying process. The content refers to the activities realized, the tasks executed and the results obtained. The evaluation of the content takes place as much on the qualitative as on the quantitative level: rough, abstract information will form a part of it along with more refined data. The variable of process adds to the preceding by urging the observation of different relationships which unite and disunite the actors involved in a given action. These

---

78 J. L. Cohen, 'Strategy or Identity: New Theoretical Paradigms and Contemporary Social Movements' (1985) 52 Social Research 663.

relationships go two ways: they unite competition and cooperation, project and counter-plans. The most important thing is to verify how content and process interact, define themselves in relation to each other. As for the third pair of variables, it places the emphasis on the double dimension of participation and of realization. The variable of participation concerns manifestations such as speech, support for projects, support for activities; that of realization pursues tangible results. Each one needs and is stimulated by the other: there cannot be any concrete achievements without effective participation, which may be facilitated in the future by attaining good results in a particular project.

How is holistic action carried out? From the moment the concept of holistic action is defined, it is advisable to examine more precisely the conditions for implementing it. In this regard, the approach adopted rests upon the hypothesis that the different forms of holistic action depend on the constitution of groups and the elaboration of strategies. The nature of the constitution of a particular group will frequently depend on the individual or collective range of objectives which it pursues. Several types of grouping are thus possible, just as many types of strategy are conceivable.

The types of grouping could correspond to the following designations: the socialization group, the interest group and the solidarity group.[79] The socialization group pursues objectives related to training, which seek to provide awareness to actors forming part of it. The accent is placed on the development of the actors by means of the group dynamic, which facilitates interpersonal exchanges and the acquisition of rules of communal life. Socialization, the purpose of this group, is manifested by various forms of learning based on, for example, the relationship with others, the requirements of life in a society and the functioning of institutional bodies. The group is thus able to function at two levels simultaneously. First, it provides a context favourable to reassuring, to freeing from guilt and to motivating individual actors who live in the same world, but who present dissimilar capacities and varied personal itineraries. Secondly, the group constitutes a limited space within which occurs the experiencing or the reexamination of norms and roles existing in a world. The socialization group acts somewhat like a guide within a transition experienced by an actor. For its actors, it represents the opportunity to experience something, an experience eventually able to direct them toward other types of grouping. An interest group views otherwise its *raison d'être*. It is structured to last for as long as is necessary in order to attain the common interests, goals and activities shared by all of its members. The group pursues targeted objectives with which its actors concur because they feel directly concerned. This explains why priority is attributed, within an interest group, to designs with which each actor identifies. Incidentally, the group can turn its attention to satisfying the needs specific to some of them, insofar as it is not detrimental to its functioning. The purposes of this type of grouping are potentially quite diversified on all levels

---

79 A. Trognon, 'L'interaction en général: sujets, groupes, cognitions, représentations sociales' (1991) 57 Connexions 9.

(purpose, scope, etc.): the fulfilment of minor productive activities, the organization of mutual aid networks, of services useful to many in daily life, finalizing demands aimed at access to collective services, and so on. In general, if the advantages resulting from participation in the group benefits primarily all the members collectively, and secondarily each one of them, they remain internal. They have no direct external reach, that is to say, extended to other actors or groups, but this docs not prevent the latter from drawing inspiration from it. As a complement to the two preceding groups, the solidarity group enjoys a very wide range of action. It unites a vast number of actors presenting similar geographical, political, economic or ethical conditions of existence. The solidarity group does not aspire directly to individual growth and development nor to the realization of interests common to the members of a given group. It tends rather to favour the collective promotion of substantial parts of a world, indeed even an entire world. The idea of collective promotion is to be understood here as extending to measures susceptible of improving the situation of a world, of solving actual problems; it may also include projects the goal of which is to perfect a situation already enviable or esteemed. In this perspective, the solidarity group fulfils a basic organizational function. This consists of developing expanded actions, that is to say, which go beyond the sole interest or the *raison d'être* of a group. Actions undertaken highlight dynamics both internal and external to different groups constituting the solidarity group. In reality, the effect of actions undertaken require recourse to the powers of each one, but also to mutual support between groups and alliances.

Holistic action does not only need the mediation of groups to ensure its implementation. It implies, in addition, recourse to one or several strategies.[80] Many types of strategy are conceivable according to the matters at stake and the contexts. A strategy may be broken down into a series of operations linked together. As such, each component constitutes a variable of which actual analysis, in relation to a particular world, is capable of revealing a quantity of information explaining the success, the failure or simply the meaning of a holistic action. The general schema of a strategy corresponds to the following operations.[81]

- *Identification of the problematic to be resolved or of the situation to be improved.* What is problematic, or what should be perfected? A holistic action is not limited to correcting situations deemed awkward or unacceptable; it serves also to reinforce situations which are already generally positive. But, under all circumstances, what is it exactly? Whom does it concern, and why? In addition to those primarily concerned, which actors assume responsibility in this case or who are likely be interested in it?

---

80 D. Rucht, 'The Strategies and Action Repertoires of New Movements' in R. Dalton & M. Kuechler, eds., *Challenging the Political Order* (New York: Oxford University Press, 1990) at 156.

81 J. Arocéna, *Le développement par l'initiative locale* (Paris: L'Harmattan, 1986).

- *Locating of actors and identifying what is at stake.* What motivates or fails to motivate actors concerned or interested? It requires an evaluation of their degree of involvement, determining the reasons which impel them to act in the face of a situation which is problematic or which requires improvement.
- *Clarification of the objectives pursued in light of the various challenges to be faced.* The objectives must be drafted in sufficiently specific terms for each actor to feel concerned, but also in sufficiently general terms in order to grasp the stakes which bring them together.
- *Formalization of the holistic action project.* To formalize the project is to subject it to discussion and to revise it in light of comments and criticisms made by the actors participating. This is an exacting step; it requires open-mindedness and humility on the part of the main or initial actors but is totally justified from the viewpoint of enriching the project.
- *Engaging in a holistic action.* It is a question here of defining the project and of structuring the process by mobilizing the actors and organizing their collaboration in light of the circumstances and the opportunities which arise.
- *Seizing opportunities.* Events, favourable circumstances, and other factors facilitate the advancement of a holistic action. It is much easier to benefit from these opportunities when the holistic action project is well formalized and its objectives well clarified. Often, these opportunities arise when a holistic action is undertaken. However, they may spring up even during the initial steps of a project.
- *Exploiting the assets of an actor, compensating for her/his weaknesses.* Are the assets really taken into account, recognized and highlighted? What are its weak points, and how can one convert them into potential assets?
- *The enhancement of each actor's potential.* Holistic action has less chance of success when the discourse has a negative tone. Enhancing each actor's potential helps iron out and surmount what may appear, at first glance, to constitute obstacles. The extent of each person's contribution does not take on determinative importance; the idea that everyone must give the utmost of her/himself is much more essential.
- *The determination of roles.* Holistic action depends on diversity and complementarity in relation to the roles assumed by various actors pursuing common goals. These roles are determined at the outset, but they remain subject to change as the process progresses.
- *Evaluation of the process and the results of a holistic action.* In the course of realization, an evaluation encourages stimulation of the holistic action process by identifying obstacles and factors which hinder its advancement and suppressing them. However, this operation of evaluation, to be truly effective, must be anticipated and planned before holistic action can actually commence.

Holistic action: which dynamic? Holistic action emerges from which type of dynamic?[82] A response of a linear nature to this question could be attempted. It would consist in explaining the dynamism of a holistic action according to a series of logical operations: starting with a prior diagnosis, one proceeds through various steps leading to a final result, each step possibly splitting up into sequences connected together. Holistic action takes shape in a protocol to be followed. Another linear response would consist of favouring the role of the actors, evaluated at diverse moments in the course of a holistic action process. Here, attention turns to the leadership exercised by the actor: one would be interested in her/his capacity to develop and structure holistic action, ensure the exercising and sharing of responsibilities and favour participation. Generally speaking, the advantages of linearity reside in its clarity and in its functional character. Things are simple to apply, utilize and analyse. They may be transposed without difficulty from one case to another. Yet an approach of this type includes serious limitations in light of the progressive dimension of the world-based argument. First, it derives its rationality from a series of deductions: if such a gesture is made, it will provoke a certain consequence, which in turn will cause a certain reaction, and so forth. However, rationality derived exclusively from deductions will adapt with difficulty to the complexity of situations normally encountered. Secondly, the decomposition into predefined and chronologically-ordered sequences may prove less operational than foreseen, especially in difficult or unexpected situations. Thirdly, emphasis placed only on the actors will occur to the detriment of a context involving many matters at stake as well as convergent and divergent interests. In reality, the progressive expression of a holistic action invites reflection concerning another type of dynamic. Its special nature rests upon the constant interactions of the processes involved in consciousness-expanding, organization and mobilization.

The consciousness-expanding process postulates that human beings are the actors of history.[83] This assumption means that each of us is potentially master of her/his existence. It is as a sentient being that one may gain understanding and thus free oneself from obstacles which hinder life and from challenges with which one is confronted. One's identity can actually develop: this is not a commonplace. In other words, consciousness-expanding refers to a process by which the actors, both individually and collectively, awaken to their socio-cultural reality and identify the alienations, the constraints to which they are subjected in order to overcome them, thus asserting themselves as subjects responsible for their own development. Consciousness-expanding may occur at several levels.[84] Among them, there is consciousness:

---

82 J. L. Beauvois, 'Les interactionnismes' in G. Mugny & D. Oberlé, eds., *Relations humaines, groupes et influences sociales* (Grenoble: Presses universitaires de Grenoble, 1996) at 138.

83 J. P. Boutinet, *Psychologie des conduites à projet* (Paris: P.U.F., 1990).

84 C. Humbert, *Conscientisation. Expériences, positions dialectiques et perspectives* (Paris: L'Harmattan, 1976).

i) of self, one's situation, one's capacity to perform deeds, having the motivation to contemplate and realize changes;

ii) of belonging to a group, organizations, a collectivity which present similar and dissimilar characteristics and interests;

iii) of the collective aspects of a problematic or situation, which allows realization that other actors are going through experiences similar to one's own;

iv) of the possibility of holistic action and of the power inherent in grouping together as opposed to isolation;

v) of the political nature of decisions about resources, opportunities and the sharing of power;

vi) of the manner in which the preoccupations of one group are bound to those of other groups; and

vii) of the links among local situations or problems and more general (economic, political and cultural) and global ones (regional, national, international).

In this sense, consciousness-expanding represents a desire or a need to know oneself, to properly understand the times in which one is living, in order to best adapt to life. This is expressed by the development of intellectual faculties, the acquisition of knowledge, a sense of initiative and responsibility and, learning of openness to differences and tolerance, etc.

The organization process serves to determine, from all the elements and facets present, the common web that must emerge in order to undertake a holistic action.[85] The quality of leadership at the basis of any process of this nature may be found in certain virtues and attitudes. These must be adequately conveyed and inculcated in the actors in order that they may reach their full potential. Included in these, one finds the *habit of daily struggle*, which hardens one and permits one to face conflict and difficulty without undue preoccupation. In this context, the energy and the will developed can be surprising, and thus prevents behaviour characterized by fatalism or resignation. The application of this virtue may prove to be quite arduous, should the actors, for one reason or another, be made childish or profit from a status which is all too comfortable. Then, the *sense of the concrete or tangible*, by constantly seeking responses to needs, develops ingeniousness, the capacity to find solutions. This does not imply foregoing reflection for reflection's sake, no more than foregoing reflection in order to discover a minimal sense of existing. However, the virtue of the concrete is there to ensure that the distance between this reflection and experienced reality not be too great for too long a time. The *thirst for dignity*,[86] the requirement of respect for oneself and for one's own person, must be added to the preceding elements. Pride and honour, a taste for success, are powerful antidotes to withdrawal and self-sufficiency, which always include a risk of decline and discredit. Finally, the *capacity for hope* confirms the

---

85 E. Friedberg, *Le pouvoir et la règle. Dynamiques de l'action organisée* (Paris: Seuil, 1993).

86 M. A. Lutz, 'Centering Social Economics on Human Dignity' (1995) 2 Review of Social Economy 171.

range of these virtues and attitudes. Its natural function is to give rise to, and to provide, the mystery upon which the construction of an imaginable possibility or a concrete utopia may be realized.

The dynamic of a holistic action finally calls upon the process of mobilization.[87] In a progressive context, a mobilizing project corresponds to that which may be called a concrete alternative.[88] By its nature, a concrete alternative sees itself as a reaction as well as resistance to all-encompassing models and paradigms. This is in keeping with the willingness to leave room for, and bring to maturity, various initiatives deemed favourable to self-fulfilment and solidarity. In this perspective, an all-encompassing paradigm is never more than temporary; it must constantly justify itself to other emerging paradigms, which, should they eventually become all-encompassing, will also be required to submit to the test of justification. The concrete alternative thus always maintains an open vista of possible changes.

---

87 N. Cannat, *Le pouvoir des exclus* (Paris: L'Harmattan, 1990).
88 P. Mann, *L'action collective. Mobilisation et organisation des minorités actives* (Paris: Armand Cloin, 1991).

Chapter 7

The Context of Justification

Prelude

The transitory conception that I described proposes self-fulfilment and solidarity as keystones of progressive human destiny. The keystone applies to the individual as well as the global dimensions of human life. To begin with, it is characterized by the insistence placed on the individual and collective capacity to choose and to satisfy aspirations, as well as on a healthy coexistence. Beyond this, its tangible significance depends on its appropriation by various worlds and on the interaction which prevails between them. Its most immediate impact on uniform law is to relativize its legitimacy. Moreover, this is the first element mentioned in the sketch of the argument which incorporates this keystone in the progressive consciousness of uniform law. The argument based on self-fulfilment and solidarity requires finding the *raison d'être* of uniform law beyond simple formulas centred on international commerce, and it plays an influential role – that is to say it exercises a dominant influence – with respect to the relational, the common good and the world-based arguments.

At this stage of the reformulation phase, the argument must be thoroughly examined with regard to two aspects. The first concerns the teleological significance of the argument itself. Certainly, an analytical exercise of this type is demanding, especially in terms of time and talent. It is nonetheless unavoidable since the second modernity treats it as a strict requirement. I will tackle this first aspect through the question *why self-fulfilment and solidarity*? The second aspect seeks to better comprehend the argument from a strategic point of view. What are the norms that lead to self-fulfilment and solidarity? My responses are strongly dependent upon the ethic of development, more especially on the works of D. Goulet on the subject.[1] Among the reasons which may be invoked to explain this orientation, I would like to mention the following: the eclecticism of his theory, the interaction it establishes between the individual and the collective in the name of a more comprehensive and integrated vision, and its deployment of certain principles of thought and modern values, all of which constitute important traits of progressive consciousness defended up to now.

---

1   D. Goulet, *Development Ethics: A Guide to Theory and Practice* (New York: Apex Press, 1995).

Structure and Content

Why Self-fulfilment and Solidarity?

To affirm that the argument based on self-fulfilment and solidarity has a teleological significance implies that it obeys a mode of reasoning or interpretation modelled on the image of the spiral. This signifies that potentially, each step of a reasoning process may lead to an additional step. Each step cannot be intrinsically finite. And returning to steps already completed is also permitted. The idea behind teleological reasoning is not to compel thought to be plunged in the depths of total uncertainty. Rather, it is to maintain the context of justification – which amounts to self-fulfilment and solidarity – on constant alert and on the lookout for that which may be found over and above what is already known and justified. As it is, the first step in this direction consists of proposing that self-fulfilment and solidarity, blended into the more general notion of human development, are, 'at a deeper level, subordinated to the good life.'[2]

According to Goulet's theory, the good life constitutes, on the one hand, the most transcendent element of the development centred on self-fulfilment and solidarity. It is the one that benefits from the greatest diffusion on all levels and in all worlds, probably because it expresses and best translates the aspirations of one and all. On the other hand, the good life represents an inspiring and unifying element. It so describes itself by abandoning the modernist analysis of development founded on a quantitative economic comparison – which gives rise to judgements expressed in terms of success or failure – to favour an analysis which 'does not start with any predetermined model,'[3] and which relies strongly on 'a discussion of the ultimate ends.'[4] In a certain way, this approach, calling upon transcendence and the leading of the good life, resembles the first strategy utilized by the conservative consciousness of uniform law to escape the phenomenon of the antinomy of truth. One may recall that this strategy worked at a very high level of generalization, in order to be able to identify the principles common to the greatest possible number of interested parties, which seems also to be the case for the good life. However, that is where the similarity ends. First, from the perspective of conservative consciousness, once the general norm is established, it must remain intact. It is not re-situated in the context, for fear that it lose its lure and its power. On the contrary, in the perspective of the good life, generality and contextualization go together. In other words, the common dimension associated with the good life is intimately linked to a pluralistic dimension which results from its obligatory and inevitable belonging to some worlds. Secondly, the good life plays the primordial role of serving as interface between various worlds, whereas

---

2   *Ibid.* at 37.
3   United Nations Development Programme, *Human Development Report* 1992 (New York: Oxford University Press, 1992) at 2.
4   *Ibid.*

the strategy of conservative consciousness in question was comparable to a monologue.

But what is the good life? What are the principles of thought and the values forming the grounds of a profound feeling of the good life? Goulet identifies three axes tracing the essentials of a good life. First, he proposes that of self-sustenance, more amply supported by the proposition to the effect that 'The nature of life is treasured by sane men and women everywhere.'[5] It is a question here of all *life-sustaining goods*, both material and immaterial, which provide vitality, energy and vigour to the existence of a world; of all life-sustaining goods which may render a world *eminently liveable*. The next axis is that of esteem. It specifies the sense and the implications of the good life by pointing out the importance, for each world, of the favourable impression that other worlds have of its merit and its value. To be an object of respect, even of deference, would seem to be a decisive element of the capacity of each world to attain self-fulfilment, to lead a good life. To this esteem felt by others may be added self-esteem, that is to say a valid opinion that a world has of itself. Here, it is plausible to anticipate that a world suffering from an inferiority complex would be more remote from the good life than another in better harmony in this regard. Finally, the axis of liberty completes the list. In Goulet's words, freedom 'signifies an expanded range of choices for societies and their members, along with the reduction of constraints in the pursuit of some perceived good.'[6] This definition confirms the comments I had already made on the subject of self-fulfilment and solidarity. It is directly related to the progressive idea according to which worlds, as human sites, are built rather than merely discovered. However, an effective construction supposes that the capacity to make a choice exists, at least potentially.

These three axes demarcating the prospect of the good life are not perfectly symmetrical. They may lead to the elaboration of many hypotheses which are entirely plausible on a theoretical level. On a practical level, one must expect that they intersect and cause adjustment in each other, as soon as they are analysed in the light of a given world. The perspective that they create correspond more to a form of impressionism than to true expressionism. Goulet acknowledges this impressionistic perspective in the following passage:

> Although development's general goals are optimal life-sustenance, esteem, and freedom, no priority ranking among these goals can be established except as a function of some particular image of the worthy or the fulfilled human life. Even this formulation remains ambiguous since for many the exercise of freedom is itself taken to be the highest form of human actualization. The interplay among development's goals is dialectical: life-sustenance, esteem, and freedom interact in ever-shifting patterns of mutual reinforcement or conflictual tension. A high degree of freedom from wants and of self-esteem is compatible with a society having low life-sustenance or low out-group esteem, provided disruptive effects from outside are weak. If a materially poor society is sheltered from competing images of the good life, and if its wants

5   Goulet, *supra*, note 1; at 41.
6   *Ibid*. at 44.

remain few and simple, it can subsist with a high degree of social cohesion and member satisfaction. 'Remote' cultures are doubtless finding it ever more difficult to isolate themselves from modernity. Nevertheless, the basic options any society takes as to goals affect its central institutions: its form of government, educational system, and economic incentives.

Conversely, economic abundance and high prestige are compatible with low levels of genuine want-satisfaction, low self-esteem, and low freedom. A 'developed' society's wants may increase so rapidly as to be insatiable. The combination of expanding wants, industrial power, and technological modernity can bring prestige to such a society while leaving its members profoundly dissatisfied and insecure as to their identity.[7]

From reading this passage, must one conclude that the teleological consequences of the argument founded on self-fulfilment and solidarity is too complicated? Will one ever, in each analysis or decision relative to uniform law, succeed in making sense of it? Is it not tempting to backtrack toward an analysis more strictly juridico-economic and quantitative? I believe it is premature to wish to answer these questions, mainly because the mode of interpretation subjacent to this argument, as it does all of progressive consciousness, has not yet been seriously tested. In effect, up to now, uniform law has been dominated by a method of interpretation favouring fragmentation, the subject-object dichotomy, simplicity, isolation, invariance, rigidity, immobilism, competition, mechanism, exactness and discontinuity. All these essentially modernist characteristics may be found at the heart of justification by correspondence, typical of conservative consciousness and of modern science in general. Yet, as has been brought out by the critique, justification by correspondence has sterilized and impoverished the discourse proper to uniform law. Moreover, it has led it to rely too easily on the scientific virtues of economics. To speak of self-fulfilment and solidarity forces uniform law to venture onto territory that is slipperier than that of conservative consciousness. The adventure opens up to complexity, variability, flexibility, cooperation, openness, looseness, continuum and globalism. But this is in keeping with the logic of the type of justification favoured by the second modernity. Reduced to its simplest expression, this type of justification based on global coherence consists in searching for the best response in all circumstances. The second modernity wagers that uniform law – and the law – will, in this manner, find a new strength which 'lies in the capacity of broadly framed ideas to interact with pre-existing conditions, and in the process, to transform those conditions for the purposes of meeting, not transcending, the needs of people.'[8]

What are Strategic Principles?

According to Goulet, 'strategic principles are normative judgements as to how development goals ought to be pursued. They provide standards for devising

---

7   *Ibid.* at 49-50.
8   Chibundu, *supra*, Introduction, note 5; at 92.

solutions to specific problems and for appraising performance.'[9] The first of these principles concerns self-fulfilment. It seeks to clarify the opposition between the fact of claiming that the human being should *possess* in sufficient amounts to lead a good life, and the fact that the good life is not synonymous with abundant possessions. Goulet enunciates the principle in the phrase *to have enough in order to be more*. The second principle is directed at solidarity. In strategic terms and first of all, this principle would consist in repudiating a form of power and domination over others in favour of that which, in one way or another, tends toward universalism. I will examine each of these two principles in turn.

To understand the first principle, one must determine, first of all, 'why humans need to "have" goods at all.'[10] The response agrees with a conception of human life – already evoked in the transitory conception – which insists on its perfectible character. The individual, society, worlds, are or should be in constant search of new projects concomitant with or consecutive to current achievements. Human beings thus have needs because they are always perfectible in the sense that they can always improve, enrich themselves or acquire more profound maturity. If humans were already perfect, they would experience no needs, thus freeing themselves from the contingencies of reality; if they were totally imperfect, they would not have the possibility of feeling needs, and would thus remain excluded from any relations with others. It is because they are found between these two extremes that human beings need to have goods. But it is also because human beings occupy a middle place that their needs and they themselves are transformed. Through the satisfaction of physical and mental needs, human beings improve the quality of their existence. In turn, this improvement opens the way to new needs and to new human beings. This dynamic is not purely internal. It is lived through contact with others, who may influence its course, as well as vice versa. In sum, at any moment of her/his existence, a human being represents less than that which she/he could be. And that which she/he may become fairly depends on what she/he possesses. From these two premises, the basic equation of self-fulfilment may be formulated as follows: 'In order to become more, [a human being] must have enough.'[11] But just how far can one push the limits of this equation? Is there no limit to wanting to become more? When is enough, enough?

Goulet discusses this problematic of limits on the basis of the notion of superfluity, by asking himself in what circumstances the fact of having more or being more is legitimate or not. He recalls that within Christianity, two contradictory versions of superfluity prevail. The first version is fraught with immobilism. It postulates that the human being is confined to a single destiny, from which she/he cannot be released. There exist several of these destinies, called *stations in life*, and each one corresponds to a level of specific self-fulfilment. Here, the human being is completely indebted to others for what she/he possesses over and above the level of self-fulfilment specific to her/his destiny. The second

9   Goulet, *supra*, note 1; at 53.
10   *Ibid.*
11   *Ibid.* at 55.

version is more progressive. It admits that human beings may pass from one station in life to another. However, it only authorizes this passage insofar as the human being redistributes to others the fruits of her/his advancement. These versions of superfluity are not particularly stimulating on the self-fulfilment level. In both cases, they rely, more particularly, on a feeling of guilt in the person who wants to become more in order to cause her/him to retire or to give everything to others. In this regard, Goulet feels that it is the feeling of responsibility that one has to graft to superfluity that ensures that the latter remains constructive. He contrasts it with feelings of guilt in this manner:

> Responsibility looks to the present and the future, and it presupposes freedom – that is, the possibility of responding to an exigency that is perceived and accepted. Responsibility is founded on the belief that human agents are not always subject to absolute determinism, but rather that they can respond to the solicitation of goals perceived by them as humanly worthy. Precisely because we are human, we are 'responsible' for creating conditions that optimize the humanization of life. Guilt, on the contrary, is the negative burden of past fault or injustice. Guilt is something passive and recriminating, not active and creative. [12]

By associating superfluity with the feeling of responsibility, I submit that the strategic principle relative to self-fulfilment obeys a dialectic based on the surpassing of oneself and relationalism. In one regard, the principle does not prevent a human being from attaining the most of which she/he is capable, of developing her/himself to the utmost. In another regard, this surpassing of oneself is conditioned by the fact that a human being must be generous toward others with all that she/he possesses, that is to say of her/his person, time, feelings and so on. This condition of generosity allows for connecting with the second strategic principle: solidarity. To be generous is to take into account others, to be selfless for them, expressing, one could say, a form of solidarity toward them. But, does solidarity mean more? If yes, what are the parameters from which it may spread? As previously indicated, Goulet relies here on a repudiation of norms and attitudes which are similar to domination and on an invocation of universalism. However, his remarks remain vague and they are far from conferring a truly strategic impact on the principle. They do not appear truly innovative – 'All persons are one by their humanity' [13] – and they act as indications of good intentions. And especially, they do not add anything of significance to the propositions I formulated in connection with the transitory conception and the outline of the argument founded on self-fulfilment and solidarity. These propositions have brought to light an approach relying upon the approval of certain values – equity, reciprocity, liberty – and on cooperation resulting from overlapping consensus of various visions of the world and of development followed more or less here and there. In spite of the lacunae in Goulet's theory, is it possible to extend these propositions by endowing

---

12   *Ibid.* at 57.
13   *Ibid.* at 63.

them with a certain pragmatic tone, as I announced in the preliminary observations to this part?

Few potential solutions exist. This scarcity is a sign that the second modernity is a work in progress, rather than a work completed. And that is particularly true in relation to the pragmatic aspect of this process, that is to say that which, starting as a reflection, results in an action. Reflection, it goes without saying, represents a step whose importance is incontrovertible and which strongly interacts with an action. However, it does not include action, any more that it may be merged with it. Reflection is possibly, at the limit, a form of action. But, by definition, the action corresponds to the materialization of reflection. Often, action can prove to be more difficult than reflection because it is confronted by an already established reality that it must change. This is the case as regards the second modernity: many ideas are present, but their implementation comes up against the *system in place*. At any event, for the present, C. Ruby is one of those who best translates the practical requirements engendered by solidarity.[14] The materialization to which he refers rests primarily on the idea of a force:

[S]olidarity goes to the root of the signification of oppositions and of social injustices, of social and political disputes actually existing, in order to raise these differences to the strongest intensity for the present. It is then that they produce a particular force, which is measured in light of the experimental commitments that they inspire.[15]

Then, to this force is linked the notion of a double power of solidarity, described as follows:

– Endlessly solicit singular or collective rural, local (in the space of relations: home, district, commune, region) and global (in their purposes) experiments; in brief, initiatives forming an archipelago – propositions of multipolar relations constantly in tension, refusing to consider that each one represents a singularity, the history of which may result in a term, while simultaneously not having to adapt to displays of social violence.
– Require, concurrently, debate within societies, dealing with the composition of these archipelagos, without limiting the field covered, more particularly without neglecting the differences, the lacunae between archipelagos; whether it is a question of identifying antagonisms, the achievements to be managed, the relationships of confrontation to be established, the choice of orientations of the action, the preventive measures to be taken, solidarity seeks to arouse public discussions, each giving rise, over and above its own specific nature, to practical schemes from which a living political horizon manifests itself.[16]

Over the short, medium and long term, the strength and power of solidarity will be indispensable to the *untying of knots* which, as R. Petrella says,[17] impede

---

14   C. Ruby, *La solidarité* (Paris: Éllipses, 1997).
15   *Ibid*. at 100.
16   *Ibid*. at 101.
17   *Supra*, Chapter 5, note 5; at 79.

the attainment of a progressive *modus vivendi,* and of which the transitory conception offers an outline.

Final Remarks

Part III of this reflection has had as its objective completing a process modelled on Koskenniemi's triptych, by proceeding to a *reformulation* of uniform law. Overall, it was intended to allow for setting out the major axes of a progressive consciousness of uniform law. On the basis of the regressive analysis effected in Part I, which revealed a conservative consciousness of uniform law, and the critique of this consciousness on a progressive foundation effected in Part II, I identified and developed the most promising arguments for the future of progressive uniform law. The relational argument is one of these promising arguments. It concerns the juridical relationship presented under the term contract. Closely linked to the idea of cooperation, the relational argument is deployed from focuses including linkage, project and osmosis. Within the same genus is found the argument of the common good. The latter renders pertinent, within progressive consciousness, various considerations which go beyond the bare advantages and interests of the parties involved in a contract. For purposes of the reformulation, I limited, but only formally, the common good argument to the question of the environment. These two arguments, combined with the 'world-based' argument – which has been examined in depth through a mode of interpretation founded on holistic action – form the context of discovery of progressive consciousness. Just as for conservative consciousness, a context of justification controls the context of discovery, but with the difference that here, it is based on self-fulfilment and solidarity.

The three first steps covered up to now might be assimilated to a long process of observation on what uniform law should be. It is now time for action and for deducing from progressive consciousness certain practical applications. That is what I will attempt in the fourth and last part of this book.

PART IV

APPLICATIONS

Preliminary Remarks

Part IV seeks to examine two applications emerging from progressive consciousness, namely an interpretive schema of uniform law and a uniformist reading of the Quebec world. This analysis requires that one first return to the notion of ideal type.

In the Introduction, I explained that the pursuit of the objectives of this reflection was bound to a methodology combining the three following processes: the utilization of Koskenniemi's triptych, subject to certain adjustments; a distinction between the context of discovery and the context of justification of the consciousness of uniform law; and an assimilation of this same consciousness to an ideal type. At this stage, the first and second processes are no longer formally necessary. They have facilitated attaining the objective consisting of proposing and justifying the elements which constitute a progressive consciousness in uniform law. The aim is now to optimize the repercussions of such a consciousness. This relates to the third process, derived from the works of M. Weber. A portion of this process has already been undertaken in the previous parts of this work. It has thus facilitated the grouping and stylization of the salient elements of the conservative and progressive consciousnesses of uniform law. Obviously, the image resulting therefrom cannot be absolute. Several versions of these consciousnesses, both as to form and as to substance, are plausible. And as is the case in any intellectual development, the one which I propose will be judged according to its persuasiveness. The process based on the ideal type has also fulfilled its proper function of comparing and measuring. From the elements specific to conservative consciousness, I have been able, first, to establish a correlation between the latter and modernity and modern law; secondly, to analyse to what extent there was a distance separating this mass of ideas from the second modernity; and, thirdly, to set out the arguments relating to progressive consciousness.

The present part brings into play an as yet unutilized portion of the third process. This portion devolves from the perspective according to which the ideal type constitutes an instrument of applied research. In this perspective, and as has already been pointed out in the Introduction, the ideal type is here called upon to act as a catalyst upon progressive consciousness. Its content is supposed to present sufficient attractiveness and luminosity to engender fruitful applications, no matter what are their nature and their appearance. In other words, the ideal type is a means of general application. Doctrinal analyses rarely, if ever, tackle this perspective of the ideal type centred on its productivity. Most often, they place the ideal type within a fairly restrictive methodological framework. The ideal type is thus connected to precise utilitarian functions, set out in advance and contributing to the harmony of Weber's thought. As an illustration, writers will present the ideal type as a component of Weber's concern to realize rigorous definitions of his concepts and numerous distinctions to better confront the problematics in which he was interested. Again writers will elaborate a description of the ideal type based on its contribution to the understanding of, according to Weber, an incommensurate, changing reality which, as a result, is beyond human comprehension.[1] In this case, the fruitful ideal type, without renouncing its other attributes of a methodological nature, determines its *raison d'être* in one of Weber's personality traits which has been strongly underlined by J. Freund. Recalling Weber's firm intention not to inspire unanimity, his wish to be vigorously contested and raise controversy, Freund declares that 'Weber remains an inspiring actor, he was never nor did he ever want to be a dominating or authoritative teacher.'[2] It is in this notion of inspiration that the ideal type finds a natural extension going beyond the mere internal methodological contribution to Weber's theory, which is presented in terms of fecundity, of a capacity to develop applications.[3]

One of these applications could have involved civil society, which forms a major theme of the second modernity.[4] It has been invoked within the metaphor of consensus, and it is present in many other aspects of the progressive consciousness of uniform law. Traditionally, civil society has been associated with a host of activities (sporting, social, community, literary etc.) and institutions (schools, churches, associations, etc.) connected to the life of a citizen. This network, within the context of liberal societies, occupies a middle road between the sphere of the State and the sphere of the marketplace. One of the more virulent criticisms levelled against modernity is to have grossly reduced the scale of civil society and thus its faculty of ensuring mediation between the State and the market-place.[5] The modern citizen must solely define her/himself in light of what the State and the market-place accomplish for her/him. She/he is torn between these two poles. She/he no longer disposes of a reserved space where she/he could assert her/himself according to her/his own wishes, that is to say, in terms of what she/he can derive from the State and the marketplace, added to what she/he is in her/his own right. To what extent does the conservative consciousness of uniform law, as a specific *corpus* of norms and principles, work toward this dilution of civil society? And to what extent can progressive consciousness revive it? These are two questions of primary importance that the ideal type process could have attempted to resolve. Without any doubt, uniform law is very present within the State sphere. It resides there quite comfortably. In effect, no matter what one says of the State today, it plays a preponderant role in the production of uniform law. This does not imply that uniform law might not also be readily found within the sphere of the marketplace. The exhortations for allowing uniform law to evolve according to the

---

1   See the comments of J. Freund in *Sociologie de Max Weber* (Paris: P.U.F., 1968) at 1ff.
2   *Ibid.* at 28.
3   This dimension is more evident in P. Bouretz's analysis, *Les promesses du monde: la philosophie de Max Weber* (Paris: Gallimard, 1996).
4   R. A. Macdonald, 'Metaphors of Multiplicity: Civil Society, Regimes and Legal Pluralism' (1998) 15 Ariz. J. Int'l & Comp. Law 69.
5   Barber, *supra*, Chapter 4, note 53; at 276ff.

likings of commercial activity and the will of dealers in international commerce are ample proof of this. In the midst of this double allegiance, few things emerge from the relationship between uniform law and civil society. It is this silence that one would have to shed light upon, in order to better ensure the general transition of contemporary society toward the second modernity.[6] Other applications of this nature merit as much attention.[7] However, I felt that it was more important to deal with the two applications mentioned at the beginning of this part, which are essential to the second major goal of this reflection.

The first application – the interpretive schema of uniform law – refers to a dominant theme of uniform law, namely its interpretation. Legal scholarship affords a preeminence to this theme insofar as it perceives in it the presence of the sword of Damocles of uniform law. Interpretation somewhat underscores the incessant peril which dogs uniform law and which, if not controlled, threatens to undermine it at any moment. Fears raised by interpretation may be found in an article entitled 'International Uniform Law in Practice – Or Where the Real Trouble Begins',[8] in which M. J. Bonell encourages those interested to consider with alacrity and attentiveness this theme fundamental to the future of uniform law. Bonell has also subsequently had occasion to tie this problem to a reflection of an existential nature articulated around the following question: 'Uniform Law: A Bridge Too Far?'[9] In brief there is a consensus on the importance of interpretation within the framework of uniform law, a consensus thus summarized by V. G. Curran: 'Uniformity of application through uniformity of interpretation has become something of a sacred mission.'[10] Analysis of conservative consciousness has provided some indications which could be considered as relating directly or indirectly to interpretation. Among these indications, one finds the notion of non-contradiction – which confers the status of a general principle of interpretation on good faith – and dualism – which seeks to avoid contamination of internationalist thought by national laws – which characterizes the argument of good faith. One may also find the principle of determinism – concerned with maintaining constancy and persistence within uniform law – connected to the argument of juridical convergence. However, these indications, and others, must be read in light of the critique and reformulation which have culminated in the elaboration of the progressive consciousness of uniform law. Likewise, this consciousness, by its very nature and content, sets out certain parameters that one must take into account concerning one theme, interpretation, the importance of which does not lose significance in the context of the second modernity. Consequently, I will develop an application relating to interpretation in Chapter 8.

---

6   D. Leydet, 'Mondialisation et démocratie: la notion de société civile globale' in *Mondialisation des échanges et fonctions de l'État*, F. Crépeau, ed. (Brussels: Bruylant, 1997) at 258.

7   See the Conclusion, below.

8   Published at (1990) 38 A.J.C.L. 865.

9   Published at (1995) 3 Tul. J. Int'l & Comp. L. 145.

10   'The Interpretative Challenge to Uniformity by Claude Witz' (1995) 15 J. L. & Com. 175 at 175.

The second application – a uniformist reading of the Quebec world – aims at demonstrating the world-based argument *in action*. It is justified on two levels. First, it allows one to give a particular colouration to the world-based argument. I have explained, in the critique and reformulation, how this argument was constituted and toward what its orientations lead. But despite these explanations, and even if it clearly falls within the foundations set out by the emerging route of law and development, the argument remains unrefined. It lacks polish and it fails to convey in terms of significance all that it may entail. Yet an exercise of this nature should, to some extent, enable one to verify and attest to the reliability of the argument. In such a case, it would only reinforce the theoretical underpinnings of the world-based argument and increase its practical usefulness. Secondly, to provide a demonstration of the world-based argument *in action* allows the establishment of a link with comparative law, which is closely related to uniform law. This close relationship implies that the present upheavals in comparative law are not without consequence nor interest with regard to uniform law in the broader sense, and vice versa. On the contrary, it can facilitate their mutual adaptation and evolution. This intimate connection was once again recently revealed by G. Teubner, in a study dealing with the *irritating* official reception of good faith in English law.[11] At the end of his analysis, Teubner declares:

> Attempts at institutional transfer seem to produce a double irritation in the new context. They irritate law's binding arrangements to society. Foreign rules are irritants not only in relation to the domestic legal discourse itself, but also in relation to the social discourse to which law is, under certain circumstances, closely coupled. As legal irritants, they force the specific epistéme of domestic law to a reconstruction in the network of its distinctions. As social irritants they provoke the social discourse to which law is closely tied to a reconstruction of its own. Thus, they trigger two different series of events whose interaction leads to an evolutionary dynamics which may find a new equilibrium in the eigen values of the discourse involved. The result of such a complex and turbulent process is rarely a convergence of the participating legal orders, but rather the creation of new cleavages in the interrelation of operationally closed social discourses.[12]

Considering what precedes, a uniformist reading of the Quebec world, although it formally comes within the province of uniform law, also corresponds to a form of comparative law. On this basis, it is in a position to be able to contribute to the advancement of this latter domain, from which uniform law has so extensively profited. I will effect this demonstration in Chapter 9.

---

11   G. Teubner, 'Legal Irritants: Good Faith in British Law or How Unifying Law Ends Up in New Divergences', (1988) 61 Modern Law Review 11.

12   *Ibid.* at 31-32.

Chapter 8

An Interpretive Schema of Uniform Law

Someone has to take a decision on a subject to which uniform law is pertinent. How does one proceed? This is the interrogation to which the interpretive schema must respond. By decision, I understand all forms of mental process in which a choice is made, a deed is accomplished, a particular orientation is favoured or a need is fulfilled. In brief, a decision marks the end of a certain deliberation. The decision of an arbitrator, the opinion of a legal professional, the project advanced by a non-governmental body, as well as the simple desire to know something, are all illustrations of a decision. The interpretive schema which I propose can be broken down into three stages. The first involves *taking cognizance* of uniform law. It seeks to determine how it is possible for anyone to embrace uniform law, to make it one's own. Once uniform law is known, the interpretive schema entails a second step devoted to *reasoning*. This step has as its goal the determination of the manner in which the party that must decide deals with, absorbs and transforms the information collected during the execution of the preceding step. In a third and final step, the decider evaluates the validity of her/his tentative decision in relation to what uniform law could have decided up to that point. This is the *situation* stage. As proposed, the interpretive schema resembles an ordered succession of steps. These would indicate a sequence which proceeds from a beginning 'x' to an end 'y'. However, one must admit that in reality, these steps overlap and influence each other.

As I indicated in my preliminary observations, the theme of interpretation is of great concern to those who have contributed to legal scholarship. This concern is most evident in connection with the Vienna Convention. There, the efforts made to properly master this crucial issue of interpretation have been significant and indeed in some cases of very great scope.[1] A form of authority devolves from them which justifies that they be integrated, to some extent, in the presentation of the interpretive schema. Such an integration may also be profitable from a heuristic point of view. In effect, it will situate the interpretive schema within the perspective of that which has already been done, thus facilitating comprehension of its trends. I could, at the same time, follow through on my statement advanced with

---

1   See, for example, A. H. Kritzer, *Guide to Practical Applications of the United Nations Convention on Contracts for the International Sale of Goods* (Deventer: Kluwer, 1989).

regard to the context of justification of the values of conservative consciousness, according to which the doctrinal representation of the international commercial case law does not conform to an ideal speech situation.[2] In light of what precedes, I feel it is preferable to present the interpretive schema as follows. For each step mentioned above, I will describe the operation that it implies – the taking cognizance step, the reasoning process or the situation – in light of its closest equivalent in legal scholarship. Next, I will qualify and critique this equivalent. This will, finally, permit me to put forward a proposition that is as faithful as possible to the progressive consciousness of uniform law.

The Taking Cognizance Step

How may one gain knowledge of uniform law? More specifically, how may one become permeated and imbued with progressive consciousness? At one level, progressive consciousness has established arguments which present a certain content. For example, the rational argument does not mean just anything. It points in various precise directions, represented by the concepts of linkage, project and osmosis. These concepts are clarified by diverse considerations – which I have assembled in a prelude – and they are rooted in the notion of cooperation. At a second level, progressive consciousness is provided with the means which act on the content of the arguments. The metaphors of the multiple, the consensus, the flexible and the relative are particularly active at this level. Other levels of progressive consciousness susceptible of having an impact on the content of arguments, such as the phenomenon of sedimentation, could also be identified. All of this creates a vast sphere of information which does not directly come to mind. Whoever seeks to gain knowledge is thus obliged to do something.

The text which I will be using to describe the taking cognizance step is that of P. Koneru, entitled 'The International Interpretation of the UN Convention on Contracts for the International Sale of Goods: An Approach Based on General Principles.'[3] Koneru initiates his analysis by affirming, 'The integrity of the Convention and its role as an international body of law to be respected and widely followed depends on how its various provisions are interpreted by the judiciary in a given country.'[4] He continues by underlining that Article 7 'is arguably the single most important provision in ensuring the future success of the Convention.'[5] More specifically, he is of the opinion that the surest way of connecting with the Vienna Convention and of respecting the provisions of Article 7 depends upon a knowledge of its general principles. Let us see in more details what he proposes.

---

2   See Chapter 2, 'The Context of Justification', above.
3   (1997) 6 Minn. J. Global Trade 105.
4   *Ibid.* at 106.
5   *Ibid.*

Description of the Process

In the first part of his text, Koneru tackles the international dimension which must clothe the interpretation of the Vienna Convention. He states, 'Many scholars agree that an international interpretation cannot be based on any legal domestic concepts. There has been less than clear guidance, however, on how to achieve the international interpretation.'[6] Obviously, the decider can consult various sources, but this does not automatically confer an international character on her/his decision. According to Koneru, the solution resides in referring to the general principles of the Vienna Convention.

> Because the general principles represent the 'common ground' on which the international delegates understand each other and agreed to join together in formulating the Convention, interpretations based on general principles are least likely to be labelled as domestic or parochial and are most likely to represent the spirit of international cooperation and understanding behind the Convention.[7]

Recourse to general principles is superior to all other approaches because it allows for filling the unavoidable gaps in the text of the Vienna Convention. This is the case, in particular, regarding good faith. Also, in order to become acquainted with the fundamental objectives of the Vienna Convention, it proves to be more dependable and evocative than the legislative history, too often unsatisfying. This is why 'it becomes imperative that the judiciary has a thorough understanding of the general principles of the Convention.'[8]

What are these general principles? This is the central question of the second part of Koneru's text. From the outset, the writer affirms that the Vienna Convention does not contain any list enunciating these principles. However, 'it is possible to discern a number of those principles from the text of the Convention and from its legislative history.'[9] Before undertaking this operation of discernment, Koneru specifies, 'In identifying those general principles, it should be kept in mind that the Convention's overall objective is to promote international trade by removing legal barriers that arise from different social, economic and legal systems of the world.'[10] Then he enumerates a series of general principles. Each one is enunciated quite briefly and is connected to one or several provisions of the Vienna Convention. The first paragraph of this enumeration, which faithfully reflects this manner of proceeding, reads as follows:

> An important general principle that has been explicitly stated in the Convention itself is the Parties' freedom of contract. 'Virtually all the provisions . . . yield to the contract made by the seller and buyer; in short, the heart of the Sales Convention is the contract

---

6   *Ibid.* at 108.
7   *Ibid.* at 115.
8   *Ibid.*
9   *Ibid.* at 116.
10   *Ibid.*

of sale'. The general principle of timely communication among the parties whenever that communication is important for the affected party is pervasive among the many provisions of the Convention. For example, Article 18(1) states that silence is not communication of an acceptance. Article 26 provides that a party cannot avoid the contract unless a declaration of avoidance of contract is communicated to the other party. A buyer's right to demand that the product conform to the contract is lost under Article 39 if the buyer does not notify the seller in a reasonable time. Article 72(2) requires a party to give reasonable notice if it wants to declare the contract avoided. The Convention requires these important messages to be communicated promptly so that the affected party can take the necessary measures to protect its interests. Not only must the communication be timely, but also it must disclose relevant information to avoid any surprises.[11]

Other principles, 'evident from the text of the Convention,'[12] complete the enumeration. This causes Koneru to ask, with regard to less obvious cases, if 'one should exercise restraint in extracting the general principles.'[13] Here, his proposition consists in saying that all matters not expressly excluded from the scope of application of the Vienna Convention, and which may be resolved by applying its general principles, must so be resolved. By way of illustration, he refers to the payment of prejudgement interest. This is a matter covered by the Vienna Convention, but concerning which no method is foreseen for determining the rate of interest. What should one do in the face of this void? After a cursory examination of the few provisions deemed pertinent, Koneru concludes as follows:

> If the mandate of Article 7(2) is followed, it also becomes apparent that the various formulations of calculating the interest rate may be unnecessary. By focussing on the full-compensation objective of the Convention, the inquiry should be which interest rate will fully compensate the aggrieved party.[14]

On the basis of this general principle, he then analyses several decisions. He concludes by tackling, in succession, the point of accrual for interests, the currency for payment and the place of payment, always according to the same general principle.

In the third and fourth parts of his analysis, Koneru explains how an approach based on general principles enables enlarging the juridical scope of good faith and reducing the extent of the exclusion of questions concerning the validity of the contract of sale from the range of application of the Vienna Convention,. In so doing, that is to say, 'by extracting general principles from the Convention,'[15] it becomes more autonomous and independent of national precedents. As a corollary, it becomes more international. And that sets the Vienna Convention in conformity with the major objective that '[t]he international delegates to the Vienna

---

11   *Ibid.* at 117-118.
12   *Ibid.* at 120.
13   *Ibid.* at 121.
14   *Ibid.* at 126.
15   *Ibid.* at 152.

Convention negotiated and compromised to the best of their abilities . . . to bring uniformity and certainty to the international trade regime.'[16]

Qualifications and Critique

I submit that the taking cognizance step of uniform law as suggested by Koneru is *passive*. The role reserved for the decider is modest. The decider may presume that the law is there present, that is to say may be found in the Vienna Convention. It suffices that the decider draw uniform law to her/him. More specifically, her/his work consists in discovering what are called the general principles and what they state. On occasion, this exercise will be relatively simple. From a simple reading, or a simple observation, the decider will be able to identify one or more general principles. In other circumstances, the exercise will be more demanding, but none the less available. This will be the case when the text of the Vienna Convention will not clearly provide a statement which resembles a general principle. In this case, the decider will glean a general principle which exists in a latent state. It matters little how the exercise is realized, a general principle will be applicable in many different situations. The involvement of the decider in the taking cognizance step of uniform law is thus minimal. In addition to being passive, this taking cognizance step is *directive or interventionist*. It directs the decider where to look and where not to look. However, the sources to which one may refer are not very extensive nor varied. One has the text of the Vienna Convention and its legislative history. But after that, the sources dry up. Likewise the taking cognizance step indicates certain points of interest for the decider, such as the promotion of international trade and that which the framers of the Vienna Convention had in mind in the course of their work. These points of interest delimit the parameters of the taking cognizance step of uniform law. They indicate to the decider just how far to go if she/he wishes to gain knowledge of uniform law. They are, in addition, already well known and are indeed apparent in the officially recognized sources of uniform law.

This passive and directive step is basically structurally deficient. It disregards all that the decider naturally projects of her/himself, on the elements upon which she/he enquires here and there. In other words, it is unaware that the enquiry of the decider is based on experience. The taking cognizance step is not limited to an assimilation of information coming from the outside world. In order for there to be knowledge of uniform law, the decider must press on and put her/himself in a position of being able to test and feel uniform law in a sensitive way. Consequently, it is not possible to believe that the decider has only to gather uniform law as it exists in a well determined place. To begin with, uniform law cannot impose itself upon her/him. Rather it behoves the decider to give it life both initially and progressively. Seen from another perspective, one could say that uniform law *can make any sense* only after the involvement of the decider. This relationship, which raises the decider above uniform law, is highlighted in a series

---

16   *Ibid.* at 151-152.

of interpretive approaches. Based on the notion of text, they share a common element in that they insist upon the indispensable role played by the reader in her/his enquiry as to a reality.[17] The act of reading is assimilated to a process by which the reader constructs, puts in concrete form, materializes or actualizes the text. After each reading, one conclusion is inevitable: the reader has grasped the text in light of what she/he is. For these approaches, the meaning of a text is thus not beyond the consciousness of the reader. The meaning of a text is determined by the reader. For S. Fish, this is explained by the nature of the text itself, which he presents as a 'structure of meanings that is obvious and inescapable from the perspective of whatever interpretative assumptions happen to be in force.'[18]

Despite what precedes, in insisting on passivity and taking a directive tone, the taking cognizance step envisioned by Koneru deludes the decider by allowing her/him to believe that the law can be localized or that it ends somewhere. In the case in point, uniform law may not only be found in the provisions of the Vienna Convention, just as it may not only be found in its general principles. It may be found within what everyone, individual or group, is capable of doing with it. Indeed, all things considered, this logic of confinement or determination should lead one to the following result: uniform law may be found in the legislative history and in the commentaries which accompany it. In effect, that is where information is most useful and complete. That is where the decider may learn the most. Yet this viewpoint is not seriously considered. In the opinion of Koneru, it is the general principles which must retain the attention of the decider. However, the underlying enquiry forces the decider to rely upon a circular process which is not necessarily enlightening. As is evident from the quotation from Koneru above, most often the enunciation of a general principle simply means, in other words, that which one may glean from the Vienna Convention. The equation confronting the decider is as follows: the general principle which states 'p' falls under article '1'; article '1' also states 'p', but in utilizing 'q'. Is she/he really any farther ahead? Certainly, the general principles solution is tempting. It evokes a vast scope of inquiry placed at the disposal of the decider. But to optimize repercussions of this scope, the nature of the taking cognizance step must be modified.

Proposition

In order to take cognizance of uniform law, the decider must play an active role. She/he must proceed from a position of dominated to dominator relative to uniform law. In priority, it is thus incumbent upon the decider to construct or mould uniform law. Straight away, one must depend upon the decider to carry out this task with originality. In my view, this active role presupposes almost total liberty as to which elements the decider may consult in order to have some notion of

---

17   See the synthesis provided by G. Moore, 'The Interpretive Turn in Modern Theory: A Turn for the Worse?' (1989) 41 Stan. L. Rev. 871.

18   S. Fish, *Is There a Text in this Class?: The Authority of Interpretive Communities* (Cambridge: Harvard University Press, 1980) at vii.

uniform law. There are no limits – natural, logical, or other– to her/his range of consultation and inspiration. This very broad room for manoeuvre is not equivalent to unbridled eclecticism. It is not a plea for confusing *laissez-faire*. In effect, an active taking cognizance step is an invitation addressed to the decider to pull her/his weight in order to always contemplate uniform law under a better light. In so doing, the taking cognizance step recovers a value to which the conservative is strongly attached, that of liberty. We have seen to what point conservative consciousness associated this value with innovation, creation, imagination, in a word, with new development. The idea of an active role devolving upon the decider also depends on these attributes. It supposes that it is normal and desirable that at this stage, the decider may view things in her/his own way.

In providing the decider with the freedom to enquire as to uniform law in her/his own manner, there is a greater likelihood that she/he will encounter the arguments which constitute the progressive consciousness of uniform law. At present, these arguments are pushed to the background by a still preponderant conservative consciousness. The decider has no access to their content. And this inaccessibility will continue as long as, from the dichotomous point of view, the decider is limited in her/his perception of reality. In effect, as long as the decider is prevented from referring to her/his personal experience, to the milieu from which she/he comes, and from looking at whatever she/he wants to in order to learn something, only fortune will permit her/him to come into contact with progressive consciousness. This can be explained by the very nature of the second modernity, which cannot be grasped, understood and modified outside the *interactions* of which it is a part. The second modernity is not made of cuts and reductions. It is composed of junctions and prolongations. And in order to multiply these junctions and prolongations, it sees in inquisitiveness an essential element of the taking cognizance step. Indeed, the inquiring decider will be the one who will not neglect any occasion to be interested in a progressive consciousness essential to the advancement of uniform law. How is this liberty of enquiry exercised? The model I have in mind, personified by a fictitious person named Mark Anthony, resembles this.

The basic foundation of Mark Anthony's enquiry is *representation*. Mark Anthony is born different and he moulds this difference throughout his life. This uniqueness leads him to interact with reality and react to it through the prism of his personality. In fact, he organizes and interprets reality in his own fashion, in order to gain direction and adapt to it. He constructs or invents reality more than he discovers it. These constructions or inventions are illustrations of representations. A representation is formed from mental tools, such as opinions, which gather and transform information. A representation results from a reconstitution of a reality before which Mark Anthony is placed, and to which he attaches a specific signification. Wishing, or called upon, to take cognizance of uniform law, Mark Anthony will realize few or many reconstitutions which will stimulate his emotions, his beliefs and values, and his behaviour.

More specifically, the reconstitutions correspond to phases during which Mark Anthony processes the information. He has read certain doctrinal writings on uniform law, has consulted the Internet site of the CNUDCI and referred to the work of R. David.[19] A moderate environmentalist, he wishes to know if uniform law has any objection with regard to a project involving the exportation of bottled soft water which would significantly reduce the ground water in his part of the world. He has not come across the words environment or nature in the literature dealing with uniform law. This silence has touched him, which is absolutely normal. An emotion manifests itself when a situation arises that contrasts, either positively or negatively, with the expectations of the decider. The manifestation of this emotion will be stronger or weaker according to the gap perceived by the decider between what is and what should be. Here, Mark Anthony does not understand. Uniform law is promoted by major international organizations such as the United Nations. He knows very well that the UN often has the environment on its agenda, or at the very least, the quality of life in general. That is why he decides to learn more about the relationship between commerce and the environment. He agrees that nature must be of some use, but he refuses to believe that uniform law can support the exportation project. His refusal rests upon values to which he adheres. In his mind, values are associated with the most durable elements. His values impel him to take a course on the management of environmental hazards. He thus participates in discussions and simulations. He realizes that commerce and the environment can be reconciled. He now has a preliminary response to his initial query. He knows that by going deeper into this answer, he could eventually formulate specific proposals to those who are responsible for the project and that his proposals could bear the seal of uniform law. He knows in advance that in order for them to be accepted, his attitude will be a determining factor. In effect, his proposals will probably go somewhat against the mainstream, especially in relation to commercial practices. He must thus enhance them as much as possible. Presented as an equation, Mark Anthony's progress may be summarized as follows: for Mark Anthony, article '1' means 'p'; but in adding 'q' to 'p', plus 'r' to (p + q), article '1' can now convey 's'.

The Reasoning Process

Let us take for granted that the applicable uniform law required in order to make a decision is now known. This knowledge remains quite useless if it is not accompanied by a grouping together of its diverse fragments. Indeed, isolated from each other, these fragments remain relatively inert. It is the task of reasoning to animate them. Already, the distinction between the context of discovery and the context of justification of progressive consciousness has shed some light on what reasoning consists of. It proceeds by distinguishing important fragments of knowledge from decisive fragments. Moreover, progressive consciousness, as presented, provides for an interrelationship between the arguments which it

---

19 See, for example, David, *supra*, Chapter 1, note 32; also, *Les avatars d'un comparatiste* (Paris: Économica, 1982).

contains. Thus, one may deduce that the project advanced by the parties is susceptible of being influenced by the concerns for the environment that are so characteristic of the common good argument. There again, one finds an illustration of what constitutes the reasoning prior to a decision. The goal here is to further the comprehension of this stage of the interpretive schema.

The description of the operation underlying the reasoning step will be carried out according to the texts of A. Boggiano and M. P. Van Alstine, entitled respectively, 'The Experience of Latin American International Sales Law'[20] and 'Consensus, Dissensus and Contractual Obligation Through the Prism of Uniform International Sales Law'.[21] In his text, Boggiano analyses the problematic of uniform interpretation of several international conventions relating to commercial matters. His analysis is both general and specific: it discusses the stakes involved as broadly as possible, while seeking to particularize them on the basis of Latin American states. Very receptive to various projects aimed at uniformization, Boggiano states, 'Nevertheless, uniformity should be balanced against the modern requirements of flexibility.'[22] For him, it would be legitimate to favour flexibility 'so as to achieve the results which the convention intended or may reasonably be presumed to have intended.'[23] In this manner, one would lean toward what he calls *an equitable uniform law*. In conformity with these introductory remarks, he then sets out a manner of reasoning peculiar to the Vienna Convention. Van Alstine's text presents a certain interest insofar as he expounds a form of *reasoning* specific to the problematics of so called partial dissensus.

Description of Process

The reasoning proposed by Boggiano is called *principled uniform law*. It rests upon four components entitled flexible uniform law, interpretation, open texture of language and general principles on which the Vienna Convention is based. The first essentially summarizes the contents of the Introduction. It refers to 'a degree of discretion'[24] which the interpreter of the Convention would have at her/his disposal. This degree of discretion would be obvious in view of the open texture of many rules provided for by the Vienna Convention. In Boggiano's mind, there is more here than a simple technical characteristic. The degree of discretion assumes a fundamental dimension insofar as it makes the Vienna Convention 'a flexible developing international instrument for doing justice.'[25] The second component – interpretation – concerns the determination of the sense of the rules enunciated in the Vienna Convention. It is evident that this determination must be made while respecting the provisions mentioned at article 7. Moreover, the meaning of these

---

20   Published in *International Uniform Law in Practice* (Rome: UNIDROIT, 1988) at 28.
21   Van Alstine, *supra*, Chapter 2, note 2.
22   Boggiano, *supra*, note 20; at 33.
23   *Ibid.* at 34.
24   *Ibid.*
25   *Ibid.*

rules is likewise connected to the content of the preparatory works as well as to the broader objectives pursued by the Vienna Convention. They are susceptible of influencing the otherwise ordinary sense of the terms used in the Vienna Convention. In the third component, Boggiano reviews the idea of the open texture of language by situating it in the perspective of needs and practices of international commerce. Over time these needs and practices inevitably evolve. And beforehand, it is impossible to know with precision the results of this evolution. To face up to this uncertainty and enjoy the required adaptive capacity, uniform law relies upon general standards. The criterion of the reasonable person is one of these. Its content, intrinsically fluctuating, may be adjusted to the new realities of international trade. This presupposes once again the exercise of a certain discretion by the interpreter. Finally, in the fourth component, Boggiano brings together and synthesizes the preceding statements, while adding to them the touch of general principles upon which the Vienna Convention is based. The following example illustrates the type of reasoning to which this may conduce:

> Party autonomy is a principle of the Convention (Article 6). It is a principle of substantive autonomy in international contracts which has particular significance. . . . This principle of party autonomy must be accommodated to the principle of equality and mutual benefit which presupposes an equitable balance of the mutual interests of the seller and the buyer along the lines of the aims expressed in the Preamble to the Vienna Convention. Both, in turn, must conform with the principle of good faith in international trade. This is a principle both of interpretation and of integration.[26]

By this example, the writer wants to highlight 'the general interplay'[27] which the interpreter must undertake in order to be able to make a decision. Extending his demonstration, Boggiano adds this:

> The principles of fairness of exchange and mutual advantage should further develop the balance between the obligations of the seller and the buyer implied by the Convention. The principle of good faith should give effect to any reasonable reliance on a declaration, conduct or significant silence, thus permitting the development of a more specific principle of responsibility which underlies several rules of the convention.[28]

Van Alstine's article supports Boggiano's analysis. His point of departure is as follows: traditionally, a contract results from a meeting of minds. Without it, no obligatory effect can be sanctioned. This is why it is important to define the contours of the common intent of the parties. As such, this exercise is not always evident. However, here Van Alstine seeks to call attention to a situation which frequently arises: even if the parties have not settled all aspects related to their agreement, they acknowledge being bound by contract and consequently intend to fulfil it. But how to determine the content and the range of this type of flexible and

---

26　*Ibid.* at 36.
27　*Ibid.*
28　*Ibid.*

informal relationship? How should one proceed in order to grapple with what Van Alstine calls a partial dissensus, which occurs when 'the dissensus between the parties is overcome by a more powerful consensus between them that they have nonetheless concluded a binding deal?'[29] This type of relationship cannot be taken without proper thought since a good number of commercial transactions are concluded in this manner. According to the writer, legal scholarship on the subject of the Vienna Convention is, up to now, in keeping with tradition: the problematic of partial dissensus is raised from the viewpoint of the offer-acceptance schema, in that the last formal declaration exchanged between the parties must be respected if they wish to follow through with their commitment. Van Alstine contests this doctrinal position. He argues for an approach favouring putting into application the pertinent values which underlie the Vienna Convention.[30] This approach leads him to propose the following solution to cases of partial dissensus:

> The result . . . in such cases is that the declarations and expressive conduct of neither party manifest unqualified assent to the formal declaration of the other. It is in such situations that the principle of party autonomy assumes its appropriate function in the hierarchy of norms of uniform international sales law. In the event of mutual performance, that principle will, first, require the recognition of enforceable contractual obligations. Party autonomy then operates to define the content of those obligations on the basis of the actual common intent that emerges from the parties' respective writings (in particular their standardized business terms) will take effect only to the extent that the writings are in agreement. Where gaps remain, the substantive provisions of the Convention respecting the rights and obligations of buyer and seller likewise assume their appropriate function of defining the 'background' to the parties' relationship.[31]

For Van Alstine, this is a 'better reasoned approach'[32] to the Vienna Convention's interpretive values.

Qualification and Critique

The type of reasoning proposed by these writers is characterized by its *broad-mindedness – largesse*. That is its primary merit. For one, Boggiano does not hesitate to connect material information contained in the Vienna Convention and immaterial information which may devolve from the idea of justice. For his part, Van Alstine explains with vigour that the reasoning must extend to including the values which underlie the Vienna Convention. On the basis of this expansion, he demonstrates a new solution to the problem of partial dissensus. For both, the broadness of the reasoning is essential to ensuring the adaptability of uniform law to the changing conditions of practices and the needs of international commerce. The second merit of their type of reasoning is its direct recourse to *interaction*. The

---

29   Van Alstine, *supra*, Chapter 2, note 2; at 2.
30   *Ibid.* at 52ff.
31   *Ibid.* at 5.
32   *Ibid.* at 103.

two writers express themselves quite clearly on this subject, and the applications which they propose present no doubt as to their interactive dimension. For example, Boggiano exposes how the principle of the autonomy of the will is susceptible of being influenced by other considerations, that the respective obligations of the buyer and seller must be considered in light of the principle of fairness and mutual advantage. And Van Alstine accurately describes the hierarchical effects of the principle of the autonomy of the will within the parameters of the juridical framework established by the Vienna Convention. Broad-mindedness and interaction suppose that the decider, starting with her/his taking of cognizance step of uniform law, has an assembly to complete and that it is large in scale.

In spite of these merits, the reasoning process proposed by these writers does not agree entirely with the progressive consciousness of uniform law. Its main defect derives from the emphasis placed on the resolution of juridical *questions*, as opposed to juridical *problematics*. The decider called upon to respond to a *question* is guided by two major axes. First, she/he is preoccupied with filling a given juridical void by a response deemed indispensable and which imposes itself upon her/him. The decider searches for the unique answer which will eliminate the juridical void. Consequently, she/he will not concurrently evaluate the arguments deemed true with those considered false. The decider will set the latter aside and reason only in light of the former. This is evident in Van Alstine's analysis. For him, the most important thing is to respect the intentions of the drafters regarding the formation values of the Vienna Convention. The true response is there. He deduces from these intentions that the concerns of communitarian theorists, who could have had some influence, have not received the support of the drafters. He thus excludes them from his analysis. Then, the decider placed in this situation knows that the soundness of her/his response will eventually be measured according to the exactness and lucidity of the deductions which it contains, as well as in light of its thoroughness and completeness. That will lead the decider, as in the passage cited from Van Alstine, to formulate a response initially in general terms, then in more specific terms, which will end with an omnibus clause covering all other possible loopholes.

In contrast, progressive consciousness requires reasoning based on juridical problematics.[33] Contrary to the juridical question, which may be resolved by a clear, precise and complete response, a juridical problematic is settled by a series of propositions which express possibilities. This call for the idea of possibilities is explainable by the fact that a problematic results essentially from the combination and aggregation of several factors. A problematic is thus a composite. The impact of its constituent factors is variable, both internally and externally. In certain cases, this impact is extremely hard to determine. This is why the solution corresponding

---

33   See, for two recent illustrations: T. D. Barton, 'Creative Problem Solving: Purpose, Meaning, and Values' (1998) 34 Cal. W. L. Rev. 273; J. M. Cooper, 'Towards a New Architecture: Creative Problem Solving and the Evolution of Law' (1998) 34 Cal. W. L. Rev. 297.

to one problematic is, in one regard, multi-level. It requires the participation of several elements which, at first sight, are perceived as not forming part of the same family. Moreover, the importance of these elements cannot be measured on the basis of a quantitative scale. Their mere presence or participation renders them important.

This is also why the solution to a problematic will always voluntarily allow one or more uncertainties to subsist. The uncertainty will eventually allow feedback on the proposed solution that validates or rejects it. If necessary, other possibilities could be grafted on to or added to the solution. Despite these conditions of relative instability, a solution can attain cohesion and a functional character. It will attain these if it succeeds in embarking on the pursuit of an end which transcends both it and the other solutions developed for other problematics.

These traits of the juridical problematic can be found in diverse segments of progressive consciousness. Thus progressive consciousness is deeply interested in the fact that the interaction between its arguments produces combinations that are varied, surprising, or merely very useful. For example, the world-based argument may provide very pertinent information for understanding the behaviour of one party to a contract. According to what she/he has experienced and learned in her/his world, a party may be more or less inclined to cooperate so that the other party may also cooperate. Yet generally speaking, progressive consciousness approaches reality with a multi-criteria and multi-factorial analytical grid. Growth and solidarity are valid as much for individuals as for collectivities. In both cases, one may understand that they are interested in leading the good life. But one may learn to better understand their concept of the good life by viewing them through the prism of the world in which they evolve. The world, for its part, refers to the idea of a code which assumes different functions of collecting and diffusing different types of information. Likewise, progressive consciousness tries to profit from uncertainty. This is evident in the notion of project which characterizes the relational argument. Here, uncertainty is seen as a possibility to maintain the project between the parties and improve rather than destroy it. Overall, progressive consciousness finds the resources to control the multiplicity and insecurity which may arise in the teleological thought which drives it. These considerations impel me to propose the following manner of reasoning, again as personified by Mark Anthony.

Proposition

I will resume the problematic-based reasoning process at the point where the taking cognizance step was interrupted. Mark Anthony then had a preliminary response. He thought that by suggesting to the parties involved in the project that they spread the development of ground water over a period of twenty years – instead of five as originally planned – everyone would be satisfied. This is not the case. Resistance by the actual parties to the contract, that is to say, a municipality, a local business and a foreign exporter, is fierce. They claim to know what they are doing and that this contract will certainly have positive repercussions. Mark Anthony understands that his preliminary response was only temporary. The taking cognizance step permitted anticipation, nothing more.

In order to extend his reasoning, Mark Anthony must define or describe the problematic in which he is interested. He will do so in two steps. First he must distinguish the various interests involved, as well as the various, apparently more neutral, components of the problematic. He is not making a diagnosis but rather identifying and understanding the reasons and circumstances at the source of the problematic. He realizes that certain factors may have a fairly strong impact on the present situation and others may remain somewhat secondary. However, he is not really anxious to distinguish the essential from the secondary. As a second step, he must draft a list of phenomena which require explaining. He submits his list to certain persons close to him in order to establish to what extent they share his view of the situation. At the end of this definition, Mark Anthony knows that he will have to elucidate why the actual parties to the contract are not listening to the opinion of those in his circle, why nature does not immediately receive commercial support and why, despite appearances, relations are so strained between the parties to the contract. On top of everything, he knows that he will have to forge or create a solution in keeping with uniform law, if he wants it to be accepted by all.

The next step is crucial. It consists in elaborating various potential solutions or hypotheses. To develop them, Mark Anthony refers to his accumulated knowledge and his provisional response, which he revives, as well as to interesting and serious explanations which are not necessary true, but which he may choose to advance. It is an opportunity to be at once creative and methodical. It is here that Mark Anthony once again realizes that his ultimate solution will not escape criticism. No matter: he says to himself that through self-questioning, he will surely arrive at a credible solution. Of the open questions which he asks himself, some will serve to guide the process of developing hypotheses: How to explain this solution? Can one reflect on other explanatory factors? Are there no other avenues to consider? Are there foreseeable repercussions on various levels? Others questions encourage investigation: Why did I think of that? What do I think of the opinion of ... ? Which reasons incite me to keep or reject this hypothesis? Finally, certain questions will serve to bring him back to what is really at stake in the problematic: Can I return to a more methodical approach? How may I summarize my view up to this point?

Which hypothesis is the best? In order to determine this, Mark Anthony must test each hypothesis by submitting its various components to the spiral test.[34] This test rests upon a postulate of a systemic nature: the sense of a whole must be understood in light of the sense of each of its parts, and the sense of each part must be understood according to the whole. In concrete terms, this implies that each component is placed along a curve and the decider goes from one to the other while mutually adjusting them. This passage allows the decider to measure to what point each component fits in with the other components of the hypothesis. This postulate of a systemic nature also supposes that the decider will shuttle between

---

34   H. G. Gadamer, *Vérité et méthode*, trans. Pierre Fruchon (Paris: Seuil, 1965) at 104ff.

the various components. She/he comes and goes between the components at irregular intervals. This creates a series of small and greater revolutions which confirm or invalidate the importance or the soundness of a component. Little by little, the decider approaches a pole which will constitute a type of maximum that a hypothesis is capable of offering. And because the pole does not delimit an absolute end, the solution proposed by a hypothesis will always be partial.

After having tested each hypothesis in this manner, Mark Anthony feels that the best solution is first and foremost one of a preventive character: we say yes to the project, provided it is preceded by an environmental impact study. He knows that uniform law will support this solution. His comings and goings among the arguments which constitute progressive consciousness has convinced him of this. The project as originally conceived cannot only concern the official parties to the contract. Through an osmotic phenomenon, the project must be open to other considerations. Included in these is the environment. Progressive consciousness does not elevate it to the level of an absolute obstacle to any project, but it remains nevertheless an essential consideration. By means of an impact study, his world will have the opportunity of expressing its point of view and demonstrating its credibility. He also thinks that the hearings which are part of the impact study will establish a climate of collaboration amongst the interested parties, especially the parties to the contract itself. Why is this solution to be preferred? Here, Mark Anthony is hesitant. He is unable to prove that it is the best solution with figures to support him. But his opinion is firm: all things considered, this is the solution which is conducive to the most stimulating *modus vivendi*.

A final point preoccupies Mark Anthony: before formally proposing his solution to the interested parties, must he put it in perspective? This is not very clear in his mind. Why, when all is said and done, would his decision be more valid than that of another? What authority does it have in light of existing decisions in similar matters and in light of those to come? Preoccupied by this, Mark Anthony will try to situate his decision before formally submitting it.

The Situation

The two prior steps have enabled the interpreter to take cognizance of uniform law and develop an argument on the basis of the information gathered. She/he must now clear a final step devoted to situating the decision that she/he has in mind, in relation to that which already exists in uniform law. Otherwise stated, her/his tentative decision must be set in a certain place within a whole, represented by uniform law. This may seem evident by the mere fact that nothing, as a general rule, ever occurs in isolation; and inversely all is connected in one way or another to something else. The step of determining the situation is nonetheless vital, because the connection to something else may, in theory, take several paths. Thus, an interpreter may, by a conscious decision, opt for the *status quo*. She/he may also favour an evolution, or indeed a revolution, in uniform law. The avenue of going back also remains open, as well as that where a decision proves simply different or dissident vis-à-vis the others. The situating step thus directly targets the major part of the heart and soul of uniform law, that is to say the notion of uniformity.

The text by M. P. Van Alstine entitled 'Dynamic Treaty Interpretation'[35] offers, in my opinion, the most thorough analysis of the situation within the context of uniform law. For this writer, 'the new generation of international conventions ..., inspired by a paradigm established in the U.N. Sales Convention, ... contemplate an active role for the courts in developing the law within their scope.'[36] As in the approach utilized by P. Koneru concerning the taking cognizance step of uniform law, Van Alstine also refers to the general principles as a primary path 'in the fashioning of solutions at an international level.'[37] He feels that the vitality particular to general principles, which moreover, is in keeping with the dynamism peculiar to present economic globalization, constitutes that which is best to 'guide the future development of the law,'[38] 'to adapt a convention to accommodate social and technological changes ... .'[39] Let us examine in greater detail what he proposes.

Description of Process

Van Alstine exhibits great confidence in the general principles of the Vienna Convention. This confidence rests largely on the lessons drawn from the process of codification of private law in Europe during the nineteenth century. This codification, he reminds us, had as a primary goal the replacement of law in force up to then. The purpose was not to renew the old but to build the new with new elements. As a corollary, this codification was characterized by its completeness. The material code which resulted from this contained all of the law. Conversely, one could say that all the law could be found therein. Moreover, this completeness enjoyed a quality of timelessness. The code was vested with a power of regeneration enabling it to last and last. One could not be assured that it immediately sets out solutions to each precise question, but one could be assured that it could offer to provide a solution adjusted to the circumstances and the needs of the moment.

Moreover, all this is rendered possible by recourse to general principles. Van Alstine feels that these characteristics form the basis of the philosophy also animating the Vienna Convention. The latter has its eyes on the future and not on the past. Its *raison d'être* is to attain a veritable transnational juridical corpus. It will succeed insofar as it is self-sufficient, without undue reliance on its predecessors, the national juridical systems. Also, its internal structure renders it capable of adapting and evolving. And, at the heart of this philosophy may be found, once again, a call to general principles. What renders these general

---

35   *Supra*, Chapter 4, note 48.
36   *Ibid.* at 692.
37   *Ibid.* at 693.
38   *Ibid.*
39   *Ibid.* at 694.

principles so indispensable may be explained, according to the writer, by their particular nature. This nature confers on the law a living and progressive dimension. The law cannot be helpless when confronted with new situations. At the same time, it benefits from a vitality which positively influences the quality of proposed responses to various problems.

In light of what precedes, Van Alstine situates general principles at the centre of the notion of dynamic jurisprudence . . . so dynamic, however, that it could become counter-productive. By definition, dynamism presents change as inherent. From this angle, it adheres closely to the view developed by Van Alstine. But, pushed further, dynamism must be understood as forces irreducible to a single mass. This presupposes that if a decision in relation to uniform law is able to go in all directions, are we not confronted by a real and inconceivable antinomy? Van Alstine is very aware of this problem. And it is precisely here that he reveals how to evaluate the validity of a decision in relation to the whole of uniform law. Van Alstine's idea, which enables him to refine his view of uniformity, rests upon a well known warning: ensure deciders do not fall back on their respective traditions to shape uniform law. From that, he enunciates 'certain procedural antidotes to this potential homesickness of national adjudicators.'[40]

The first antidote is qualified as backward-looking. For the interpreter it consists of 'giving deference to prior decisions by adjudicators of other countries on the same or similar issues.'[41] In this manner, a link is forged between the national tribunals, which otherwise remain independent of one another. This link must lead them to 'view their own interpretative discretion as constrained by the decisions of the courts of other contracting states.'[42] The second antidote takes a different path, qualified as forward-looking. Van Alstine sees it as 'an instruction that an adjudicator consider the likelihood that a particular interpretation will find international acceptance.'[43] In other words, the decider must consider the 'consensus capacity'[44] of her/his view of things. As it is, Van Alstine feels that this capacity will be increased if the decider takes care to fully justify her/his interpretation. Finally, the third antidote 'is found in an expanded view of the relevant interpretative community.'[45] In practical terms, this expansion signifies that the decider must take legal scholarship into account. This scholarship, like the role it plays in regard to codified law, is probably a very useful source in order to build the necessary consensus. These three antidotes are at the source of the dynamism contemplated by Van Alstine. In the absence of an international jurisdiction, uniformity depends upon actual communication between national authorities: that is what the antidotes establish.

---

40   *Ibid.* at 787.
41   *Ibid.*
42   *Ibid.*
43   *Ibid.* at 787-788.
44   *Ibid.* at 788.
45   *Ibid.*

Then, Van Alstine devotes particular attention to the temporal dimension of the development of a dynamic international jurisprudence. As he acknowledges, 'In the early stages of this process, the force of the justificatory arguments in individual decisions will play the significant unifying role.'[46] However, it would be illogical and premature to confer greater authority than that on the first decisions on a given subject. The reason is that, with the passing of time, a stabilizing phenomenon will come into play:

> As the case law on an issue grows in mass, so too in the course of time will its gravitational force. And as an international consensus emerges on a given issue, the express legislative direction in GISG article 7(1) that courts defer to the needs of international uniformity will give that gravitational force all the practical effect of precedent.[47]

Van Alstine thus depends on 'the attractive power of the international consensus'[48] and on 'the magnetic influence of the needs of uniformity'[49] to preserve the international character of the Convention. It is only once these sources are completely exhausted that the decider may turn to national sources to justify an interpretation. He also counts on these driving forces as primary guides for the person or the court which must situate a tentative decision within the whole of uniform law.

Qualification and Critique

The situation proposed by Van Alstine essentially rests on general principles. The first mission of these principles is to endow uniform law with a *foundation*. Despite all the dynamism one can attribute to them, their prospect is to succeed in creating precedents. In other words, their objective is to create one acceptable well-defined law, whose goals and functioning are universally legitimate. This foundation has yet to be set. It does not yet repose on an already established or antecedent stratum. It must thus resolutely turn to the future. And this future seems to be the same for all. The foundation to be set out inspires confidence because it falls under the same philosophy as an historical event which has known much success, that of codification. Progressive consciousness refutes this idea of a foundation. More specifically, it refuses to attribute much prestige to juridical security resulting from such a foundation. For it, juridical security is not a goal in itself. It knows quite well that for someone to know what to do and what not to do is not automatically synonymous with justice. In order to avoid this snag, progressive consciousness abandons precedent in order to rely on the subsequent. This signifies that first, each decision is evaluated according to its intrinsic value in the eyes of those to whom it is addressed, that is to say to its immediate audience. Secondly, each decision is

---

46 *Ibid.* at 789.
47 *Ibid.* at 790.
48 *Ibid.*
49 *Ibid.* at 791.

evaluated according to the qualitative degree of advancement that it procures for uniform law in general. It must demonstrate a willingness to improve a situation by having it climb the ladder of the good life.

One may respond that the doctrine of the subsequent confers an excessively broad discretion on the decider. I am not so sure this is the case. On the one hand, it is an incentive to do better than before. While the precedent crystallizes and comforts, the subsequent leads to calling into question and looking ahead. In the commercial and developmental spheres, where innovation is of the first importance, to speak of precedent is paradoxical. On the contrary, to speak of the subsequent is more normal: links with the past exist, but all opens to the new. In addition, a decider who takes progressive consciousness seriously is not abandoned. She/he is not authorized to think that progressive consciousness does not pursue determined or determinable ends, or that these goals may not be identified by means of appropriate enquiry and reasoning. Nor is she/he authorized to subjectively produce uniform law by choosing, without constraint and according to personal preferences, political, economic and moral convictions, solutions which she/he prefers. The decider who takes progressive consciousness seriously knows that she/he must construct a decision which respects the principles of thought and the values underlying the arguments found in the context of discovery and the context of justification. She/he also knows that her/his decision will be recognized and validated insofar as it reflects, as interestingly as possible, progressive consciousness. If this reflection is negative, her/his decision will be downgraded.

Progressive consciousness is thus unsceptical. It believes in something. But it is not an incontestable objective verity nor an impassable standard. The truth of progressive consciousness, if there is one, corresponds to a form of vigilance and emancipation in light of reality. For example, the relational argument places emphasis on the values and circumstances suitable for enriching the relationship between the parties rather than render it unproductive. The argument of the common good provides attentive supervision, with the least possible lapses, over situations which obstruct the achievement of well-being. The world-based argument exists to manifest and render visible the aspirations, fears and despairs of a world. And the argument based on self-fulfilment and solidarity is there to recall that trade is not an end in itself, and its merit depends on its assistance in attaining more honourable objectives than mere growth. Contrary to what Van Alstine proposes, vigilance and emancipation cast a critical light on the current significance of the experience related to codification. Nothing proves that this experience, and its underlying motivation, suits today's and tomorrow's situations. And nothing proves that a code has, within itself, the certainty of providing good law. The problematic which consists in knowing if a law is right is always present and topical, and the response which one gives to this problematic is always provisional.

In opting for precedent, the dynamic interpretive approach proposed by Van Alstine risks creating uniformization functioning on a method of formal recognition. In this context, a decision is valid if it compares favourably with those rendered up to now. One seeks actual or similar indices or information, as well as invariability. Little by little, in order to facilitate the operation, to aid communication between interested parties and optimize purer uniformity, the number of elements allowed to be compared diminish. National precedents are already excluded. By diluting its force in this manner, uniform law may certainly better accommodate the social and technological changes of which Van Alstine speaks, because it will eventually lose its ascendancy and its impact on reality. At the outside, it will have very little to say, as is the case with conservative consciousness. It will fall back on the autonomy of the will and on juridical convergence. Progressive consciousness would dispute this tendency. Even at the cost of – apparent – complexification of uniform law, it views otherwise this stage of the situation. For it, to situate a decision should not be equivalent to placing it in a prefabricated mould. This is what Mark Anthony must attempt.

Proposition

At the close of his process of reasoning, Mark Anthony arrived at 'the most consistent and coherent package which best squares with everything.'[50] He has read much and reflected on what is done here and there. He has thus taken into account and integrated into his reasoning existing solutions and decisions which exist in similar matters and anticipate the future. In a certain way, his decision is already in place or situated with regard to uniform law. But he knows that overall it has a distinctive character in comparison with the rest of this whole that is uniform law. Is it valid? He hopes so, inasmuch as according to the feedback he has received, all interested parties would be in agreement with his solution. Unknown to him, a reclusive but famous decider known as Hercules has the answer to his question.[51] According to Hercules, the distinctive character of Mark Anthony's decision does not constitute a problem. Fundamentally, this character is equivalent to that which Hercules conceptualizes under the term of *differentiation*. Now the pluralism inherent in progressive consciousness is very receptive to this idea. It converts it into what is commonly called a principle. For progressive consciousness, differentiation is synonymous with progress and evolution. The decision which differs draws attention, stimulates the outside and lays the foundation for new experiences. However, to be completely valid, it must overcome three objections.

The first objection consists in saying that the adding up of differentiations would create too imposing a mass of information and data. By constantly adding to what precedes, the differentiated decision cannot do otherwise than increase the extent of this mass. Eventually, that increase will produce a result which will be too cumbersome for uniform law to handle. To remain functional, uniform law can only store, over a period of time, a finite quantity of material. Thus, when, at a certain moment, uniform law opens a parenthesis, the latter is already closed. It is

---

50   Kei Nielsen, 'In Defense of Wide Reflective Equilibrium', in D. Odegard (ed.), *Ethics and Justification* (Edmonton: Academic Printing and Publishing, 1998) 19 at 22.
51   The image I have in mind is the famous justice derived from the theory of R. Dworkin in *Law's Empire* (Cambridge: Belknap, 1986).

the equation $(x + \ldots + \ldots)$. The length of the equation is variable but it denotes limited storing capacity. This fear and the underlying premise are ill-founded. For progressive consciousness, uniform law is a process for which the density of the mass of information is not an obstacle. This is not because there is an unlimited storage capacity. That would be mere illusion. Rather, it is possible to compact the information available. The information remains present within uniform law; it is not impoverished nor reduced, it is simply compressed. When uniform law opens a parenthesis, the parenthesis stretches until a compacting operation is deemed opportune. The equation $(x + x + x)$ may become $3x$ and then be submitted to other compacting operations. In any case, the initial information may always be recovered by de-compacting. On this level, Mark Anthony's decision is, according to Hercules, easily assimilated by uniform law.

The second objection is that over time, the accumulation of differentiated decisions will lead to chaos. It would be very difficult to situate a decision within the whole of uniform law. At best, its situation would be precarious: it would tend to drift instead of being firmly implanted. First and foremost, the effect of this objection is powerful. How to get one's bearings if uniform law is made up of decisions which do not share the same vision, which trace varied lines of conduct, which create, finally, a divergent juridical corpus? If pluralism leads to the incommensurable, that is to say, if each decision is in conflict with another to the point of excluding it, are we not risking anarchy or confusion? The answer is no: in effect, progressive consciousness holds to a reversed perspective of what one can expect in relation to the accumulation of differentiated decisions. For progressive consciousness, uniform law constitutes a naturally expansive body. This body possesses the faculties needed to sufficiently expand in order to integrate decisions hitherto unknown. The faculties in question derive their most exact synthesis from the notion of polyvalence, which I had discussed in the first part of this reflection.[52] A polyvalent uniform law is necessarily unresolved and incomplete at all times. It has constantly to be made and remade, and its experience corresponds more to clashes of ideas than to their harmonious bonding. At any time, its decentred nature thus leaves open spaces for new contributions, such as that of Mark Anthony.

Finally, the third objection underlines the fact that differentiation constitutes a very poor method of communication. In order for an exchange to succeed between persons or entities, a community must exist between them, a unique medium must unite them. Optimal communication depends on an identity between the diverse components of the whole or of the system in question. In the absence of this identity, the components remain isolated from each other in such a way that there is no contact between them. This objection fails to recognize the true nature of the differentiation. A differentiated decision is not pure, born in abstraction from actions of some authority. It is the fruit of taking cognizance and of reasoning which have led it to borrow from opinions, discussions and arguments. When one is at the situating step, the differentiated decision is consequently bound to other external elements. Its composite nature places it in a position of connection rather

---

52   Part I, Preliminary Remarks, 'A Poly-background', above.

than of detachment with regard to that which surrounds it. This position affirms that a differentiated decision is in communication with the others. However, even seen in this light, does not the difference remain an irritant? No, because it possesses a faculty of reverberation and reflexibility greater than similarity. In the presence of identical decisions, there is little or no advantage to the decider in informing her/himself as to what is done elsewhere. The decider does not have to talk or converse with whomever. She/he only has to follow the road set out, setting aside all efforts to initiate a dialogue. By opposition, the difference may sow doubt in the person who must decide and may incite her/him to look elsewhere. All cannot be the same everywhere. In so doing, the chances are better that the decider turns her/his thought over and over in her/his mind in order to thoroughly examine the problematic in which she/he is interested. That is what Mark Anthony did. Hercules recognizes this without any reservations.

Chapter 9

A *Uniformist* Reading of the Quebec World

As mentioned in the Preliminary Remarks to Part IV, the objective of the uniformist reading of the Quebec world consists in making a demonstration of the world-based argument in action. In order to reach this objective, it is necessary to go back to the structure and the content of the world-based argument.[1] As will be recalled, this structure and this content rest on a central concept, the concept of holistic action. At the stage of reformulation of uniform law, I discussed this concept according to three considerations: its significance, its implementation and the dynamics that animate it. These considerations showed a considerable amount of data and variables susceptible of helping in the analysis of the elements of innovation, diffusion and aspiration that are part of the *raison d'être* of the world-based argument. At the end of the day, these elements constitute what I qualified as the mental foundation of uniform law in every given world.

Of course, more than one type of holistic action can be considered in reading the Quebec world, in a uniformist way. Like all worlds, this one is the fruit, in constant maturation, of the combined interplay of actors, activities and links between these actors and these activities. This interplay defines, stimulates and modifies, all naturally, a plurality of holistic actions. In corollary, it would be an exaggeration to pretend being able to make a complete uniformist reading of the Quebec world from only one holistic action, whatever it may be. Any uniformist reading cannot provide a comprehensive understanding of the Quebec world: *it can only bring a progression in the understanding of the Quebec world or any other world, as opposed to a complete understanding.*

In the circumstances, the holistic action that will serve as the main thread of this chapter will be represented by the theme of regional development. To opt for this theme implies, first, a particular way of *seeing* the Quebec world. Here, to look at Quebec means visualizing an entity divided up into regions. Indeed, due to historic, economic, geographical, political and other kinds of factors, the Quebec world is broken up into settings and concentrations that correspond to what one commonly calls regions. Beyond this factual dimension, regional development supposes, secondly, a vision of *how to conceive* the Quebec world. In an age of internationalization and economic integration, and of the redefinition – now

---

1   Chapter 6, 'The World-based Argument', above.

probably on the downturn – of Quebec's role as a state,[2] regions are seen as indispensable loci for what the Quebec world could be now and could become in the future.

The choice of regional development and, at a broader level, the Quebec world may seem surprising or not immediately persuasive. Why these and not others? The answers have to do with logic and affect first, and daring next. Logic and affect explain the choice of the Quebec world. This is the world I know best. The intimacy of this knowledge is, in my view, sufficient to justify my reliance on it for my demonstration of the argument of the world in action. The theoretical soundness and practical potential of the approach are likely to be more evident than if I advanced a different world for my analysis. The resulting pedagogical benefits are of the first importance in a reflection that puts forward new avenues for thought. As for the daring, it explains the choice of regional development. The goal here is to rise to the challenge of making a clear and convincing case that uniform law is interrelated with a set of activities that would appear to be foreign to it and far removed from it. To meet this challenge is to act in tune with the notion that progressive consciousness sees in uniform law a permeable whole that extends to infinity and toward which influences of all kinds themselves extend.

Considering the previous remarks, and in order to reach the objective pursued here, this chapter has been structured as follows. By reason of their importance within the world-based argument, elements of innovation, diffusion and aspiration form the main structure of the chapter. They will therefore be analysed successively. With respect to each element, I will first describe – with the help of the concept of holistic action – a variable drawn from the theme of regional development. This description must be understood as the result of my own synthesis – and sometimes interpretation – of information and commentaries contained in the Quebec literature on regional development. As such, it proceeds more from conventional wisdom than assertions of fact about regional development. Secondly, I will proceed to an evaluative uniformist reading of the variable in question. It will be the occasion to put in parallel the Quebec world and the progressive consciousness of uniform law and to take note of some relevant aspects in relation to innovation, diffusion and aspiration. Thirdly, a prospective uniformist reading will explore possibilities of renewal and consolidation of the ties between the Quebec world and progressive consciousness.

Before going any further, a question deserves attention: does the Quebec world exist? Since the beginning of this reflection, I have been assuming that such a world existed. Do I have to push the investigation further and bring back the proof of this existence? In the event of an affirmative answer, I would have to establish positively and substantially, in accordance with principles of the transitory conception, that a code sufficiently unites and underlies various components to the point of being able to speak of a Quebec world.[3] In spite of the

---

2   S. Coulombe & G. Paquet, eds., *La réinvention des institutions et le rôle de l'État* (Montreal: A.S.D.E.Q., 1996).

3   See Chapter 5, 'The Transitory Conception', above.

manifest importance taken on by the concept of world within the progressive consciousness of uniform law, I do not believe that it is necessary to perform this exercise. I submit that, as a hypothesis, it can be reasonably admitted that a Quebec world exists. Signs and reference marks of all kinds, in spite of their volatility and the present controversies on what Quebec is, are numerous and strong enough to purely and simply admit this hypothesis.[4]

Innovation

Innovation is not synonymous with novelty. In my opinion, it would be too simplistic to hold to this correspondence, since it would imply that the analysis turns into a search for what appears or may appear for the first time. Innovation is defined rather according to three faculties, aptitudes or predispositions characteristic of a human being or of any other entity.[5] In this sense, and in the first place, innovation can be understood as an adaptability to the normal fluctuations that occur on a daily basis. Even if extensive planning has preceded a given topic or project, even though thorough reflection has preceded the coming into force of a given norm, adjustments are unavoidable: it is the order of things that commands it. In a more accentuated way, innovation further refers to a capacity of reaction in the face of the unexpected. The unexpected event can present itself under the cover of a problematic or of an opportunity, a chance. In both cases, it will be possible to speak of innovation inasmuch as an adequate reaction has been deployed in order to solve the problematic, or inasmuch as the unsuspected opportunity has been seized to the advantage of someone or something. Finally, innovation is the feature of any ability to foresee and think the future. More specifically, this ability permits us to anticipate the course of events. Normally, the sense of anticipation should ensure a better control of what is coming, that is, the future, and permit a greater influence on it.

In the framework of regional development, it is the concept of small and medium-sized enterprise[6] that embodies the most meaningful variable as regards innovation. Indeed, SMEs are perceived as the driving force behind innovative actions whose spinoff effects can improve a region's fate.[7] But despite the significance of the SME, it is a very difficult entity to define quantitatively. For example, how can we determine the number of employees beyond which an SME is no longer considered one? Or how can we fix the turnover characteristic of the SME? This kind of difficulty is no less evident in the qualitative realm. This is so

---

4   F. Dumont, *Raisons communes* (Montreal: Boréal, 1995); F. Dumont, ed., *La société québécoise après 30 ans de changements* (Québec: I.N.R.S., 1990).

5   T. Gaudin, *Le temps du germe: philosophie de l'innovation* (Strasbourg: Sophon, 1987).

6   Hereafter called SME.

7   P. A. Julien & M. Marchesnay, *L'entrepreneuriat* (Paris: Économica, 1996); D. Maillat & J. C. Perrin, eds., *Entreprises innovatrices et développement territorial* (Neuchâtel, E.D.E.S., 1992).

because of the fact that an SME, though different from a large enterprise, shares several features with it, for example management, specialization, strategies and the integration of technology. Not to mention that SMEs differ among themselves in terms of organizational structure, product, progress of growth and causes of start-up. Despite these difficulties, for the present purpose I intend to use a functional definition of the SME[8] according to which it consists of economic activities conducted by an entity with fewer than 200 employees, having these features:

i)   the manager's vision is the determining factor in the enterprise's development;
ii) the enterprise has the capacity to adjust rapidly to the economic and industrial environment;
iii) its financial limitations oblige it to operate creatively with regard to methods of work, management approach and the use of financial, material and human resources;
iv) recourse to outside partners is essential to its functioning, whether in dealing with excess work, handling crises, or obtaining valuable information in various fields.

Description of the Variable

At present, the Quebec SME is more often than not analysed under the point of view of an entity obliged to redefine itself in order to meet the challenges resulting from market liberalization.[9] These challenges are usually channelled in the so called imperative of competitiveness.[10] This imperative forces the SME to think and to act with respect to a number of factors which are likely to help it withstand the increased competition prompted by the liberalization of economic activity. Although it is too early to make a final observation on the question, it appears that, until now, the SME has managed relatively well in this new context.[11] However, this observation implies that some SMEs do not succeed in sustaining themselves, and that, generally, training in the field of internationalization must continue. That

---

8   P. A. Julien, 'Pour une définition des PME' and 'Théorie économiques des PME' in P. A. Julien, ed., *Les PME. Bilan et perspectives* (Paris: Économica, 1994) at 21 and 41; Institut de la statistique du Québec, *Les PME au Québec. État de la situation*, 1999 (Québec: Éditeur officiel, 2000).

9   R. Poisson, *La stratégie d'internationalisation des PME: état actuel des recherche et perspectives* (Québec, Université Laval, 1996); P. A. Julien, *PME et grands marchés: PME québécoises et françaises face à l'ALENA et au Marché unique* (Paris: L'Harmattan, 1995); P. A. Julien & J. Chicha, *La belle entreprise: la revanche des PME en France et au Québec* (Montreal: Boréal, 1986).

10 A. Joyal, *Des PME et le défi de l'exportation* (Cap-Rouge: Presses Inter Universitaires, 1996).

11 P. A. Julien & M. Morin, *Mondialisation de l'économie et PME québécoises* (Sainte-Foy: Presses de l'Université du Québec, 1996); Ministère de l'Industrie, du Commerce, de la Science et de la Technologie, *Les PME au Québec: état de la situation, 1996* (Québec: Éditeur officiel, 1996).

is why intense efforts are made in order to identify the characteristic features of the successful SME.[12] In my view, two important axes emerge from the synthesis of these features.

The first axis refers to norms of behaviour that the SME must satisfy if it wants to be at its best within the new economy.[13] The Quebec SME which symbolizes the model to follow represents an actor who behaves or acts in a certain manner. Thus, the good SME refers to an image of an actor who shows leadership in its region.[14] The SME is stripped here of its usual economic connotation to take advantage of a more comprehensive status of good corporate citizen. Like other actors, it shows off as a leader capable of mobilizing and guiding the population of a region in its development. The SME acquires this status by adopting conduct and making gestures of the following kind: it provides some stimulating future perspectives; it favours partnerships between enterprises; it gives sense to events and phenomena that occur in the region; it contributes to create an atmosphere of confidence within the population; and it is concerned with the quality of life prevailing on its immediate territory. Leadership will be all the more strong and efficient when combined with the credibility of the SME. This credibility is expressed in terms of expertise and compatibility. An SME is able to exercise leadership if its expertise is judged relevant and useful in relation to the development of a region and if the faculties that it puts forward are judged favourably by the population. But things do not stop at leadership. The successful SME possesses a very specific personality. Among the most important facets of its personality, are sixth sense and intuition. The SME feels what happens in its field of economic activity. It is capable of identifying some latent needs, it senses opportunities with interesting potential. While knowing how to sense good opportunities, a winning SME acts with prudence. It evaluates the consequences of the gestures it is about to make. Thus, the typical behaviour of the successful SME is recognizable by the suppleness of mind, the discernment and the common sense that it displays. It adds to these an almost infinite capacity for tenacity and resourcefulness. This helps it to optimize the spinoffs from its pragmatism, which brings us back to its astonishing capacity to identify what can be useful and what is capable of giving results. In the end, the talent of the SME for communication is striking. To know how to express itself and to know how to listen constitute two norms of behaviour of the SME which, against all the odds, knows how to preserve an enviable position within the network of which it is part.

---

12 Y. Laprade, *L'histoire des meilleures PME au Québec* (Outremont: Québécor, 1996).

13 G. d'Ambroise, *Quelle gestion stratégique pour la PME?* (Cap-Rouge: Presses Inter Universitaires, 1997).

14 For more on this topic, see U. Witt, 'Imagination and Leadership – The Neglected Dimension of an Evolutionary Theory of the Firm' (1998) 35 Journal of Economic Behavior and Organization 161.

The second axis depicts an SME that maintains an extremely strong connection with knowledge or learning.[15] This connection makes the SME an intelligent entity, in the sense that it possesses the necessary faculties or assets to capture and to master information, and then to produce new information that is more advanced and effective.[16] In a general way, this profile of the SME corresponds to that of an organization in the vanguard of research, science and technology.[17] The entity which we face is one at the leading edge of what scientific progress can offer. A very positive image comes out of these attributes. Endowed with the faculties to know, to understand, in short with complete intellectual capacities with respect to knowledge, the model SME personifies the leader of all the good that the future holds for a region. From the moment it becomes a consumer and producer of knowledge, there is not the slightest doubt about its competitiveness. And, in principle, it should be capable of preserving its competitive advantages as long as it remains intelligent. In concrete terms, the Quebec SME which becomes famous in this regard intervenes on three levels. First, it knows how to adopt an adequate organization of labour. Usually, it will be said that the development of new products and services, the development of new processes and the increase in productivity must be accompanied by changes in the organization of labour. It means that the different processes that the SME puts in action to achieve its mission are subject to a constant review.[18] Then, the SME intervenes with respect to research and development. The golden rule is that the SME which invests in research and development succeeds better than that which does not. In a period of economic growth, it contributes more to the creation of jobs, whereas in a period of stagnation or decrease, it loses fewer of them. Finally, the Quebec SME knows how to innovate by profiting from the constantly evolving technologies that exist on the market or from what it conceives by itself.[19] These technologies do not only consist of technical outfitting. Sometimes, they can be immaterial acquisitions, such as intellectual property or, again, advanced management practices such as ISO norms.[20]

---

15   P. A. Julien, *Économie du savoir, emploi et PME* (Trois-Rivières, U.Q.T.R., 1997). For more on this topic, see F. Machlup, *Knowledge: Its Creation, Distribution and Economic Significance* (Princeton: Princeton University Press, 1983).

16   J. P. Bruneau, *Création, développement et continuité des PME: psychanalyse et entreprises* (Montreal: Agence d'ARC, 1990).

17   Ministère de la Recherche, de la Science et de la Technologie, *Québec. Objectif emploi. Vers une économie d'avant-garde* (Québec: Gouvernement du Québec, 1999).

18   J. Brunelle, *Le management de la PME* (Montreal: Éditions Bo-pré, 1985).

19   P. A. Julien, ed., *Pour des PME de classe mondiale: recours à de nouvelles technologies* (Montreal: Éditions Transcontinentales, 1994); R. Chaussé, *La gestion de l'innovation dans la PME* (Montreal: G. Morin, 1987).

20   J. L. Malouin & Y. Gasse, *L'innovation technologique dans les PME manufacturières* (Québec: I.R.P., 1992).

Evaluative Reading

The innovative Quebec SME is one that meets high standards of behaviour and shows intelligence. In this sense, it is an actor which positions itself well, in principle, in the face of requirements and qualifications prescribed by the relational argument. The latter, as presented, insists a great deal on the quality and the durability of contractual relations. To that effect, it imposes on the partners a heavy enough burden as to the rightness and the appropriateness of their conduct. However, without any doubt, the Quebec SME depicted above possesses a strong and attractive personality. But is it sufficient to admit without hesitation that this SME will know how to act with dignity as regards the statements of the relational argument?

This question underlines the fact that the emphasis of the relational argument on representing the contract as a union, a convergence of interests willing to collaborate, does not imply an underestimation of the substantial degree of tension, opposition and differentiation that can prevail between the partners. To think otherwise would amount to conferring a surrealist character on the argument. This fact proves to be especially important because it reflects a very concrete reality, whose acuteness is reinforced by the liberalization of international trade. This reality is that the relationship of traders from different cultures creates a broader range of strategies and motivations than before.[21] In turn, this range provokes the emergence of a predominance of contractual relations that may be qualified as *asymmetric*.[22] By definition, such a relation occurs when partners are united by divergent incentives and a different involvement in one particular project. The will of one to privilege the commercial success of the partnership (importance of the turnover achieved, number of contracts concluded for the supply of materials, etc.) will correspond to the will of the other to aim for a more global success, that is to say that goes beyond the simple sharing of market opportunities and the pecuniary gains (implementation of a real process of production, assimilation of new technology, etc.).[23] The Quebec SME, in spite of its qualities and advantages, is confronted by this asymmetry. And the capacity of the Quebec SME to fully assume the requirements derived from the relational argument is susceptible of being severely tested by this asymmetry. To cooperate, in the context of a linkage and a project with symmetrical contours, constitutes an interesting challenge, no more than that. However, in an asymmetric context, the challenge risks being considerable, even huge.

The predominance of asymmetry is also present when one considers international commercial relations in the intelligence-based perspective that

---

21 See, in general, C. Durand, *La coopération technologique internationale* (Brussels: De Boeck, 1994).

22 K. R. Kerrigan, 'Strategic Alliances and Partner Asymmetries' (1988) 16 Management International Review 53.

23 C. E. Schillaci, 'Designing Successful Joint Ventures' (1987) 8 Journal of Business Strategy 59.

characterizes the Quebec SME. This perspective leads us to suppose that the establishment of relationships between partners is strongly bound to a process of creation and coordination of knowledge. The linkage and the project will allow a partner to bring her/his stock of knowledge and permit it to bear fruit. And this is equally true for the other partner.[24] However, it is sufficient to think about the private commercial relations between partners of the North and the South to realize that, from the intelligence point of view, a very big gap can separate partners.[25] From then on, one can wonder how partners with heterogeneous and unequal knowledge can cooperate, that is to say, share their objectives and adopt some compatible behaviours to reach them.[26] Very often, scholarship – economic, legal or other – takes us back to the notion of confidence to justify and explain, in spite of asymmetry, the engagement of partners in relations of production and exchange, their respect for their promises and the success of their cooperation. But to what type of confidence are we referring?[27] The answer to this question is important. By reason of its influence, it can impel the Quebec SME to modify its personality in a direction that does not conform with the real essence of the relational argument.

A popular type of confidence is proposed by R. Wintrobe and A. Breton,[28] as well as by D. M. Kreps.[29] These writers mobilize the notion of confidence in their studies on modes of cooperation between agents while preserving the setting of reference to the modern analysis. Thus, they keep the central hypothesis of the rational agent, anxious to maximize her/his gains. However, they propose to enrich this setting while rejecting the assumption of the perfect definition of the partners' rights and liabilities at any stage of the linkage or realization of the project. Indeed, in their view, most transactions are created on the basis of informal engagements that cannot be specified in a contract. It is the role of confidence to ensure the functional character of the project in spite of these grey zones. This confidence rests on the existence of threats that force agents to respect their deals. Beyond this common point, the positions of the writers diverge. Whereas Wintrobe and Breton make the confidence depend on the repetition of bilateral transactions between the

---

24 G. Hamel, 'Competition for Competence and Interpartner Learning within International Strategic Alliances' (1991) 12 Strategic Management Journal 83.

25 S. Mappa, *Ambitions et illusions de la coopération Nord-Sud: Lomé IV* (Paris: L'Harmattan, 1991).

26 B. Snoy, 'Entreprises conjointes et coopération Nord-Sud, expérience de la Banque mondiale' in A. Jacquemin, ed., *Coopération entre entreprises* (Brussels: De Boeck, 1988) at 140.

27 B. Lyons & J. Mehta, 'Contracts, Opportunism and Trust: Self Interest and Social Orientation' (1997) 21 Cambridge Journal of Economics 21; C. Schmidt, 'Confiance et rationalité' (1997) 107 Revue d'Économie Politique 32.

28 R. Wintrobe & A. Breton, *The Logic of Bureaucratic Conduct: An Economic Analysis of Competition, Exchange, and Efficiency in Private and Public Organizations* (Cambridge: Cambridge University Press, 1982).

29 D. M. Kreps, 'Corporate Culture and Economic Theory' in J. Alt & K. Shepsle, eds., *Perspectives on Positive Political Economy* (Cambridge: Cambridge University Press, 1990) at 134.

same agents, Kreps considers that this condition is not necessary. In his opinion, the mechanism of reputation can be sufficient to ensure confidence. For Wintrobe and Breton, the perspective of future exchanges between the agents determines the necessary condition for one agent to have confidence in the other. For Kreps, it can be in agent X's own interests to be honest and inspire confidence even though he will only deal with agent Y this one time. In effect, in the event that the subsequent partners of Y learn of X's behaviour, X's reputation will be enhanced. In short, these analyses suggest the following definition of confidence: X's confidence in Y means that X knows, in a certain or likely manner, that the maximization by Y of her/his own interests will encourage her/him to respect her/his engagements.

I would qualify this type of confidence as sombre and reducing. In the examined works, the assumption is the following: confidence rests on the existence of a threat that the partner is susceptible of putting into execution, a threat that makes the opportunist agent regret the disrespect of her/his promises and engagements. In other words, one supposes that the agent cooperates if the maximization of her/his own interests forces her/him to be faithful and honest, and that she/he does not cooperate in the opposite situation. In this context, to affirm that agents are ready to have confidence in each other is ambiguous.[30] At the very least, the affirmation points in a direction different from the one privileged by the relational argument, where the support for confidence and cooperation is constituted by a rationality that does not come exclusively from calculation, but also from certain stimulating principles: equality, equilibrium and collaboration. Besides, these works prove to be too constraining and restrictive about the requisite conditions for generating confidence. Consequently, I submit that the above-mentioned solution to the problematic of asymmetry is not appropriate, and that the Quebec SME must resist the temptation to derive inspiration from it. In this respect, a prospective reading is necessary to open up a more promising solution to the question.

Prospective Reading

Is it possible to propose another definition of confidence, which would take into account the plurality of incentives and the heterogeneity of partners involved in contractual relationships? In light of the work of A. K. Sen, I consider that it is indeed possible.[31] Sen distinguishes three elements which shape individual motivation: the well-being of the individual, her/his goal and her/his choice. In the classic theory, these elements are united under the hypothesis of rationality. Sen shows that this theory adopts the following assumptions:

i)   the well-being of the individual is centred on her/himself;

---

30 O. E. Williamson, 'Calculativeness, Trust and Economic Organization' (1993) 36 Journal of Law and Economics 469.

31 A. K. Sen, 'Goals, Commitment, and Identity' (1985) 1 Journal of Law, Economics, and Organization 75.

ii) this well-being determines her/his goal; and
iii) this goal determines the choice made by the individual.

Sen criticizes the classic theory by suggesting that each of its assumptions can be questioned. Concerning the first assumption, he affirms that it must be enriched by a variable expressing care for others, in order to translate the fact that individual satisfaction is responsive to the satisfaction felt by others. As to the second assumption, Sen refutes the classic theory while advancing the view that the goal of the individual can include objectives other that the maximization of her/his own well-being. He mentions the example of an individual whose goal includes the relief of human misery even if she/he does not suffer from it her/himself. The questioning of the third assumption flows from the idea that there exist rules of conduct which are fairly independent of the goals pursued by the individual. We must distinguish, here, between the principles used by the individual in the determination of her/his goal and the principles she/he uses in making a choice. One can illustrate this distinction by identifying two possible types of individual, both of them displaying trustworthy behaviour. The first acts honestly because she/he considers that honesty is the best attitude, the attitude that permits her/him to hope for the biggest gains. The second acts honestly merely because she/he is honest: for her/him, honesty is a principle which guides her/his choice, regardless of the effects of this choice on her/his own gains. From these considerations ensue a new definition of confidence, more reflective of the reality of the asymmetry and of the establishment of the principle of cooperation, according to which a partner cooperates so that the other will cooperate. Also, this definition is potentially more fruitful in the search for factors which can explain why a project does or does not constitute a real symbiosis of co-development for partners. It could read as follows: the confidence of X in Y means that X considers that Y will respect her/his engagements, even when Y thinks that it is not in her/his own interests to act in this particular way.

However, a practical difficulty can be raised in opposition to this *new* confidence and constitute an objection to it. This difficulty is that, to have confidence, an individual must, to a certain extent, believe in her/his capacity to identify, among her/his potential partners, those who are honest. However, at first glance, the identification of the true nature of a partner is uncertain or, at the very least, demanding. For example, it is in a dishonest partner's own interests, as long as it suits her/him, to conceal her/his real nature. Given the impossibility or the unreasonable character of a process that would consist in filtering partners according to their type, the new confidence would therefore be a lure. This objection can be dismissed with the help of the work of C. W. Morris, who critiques such a position.[32] Morris reiterates the distinction mentioned above between the two types of trustworthy individuals, to whom he applies the concept

---

32   C. W. Morris, 'What Is This Thing Called Reputation', Working Paper, *Limitation de la rationalité et constitution du collectif*, Colloquium, Cerisy, June 5-12 1993, 9 at 9-10.

of limited rationality. This concept means that individuals are incapable of possessing an exact and exhaustive knowledge of a given situation, knowledge that would allow them to make absolutely sure choices. Besides, were they to possess the necessary information, the cost of taking all of it into consideration would be excessive. Morris suggests that, because of this limited rationality, it is difficult for an individual of the dishonest type to know when it is in her/his own interest to cooperate, thereby letting others believe that she/he is of the honest type, and when it is in her/his own interest to deceive others, thereby revealing her/his true type. In particular, Morris suggests that the dishonest individual is probably subject to benefit from the appealing opportunities of short-term defection, without thinking about the long-term opportunities. She/he can be mistaken then, by choosing present opportunism at the expense of future opportunism that would bring her/him more, but that would require that she/he cooperate in the present. Thus, in the long term, repeated interactions between individuals may result in the filtering out of the dishonest individuals and the pairing of honest individuals. In this perspective, the new confidence can be a credible notion and be felt concretely in commercial relations. And it is this new confidence that must inspire the Quebec SME in its contractual relations.

An important lesson can be learned from the above discussion about asymmetry. As presented, asymmetry testifies to the complexity surrounding the establishment of business relationships in an open world. In these conditions, one could say that the success of a project is more a matter related to tact, subtlety and diplomacy than a matter of brutality and contempt. These conditions are not innate for anybody. They are rather a matter of art, which is developed through practice and experience. In this sense, the lesson to be learned from asymmetry consists in assimilating innovation to a constant apprenticeship to which the Quebec SME must be committed. This training is of a cognitive order – to achieve its projects, the SME must acquire knowledge and must educate itself – and of an emotional order – implying the control of certain values and faculties. In my opinion, it is this dimension of training, especially through the relational argument, that can continue to confer such a good image on the Quebec SME. A learning SME possesses an open-mindedness and a greater capacity for self-criticism than another whose maturation is apparently complete. Not just the content, but the dynamic, of the relational argument play a clear part in this evolutionary tendency. In effect, this dynamic has an interest in making of every linkage a real source of advancement for the partners involved, and in transforming the unavoidable situations of instability and imbalance into advantages for partners and the project they pursue. These objectives are perfectly suited to a personality like that of the Quebec SME, which projects an intense desire to learn and possesses the faculties and assets to learn well. And to complete its ongoing training, the Quebec SME is not alone nor confined to itself any more. It can count on the resources available on its territory.

Diffusion

From the point of view of both the action and the results to which it leads, diffusion is a phenomenon that can easily elude satisfactory capture. At its very basis, it must be understood with the aid of the idea of propagation, which describes any movement by which information, whatever its nature, moves away from its point of origin. What happens to the data, how is it transformed as it propagates? Even a superficial analysis of the propagation of given data quickly reveals the intense, even extreme, dynamism that characterizes diffusion. And this is so for all types of diffusion, with very few exceptions. Molecular diffusion in gaseous bodies is a revealing example. There, molecules are in perpetual agitation: they are attracted to each other because of Newtonian attraction, but they also push away from each other after having been knocked against one another.[33] Mental or rational data, as vectors of communication and sources of information, are also subject to the dynamism of diffusion.[34] In this case, to speak of diffusion entails three considerations:

i)   the passage of data from a point of emission to a point of reception;
ii) the determination of what is understood by the point of reception; and,
iii) verification of the degree to which the data is a source of enrichment for the
     point of reception.

In regional development, it is the concept of territory that provides the foundation and the most sensitive variable for diffusion. More particularly, it is not possible to consider the SME without referring, expressly or implicitly, to a territory. There exists a very strong connection between the two. This connection implies that the SME derives from its rooting and adherence to a territory a large proportion of the conditions necessary for the pursuit of its ends and the maintenance of its vitality.[35] Let us study further both the meaning and the reach of this *territory* as a variable.

Description of the Variable

In many respects, territory is meaningful both for an SME and for regional development generally. The relevance of territory is clearly established from the common observation of certain facts. The proximity of a market for the outflow of production and the supplying of services, the existence of institutions devoted to training and research and the availability of modern infrastructure (roads, airports,

---

33 J. M. Ziman, *Models of Disorder: The Theoretical Physics of Homogeneously Disordered Systems* (Cambridge: Cambridge University Press, 1979).
34 G. Vinsonneau, *Culture et comportement* (Paris: Armand Colin, 1997); J. Demorgon, *Complexité des cultures et de l'interculturel* (Paris: Anthropos, 1996).
35 M. S. Gertler, 'Capital, Technology and Industrial Dynamics in Regional Development' (1987) 8 Urban Geography 251.

etc.) constitute facts that can be situated in, or linked, to a territory. They are susceptible of conferring an attractiveness on this territory and increasing its capacity to promote initiatives in a given region. However, I consider that beyond these facts, regional development sees in territory an informational variable. The *raison d'être* of territory ensues from both the quantity and the quality of information that can be, actually or potentially, found in it. More specifically, the relation of territory to information can be analysed under three linked angles.

The first concerns territory as creator of information.[36] This angle is interested in the various ways in which information is created in a territory. The typical strategy consists in multiplying the number of interested actors and inviting them to participate in forums, with a view to developing the greatest possible synergy among them. The principle of free discussion orients this creation of information. The desire to place actors on an equal footing is omnipresent. The rationale behind this strategy is the premise that information will gain both richness and relevance if it is shared rather than withheld. Therefore, territory is used to systematize and formalize processes and modes intended to inform actors, to provide them with information of all kinds. This first angle opens up on different perspectives. In certain cases, the creation of information is simply seen as useful for continuing to go in the right direction. This is the case of the Beauce region, which still stands as a model of success with respect to regional development in Quebec.[37] However, in other cases, the perspective will be of a preventive or emergency-based nature: the decline, either anticipated or real, of a region will bring actors in it to create or reinforce the dialogue among themselves. In this respect, the Montreal region provides a compelling example. As the economic driving force of Quebec, this region tries to bring in new energy by encouraging all possible exchanges among its various actors.[38]

Under the second angle, territory is a channel through which the previously generated information is used to certain ends. Territory is thus used to either effectively construct or achieve something. Its function consists in finding and transforming information simply available here and there, with a view to engendering repercussions to the benefit of the region concerned. Besides, this channel is not neutral. It is tinged with all the elements integrated into the so called *regional culture*. This particular tinge is seen as a strength, a strategic advantage

---

36 P. Veltz, 'Nouveaux modèles d'organisation de la production et tendances de l'économie territoriale' in G. Benko, ed., *La dynamique spatiale de l'économie contemporaine* (Paris: Éditions de l'espace européen, 1990) at 53.

37 A. Billette & M. Carrier, 'Régulation socio-identitaire des activités économiques beauceronnes' (1993) 34 Recherches sociographiques 261; by the same authors, 'L'entrepreunariat beauceron: les ingrédients du succès' (1992) 2 Revue Organisation 27. F. Bélanger, *La Beauce et les Beaucerons: portraits d'une région, 1737-1987* (Saint-Joseph-de-Beauce: Société du patrimoine des Beaucerons, 1990).

38 L. N. Tellier, *Les défis et les options de la relance de Montréal* (Sainte-Foy: Presses de l'Université du Québec, 1997); Groupe de travail sur Montréal et sa région, *Montréal, une ville-région: efficace, prospère et vibrante, à vocation internationale, au service de ses citoyens* (Montreal: Le Groupe, 1993).

for the region. On the one hand, it provides SMEs with different opportunities to put distinctive products and services on the market. On the other hand, it constrains these SMEs to be respectful of the characteristic facets of their immediate environment. In a way, the channel creates a marriage between regional culture and the economic vitality of the region. At present, the message sent to all is the following: Internationalization, in spite of the fears that it generates, would create some unsuspected possibilities. These would result notably from the deep diversification of needs and expectations of consumers.[39] Henceforth, one would search for singular, original or even personalized products and services. Consequently, methods and techniques of mass production would be a thing of the past in an increasing number of sectors. The future would belong to a production constituted of subtlety and that possesses a real identity, contrary to the artificial identity of mass production. From then on, for example, nothing would prevent regional producers of refined cheeses from carving a place for themselves in the North American market. In the same way, there would be reason to believe that small breweries can benefit from the opening of markets, because demand becomes segmented and more and more specialized. In short, under this angle, a territory represents an appreciable increment in the development process of a region.[40]

Finally, the third angle considers territory on the basis of the composite nature of information that it contains. In this case, territory refers to an open variable or a variable connected to different sources of information. The starting point of these sources is difficult to determine; but one understands that it is not unique and that the trajectory of these sources is more meandering rather than straight. On the internal level, the contribution of these sources to the material and emotional enrichment of a region is not evaluated on the basis of a relationship of cause and effect. The important thing is that one can seriously link them to the general picture of a region. The best example of such a way to analyse the territory is provided by the experience of the city of Drummondville. This city has passed in a few years from the unenviable status of laughingstock of Quebec to the status of a city envied and imitated in all aspects. Its cultural, economic and communitarian vitality are impressive and in some respects astonishing. They are usually illustrated with the city's yearly world festival of folklore. This festival is a strong success because of the quality of its organization, the enthusiasm of its volunteers and the richness of its programme. Founded in 1982, it is perceived as a catalyst of the renewal of the city of Drummondville.[41] Thus, one may say that it constituted, without necessarily having been planned this way, a tool for insertion of the regional territory into a global network. It multiplied points of contact between this territory and the rest of the world. It allowed the *Drummondvillois* to come out of their darkness and their torpor, and this was reflected in the economic activities carried out on the territory.

39   Julien & Marchesnay, *supra*, note 7; at Chapter 3.
40   P. Aydalot, *Dynamique spatiale et développement inégal* (Paris: Économica, 1980).
41   A. Lavallée & C. Lafond, 'Les festivals au Québec: entre économie et identité. Le cas d'un festival mondial de folklore' (1998) 21 Loisir et société 213.

Overall, the city of Drummondville projects an image of a regional capital in full expansion, whose experience can teach a great deal.

Evaluative Reading

This description illustrates the incontestable role played by territory in regional development, a role that is distinctive to the Quebec world. Territory is a diffuser of information to which the development of a region reacts favourably. This region needs the information generated by the territory, which influences, discreetly or conspicuously, its degree of vitality. In spite of this, the conservative consciousness of uniform law would consider the contribution of the territory as an anomaly. Applied to the theme under study, the conservative approach would take for granted that the *general processes* of development and transformation are clearly predominant with regard to economic, cultural, political and environmental conditions and factors specific to every regional reality. Thus, the development of the region would be considered in relation to the action of exogenous strengths and factors, that is to say, strengths and factors which come from the outside.[42] In the final analysis, only those factors and strengths coming from elsewhere would be considered relevant. In addition, conservative consciousness, itself exogenous, would put forward a standard model of development. This standardization would express development in terms of organized relations, whose future display is foreseeable. At the internal level, the region would therefore be limited to receiving information and applying its prescriptions. Its mission would consist in fulfilling a function defined at a superior level over which it does not have any ascendancy. All in all, the diffusion of the received model would operate on the basis of a levelling of the particular conditions linked to the territory. And if the latter ever offered any resistance, they would be assimilated to obstacles. In any event, their persistence would not call into question the unifying effect of the model thus diffused.

The progressive consciousness of uniform law would see this interpretation of the impact of territory as a major practical and theoretical flaw. In progressive consciousness, territory constitutes a normal variable, which means something in the contrasted orientations of the development of the different regions of Quebec. In the progressive perspective, the facts presented in the above description would permit the following reply to conservative consciousness: the exogenous strengths – external or coming from the top – are powerless to wholly explain the development of a region. The internal dynamics of the region, which flow from the fact that the conditions particular to the territory are enhanced, must also be taken

---

42   For more on this topic, see J. G. Williamson, 'Regional Inequality and the Process of Natural Development: Description of the Pattern' (1965) 13 Economic Development and Cultural Change 3; G. Myrdal, *Economic Theory and Underdeveloped Regions* (London: Duckworth, 1957).

into consideration.[43] These conditions are called endogenous, that is to say local, internal, or coming from the bottom. In short, territory is a positively relevant variable, and is not merely a contingency to be eliminated or underestimated.

In a detailed manner, the relevance of territory is dependent upon the emergence of a juridico-commercial reality which is in opposition to the idea of a standardizing model of development. The Quebec world, and in particular its regional development, are part of this emerging reality, which is very sensitive to the technological revolution presently in progress.[44] This revolution is based on the use of micro-electronics and telematics in processes of production. It brings about a developed integration between the different technologies and creates increased pressure on research and development activities and a decrease in the life cycle of products. At the same time, it causes a division of labour and an increase in the collaboration between a growing number of actors, such as the SMEs, research organizations and universities, etc. With respect to actors more directly in competition, as in the case of the enterprises, these transformations facilitate the institution of relations based on networking. These relations translate into co-management dealings of all kinds: strategic alliances, long-term agreements, coenterprises, etc. In this context, the competitiveness of an enterprise results less from a dominant position, whether oligopolistic or other, than from a combination between its control of technological progress and the quality of the interdependence it maintains with other enterprises.[45] However, in the background of this competitiveness, the territory is not an indifferent variable. On the contrary, it is at the heart of the polycentric articulation that goes hand in hand with the establishment of any network. It means that every region to which a given territory corresponds will be solicited for all the advantages that it can offer, as well as on the basis of the complementarity it maintains with the other territories of the network.

Thus, in the perspective of progressive consciousness, it is normal for the variable of territory to play an ad hoc and active role, as opposed to an already predetermined and passive role, in the regional development of Quebec. It is normal that this territory seeks to create information, that it channels it in the light of existing conditions and that it is permeable by information available elsewhere. Indeed, in this perspective, space is necessarily a place of variable geometry,[46] which renders impossible the development of any extensive model, as advocated

---

43 P. Fortin, *Innovation endogène et croissance: conséquences du point de vue canadien* (Ottawa, Industrie Canada, 1995); C. T. Huynh, *Développement endogène: aspects qualitatifs et facteurs stratégiques* (Paris: UNESCO, 1988).

44 R. Petrella, 'La mondialisation de la technologie et de l'économie: une hypothèse' (1989) *Futuribles* 3; C. Freeman & C. Perez, 'Structural Crises of Adjustment: Business Cycles and Investment Behaviour' in G. Dosi, ed., *Technical Change and Economic Theory* (London: Pinter, 1988) at 38.

45 K. Ohmae, 'The Global Logic of Strategic Alliances' (1989) 24 Harvard Business Review 143.

46 M. Castells, *The City and the Grassroots* (Berkeley: University of California Press, 1983).

by conservative consciousness. If there is to be a model, it should be interpreted under the angle of incompleteness and incompletion: for example, the case of the city of Drummondville, in principle, could not be transposed elsewhere and produce the same results, even if we attempted to follow each and every condition of its success. It will be adapted and filtered by the other interested territories.

By the same token, progressive consciousness unveils somewhat more of its position with respect to contemporary economic development: it does not exist to encourage the extension and reinforcement of the large enterprise, animated by objectives valuing the suppression of differences and the production of goods for unified markets. Rather, it encourages a variety of approaches and accomplishments by the actors involved. To the pure and simple concentration of these actors, it opposes the development among them of chains of values through the creation of partnerships.[47] At this level, the territory acts as an interface between what we commonly call *the local and the global*. This is essentially a constantly evolving role that a prospective reading will permit us to explore further.

Prospective Reading

The local-global nexus recalls the endogenous-exogenous link already mentioned. It expresses a relation between forces whose points of origin are opposed, but which come into contact in the end. What forces win when contact occurs?[48] This is one of the important questions debated under the theme of internationalization. Do the forces at the top always win, in which case internationalization would be synonymous with progressive homogenization? Or do the forces at the bottom win, in which case internationalization would correspond to a process of fragmentation? The role of diffuser of information assumed by territory, as described previously, does not rule in favour of any of these positions. In my view, this role suggests, at most, that territory acts as a common limit to the local and the global, or that it establishes a junction between them. It is a third force that mediates between the forces at the top and those at the bottom. In other words, it is an interface which, according to information it contains and its configuration, will give a particular colour to the object studied. In effect, the interface has a subjective connotation: it is shaped by different actors, faced with particular stakes and interested in satisfying specific needs. In the present case, I submit that the place conceded to territory by progressive consciousness leads to the following conclusions about regional development in Quebec.

---

47   R. Camagni, 'Inter-firm Industrial Networks: The Costs and Benefits of Co-operative Behaviour' (1993) 1 Journal of Industry Studies 1.

48   See, for an example in relation to urban matters, M. Cohen, *Preparing for the Urban Future: Global Pressures and Local Forces* (Washington: Johns Hopkins University Press, 1996).

The first conclusion concerns regional belonging or rootedness.[49] This could be defined on a macroscopic level. One would then look for signs attesting to an actor's formal presence in a region, such as an incorporation with the competent authority. We can qualify these signs as heavy, obvious or unequivocal. However, the interface idea implies that this search should be extended to the other observable elements in the informational variable that a territory is. At that moment, regional belonging does not rest any more on a rigid dichotomy between, for example, a local enterprise and non-local enterprise; it relies rather on the different forms and intensities of rooting of these enterprises. It is helpful to refer, at this point, to signs which are more diffuse and considered lighter or less obvious than the previous signs, but which are more meaningful to the development of the region. With respect to small enterprise, the differences could manifest as rootedness that is *natural* (directly influencing the type of production), *totalizing* (comprehending its whole structure), and *very dependent* on the network for its expansion. For the medium-sized enterprise, rootedness could relate to a *project* – that is to say, it might emerge from the prior choice of location; could be *selective* – interacting with the region in different ways according to context; and be *greatly influential* on the network. In this setting, the co-evolution between the enterprise and the region constitute both a condition of development for the Quebec SMEs and a factor of reproduction of regional particularities.

The second teaching concerns regional competitiveness.[50] As such, taken alone, rooting is not sufficient to produce some positive repercussions for the region. It becomes an advantage from the moment when the SME integrates in its strategic behaviour some informational data diffused by the intervention of the territory.[51] From this point of view, the region loses its presumed complexion of objectivity to become the strategic ally of the SME, an alliance that it reinforces by establishing collaborations with other enterprises and actors. This alliance is strengthened by a double assumption: on the one hand, the region is not a mere expression of an autonomous historic evolution, but remains influenced by the strategies of economic actors; on the other hand, the SME cannot be reduced to an entity evolving in isolation and instituting hegemonic relations with the region. The reciprocity therefore governs the relations between the region and the SME; everyone can expect to benefit from these relations. And the more this reciprocity proves to be intense, the more the region proves to be competitive. Indeed, by definition, the mutual relations between SMEs and regions create advantages, for a region, which are not instantaneously reproducible elsewhere. This can be explained by the fact that the interface, represented by the territory, in a sense

---

49 N. Granovetter, 'Economic Action and Social Structure: The Problem of Embeddedness' (1985) 91 American Journal of Sociology 481.

50 S. Conti, E. J. Malecki & P. Oinas, 'Introduction: Rethinking the Geography of Enterprise' in S. Conti, E. J. Malecki & P. Oinas, eds., *The Industrial Enterprise and Its Environment* (Aldershot: Avebury, 1995) at 1.

51 P. A. Julien, 'Globalization: Different Types of Small Business Behavior' (1995) 10 Journal of Business Venturing 459.

crystallizes these relations, or gives them a specific complexion. Hence, this crystallization makes impossible the reproduction of these relations elsewhere, in real time. This outline corresponds to the Quebec experience mentioned above, and it accords with the principle according to which diversity is 'the basis of the competitive advantage and the key instrument to produce economic value.'[52]

The third teaching concerns regional highlighting.[53] By sanctioning the relevance of specificities of historic, social and ethical orders, the territorial interface defines a regional logic. This logic, contrary to the general logic advocated by conservative consciousness, demonstrates the importance of interdependencies between the SMEs and the other actors – institutional, communal, etc. – that influence a region. This demonstration provides the premise necessary to defend the idea of a development based no longer on a unique process of transformation that should inevitably spread inside everything and everywhere, but on a plurality of possible conditions and modes of development. In this perspective, the region, in Quebec, is highlighted from the moment when it can put forward *its own* model of development. I would say that, in its case, the tandem self-fulfilment-solidarity promoted by progressive consciousness is translated as the search for a relational autonomy. In one respect, the region tries to determine its future as freely as possible. In order to do that, it draws here and there, on its territory, elements considered the most relevant ones. In this search for autonomy, in another respect, its territory brings it into contact with other regions. The result that it reaches can only obey, in all circumstances, the laws of complexity. Too many elements intervene and overlap for a single method to totally explain it. This is why, more often than not, the best way to understand or to present this result will be to proceed to what C. Geertz calls a *thick description*.[54] In any event, the reading of such a thick description could be the occasion to know a little bit more about the aspiration of the region, or at the very least to establish a tie with it.

Aspiration

Viewed as succinctly as possible, I would say that an aspiration is like an impetus, appreciable individually and/or collectively, which tends toward something.[55] The content of this impetus is made of the different materials that one can extricate from consciousness or the mind. Feelings, beliefs, habits are therefore some of its essential components. These contribute to establish the consistency of the process underlying the impetus, and to define the goal to be reached. The aspiration

---

52 *Ibid.* at 3-4.
53 A. Scott & R. Storper, 'Le développement régional reconsidéré' (1992) 66 Espace et Sociétés 7.
54 C. Geertz, 'Thick Description: Toward an Interpretive Theory of Culture' in *The Interpretation of Cultures, supra*, Introduction, note 9; at 3.
55 J. Stanley, *La motivation par l'action: outil essentiel aux fonceurs et aux bâtisseurs de réseaux* (Saint-Hubert: Éditions Un monde différent, 1997); D. C. McClelland, *The Achieving Society* (Princeton: Van Nostrand, 1961).

emerges mainly in two ways. At a first level, its demonstrations will take the shape of desires. With regard to a variable in particular, to feel desires will mean that it tends consciously toward an object to possess or a state to assume. This object or this state may already exist when they are desired by the variable, but they may as well be completely or partially imagined. As such, there is no reason to discriminate between these types of desires: they are both admissible and worthy. At a second level, the aspiration appears by means of ambitions. Ambitions can be distinguished from desires, mainly by their reach. As a matter of fact, an ambition is first and foremost characterized by the will of a variable to rise above others, or above the context in which it finds itself. This elevation, in accordance with progressive thought, is not automatically justified. To become so, it must express a pursuit of what appears honourable to do in the circumstances. Generally, an action will be honourable if it succeeds in attracting consideration and respect, or if it promotes human dignity in general.

An analysis which combines regional development and aspiration cannot but acknowledge that the region, as a variable, is inescapable. Basically, the region corresponds to a social milieu and a way of life. It results from the accumulation and the overlapping of a series of components whose different origins and facets are manifold. The *portrait* of a region can be explained by its population, its resources, its history, its geography and so forth. In sum, the region is the variable which, among all those that constitute the theme of regional development, can best aspire to something. Let us see how the matter stands with regard to the Quebec world.

Description of the Variable

To what does the region aspire? What are its desires and ambitions? Every Quebec region has its own idea on that question, and it expresses it in its own way. This specificity does not prevent resemblances from being observable from one region to another. In this context made of likenesses and dissimilarities, how can we draw the contours of the region as a variable? In my view, this exercise is facilitated by the fact that the aspirations of the Quebec regions, whatever they may be, are currently centred on a specific problematic: the search for and the definition of an identity.[56] Wherever one looks, reality remains the same. Landmarks still exist, but they are old and timeworn. Thus, it is strange to note that very often, the problematic surrounding the quest for a region identity rapidly becomes that of

---

56 J. Létourneau, 'Nous autres les Québécois. La voix des manuels d'histoire' in L. Turgeon & J. Létourneau, eds., *Les Espaces de l'identité* (Sainte-Foy: Presses de l'Université Laval, 1997) at 99; C. Beausoleil, *Le motif de l'identité dans la poésie québécoise, 1830-1995* (Ottawa: Le Groupe de création Estuaire, 1996); G. Laforest, 'Identité et pluralisme libéral au Québec' in S. Langlois, ed., *Identité et cultures nationales. L'Amérique française en mutation* (Sainte-Foy: Presses de l'Université Laval, 1995) at 313; J. Mathieu, *Approches de l'identité québécoise* (Québec: CELAT, 1985).

Quebec as a whole.[57] Such a debate originates in such a region and, for one reason or another, it attracts everybody's attention everywhere in Quebec and everybody feels concerned by what it raises. In the end, the identity quest of every region becomes that of Quebec. This is probably a tangible proof of the existence of a Quebec world. In any event, the turmoil, the insecurity, the ardour and the perseverance aroused by the problematic of identity appear as follows.

First, they denote an ambiguous relationship between the social milieu and history, and time in general.[58] Until recently, Quebec's past could be explained quite clearly and simply. There were little or no variations in the history of Quebec. Some periods were reputed positive and others were not. This history seemed crystallized around some personalities and episodes. There was nothing to hint that it could be reread and rediscovered. Quebec had a good memory, and it did not have to worry about the fact that it could decline. At the present time, everything is changing.[59] The main cause behind this movement lies in what I would call disappointed hopes. Several examples could illustrate this phenomenon. I will consider the example of modern Quebec as the heir to the Quiet Revolution. During this epoch, which goes back to the beginning of the 1960's, the Quebec world emerged from the years of great darkness to embark upon a very important process of reforms. Everything was permitted then, even dreaming. Today however, we are left with a memory of this adventure which is not worthy of what it predicted.[60] Some now advance the view that perhaps the acts accomplished in the past were not appropriate. Facing the future, Quebec is henceforth hesitant, because of a past more fragile than it thought.[61]

Secondly, the problematic of identity is felt on the basis of a paradoxical relationship between the social milieu and nature.[62] In one respect, nature is the object of care and protection. Here and there, people know that it is precious, and people try to preserve it. Nature is considered an indispensable ally of the quality

---

57　See, for example, the debate about the creation of a megalopolis including all the municipalities situated on the Island of Montreal: É. Desrosiers, 'Une île, une ville est accueilli froidement' Le Devoir (27 May 1999) A1; K. Lévesque, 'Une île, une ville: l'analyse de Harel est contestée' Le Devoir (23 June 1999) A3; K. Lévesque, 'Une autre superstructure? On est en train de créer un monstre' Le Devoir (26 August 1999) A1.

58　G. Bouchard, *La nation québécoise au futur et au passé* (Montreal: VLB Éditeur, 1999).

59　L. Cardinal, C. Couture & C. Denis, 'La révolution tranquille à l'épreuve de la "nouvelle" historiographie et de l'approche post-coloniale. Une démarche exploratoire' (1999) 2 Globe. Revue internationale d'études québécoises 75.

60　F. Dumont, 'Quelle révolution tranquille' in F. Dumont, ed., *La société québécoise après 30 ans de changements* (Québec: I.Q.R.C., 1990) at 13.

61　F. Dumont, *L'Avenir de la mémoire* (Québec: Nuit blanche, 1995); J. Mathieu & J. Lacoursière, *Les mémoires québécoises* (Sainte-Foy: Presses de l'Université Laval, 1991).

62　J. M. Bergeron & S. Sève, *La cause verte au Québec* (Sherbrooke: Presses de l'Université de Sherbrooke, 1993); S. Mongeau, *Pour que demain soit: l'écologie sociale en action* (Montreal: Éditions Écosociété, 1993).

of life. It is with strong satisfaction, sometimes with deep emotion, that the social milieu maintains its relation with nature. Here, the essence of the Quebec world is a matter of symbiosis between its actors and nature.[63] In another respect, this same nature finds itself in a precarious state of inferiority vis-à-vis the human environment.[64] In many respects, it is not treated in a way consistent with sustainable development. Planning of its management is weak or non-existent. The recent movie by R. Desjardins entitled *L'erreur boréale* denounced this kind of attitude as evident in the management of the Quebec boreal forest. But this movie also expressed the fact that, overall, Quebec-nature ties still remain quite precarious.[65]

Thirdly, it is clear that the relationship to others which underlies the search for, and the definition of, identity is marked by uncertainty.[66] Who is who within the nation, the people, Quebec society? Who is *authorized*, and by what, to be part of one or the other of these points of reference of the Quebec world? Is it language, ethnic origin, or some other criterion that permits the identification of the Quebec world? And what are the consequences ensuing from the criteria chosen regarding the status of very visible actors, such as the French-speaking majority, the English-speaking minority and the Native people? In my opinion, the proponents of pluralism offer the wisest and most realistic answers to these questions. The pluralistic path sanctions a notion of citizenship composed of three parts.[67] First of all, it consists in putting into effect, by the recognition of institutions or other measures, a principle of protection of minorities. Then, citizenship supposes the building of a shared history, that is to say a history that grants a place to all and that underlines each one's contribution to the well-being of the community. Finally, the firmness of the identity to be shaped depends on the full and complete execution of a duty of involvement in public life. The pluralistic path is certainly not unanimously accepted. But I think that its main advantage is that it corresponds empirically better than one believes to the Quebec situation, already pluralistic

---

63 D. Forget & P. Goulet, *Plan d'action vers un développement durable* (Québec: ÉcoSommet, 1997); P. Dansereau, *L'envers et l'endroit: le désir, le besoin et la capacité* (Saint-Laurent: Fides, 1994).

64 J. G. Vaillancourt & C. Gendron, *L'énergie au Québec: quels sont nos choix?* (Montreal: Éditions Écosociété, 1998).

65 L. G. Francoeur, 'La forêt boréale est menacée, constate le Sénat', Le Devoir (30 June 1999) A1; L. G. Francoeur, 'L'avenir de la forêt : la quantité ou la qualité?', Le Devoir (18 June 1999) C1; L. G. Francoeur, 'L'Erreur boréale a relancé un débat public', Le Devoir (4 January 1999) A2.

66 J. Maclure, 'Authenticités québécoises. Le Québec et la fragmentation contemporaine de l'identité' (1998) 1 Globe. Revue internationale d'études québécoises 9.

67 M. Seymour, 'Pour un Québec multiethnique, pluriculturel et multinational' in M. Sarra-Bournet, ed., *Le pays de tous les Québécois. Diversité culturelle et souveraineté* (Montreal: VLB Éditeur, 1998) at 219; G. Rocher, 'Droits fondamentaux, citoyens minoritaires, citoyens majoritaires', paper presented at the Colloquium entitled *Droits fondamentaux et citoyenneté*, Onati, May 4-5 1998; G. Bourque, 'Le discours sur la nation' (1997) 38 Recherches sociographiques 532.

from several points of view.[68] Besides, its intellectual credibility is beyond doubt, as evidenced in a series of commentaries written by first-class Quebec thinkers and recently published in the Montreal daily *Le Devoir*.[69]

Fourthly, the constantly evolving identity reveals a cold, distrustful relationship toward the virtues attributed to pure market economy and their implications at the national and international levels. Neoliberal doctrine is not readily accepted by actors, groups and institutions which compose the Quebec world, and it is not readily integrated in their strategies either.[70] The collaboration of the market is welcomed in the resolution of problems linked to unemployment, the future of youth, the eradication of poverty, etc. But it must cohabit with other considerations put forward by, for example, the Quebec state. As a matter of fact, the Quebec state maintains moderate interventionism in the economy of Quebec, through various programmes of subsidies and state institutions under its control.[71] In a similar way, the community movement assumes considerable leadership in social regulation, and it knows how to make itself heard when the time is right.[72] The coldness and the distrust that permeate this fourth relationship does not mean that the Quebec world refuses to change and, in particular, to participate in efforts at economic integration.[73] But the angle under which it analyses the merits of integration is not solely economic; it definitely appeals to other factors contained in its present identity, as unsteady as it might be, and in its coming identity.[74]

---

68   G. Bouchard, 'Représentations de la population et de la société québécoises: l'apprentissage de la diversité'(1990) 19 Cahiers québécois de démographie 7.

69   On the theme of 'Penser la nation québécoise', see the following contributions: G. Bouchard, 'Construire la nation québécoise' (4 September 1999) A9; D. Juteau, 'Le défi de la diversité' (28 August 1999) A9; J. Jenson, 'De la nation à la citoyenneté' (31 July 1999) A8; D. Delâge, 'Les trois peuples fondateurs du Québec' (24 July 1999) A9; G. Bourque, 'La nation, la société, la démocratie' (3 July 1999) A10; C. Taylor, 'De la nation culturelle à la nation politique' (19 June 1999) A10.

70   G. Bourque, J. Duchastel & A. Kuzminski, 'Les grandeurs et les misères de la société globale au Québec' (1997) 28 Cahiers de recherche sociologique 7.

71   J. Hamel, 'L'économie francophone au Québec à la lumière de la théorie sociologique de la transition' (1990) 22 Sociologie et sociétés 163; P. Bélanger & B. Lévesque, 'La modernité par les particularismes' in J. P. Dupuis, ed., *Le modèle québécois de développement économique* (Cap-Rouge: Presses Inter Universitaires, 1995) at 115.

72   P. Prévost, *Entrepreneurship et développement local: quand la population se prend en main* (Montreal: Éditions transcontinentales, 1993); Y. Leclerc & M. Blanchet, *Un Québec solidaire: rapport sur le développement* (Boucherville: G. Morin, 1992); H. Lamoureux & J. Panet-Raymond, *L'intervention communautaire* (Montreal: Éditions Saint-Martin, 1984).

73   P. P. Proulx, 'L'intégration économique dans les Amériques: quelles stratégies pour tenter d'assurer l'américanité du Québec plutôt que l'américanisation du Québec?' (1999) 18 Politique et sociétés 129.

74   O. Atkouf, R. Bédard & A. Chanlat, 'Management, éthique catholique et esprit du capitalisme: l'exemple québécois' in J. P. Dupuis, ed., *supra*, note 71; at 97; G. Houle & J. Hamel, 'Une nouvelle économie politique québécoise francophone' (1987) 12 Cahiers canadiens de sociologie 42.

Evaluative Reading

The four relationships just described clearly demonstrate that the region – or, rather, the whole Quebec world – aspires to something. In the face of time, nature, others and the market, it undoubtedly shows desires and ambitions. For the time being, these desires and ambitions reveal a dominant aspiration: the Quebec world wants to know who it is. This questioning participates, with both other variables – the SME and the territory – in the dynamic of global action represented by regional development. The content and effects of identity, be they felt regionally or on a pan-Quebec level, are bound to the other elements which can be observed inside the SME and the territory. To use a very simplified formula, one could put forward the following: Quebec's identity influences and will influence the information contained within the territory, which can influence the behaviour of the SME. However, I submit that the most important observation to emerge from this analysis is the following: the combination of the problematic of identity with the data collected at the time of the description of the other variables raises the veil on the conception of the good life as cherished by the Quebec world. According to progressive consciousness, it would be correct to make this observation, because of the fundamental place it grants to the concept of world and the vision it has of it. Therefore, according to progressive consciousness, it would be correct as well to make a similar statement were we to study a different world. In sum, it agrees with the assumption that competing conceptions of the good life exist. From this point, we can ask ourselves what the value of the Quebec conception of the good life is, as compared with that of other worlds. Correlatively, what should be the attitude of progressive consciousness in the face of the multiplicity of conceptions of the good life?

Logically, one would expect the attitude of progressive consciousness to be governed by a principle of neutrality.[75] From the moment when development no longer rests on a hierarchy between advanced societies and remote societies – where the latter are forced to imitate the former – but founds its *raison d'être* on the intrinsic richness of human diversity, it is normal for the basic assumption of progressive consciousness to reflect a lack of interest in sanctioning one or many conceptions of life as truly good. In short, the principle of neutrality forbids progressive consciousness – and all those who make decisions in its light – an appeal to any conception to justify its actions. From this point of view, the Quebec world should not fear that its conception of the good life will be put into question or be attacked merely because another conception is judged superior. However, this neutrality as regards justifications does not carry with it a neutrality as regards consequences.[76] This means that a decision taken by virtue of uniform law will

---

75 B. Ackerman, 'Neutralities' in R. Douglas, ed., *Liberalism and the Good* (New York: Routledge, 1993) at 193; J. Waldron, 'Legislation and Moral Neutrality' in R. Goodin & A. Reeve, eds., *Liberal Neutrality* (London: Routledge, 1989).

76 C. Larmore, *Patterns of Moral Complexity* (Cambridge, Cambridge University Press, 1987) at 43.

remain legitimate even though it has uneven consequences on conceptions of the good life existing here and there. In fact, every decision will inevitably either facilitate or put obstacles in the way of the realization of the different conceptions of the good life, because it could not be otherwise: trying to rectify some uneven consequences would probably give rise to effects as uneven as the consequences. But if the neutrality of consequences is not practicable, it is no longer desirable. Among the reasons that could be advanced to support this position, I will limit myself to pointing out the following: the neutrality of consequences is incompatible with the idea that every world is responsible for the choice of life that it has made. In other words, the Quebec world would not have the right to force its neighbourhood to pay for the costs of the good life that it has chosen for itself. If it finds itself in the difficult situation of being afflicted with bad health, it should accept the consequences. By contrast, if it finds itself in a troublesome position because of circumstances outside of its control, it should be permitted to receive more support from its neighbourhood. To accept the neutrality of consequences implies an identical answer in all cases, which is in opposition to minimal justice; to refuse it allows for a differentiated answer, which is therefore more just.[77]

It follows that the principle of neutrality does not make a passive matter of progressive consciousness, which would refrain from acting to rely exclusively on the will of the worlds to carry on a good life. On the contrary, the principle exists to serve as a guide for action.[78] Its role is not to force progressive consciousness to aim at a neutrality of consequences ensuing from its actions. It consists rather in bringing it to justify its actions in an acceptable manner for as many worlds as possible. Therefore, it is prevented from resorting to considerations as intimate and relative as those comprised in a world conception of the good life. But, having chosen neutrality as regards justifications, progressive consciousness will still have to decide if it will be neutral toward the worlds or toward the conceptions of the good life that they can choose.[79] At first glance, one could consider that this is a non-issue. Progressive consciousness could judge itself capable of being neutral at all times, toward the various worlds as well as in relation to conceptions of the good life. I submit that in so doing, progressive consciousness would overestimate itself. In fact, being neutral toward the worlds implies respect for their capacity to choose a conception of the good life.[80] In my view, this statement is axiomatic, especially when one resituates it in the perspective of the transitory conception. Neutrality toward conceptions of the good life does not have the same standing. If the case arose, it would give total freedom to all sorts of life plans, even those that limit the liberty of the worlds to choose their aspirations. To avoid such a situation, the principle of neutrality must therefore be clarified as follows. A neutral progressive consciousness will not be allowed to raise objections to the realization

---

77   T. Nagel, *Equality and Partiality* (Oxford: Oxford University Press, 1991) at 155.

78   Larmore, *supra*, note 76, at 44.

79   Ackerman, *supra*, note 75, at 37.

80   P. De Marneffe, 'Liberalism, Liberty, and Neutrality' (1990) 19 Philosophy and Public Affairs 253.

of a conception of the good life specific to a given world – such as that which characterizes the Quebec world – on the basis of an assessment of its intrinsic qualities; but it will make them (thus avoiding the hegemony of the Quebec world) if this realization undermines the capacity of the other worlds to choose their aspirations. I believe this is the best way to synthesize and apply to the question of neutrality the lessons derived from the argument of progressive consciousness based on self-fulfilment and solidarity.

Prospective Reading

Let us push the analysis of the aspiration further, by joining it to the entire uniformist reading of the Quebec world achieved so far. From this reading, a general proposition should be admitted: progressive consciousness is in a position to support regional development in Quebec. The argument in support of this proposition could be presented as follows:

i)   progressive consciousness protects, up to a certain point, the conception of the good life connected to the regional or pan-Quebec quest for identity;
ii)   it recognizes the vital role played by territory;
iii) it perceives positively the behaviour of the SME;
iv)   yet, since these three variables overlap in a holistic action devoted to regional development, it follows that progressive consciousness is an ally rather than an opponent of this development.

However, this general proposition risks facing an important objection: trade – let us say the market – which is an inseparable partner of uniform law, is presently incapable of endorsing the position of progressive consciousness. It is therefore illusory to think that Quebec regional development, as read and interpreted, will have interesting results. Why is this so? Essentially, because the market is insensible or allergic to all types of subjective data. The market favours and adheres to reason – understood in terms of efficiency in the satisfaction of needs; abstraction – demonstrated by a universal passion for wealth; and utility – which is manifested in the levelling of contingencies reputed to hinder the maximization of wealth. Therefore, the market is not interested in the intelligent behaviour of the SME and in the asymmetry of its contractual relations, it cannot take into account volatile and emotional information such as that which transits through the territory, and it would deem it irrational to consider something as personalized as regional or pan-Quebec identity; all simply on the grounds that these all relate to subjective data. How can we answer this objection?

To begin with, I would use an argument derived from the Western legal tradition. From a legal point of view, the perspective of the market that I have just described confers a technical function on law, be it uniform law or another law. Law serves the market. And it is undeniable that this perspective as well as this function stick to the reality of the conservative consciousness of uniform law.[81] The imperatives of the market dominate this reality; the nature and content of uniform law are subordinated to these imperatives, they are modelled by them. That this situation should be assimilated to one of malaise – *faux pas*? – prompted by modernity and modern law is no surprise. Nevertheless, I think that modernity and its modern law carry with them part of the solution to the problematic raised by the objection mentioned above. Following C. Taylor, I would suggest that the solution partially depends on the resurgence of what he would call an unarticulated, that is to say, unrecognized or misunderstood dimension of the modern tradition.[82] This dimension sees modern law as a mosaic, that is to say a law irreducible to an exclusive end or essence.[83] It conceives it as a juxtaposition that presents an insurmountable challenge to any attempt at definitive classification and categorization. One could approach law under the angle of an ideology, of a social fact, of a custom, of values, of emotions, etc., and all these approaches would provide meaningful findings. In the perspective of the unarticulated dimension, this separation confers on law a very large receptiveness with regard to all possible phenomena; in return, law has an enormous power over these same phenomena, including the market. As a matter of fact, the law-market juxtaposition is equivalent to saying that, potentially, what law decides can also apply to the market.[84] Thus, the resurgence of the dimension in question would lead to the belief that, faced with support by progressive consciousness for Quebec regional development, the market would have no choice but to be conciliatory. Therefore, it should facilitate this development more than it presently does. But will there be resurgence?

One could doubt it. An unarticulated dimension can go from a latent state to a concrete or actual state thanks to the contribution of many forces, including luck. But obviously no guarantee exists as to the effectiveness of this transformation. I am nevertheless tempted to be optimistic in that respect. In my view, a particular force can stimulate the expected resurgence. This force derives from one of the main hypotheses of the present reflection, which is the progressive entry of the contemporary world into the second modernity. The presumed impact of this force on the market can be understood in the light of the following argument. First of all, we have to conceive the market, like all other institutions of modernity, as equivalent to a large narrative or story.[85] This equivalence is synonymous with invincibility – the market cannot be put in question; with irresistibility – the market has an answer to everything; and with equilibrium – the market tends inexorably toward constancy. Being, by definition, a large narrative, the market cannot adapt

---

81   See Chapter 2, above.
82   See Chapter 4, 'The Rupture in Conservative Consciousness', above.
83   See the conclusion of H. Berman in *Law and Revolution, supra*, Chapter 3, note 2; at 520ff.
84   *Ibid.* at 556-558.
85   J. Friedman, 'Global System, Globalization and the Parameters of Modernity' in J. Friedman, ed., *Cultural Identity and Global Process* (London: Sage, 1994).

to small or local narratives and stories. It does not have any place for as singular a narrative as that of Quebec regional development, for example. However, in the context of the emergence of the second modernity, things arise differently. We leave a situation in which only grand discourses have a right to be accepted and are present in a limited number, to accede to a situation in which they proliferate. As observed by J. Habermas, this proliferation permits speeches which had stayed in the background until then to come to the surface.[86] Moreover, not only are they found in great numbers but they have an effect. In this respect, the second modernity is assimilated to an accelerator of discourses which bombard everything in their way. This creates a certain fissuring of the market as a grand narrative. Spaces open up to welcome more modest stories. What is the actual result of all this? It is possible to associate the market and culture or trade and subjective data – such as those issued from the Quebec regional development –, without committing heresy. The representations, varying from one country to another, of an actor apparently as insensitive as McDonald's are but one example – very modest indeed – of the fraternity that can characterize the relationships between the market and other constituents of human life, including uniform law.[87] In sum, by combining this fraternity, though fragile, with the unarticulated dimension presented above, the objection regarding the market would lose still more force, and Quebec regional development would be in an even better position. But would this combination be strong enough to move the market in the desired direction?

It is not possible to know with certainty if the unarticulated dimension examined above will reappear, nor to know if the second modernity will effectively take root. Consequently, a last strategy must be put forward to thwart the effects of the objection under study. It consists in appealing to both the public sphere of human relations and civil society, with the following intention: to force the market to modify its functioning so that it integrates and protects, among other things, what I called subjective data. Both the public sphere and civil society have a real power to act to this end.[88] Both possess the faculty to influence the finalities of the market, to the extent that they are dynamic. As a matter of fact, debates and discussions which take place in both spheres, on topics as varied as the protection of environment and the human rights, have already proved their capacity to constrain the market to function in such or such a way.[89] In my view, it goes without saying that the second modernity is interested in taking up the challenge this strategy imposes. In this respect, we may simply recall the comments quoted from C. Ruby: he counted on the public sphere to generate all the advantages of the

---

86   See Chapter 4, 'Some Legal Elements of Rupture', above.

87   J. C. Usunier, *Commerce entre cultures: une approche culturelle du marketing international* (Paris: P.U.F., 1992).

88   T. L. Fort, 'The First Man and The Company Man: The Common Good, Transcendance, and Mediating Institutions' (1999) Am. Bus. L. J. 391.

89   S. Charnovitz, 'The Universal Declaration of Human Rights at 50 and The Challenge of Global Markets: The Globalization of Economic Human Rights' (1999) 25 Brooklyn J. Int'l L. 113; J. M. Wagner, 'International Investment, Expropriation and Environmental Protection' (1999) 29 Golden Gate U. L. Rev. 465.

second modernity.[90] But what does that imply for uniform law, which is an actor identified with the private sphere of human relations? Does this mean that uniform law is totally unable to participate in the strategy recommended in the circumstances? It will perhaps be suggested that it is already present on the public scene: the decisions in which it plays a role are accessible, the institutions which promote it are open, etc. With respect, however, I submit that uniform law jurists (to speak only of them) could do more at this level. A progressive ethic requires that they realize, first, that the progressive consciousness of uniform law is fluid and soluble and therefore that its effects are not fundamentally confined to the private sphere of human relations. Then, this ethic must incite them to make use of these characteristics to either criticize or denounce, publicly, on the Internet or otherwise, resistance by the market to what they consider appropriate to accomplish in certain circumstances. Thus, if a jurist thinks that progressive consciousness views Quebec regional development positively, this means that concrete gestures – papers, demonstrations, involvement in non-governmental organizations, etc. – can be made in support of this view in venues beyond the strictly private sphere.[91] With the aid of the other strategies presented above, it may well be that the market will end up giving up and endorse the position of progressive consciousness in the face of regional development in Quebec, if need be.

---

90 *Supra*, Chapter 7, note 14.
91 For further analysis of the role of jurists in general, see A. Kronman, *The Lost Lawyer: Failing Ideals of the Legal Profession* (Cambridge: Harvard University Press, 1995).

Final Remarks

Part IV aimed to further the ideal type of the process undertaken in the previous parts through the analysis of two applications derived from the progressive consciousness of modern law. These applications consisted in an interpretive schema of uniform law and a uniformist reading of the Quebec world. On the one hand, the interpretive schema has shown how progressive consciousness could be actualized and given concrete form in each situation where a decision concerning uniform law must be taken. On the other hand, the uniformist reading of the Quebec world has given the world-based argument a chance to speak with its own voice, through the medium of my own human site.

Other applications will be added, in future, to those presented in this part. In my view, the applications as I have defined them are vital from the point of view of the progressive consciousness of uniform law. Because of the information they contain, the discoveries they prompt and the feedback they provoke, they represent an indispensable source of dynamism. They exist in order to facilitate the maturity of progressive consciousness while maintaining a state of awareness. But before I personally add other applications, it is time to pause and prepare to conclude this reflection.

Conclusion

A Fresh Look at Uniform Law, with a View to Better Knowing the Nature of Law and Human Life

For some time, the contemporary world has been undergoing transition. In its simplest expression, this transition expresses a changeover from modernity to a second modernity. This changeover is currently taking place. It is real and current. It represents an interval between a starting point and a target point. Moreover, the intermediate period that we are currently undergoing is marked by a strong ambivalence. On the one hand, it fosters a very high sense of hope and longing. More than ever, anything is possible. Science, on its own, by continually expanding the frontiers of discovery, comprehension and creation, powerfully encourages a profound sense of belief in the future. To these we may add an innumerable number of aesthetic, literary, political and social accomplishments, whose contributions to what is usually called the progress of humanity are indubitable. On the other hand, the interval we are currently experiencing is tainted with *mal de vivre*. We clearly know, deep down in our hearts and minds, that certain situations are intolerable and incomprehensible with respect to the seemingly unequalled magnitude of our human and material heritage, both in space and time. This ambivalence is helpful in several respects. It serves to explain our state of mind as well as the efforts that we are ready to deploy for any given end. However, it does not inform us of every detail. I would even go as far as to state that one must favour a different perspective on the present. This perspective forsakes ambivalence and places the emphasis on the following consensus: the current transition features a multitude of conflicts and disagreements because it is chaotic, agitated, obscure and barely comprehensible. The reason for this discomfort resides in our faulty perception of the advantages linked to the movement in general, and in particular the movement toward the second modernity.[1] However, one can write that with regard to the focal point of this reflection, this movement allows one to pass from uniform law based on inanimate matter – *d'un droit uniforme à la mesure d'une matière inanimée* – to uniform law based on an ideal of humanity – *à un droit uniforme à la mesure de l'être humain*.

Uniform law based on inanimate matter refers to conservative consciousness as presented in Part I. On the level of principles of thought, stability, precision and simplicity are extolled by conservative consciousness. Moreover, these three pillars are strengthened by instrumental reason. The latter bestows a strategic role on uniform law. It considers uniform law as a lever so indispensable in the quest for opulence that it turns out to be automatically and permanently legitimized. The

---

1   G. Balandier, *Le désordre: éloge du mouvement* (Paris: Fayard, 1988).

level of values does not offer a much more elevated degree of vitality. In themselves, these values are not necessarily to be discredited. However, their comprehensive dynamic, founded on communication, ultimately reveals itself as artificial, if not ineffective. Consequently, what should be done to animate uniform law? An exposition of conservative consciousness was achieved through a regressive analysis based on the work of M. Koskenniemi. In order to elaborate an animated uniform law, I first proceeded, in Part II, by setting out a critique of conservative consciousness. This *critique, as legal imagination*, was developed in three steps. First, it established an inherent relationship between conservative consciousness on the one hand and modernity and modern law on the other. On the basis of this correlation, it analysed, secondly, the factors of rupture of this consciousness, as well as a series of oppositions and of metaphors capable of adequately redirecting its course. And thirdly, it ventured onto the ground of utopia, where one could see the seeds of a new consciousness of uniform law, turned this time toward a second modernity. It is from the reformulation effected in Part III that uniform law modelled on the human being has truly emerged, that it has adopted more realistic human dimensions. Some new arguments, components of progressive consciousness, came to light and were developed. Through an accent on cooperation, osmosis, nature, holistic action, surpassing and generosity, and the relational, common good and world-based arguments, as well as one founded on self-fulfilment and solidarity, a strong human dimension was introduced into the heart of uniform law. Part IV, reserved for an interpretative schema and a uniformist reading of the Quebec world, has completed the picture.

The alignment on an ideal of humanity changes the internal nature of uniform law. Henceforth, it is no longer possible to see and treat it as before. Alone, the appearance of systemic, complex and dialectical thoughts, and their connection with teleological thought, considerably change uniform law as a juridical field. But this change, which I attempted in particular to illustrate by means of an interview relating to the history of uniform law, may and must also be felt with regard to other juridical fields. Moreover, in the Introduction, I had indicated that the principal objectives of the reflection presented in this book were intended as a *right* follow-up for the emerging route of law and development. This bond between uniform law and law and development anticipated, to some extent, the remarks I made later on. These opened up uniform law, caused it to expand. One could object on this score that there is nothing more open than uniform law as it presently stands. As proof, one may point out that it could not have been that which it has become, that is to say a harmonious marriage of juridical cultures existing throughout the world, without an intrinsic quality of openness. Again, it will be argued that it participates intensely in the exchange of goods and services and that it creates, as a result, a wealth which necessarily spreads to all levels and on all planes. To these objections I would reply the following: I have fully and amply *deconstructed* the assertions they contain. The dominant face of uniform law, as revealed by conservative consciousness, is reduced to certain narrow ends which no longer correspond to the needs of the present and the future. What uniform law is most receptive to is modernity and modern law. Yet these belong more to a past that one must preserve as a legacy, but without attributing to it the nature of a testament.

Greatly expanded and fragmented, uniform law takes up a transverse position in relation to other fields of law. In the case in point, it acts as a serious interlocutor in relation to law and development. More specifically, it permits one to know more about *what law has to say to economic, sociocultural and political development, and vice versa.* In conformity with the way paved by the emerging route, progressive uniform law attests to the possibility of conceiving law otherwise than as the sole emanation of the State. The law is midway between the formal and the informal. It is recognizable as much by what is said and written, as by what is predicted, guessed and perceived. It discovers its roots in semi-autonomous and semi-intersected human environments or milieus. Progressive uniform law also attests to the significant sensitivity and porousness of juridical rules. It is not plausible that juridical rules can be understood without recourse to other sources of information. This dependence is explained by the fact that the rules do not at the outset possess a pre-constituted and ready-to-use meaning. Contrary to what one may think, this dependence is not a sign of weakness. In fact, it can only enhance and consolidate the credibility of the law. In the same vein, progressive uniform law demonstrates that it is possible to believe in juridical interactivity, that the law is not reduced to being transplanted from one world to another. Besides, it suffices to compare the picture of conservative consciousness, made up of universality, neutrality, abstraction and constancy, to that of progressive consciousness, made up of diversity and impressionism, in order to realize the stronger allure and attraction of the latter. Finally, progressive uniform law proves that by favouring an interpretative approach based on the quest for the best response, the law remains just as reliable even if it no longer responds to the classic truth criteria of sciences.

If greatly expanded and fragmented, would uniform law become repulsive? Does the reorientation required so that it will be in keeping with the second modernity render it unrecognizable? Does the – *theoretical?* – argument which I proposed in the course of this reflection too greatly complicate things, or is it equivalent to setting the cat among the pigeons – *jeter un pavé dans la mare*? Expressing himself in a general manner on international commercial law, M. Mustill declares he believes 'that many of the possibilities for new thinking in a purely theoretical mode have by now been largely exhausted.'[2] For my part, I feel that theoretical argumentation and all observations so labelled are the surest means of seeing clearly and remaining perspicacious in the presence of a reality whose density ceaselessly increases. Were I seeking to reassure, I would say that the important thing is not the length of the argument. In any case, we are always left with 'incompletely theorized arguments.'[3] The most important thing is to avoid falling into the trap of interpretative intuitionism identified by Koskenniemi, which induces us, unconsciously and perhaps against our will, to reproduce the old rather

---

2   M. Mustill, 'Keynote Speech' in A. J. van den Berg, ed., *International Congress for Commercial Arbitration* (Kluwer, Deventer, 1993) 20 at 23.

3   C. R. Sunstein, 'Incompletely Theorized Arguments' (1995) 108 Harv. L. Rev. 1733.

than produce the new. In this case, legal scholarship errs when it associates uniform law with novelty and progress. This uniform law, unless it changes, remains quite classic, in the sense of very modern. It repeats most of the conceptual categories already known to juridical experience. As a movement, it proceeds on the foundation which enabled the construction of Western national legal systems. Its consciousness, conservative, faithfully reflects the precepts and ideals of modernity. This classicism of uniform law may, through the phenomenon of sedimentation,[4] continue to offer the best of that which it contains for the future. But the survival of certain elements is no reason to justify the present attitude of legal scholarship.

In fact, a greatly expanded and fragmented uniform law takes sides in the debates presently raging, the results of which tell us, each in their own fashion, *what we are aiming for*. In this regard and contrary to appearances, expanded and fragmented uniform law appears to be eminently practical. It is capable of identifying the true issues, the actual problematic and the most likely components of a solution. Its progressive consciousness enjoys the faculties needed to do so. For anyone wishing to be imbued with it, this progressive consciousness is capable of enabling one to grasp that all is not limited to what may be read and understood in legislation, case law and legal scholarship related to uniform law. Behind these *sources* and ahead of them, discussions, deliberations and choices concerning uniform law are scattered and intertwined, seeking only to become integrated into it, an integration that progressive consciousness can achieve. It is difficult to believe, for example, that uniform law can significantly contribute to world peace and harmony, without doctrinal discussion developing the slightest serious statement on the subject. This situation creates divergences and gaps between state law, *lex mercatoria* and intermediate law, on the one hand, and *real life*, on the other, which risk downgrading uniform law in two respects. First, uniform law divorced from real life would be an object of suspicion. One might fear it would serve to *colonize the factual world*, in the words of J. Habermas,[5] only in favour of certain persons. Secondly, uniform law would be unduly removed from its primary users, the traders. Moreover, in his celebrated article entitled 'Non-Contractual Relations in Business: A Preliminary Study',[6] S. Macaulay emphasizes a fact disturbing to jurists: the law of contracts is frequently disregarded or unused in business relations. There is no reason to believe that uniform law is protected from this danger of exclusion. In my opinion, if it maintains a conservative consciousness, it has a greater chance of becoming an irrelevant rather than a relevant juridical corpus in the eyes of its users.[7]

---

4   See Part III, Preliminary Remarks, above.

5   J. Habermas, *The Theory of Communicative Action* (Boston: Beacon, 1984).

6   (1963) 28 Am. Soc. Rev. 55.

7   See V. Behr, 'The Sales Convention in Europe: From Problems in Drafting to Problems in Practice' (1998) 17 J. L. & Com. 263 at 264.

In what debates would a greatly expanded and fragmented uniform law be interested? In the immediate future, the debates surrounding globalization,[8] a redefinition of the law of contracts,[9] liberalism,[10] justice,[11] the expansion of democracy[12] and the prevention and settlement of disputes[13] would seem to me to have priority. All of them have been directly or indirectly touched upon in this reflection. Consequently, each represents a way of pursuing research and reflection which I have undertaken in this study. But more particularly, each represents a clear opportunity for uniform law to take an interest in fundamental considerations, the practical implications of which are evident and manifest. A. Chua provides us with an example of this in the following passage relating to the expansion of the market economy and of democracy:

> Marketization and democratization have each been the site of massive Western legal intervention in the developing world. Legal work on marketization ranges from structuring international project finance to drafting market-oriented laws to developing regimes that facilitate the transition from command to market economies. Work on democratization includes not only writing constitutions but also grappling with formidable issues such as the transplantability of Western social and political institutions and postcommunist state building.
>
> But there is one constituent element of developing societies that these interventions repeatedly overlook. Entrenched ethnic divisions permeate most developing countries, and these divisions bear a distinctive and potentially subversive relationship to the project of marketization and democratization. . . . In the developing world, . . . [m]arkets often reinforce the economic dominance of certain ethnic minorities [and] democracy characteristically pits a powerful but impoverished 'indigenous' majority against an economically dominant ethnic minority.[14]

Insofar as uniform law is a central element of the projects of marketization and democratization, it becomes indispensable that its consciousness possess the qualities required to bring them to a successful conclusion and that it ask the proper questions. This is also true for globalization – to what extent does uniform law conform to the intuition of D. Kennedy according to which internationalization

---

8   J. N. Pieterse, 'Globalisation as Hybridisation' (1994) 9 International Sociology 161.

9   A. M. Burley, 'Liberal States: A Zone of Law', Paper presented to the Annual Meeting of the American Political Science Association, September 3-6, 1992, Chicago.

10 M. W. Zacher, R. A. Matthew, 'Liberal International Theory: Common Threads, Divergent Strands', in C. W. Kegley, *Controversies in International Relations Theory: Realism and the Neoliberal Challenge* (New York: St. Martin's, 1995) at 107.

11 L. Brilmayer, 'International Justice and International Law' (1996) 98 W. Va. L. Rev. 611.

12 A. Chua, 'Markets, Democracy, and Ethnicity: Towards a New Paradigm for Law and Development', Law and Economics Workshop Series, Faculty of Law, University of Toronto, September 16, 1998.

13 A. Connerty, 'The Role of ADR in the Resolution of International Disputes' (1996) 1 Arbitration International 41; C. Menkel-Meadow, 'The Trouble with the Adversary System in a Post-Modern, Multi-Cultural World' (1996) 1 J. Inst. Stud. Leg. Eth. 49.

14 *Supra*, note 12, at 3-4.

strengthens the private and the technocratic?[15] And it is true, too, for the redefinition of the law of contracts – to what extent does uniform law truly reflect commercial practices and can it adapt to them? And for liberalism – to what extent is uniform law a free-exchange doctrine? And for international justice – to what extent does uniform law consolidate this level of justice in evolution? And for the prevention and settlement of disputes – to what extent does uniform law have at its disposal the institutions required to be effective and useful? These debates and these questions dictate the future orientations of my work.

For the time being, one must return to the question posed in the Preamble. *Why is there international uniform commercial law rather than nothing?* The response I have sought to present does not seek to reject the notion of uniform law. Rather, it defends a vision of this great project that could be called normative, that is, a vision that emphasizes the search for principles of thought and for values that will enable uniform law to be considered a virtue in and of itself. In my view, the gradual entry of the contemporary world into a second modernity justifies this emphasis, if only for the sake of the search for meaning that underlies this movement. As a complement to this point, it must be admitted that certain positive considerations can in their turn contribute to supporting the ongoing creation of uniform law. That uniform law should contribute, directly or indirectly, to the attainment of certain goals deemed to be desirable, such as the promotion of a common language of trade, the rapid and efficient completion of business transactions and so on, does not conflict with the vision of it that I have put forward. There is thus no question of suggesting that the normative vision and the positive one are mutually exclusive. Nevertheless, our current context seems to me to argue in favour of paying greater attention to the former than to the latter. In the present case, just such attention has enabled me to defend a vision linking numerous concerns and establishing connections among them. In particular, it links the simplicity of what J. Rawls calls *considered judgements*[16] – carefully weighed convictions such as those associated with the notions of self-fulfilment and solidarity – to the complexity of life on earth, as found in the world-based argument. I do not believe that it results in an indigestible mixture, especially for those to whom it is primarily addressed, namely traders. Traders are used to navigating ambiguity, and in the world of commerce and industry, the contract is already a highly technologically sophisticated instrument, which stores and processes impressive quantities of data of a fluctuating and imprecise nature. In a word, the principle of juridical security, which has attained the status of dogma, will not suffer from a *correct* response that warns of potential change to the legal framework for commercial activity. Nevertheless, the fact remains that this reflection offers only the germs of a response to the question raised in the title. Each germ is interesting in itself, but, even combined, they provide only a partial truth. As I bring this reflection to a close, I am inclined to say that the most truthful response to the question paraphrased from M. Heidegger is this phrase, understood

---

15   D. Kennedy, 'Receiving the International' (1994) 10 Conn. J. Int'l L. 1.
16   Rawls, *supra*, Introduction, note 4; at 14ff.

as the leitmotiv that expresses the aspiration of uniform law: to better know the nature of law and human life. Uniform law exists in order to provide both law and human existence with ever more refined meaning, an ever more solid foundation. This quest for meaning forms the mystery of uniform law, the mystery of law in general and the mystery of life. I intend to further explore these mysteries, prompted by the posture of astonishment which must underlie any such undertaking.

Bibliography

This bibliography includes only the works cited or referred to in the reflection. It is not a list of all works consulted.

Books

Adams, W. M. (1996), *Future Nature: A Vision for Conservation*, Earthscan, London.

Adler, R. A., and Rosenfeld, L. B. (1983), *Interplay: The Process of Interpersonal Communication*, Holt, Rinehart, and Winston, New York.

Adorno, T. (1978), *Dialectique négative*, Payot, Paris. (Trans. G. Coffin of *Negative Dialektik*.)

Altman, A. (1990), *Critical Legal Studies: A Liberal Critique*, Princeton University Press, Princeton.

Apter, D. E. (1987), *Rethinking Development: Modernization, Dependency, and Post Modern Politics*, Sage, New York.

Arendt, H. (1961), *Condition de l'homme moderne*, Calmann-Lévy, Paris. (Trans. G. Coffin of *The Human Condition*.)

Arnaud, A. J. (1998), *Entre modernité et mondialisation. Cinq leçons d'histoire de la philosophie du droit et de l'État*, Librairie Générale de Droit et de Jurisprudence, Paris.

Arocéna, J. (1986), *Le développement par l'initiative locale*, L'Harmattan, Paris.

Aron, R. (1969), *Les désillusions du progrès: essai sur la dialectique de la modernité*, Calmann-Lévy, Paris.

Arrow, K. J. (1963), *Social Choice and Individual Values*, Yale University Press, New Haven.

Atias, C. (1990), *Savoir des juges et savoir des juristes. Mes premiers regards sur la culture juridique québécoise*, Centre de recherche en droit privé et comparé du Québec, Montreal.

Attfield, R. (1991), *The Ethics of Environmental Concern*, University of Georgia Press, Athens.

Axelrod, R. (1984), *The Evolution of Cooperation*, Basic Books, New York.

Aydalot, P. (1980), *Dynamique spatiale et développement inégal*, Économica, Paris.

Bachelard, G. (1991), *Le nouvel esprit scientifique*, 4th ed., Presses Universitaires de France, Paris.

Bacon, F. (1991), *Du progrès et de la promotion des savoirs*, Gallimard, Paris. (Trans. M. Le Doeuff of *The Advancement of Learning*.)

Bakhtin, M. (1981), *The Dialogical Imagination*, University of Texas Press, Austin. (Trans. C. Emerson and M. Holquist of *Voprosy literatury i 'estetiki*.)

Balandier, G. (1988), *Le désordre: éloge du mouvement*, Fayard, Paris.

Barber, B. (1995), *Jihad vs. McWorld,* Times Books, New York.

Barber, B. (1983), *The Logic and Limits of Trust*, Rutgers University Press, New Brunswick.

Barnet, R. J., and Cavanagh, J. (1995), *Global Dreams: Imperial Corporations and the New World Order*, Simon & Schuster, New York.

Bartoli, H. (1991), *L'économie multidimensionnelle*, Économica, Paris.

Beausoleil, C. (1996), *Le motif de l'identité dans la poésie québécoise, 1830-1995*, Le Groupe de création Estuaire, Ottawa.

Bélanger, F. (1990), *La Beauce et les Beaucerons: portraits d'une région, 1737-1987*, Société du patrimoine des Beaucerons, Saint-Joseph-de-Beauce.

Belley, J. G. (1996), *Le droit soluble: contributions québécoises à l'étude de l'internormativité*, Librairie Générale de Droit et de Jurisprudence, Paris.

Bergeron, J. M. (1993) and Sève, S., *La cause verte au Québec*, Presses de l'Université de Sherbrooke, Sherbrooke.

Berman, H. J. (1983), *Law and Revolution: The Formation of the Western Legal Tradition*, Harvard University Press, Cambridge.

Bertalanffy, L. von (1973), *Théorie générale des systèmes*, Dunod, Paris. (Trans. J. Chabrol of General Systems Theory.)

Birnbacher, D. (1995), *La responsabilité envers les générations futures*, Armand Colin, Paris.

Bonell, M. J. (1994), *An International Restatement of Contract Law: The Unidroit Principles of Commercial Contracts*, Transnational Juris Publications, Irvington.

Bonnefous, E. (1990), *Réconcilier l'homme et la nature*, Presses Universitaires de France, Paris.

Bouchard, G. (1999), *La nation québécoise au futur et au passé*, VLB Éditeur, Montreal.

Boudon, R. (1986), *L'idéologie*, Fayard, Paris.

Bourdieu, P. (1994), *Raisons pratiques: sur la théorie de l'action*, Seuil, Paris.

Bouretz, P. (ed.) (1991), *La force du droit: panorama des débats contemporains*, Éditions Esprit, Paris.

Boutinet, J. P. (1990), *Psychologie des conduites à projet*, Presses Universitaires de France, Paris.

Bruneau, J. P. (1990), *Création, développement et continuité des PME: psychanalyse et entreprises*, Agence d'ARC, Montreal.

Brunelle, J. (1985), *Le management de la PME*, Éditions Bo-pré, Montreal.

Brunet, P. (1970), *L'introduction des théories de Newton en France au XVIIIe siècle*, Slatkine, Geneva.

Bruttin, M. D. (1999), *Philosophie politique et justice sociale: une mise en perspective typologique du débat contemporain autour de John Rawls*, Librairie de l'Université, Geneva.

Buchanan, J. M. (1991), *The Economics and the Ethics of Constitutional Order*, University of Michigan Press, Ann Arbor.

Callicott, J. B. (1986), *Defense of Land Ethic: Essays in Environmental Philosophy*, State University of New York Press, Albany.

Cannat, N. (1990), *Le pouvoir des exclus*, L'Harmattan, Paris.

Carbonneau, T. E. (ed.) (1998), *Lex Mercatoria and Arbitration: A Discussion of the New Law Merchant*, Juris Publishing, New York.

Carrilho, M. M. (1997), *Rationalités: les avatars de la raison dans la philosophie contemporaine*, Hatier, Paris.

Carty, A. (1990), *Post-Modern Law: Enlightenment, Revolution, and the Death of Man*, Edinburgh University Press, Edinburgh.

Castells, M. (1983), *The City and the Grassroots*, University of California Press, Berkeley.

Chappuis, R. (1994), *Les relations humaines: la relation à soi et aux autres*, Vigot, Paris.

Chattopadhyaya, D. P. (1989), *Knowledge, Freedom, and Language: An Interwoven Fabric of Man, Time, and World*, Motilal Banarsidass Publishers, Delhi.

Chaussé, R. (1987), *La gestion de l'innovation dans la PME*, G. Morin, Montreal.

Cohen, M. (1996), *Preparing for the Urban Future: Global Pressures and Local Forces*, John Hopkins University Press, Washington, DC.

Collin, P. and Mongin, O. (1998), *Un monde désenchanté?: débat avec Marcel Gauchet sur le 'Désenchantement du monde'*, Éditions du Cerf, Paris.

Charpentier, É. M. and Crépeau, P. A. (1998), *The UNIDROIT Principles and the Civil Code of Québec: Shared Values?*, Carswell, Toronto.

Coulombe, S. and Paquet, G. (eds.) (1996), *La réinvention des institutions et le rôle de l'État*, ASDEQ, Montreal.

D'Ambroise, G. (1997), *Quelle gestion stratégique pour la PME?*, Presses Inter Universitaires, Cap-Rouge.

Dansereau, P. (1994), *L'envers et l'endroi: le désir, le besoin et la capacité*, Fides, Saint-Laurent.

David, R. (1968), *Cours de droit privé comparé*, Les Cours de droit, Paris.

David, R. (1982), *Les avatars d'un comparatiste*, Économica, Paris.

David, R. (1987), *Le droit du commerce international: réflexions d'un comparatiste sur le droit international privé*, Économica, Paris.

Demorgon, J. (1996) *Complexité des cultures et de l'interculturel*, Anthropos, Paris.

Dezalay, Y., Garth, B. G., and Bourdieu, P. (1998), *Dealing in Virtue: International Commercial Arbitration and the Construction of a Transnational Legal Order*, Chicago University Press, Chicago.

Dinwiddy, J. R. (1989), *Bentham*, Oxford University Press, Oxford.

Dixit, A. K. and Norman, V. D. (1980), *Theory of International Trade: A Dual, General Equilibrium Approach*, J. Nisbet, Welwyn.

Domenach, J. M. (1995), *Approches de la modernité*, Ellipses, Paris.

Douzinas, C. and Warrington, R. (1991), *Postmodern Jurisprudence. The Law of the Text in the Texts of Law*, Routledge, London.

Dumont, F. (ed.) (1990), *La société québécoise après 30 ans de changements*, Institut national de la recherche scientifique, Québec.

Dumont, F. (1995), *L'Avenir de la mémoire*, Nuit blanche, Québec.

Dumont, F. (1995), *Raisons communes*, Boréal, Montreal.

Durand, C. (1994), *La coopération technologique internationale*, De Boeck, Brussels.

Dworkin, R. (1986), *Law's Empire*, Belknap, Cambridge.

Elster, J. and Roemer, J. E. (1991), *Interpersonal Comparisons of Well-Being*, Cambridge University Press, Cambridge.

Enderlain, F. and Maskow, D. (1992), *International Sales Law*, Oceana: New York.

Engelhard, P. (1996), *L'homme mondial. Les sociétés humaines peuvent-elles survivre?*, Arléa, Paris.

Epstein, J. J. (1977), *Francis Bacon: A Political Biography*, Ohio University Press, Athens.

Ferry, L. (1995), *The New Ecological Order*, University of Chicago Press, Chicago. (Trans. C. Volk of *Le nouvel ordre écologique: l'arbre, l'animal et l'homme*.)

Fillieule, O. and Péchin, C. (1993), *Lutter ensemble. Les théories de l'action collective*, L'Harmattan, Paris.

Finnis, J. (1980), *Natural Law and Natural Rights*, Clarendon Press, New York.

Fish, S. (1980), *Is There a Text in this Class?: The Authority of Interpretive Communities*, Harvard University Press, Cambridge.

Flax, J. (1990), *Thinking Fragments: Psychoanalysis, Feminism, and Postmodernism in the Contemporary West*, University of California Press, Berkeley.

Forget, D. and Goulet, P. (1997), *Plan d'action vers un développement durable*, ÉcoSommet, Québec.

Fortin, P. (1995), *Innovation endogène et croissance: conséquences du point de vue canadien*, Industrie Canada, Ottawa.

Fourastier, J. (1996), *Les conditions de l'esprit scientifique*, Gallimard, Paris.

Freund, J. (1968), *Sociologie de Max Weber*, Presses Universitaires de France, Paris.

Fried, C. (1981), *Contract as Promise: A Theory of Contractual Obligation*, Harvard University Press, Cambridge.

Friedberg, E. (1993), *Le pouvoir et la règle. Dynamiques de l'action organisée*, Seuil, Paris.

Frye, N. (1973), *The Critical Path: An Essay on the Social Context of Literary Criticism*, Indiana University Press, Bloomington.

Gadamer, H. G. (1965), *Vérité et méthode*, Seuil, Paris. (Trans. P. Fruchon of *Wahrheit und Methode.*)

Galbraith, J. K. (1970), *L'ère de l'opulence*, Calmann-Lévy, Paris. (Trans. G. Coffin of *The Affluent Society.*)

Gaudin, T. (1987), *Le temps du germe: philosophie de l'innovation*, Sophon, Strasbourg.

Gauthier, D. P. and Sugden, R. (1993), *Rationality, Justice and the Social Contract: Themes from 'Morals by Agreement'*, University of Michigan Press, Ann Arbor.

Gay, P. (1967), *The Enlightenment: An Interpretation – The Rise of Modern Paganism*, Knopf, New York.

Geertz, C. (1973), *The Interpretation of Cultures*, Basic Books, New York.

Geertz, C. (1983), *Local Knowledge*, Basic Books, New York.

Gérard, P. (1995), *Droit et démocratie. Réflexions sur la légitimité du droit dans la société démocratique*, Facultés universitaires Saint-Louis, Brussels.

Giddens, A. (1994), *Les conséquences de la modernité*, L'Harmattan, Paris. (Trans. O. Meyer of *The Consequences of Modernity.*)

Goodman, N. (1978), *Ways of Worldmaking*, Hackett Pub., Indianapolis.

Gordon, I. G. (1989), *Changing the Face of the Earth: Culture, Environment, History*, Blackwell, New York.

Gould, S. J. (1996), *Réflexion sur l'histoire naturelle*, Seuil, Paris. (Trans. M. Blanc of *Ever Since Darwin: Reflections in Natural History.*)

Goulet, D. (1995), *Development Ethics. A Guide to Theory and Practice*, Apex Press, New York.

Griffon, K. and Knight, J. (1990), *Human Development and the International Development Strategy for the 1990s*, Macmillan, London.

Grisoni, D. and Maggiori, R. (1973), *Lire Gramsci*, Éditions Universitaires, Paris.

Grzegorczyk, C. (1992), *Le positivisme juridique*, E. Story-Scientia, Brussels.

Habermas, J. (1984), *The Theory of Communicative Action*, Beacon, Boston. (Trans. F. Lawrence of *Theorie des Kommunikativen Handels.*)

Habermas, J. (1986), *Autonomy and Solidarity*, Verso, London.

Habermas, J. (1987), *The Philosophical Discourse of Modernity*, MIT Press, Cambridge. (Trans. F. Lawrence of *Philosophische Diskurs der Moderne.*)

Habermas, J. (1990), *Moral Consciousness and Communicative Action*, MIT Press, Cambridge. (Trans. C. Lehnhardt of *Moralbewusstsein und Kommunikatives Handeln.*)

Habermas, J. (1992), *De l'éthique de la discussion*, Éditions du Cerf, Paris. (Trans. M. Hunyadi of *Erläuterungen zur Diskursethik.*)

Hamlin, A. P. (1986), *Ethics, Economics and the State*, St. Martin's Press, New York.

Hampel, C. G. (1965), *Aspects of Scientific Explanation*, Free Press, New York.

Hampson, N. (1968), *The Enlightenment*, Harmondsworth, London.

Harrison, J. (1976), *Hume's Moral Epistemology*, Clarendon, Oxford.

Hayli, A. (1970), *Newton*, Seghers, Paris.

Heidegger, M. (1951), *Qu'est-ce que la métaphysique?*, Gallimard, Paris. (Trans. H. Corbin of *Was ist Metaphysik?*)

Heuzé, V. (1992), *La vente internationale de marchandises. Droit uniforme*, GLN Joly, Paris.

Hodgson, D. H. (1967), *Consequences of Utilitarianism: A Study in Normative Ethics and Legal Theory*, Clarendon, Oxford.

Hollinger, R. (1985), *Hermeneutics and Praxis*, University of Notre Dame Press, Notre Dame.

Honnold, J. O. (1991), *Uniform Law for International Sales under the 1980 United Nations Convention*, Kluwer, Deventer.

Horkheimer, M. (1974), *Critique of Instrumental Reason: Lectures and Essays since the End of World War II*, Seabury Press, New York. (Trans. M. O'Connel of *Zur Kritik der instrumentallen Vernunft*.)

Horkheimer, M. (1974), *Éclipse de la raison*, Payot, Paris. (Trans. E. Kaufholz of *Dialektik der Reason*.)

Humbert, C. (1976), *Conscientisation. Expériences, positions dialectiques et perspectives*, L'Harmattan, Paris.

Huynh, C. T. (1988), *Développement endogène: aspects qualitatifs et facteurs stratégiques*, UNESCO, Paris.

Institut de la statistique du Québec (2000), *Les PME au Québec. État de la situation 1999*, Éditeur officiel, Québec.

Jacobs, I. (1995), *Systèmes de survie. Dialogue sur les fondements moraux du commerce et de la politique*, Boréal, Montreal. (Trans. C. Teasdale of *Systems of Survival. A Dialogue on the Moral Foundations of Commerce and Politics*.)

Jonas, H. (1995), *Le principe responsabilité. Une éthique pour la civilisation technologique*, Éditions du Cerf, Paris. (Trans. J. Greisch of *Das Prinzip Verantwortung*.)

Joyal, A. (1996), *Des PME et le défi de l'exportation*, Presses Inter Universitaires, Cap Rouge.

Julien, P. A. (ed.) (1994), *Pour des PME de classe mondiale: recours à de nouvelles technologies*, Éditions Transcontinentales, Montreal.

Julien, P. A. (1995), *PME et grands marchés: PME québécoises et françaises face à l'ALENA et au Marché unique*, L'Harmattan, Paris.

Julien, P. A. (1997), *Économie du savoir, emploi et PME*, Université du Québec à Trois-Rivières, Trois-Rivières.

Julien, P. A. and Chicha, J. (1986), *La belle entreprise: la revanche des PME en France et au Québec*, Boréal, Montreal.

Julien, P. A. and Marchesnay, M. (1996), *L'entrepreneuriat*, Économica, Paris.

Julien, P. A. and Morin, M. (1996), *Mondialisation de l'économie et PME québécoises*, Presses de l'Université du Québec, Sainte-Foy.

Kant, I. (1971), *Métaphysique des moeurs*, Vrin, Paris. (Trans. V. Delbos of *Grundlegung zur Metaphysik der Sitten*.)

Kassis, A. (1984), *Théorie générale des usages du commerce*, Librairie Générale de Droit et de Jurisprudence, Paris.

Kassis, A. (1993), *Le nouveau droit européen des contrats internationaux*, Librairie Générale de Droit et de Jurisprudence, Paris.

Kealey, D. A. (1990), *Revisioning Environmental Ethics*, State University of New York Press, Albany.

Kelman, M. (1987), *A Guide to Critical Legal Studies*, Harvard University Press, Cambridge.

Kokis, S. (1996), *Les langages de la création*, Nuit blanche, Montreal.

Koskenniemi, M. (1989), *From Apology to Utopia: The Structure of International Argument*, Lakimiesliiton Kustannus, Helsinki.

Kritzer, A. H. (1989), *Guide to Practical Applications of the United Nations Convention on Contracts for the International Sale of Goods*, Kluwer, Deventer.

Kronman, A. (1995), *The Lost Lawyer: Failing Ideals of the Legal Profession*, Harvard University Press, Cambridge.

Kukathas, C. and Pettit, P. (1990), *Rawls: A Theory of Justice and its Critics*, Stanford University Press, Stanford.

Lamoureux, H. and Panet-Raymond, J. (1984), *L'intervention communautaire*, Éditions Saint-Martin, Montreal.

Lapidus, A. (1986), *Le détour de valeur*, Économica, Paris.

Laprade, Y (1996), *L'histoire des meilleures PME au Québec*, Québécor, Outremont.

Larmore, C. (1987), *Patterns of Moral Complexity*, Cambridge University Press, Cambridge.

Larrère, C. (1997), *Les philosophies de l'environnement*, Presses Universitaires de France, Paris.

Larrère, C. and Larrère, R. (1997), *Du bon usage de la nature. Pour une philosophie de l'environnement*, La Découverte, Paris.

Laslett, P. and Fiskin, J. S. (1992), *Justice between Age Groups and Generations*, Yale University Press, New Haven.

Lauesen, M. (1943), *Le temps de l'opulence*, Stock, Paris.

Le Roy, É., Rouland, N., and Anton, D. J. (1995), *Diversity, Globalization and the Ways of Nature*, International Development Research Centre, Ottawa.

Leclerc, Y. and Blanchet, M. (1992), *Un Québec solidaire: rapport sur le développement*, G. Morin, Boucherville.

Lehman, D. (1992), *Signs of the Times: Deconstruction and the Fall of Paul DeMan*, Poseidon Press, New York.

Ly, F. de (1992), *International Business Law and Lex Mercatoria*, Elsevier Science, North Holland.

Machlup, F. (1983), *Knowledge: Its Creation, Distribution and Economic Significance*, Princeton University Press, Princeton.

MacIntyre, A. (1984), *After Virtue: A Study in Moral Theory*, 2nd ed., University of Notre Dame Press, Notre Dame.

MacKinnon, C. A. (1989), *Toward a Feminist Theory of the State*, Harvard University Press, Cambridge.

Macneil, I. R. (1980), *The New Social Contract: An Inquiry into Modern Contractual Relations*, Yale University Press, New Haven.

Maillat, D. and Perrin, J. C. (eds) (1992), *Entreprises innovatrices et développement territorial*, Éditions de la Division Économique et Sociale, Neuchâtel.

Malouin, J. L. and Gasse, Y. (1992), *L'innovation technologique dans les PME manufacturières*, Institut de Recherches Politiques, Québec.

Mann, P. (1991), *L'action collective. Mobilisation et organisation des minorités actives*, Armand Cloin, Paris.

Mannheim, K. (1959), *Ideology and Utopia*, Harcourt, Brace, New York.

Mappa, S. (1991), *Ambitions et illusions de la coopération Nord-Sud: Lomé IV*, L'Harmattan, Paris.

Martin, R. M. (1979), *Pragmatics, Truth, and Language*, D. Reidel, Boston.

Mathieu, J. (1985), *Approches de l'identité québécoise*, CELAT, Québec.

Mathieu, J. and Lacoursière, J. (1991), *Les mémoires québécoises*, Presses de l'Université Laval, Sainte-Foy.

Max-Neef, M. A. (1991), *Human Scale Development: Conception, Applications and Further Reflections*, Apex, New York.

McClelland, D. C. (1961), *The Achieving Society*, Van Nostrand, Princeton.

Minda, G. (1995), *Postmodern Legal Movements. Law and Jurisprudence at Century's End*, New York University Press, New York.

Ministère de l'Industrie, du Commerce, de la Science et de la Technologie du Québec (1996), *Les PME au Québec: état de la situation, 1996*, Éditeur officiel, Québec.

Ministère de la Recherche, de la Science et de la Technologie du Québec (1999), *Québec. Objectif emploi. Vers une économie d'avant-garde*, Gouvernement du Québec, Québec.

Misztal, B. A. (1996), *Trust in Modern Societies: The Search for the Bases of Social Order*, Polity, Cabridge.

Moessinger, P. (1996), *Irrationalité individuelle et ordre social*, Droz, Geneva.

Moles, A. A. and Rohmer, E. (1986), *Théorie structurale de la communication et société*, Masson, Paris.

Mongeau, S. (1993), *Pour que demain soit: l'écologie sociale en action*, Éditions Écosociété, Montreal.

Morin, E. (1990), *Introduction à la pensée complexe*, ESF Éditeur, Paris.

Morin, E. and Naïr, S. (1997), *Une politique de civilisation*, Arléa, Paris.

Mucchielli, A. and Corbalan, J. A. (1998), *Théorie des processus de la communication*, Armand-Colin, Paris.

Myrdal, G. (1957), *Economic Theory and Underdeveloped Regions*, Duckworth, London.

Naess, A. (1989), *Ecology, Community and Lifestyle: Outline of an Ecosophy*, Harvard University Press, Cambridge.

Nagel, T. (1991), *Equality and Partiality*, Oxford University Press, Oxford.

Norton, B. (1987), *Why Preserve Natural Variety?*, Princeton University Press, Princeton.

Nussbaum, M. and Sen, A. K. (1990), *The Quality of Life*, Clarendon, Oxford.

O'Donnell, R. (1990), *Adam Smith's Theory of Value and Distribution: A Reappraisal*, St. Martin's Press, New York.

Ollivier, B. (1995), *L'acteur et le sujet: vers un nouvel acteur économique*, Desclée de Brouwer, Paris.

Osman, F. (1992), *Les principes généraux de la lex mercatoria. Contribution à l'étude d'un ordre juridique anational*, Librairie Générale de Droit et de Jurisprudence, Paris.

Ost, F. (1995), *La nature hors la loi. L'écologie à l'épreuve du droit*, La Découverte, Paris.

Passet, R. (1996), *L'économique et le vivant*, Économica, Paris.

Pearce, D. and Moran, D. (1994), *The Economic Value of Biodiversity*, Earthscan, London.

Perelman, C. and Olbrechts-Tyteca, L. (1988), *Traité de l'argumentation. La nouvelle rhétorique*, 5th ed., Presses Universitaires de France, Paris.

Petrella, R. (1996), *Le bien commun. Éloge de la solidarité*, Labor, Brussels.

Pitcher, P. (1997), *Artistes, artisans et technocrates dans nos organisations*, Québec-Amérique, Montreal. (Trans. J. P. Fournier of *Artists, Craftsmen, and Technocrats*.)

Poisson, R. (1996), *La stratégie d'internationalisation des PME: état actuel des recherche et perspectives*, Université Laval, Québec.

Popper, K. (1982), *La connaissance objective*, Éditions Complexe, Brussels. (Trans. C. Bastyns of *Objective Knowledge*.)

Popper, K. (1985), *Conjectures et réfutations: la croissance du savoir scientifique*, Payot, Paris. (Trans. M. de Launay of *Conjectures and Regutations: The Growth of Scientific Knowledge*.)

Prévost, P. (1993), *Entrepreneurship et développement local: quand la population se prend en main*, Éditions transcontinentales, Montreal.

Prigogine, I. (1996), *La fin des certitudes*, Odile Jacob, Paris.

Prigogine, I. and Stengers, I. (1979), *La nouvelle alliance: métaphore de la science*, Gallimard, Paris.

Putnam, H. (1984), *Raison, vérité et histoire*, Éditions du Minuit, Paris. (Trans. A. Gerschenfeld of *Realism and Reason*.)

Quinton, A. (1973), *The Nature of Things*, Routledge, London.

Rae, D. (1981), *Equalities*, Harvard University Press, Cambridge.

Rawls, J. (1971), *A Theory of Justice*, Harvard University Press, Cambridge.

Regan, D. (1980), *Utilitarianism and Co-operation*, Clarendon, New York.

Reichenbach, H. (1938), *Experience and Prediction*, The University of Chicago Press, Chicago.

Reichenbach, H. (1955), *L'avènement de la philosophie scientifique*, Flammarion, Paris.

Reiss, T. J. (1988), *The Uncertainty of Analysis: Problems in Truth, Meaning, and Culture*, Cornell University Press, Ithaca.

Reynaud, J. D. (1989), *Les règles du jeu. L'action collective et la régulation sociale*, Armand-Colin, Paris.

Ricoeur, P. (1995), *Le Juste*, Éditions Esprit, Paris.

Riley, J. (1998), *Liberal Utilitarianism: Social Choice Theory and J. S. Mill's Philosophy*, Cambridge University Press, Cambridge.

Robinson, G. and Rundell, J. (eds.) (1994), *Rethinking Imagination. Culture and Creativity*, Routledge, London.

Romano, S. (1975), *L'ordre juridique*, Dalloz, Paris.

Roose, F. de and Parijs, P. van. (1991), *La pensée écologiste. Essai d'inventaire à l'usage de ceux qui la pratiquent comme de ceux qui la craignent*, De Boeck, Brussels.

Roseneau, P. M. (1992), *Post-Modernism and the Social Sciences. Insights, Inroads, and Intrusions*, Princeton University Press, Princeton.

Rothenberg, D. (1993), *Is it Painful to Think? Conversations With Arne Naess*, University of Minnesota Press, Minneapolis.

Ruby, C. (1997), *La solidarité*, Éllipses, Paris.

Samek, R. A. (1981), *The Meta Phenomenon*, The Philosophical Library, New York.

Sartorius, R. E. (1975), *Individual Conduct and Social Norms: A Utilitarian Account of Social Union and the Rule of Law*, Dickenson Publishing, Encino.

Sartre, J. P. (1998), *La responsabilité de l'écrivain*, Verdier, Paris.

Sautet, M. (1995), *Un café pour Socrate*, Robert Laffont, Paris.

Schouls, P. A. (1989), *Descartes and the Enlightenment*, McGill-Queen's University Press, Kingston.

Sen, A. K. (1982), *Choice, Welfare, and Measurement*, MIT Press, Cambridge.

Sen, A. K. (1985), *Commodities and Capabilities*, North Holland, Amsterdam.

Sériaux, A. (1993), *Le droit naturel*, Presses Universitaires de France, Paris.

Sikora, R. I. and Barry, B. (1978), *Obligations to Future Generations*, Temple University Press, Philadelphia.

Simon, Y. and Kuic, V. (1992), *The Tradition of Natural Law: A Philosophe's Reflections*, Fordham University Press, New York.

Smart, C. (1989), *Feminism and the Power of Law*, Routledge, London.

Smart, J. J. C. and Williams, B. (1997), *Utilitarisme: le pour et le contre*, Labor, Geneva. (Trans. H. Poltier of *Utilitarianism, For and Against*.)

Smith, N. K. (1983), *The Philosophy of David Hume*, Garland Publishing, New York.

Sousa Santos, B. de (1995), *Toward a New Common Sense: Law, Science and Politics in the Paradigmatic Transition*, Routledge, New York.

Stanley, J. (1997), *La motivation par l'action: outil essentiel aux fonceurs et aux bâtisseurs de réseaux*, Éditions Un monde différent, Saint-Hubert.

Starr, R. M. (1989), *General Equilibrium Models of Monetary Economics: Studies in the Static Foundations of Monetary Theory*, Academic Press, Boston.

Stoffel-Munck, P. (1994), *Regards sur la théorie de l'imprévision: vers une souplesse contractuelle en droit privé français contemporain*, Presses universitaires d'Aix-Marseille, Aix-en-Provence.

Stoyanovitch, C. (1964), *Marxisme et droit*, Librairie Générale de Droit et de Jurisprudence, Paris.

Tarnas, R. (1991), *The Passion of the Western Mind*, Ballantine, New York.

Taylor, C. (1975), *Hegel*, Cambridge University Press, New York.

Taylor, C. (1989), *Sources of the Self: The Making of the Modern Identity*, Harvard University Press, Cambridge.

Taylor, C. (1992), *Grandeurs et misères de la modernité*, Bellarmin, Montreal. (Trans. C. Melançon of *The Malaise of Modernity*.)

Tellier, L. N. (1997), *Les défis et les options de la relance de Montréal*, Presses de l'Université du Québec, Sainte-Foy.

Todorov, T. (1984), *Critique de la critique: un roman d'apprentissage*, Seuil, Paris.

Touraine, A. (1984), *Le retour de l'acteur*, Fayard, Paris.

Touraine, A. (1992), *Critique de la modernité*, Fayard, Paris.

United Nations (1997), *Loi type de la CNUDCI sur le commerce électronique et Guide pour son incorporation 1996*, United Nations, New York.

United Nations Development Program (1992), *Human Development Report 1992*, Oxford University Press, New York.

Usunier, J. C. (1992), *Commerce entre cultures: une approche culturelle du marketing international*, Presses Universitaires de France, Paris.

Vaillancourt, J. G. and Gendron, C. (1998), *L'énergie au Québec: quels sont nos choix?*, Éditions Écosociété, Montreal.

Veyret, Y. (1993), *L'homme et l'environnement*, Presses Universitaires de France, Paris.

Vinsonneau, G. (1997), *Culture et comportement*, Armand Colin, Paris.

Vuillemin, J. (1971), *La logique et le monde sensible: étude sur les théories contemporaines de l'abstraction*, Flammarion, Paris.

Wallerstein, I. (1995), *Impenser la science sociale: pour sortir du XIXe siècle*, Presses Universitaires de France, Paris. (Trans. A. E. Demartini and X. Papaïs of *Unthinking Social Science: The Limits of Nineteenth-century Paradigms*.)

Waluchow, W. J. (1994), *Inclusive Legal Positivism*, Clarendon Press, Oxford.

Weber, M. (1968), *Basic Concepts in Sociology*, Owen, London. (Trans. H. Secher of *Wirtschaft und Gesellschaft*.)

Weber, M. (1995), *Économie et société*, Pocket, Paris. (Trans. J. Freund of *Wirtschaft und Gesellschaft*.)

Weintraub, E. R. (1985), *General Equilibrium Analysis: Studies in Appraisal*, Cambridge University Press, Cambridge.

Westfall, R. S. (1980), *Never at Rest: A Biography of Isaac Newton*, Cambridge University Press, Cambridge.

Wintrobe, R. and Breton, A. (1982), *The Logic of Bureaucratic Conduct: An Economic Analysis of Competition, Exchange, and Efficiency in Private and Public Organizations*, Cambridge University Press, Cambridge.

Ziman, J. M. (1979), *Models of Disorder: The Theoretical Physics of Homogeneously Disordered Systems*, Cambridge University Press, Cambridge.

Zoll, R. (1992), *Nouvel individualisme et solidarité quotidienne*, Kimé, Paris.

Official Documents

UNIDROIT (1994), *UNIDROIT Principles for International Commercial Law*, UNIDROIT, Rome.

United Nations (1980), *Vienna Convention on Contracts for the International Sale of Goods*, April 11, UN Doc. A/CONF.97/18, Annex I (1980).

United Nations Commission on International Trade (1970), *The International Yearbook of the United Nations Commission on International Trade*, UN Doc. a/CN.9/SERA/1970.

United Nations General Assembly (1966), *General Assembly Resolution 2205 (XXI)*, UN Doc. A/6396.

United Nations Secretary-General (1966), *Progressive Development of the Law of International Trade: Report of the Secretary-General*, UN GAOR, UN Doc. A/6396, 21.

United Nations Secretary-General (1994), *World Summit for Social Development: An Overview Report of the Secretary-General*, UN Doc. A/Conf. 166/PC/6.

Articles

Ackerman, B. (1993), 'Neutralities', in R. Douglas (ed.), *Liberalism and the Good*, Routledge, New York, pp. 193-211.

Amissah, R. (1997), 'The Autonomous Contract', online: University of Tromso <http://ananse.irv.uit.no/trade_law...s.Contract.03.10.1997.Amissah.html>.

Amselek, P. (1968), 'L'étonnement devant le droit', *Archives de philosophie du droit*, Vol. 13, pp. 165-6.

Amselek, P. (1989), 'Le droit dans les esprits', in P. Amselek and C. Grzegorczyk (eds.), *Controverses autour de l'ontologie du droit*, Presses Universitaires de France, Paris, pp. 40-504.

Arnold, B. (1993), 'Challenges Facing Economists in the 21st Century', *Review of Social Economy*, Vol. 48, pp. 48-72.

Atkouf, O., Bédard., R. and Chanlat, A. (1995), 'Management, éthique catholique et esprit capitaliste: l'exemple québécois', in J. P. Dupuis (ed.), *Le modèle québécois de développement économique*, Presses Inter Universitaires, Cap-Rouge, pp. 97-112.

Attfiled, R. (1997), 'Global Warming and International Equity', in J. Parker (ed.), *The European Moral Community*, Avebury, Aldershot, pp. 142-164.

Audit, B. (1990), 'The Vienna Sales Convention and the *Lex Mercatoria*', in T. E. Carbonneau (ed.), *Lex Mercatoria and Arbitration*, Transnational Juris Publications, New York, pp. 139-159.

Axelrod, R. (1981), 'The Emergence of Cooperation Among Egoists', *American Political Review*, Vol. 76, pp. 306-54.

Bannes, F. M. (1996), 'L'impact de l'adoption des *Principes* Unidroit 1994 sur l'unification du droit commercial international: réalité ou utopie?', *Revue de la Recherche. Droit prospectif*, Vol. 21, pp. 933-67.

Baptista, L. O. (1995), 'The Unidroit Principles for International Commercial Law Project: Aspects of International Private Law', *Tulane Law Review*, Vol. 69, pp. 1209-24.

Barnett, R. E. (1992), 'Conflicting Visions: A Critique of Ian Macneil's Relational Theory of Contract', *Virginia Law Review*, Vol. 78, pp. 1175-206.

Barry, B. (1979), 'Justice between Generations', in P. Hacker (ed.), *Law, Morality and Societies: Essays in Honor of H. L. A. Hart*, Oxford University Press, Oxford, pp. 272-94.

Barton, T. D. (1998), 'Creative Problem Solving: Purpose, Meaning, and Values', *California Western Law Review*, Vol. 34, pp. 273-96.

Beauvois, J. L. (1996), 'Les interactionnismes', in G. Mugny and D. Oberlé (eds), *Relations humaines, groupes et influences sociales*, Presses universitaires de Grenoble, Grenoble, pp. 138-65.

Béguin, J. (1985), 'Le développement de la *lex mercatoria* menace-t-il l'ordre juridique international', *McGill Law Journal*, Vol. 30, pp. 478-538.

Behr, V. (1998), 'The Sales Convention in Europe: From Problems in Drafting to Problems in Practice', *Journal of Law and Commerce*, Vol. 17, pp. 263-99.

Bergh, G. C. J. J. van den (1984), 'What Law for Whose Development? – Some Theoretical Reflections on Law and Development', in E. Hondius (ed.), *Unification and Comparative Law in Theory and Practice: Contributions in Honour of Jean Georges Sauveplanne*, Kluwer, Boston, pp. 29-44.

Bergson, H. (1960), *Dictionnaire encyclopédique universel*, Vol. 5, Quillet et Grolier, Paris.

Bélanger, P. and Lévesque, B. (1995), 'La modernité par les particularismes', in J. P. Dupuis (ed.), *Le modèle québécois de développement économique*, Presses Inter Universitaires, Cap-Rouge, pp. 115-45.

Berman, H. (1995), 'The Role of International Law in the Twenty-first Century: World Law', *Fordham International Law Journal*, Vol. 18, pp. 1617-22.

Berthout, A. (1994), 'Remarques sur la rationalité instrumentale', *Cahier d'économie politique*, Vols. 24 & 25, pp. 105-30.

Billette, A. and Carrier, M. (1993), 'Régulation socio-identitaire des activités économiques beauceronnes', *Recherches sociographiques*, Vol. 34, pp. 261-86.

Billette, A. and Carrier, M. (1992), 'L'entrepreneuriat beauceron: les ingrédients du succès', *Revue organisation*, Vol. 2, pp. 27-38.

Birnbacher, D. (1987), 'Ethical Principles versus Guiding Principles in Environmental Ethics', *Philosophica*, Vol. 39, pp. 59-69.

Bloch, E. (1976), Comments on 'La conscience anticipante', in E. Bloch (ed.), *Le Principe Espérance*, Gallimard, Paris, pp. 61-89.

Boggiano, A. (1988), 'The Experience of Latin American International Sales Law', in *International Uniform Law in Practice*, UNIDROIT, Rome, pp. 28-45.

Boltanski, L. and Thévenot, L. (1987), 'Les économies de la grandeur', *Cahiers du centre d'études de l'emploi*, Vol.4, pp. 14-44.

Bonell, M. J. (1987), 'Introduction to the Convention', in M. J. Bonell and G. M. Bianca (eds.), *Commentary on the International Sales Law: The 1980 Vienna Sales Convention*, Guiffré, Milan.

Bonell, M. J. (1990), 'International Uniform Law in Practice – Or Where the Real Trouble Begins', *American Journal of Comparative Law*, Vol. 38, pp. 865-890.

Bonell, M. J. (1995), 'Uniform Law: A Bridge Too Far?', *Tulane Journal of International and Comparative Law*, Vol. 3, pp. 145-175.

Bonell, M. J. (1997), 'The Unidroit Principles in Practice: The Experience of the First Two Years', *Revue de droit uniforme*, Vol. 25, pp. 30-60.

Bouchard, G. (1990), 'Représentations de la population et de la société québécoises: l'apprentissage de la diversité', *Cahiers québécois de démographie*, Vol. 19, pp. 7-70.

Bourdieu, P. (1986), 'La force du droit. Éléments pour une sociologie du champ juridique', *Actes de la recherche en sciences sociales*, Vol. 64, pp. 3-30.

Bourque, G. (1997), 'Le discours sur la nation', *Recherches sociographiques*, Vol. 38, pp. 532-55.

Bourque, G., Duchastel, J., and Kuzminski, A. (1997), 'Les grandeurs et les misères de la société globale au Québec', *Cahiers de recherche sociologique*, Vol. 28, pp. 7-67.

Brilmayer, L. (1996), 'International Justice and International Law', *West Virginia Law Review*, Vol. 98, pp. 611-34.

Brudner, A. (1993), 'Reconstructing Contracts', *University of Toronto Law Journal*, Vol. 43, pp. 1-64.

Buchanan, J. M. (1954). 'Individual Choice in Voting and the Market', *Political Economy*, Vol. 64, pp. 334-365.

Burley, A. M. (1992), 'Liberal States: A Zone of Law', Paper presented to the Annual Meeting of the American Political Science Association, September 3-6, 1992, Chicago.

Burton, T. D. (1998), 'Troublesome Connections: The Law and Post-Enlightenment Culture', *Emory Law Journal*, Vol. 47, pp. 163-236.

Camagni, R. (1993), 'Inter-firm Industrial Networks: The Costs and Benefits of Co-operative Behaviour', *Journal of Industry Studies*, Vol. 1, pp. 1-34.

Carbonneau, T. E. (1984), 'Étude historique et comparée de l'arbitrage: vers un droit matériel de l'arbitrage commercial international fondé sur la motivation des sentences', *Revue Internationale de Droit Comparé*, Vol. 36, pp. 727-81.

Cardinal, L., Couture, C., and Denis, C. (1999), 'La révolution tranquille à l'épreuve de la "nouvelle" historiographie et de l'approche post-coloniale. Une démarche exploratoire', *Globe. Revue internationale d'études québécoises*, Vol. 2, pp. 75-123.

Carraso, E. R. (1994), 'Law, Hierarchy, and Vulnerable Groups in Latin America: Towards a Communal Mode of Development in a Neoliberal World', *Stanford Journal of International Law*, Vol. 30, pp. 221-314.

Cattaui, M. L. (1997), 'The global economy – an opportunity to be seized', online: Business World <http://www.iccwbo.org/html/globalec.htm>.

Charnovitz, S. (1999), 'The Universal Declaration of Human Rights at 50 and the Challenge of Global Markets: The Globalization of Economic Human Rights', *Brooklyn Journal of International Law*, Vol. 25, pp. 113-24.

Chibundu, M. O. (1997), 'Law in Development: On Tapping, Gourding and Serving Palm-Wine', *Case Western Reserve Journal of International Law*, Vol. 29, pp. 167-260.

Chua, A. (1998), 'Markets, Democracy, and Ethnicity: Towards a New Paradigm for Law and Development', Law and Economics Workshop Series, Faculty of Law, University of Toronto, September 16.

Coase, R. (1998), 'Industrial Organization: A Proposal for Research', in R. Coase (ed.), *The Firm, The Market and The Law*, University of Chicago Press, Chicago, pp. 57-83.

Cohen, J. L. (1985), 'Strategy or Identity: New Theoretical Paradigms and Contemporary Social Movements', *Social Research*, Vol. 52, pp. 663-700.

Connerty, A. (1996), 'The Role of ADR in the Resolution of International Disputes', *Arbitration International*, Vol. 1, pp. 41-60.

Conti, S., Malecki, E. J., and Oinas, P. (1995), 'Introduction: Rethinking the Geography of Enterprise', in S. Conti, E. J. Malecki and P. Oinas (eds), *The Industrial Enterprise and its Environment*, Avebury, Aldershot, pp. 280-310.

Cook, V. S. (1997), 'The U.N. Convention for the International Sale of Goods: A Mandate to Abandon Legal Ethnocentricity', *Journal of Law and Commerce*, Vol. 16, pp. 49-82.

Coombe, R. J. (1995), 'The Cultural Life of Things: Anthropological Approaches to Law and Society in Conditions of Globalization', *American University International Law Journal*, Vol. 10, pp. 791-864.

Cooper, J. M. (1998), 'Towards a New Architecture: Creative Problem Solving and the Evolution of Law', *California Western Law Review*, Vol. 34, pp. 297-323.

Cornell, D. (1985), 'Toward a Modern/Postmodern Reconstruction of Ethics', *University of Pennsylvania Law Review*, Vol. 133, pp. 291-380.

Cuerrier, A. (1997), 'Le nouvel esprit scientifique', *Interface*, 18(6), pp. 16-24.

Curran, V.G. (1995). 'The Interpretative Challenge to Uniformity by Claude Witz', *Journal of Law and Commerce*, Vol. 15, pp. 175-194.

Dare, T. (1994), 'Kronman On Contract: A Study in the Relation Between Substance and Procedure in Normative and Legal Theory', *Canadian Journal of Law and Jurisprudence*, Vol. 7, pp. 331-48.

De Marneffe, P. (1990), 'Liberalism, Liberty, and Neutrality', *Philosophy and Public Affairs*, Vol. 19, pp. 253-74.

Delaume, G. (1988), 'The Proper Law of State Contracts and the *Lex Mercatoria*: A Reappraisal', *International Center for the Settlements of Investment Disputes Review*, Vol. 14, pp. 79-101.

Delaume, G. (1989), 'Comparative Analysis as a Basis of Law in State Contracts: The Myth of *Lex Mercatoria*', *Tulane Law Review*, Vol. 63, pp. 575-613.

Derains, Y. (1976), Observations on Sentence CCI 2291, *Journal du Droit International*, pp. 991-993.

Devall, B. (1980), 'The Deep Ecology Movement', *Natural Resources Journal*, Vol. 20, pp. 299-333.

Dodgson, M. (1993), 'Learning, Trust, and Technological Collaboration', *Human Relations*, Vol. 46, pp. 77-95.

Dubouchet, P. (1994), 'Herméneutique et théorie normative du droit', *Revue de la recherche juridique. Droit prospectif*, Vol. 3, pp. 735-60.

Dumont, F. (1990), 'Quelle révolution tranquille', in F. Dumont (ed.), *La société québécoise après 30 ans de changements*, Institut québécois de recherche sur la culture, Québec, pp. 13-36.

Emirbayer, M. (1997), 'Manifesto for a Relational Sociology', *American Journal of Sociology*, Vol. 103, pp. 281-311.

Fallon, R. H. (1997), 'The Rule of Law as a Concept in Constitutional Discourse', *Columbia Law Review*, Vol. 97, pp. 1-56.

Feinman, J. M. (1983), 'Critical Approaches of Contract Law', *University of California at Los Angeles Law Review*, Vol. 30, pp. 829-60.

Feltham, J. D. (1981), 'The United Nations Convention on Contracts for the International Sale of Goods', *Business Law Journal*, pp. 346-374.

Ferrari, F. (1998), 'CISG Case Law: A New Challenge for Interpreters', *Journal of Law and Commerce*, Vol.17, pp. 245-61.

Fort, T. L. (1999), 'The First Man and the Company Man: The Common Good, Transcendence, and Mediating Institutions', *American Business Law Journal*, Vol. 36, pp. 391-435.

Freeman, C. and Perez, C. (1988), 'Structural Crises of Adjustment: Business Cycles and Investment Behaviour', in G. Dosi (ed.), *Technical Change and Economic Theory*, Pinter, London, pp. 38-55.

Friedman, J. (1994), 'Global System, Globalization and the Parameters of Modernity', in J. Friedman (ed.), *Cultural Identity and Global Process*, Sage, London, pp. 10-35.

Gaillard, E. (1995), 'Trente ans de *lex mercatoria* – Pour une application sélective de la méthode des principes généraux du droit', *Journal du Droit International*, Vol. 122, pp. 625-640.

Garro, A. M. (1995), 'The Contribution of the UNIDROIT Principles to the Advancement of International Commercial Arbitration', *Tulane Journal of International and Comparative Law*, Vol. 3, pp. 93-128.

Gertler, M. S. (1987), 'Capital, Technology and Industrial Dynamics in Regional Development', *Urban Geography*, Vol. 8, pp. 251-75.

Gessner, V. (1994), 'Global Legal Interaction and Legal Cultures', *Ratio Juris*, Vol. 7, pp. 132-60.

Giardina, A. (1995), 'Les Principes UNIDROIT sur les contrats internationaux', *Journal du Droit International*, Vol. 122, pp. 547-84.

Glenn, H. P. (1987), 'Persuasive Authority', *McGill Law Journal*, Vol 32, pp. 261-98.

Glenn, H. P. (1989), 'Le droit comparé et la Cour suprême du Canada', *Mélanges Louis-Philippe Pigeon*, Collection Bleue, Ottawa, pp. 199-214.

Glenn, H. P. (1989), 'Unification of Law, Harmonization of Law and Private International Law', in *Liber Memorialis François Laurent*, E. Story-Scientia, Brussels, pp. 781-799.

Glenn, H. P. (1995), 'Harmonization of Private Law Rules Between Civil and Common Law Jurisdictions', *Contemporary Law: Canadian Reports to the 1994 International Congress of Comparative Law*, Éditions Yvon Blais, Cowansville, pp. 79-101.

Goldman, B. (1964), 'Frontières du droit et lex mercatoria', *Archives de philosophie du droit*, Vol. 9, pp. 747-767.

Goldman, B. (1979), 'La *lex mercatoria* dans les contrats et l'arbitrage internationaux: réalité et perspectives', *Journal du Droit International*, Vol. 106, pp. 475-505.

Gordley, J. (1981), 'Equality in Exchange', *California Law Review*, Vol. 69, pp. 1587-656.

Gordon, R. (1985), 'Macaulay, Macneil, and the Discovery of Solidarity and Power in Contract Law', *Wisconsin Law Review*, pp. 565-79.

Granovetter, N. (1985), 'Economic Action and Social Structure: The Problem of Embeddedness', *American Journal of Sociology*, Vol. 91, pp. 481-513.

Griffith, W. B. (1994), 'Equality and Egalitarianism: Framing the Contemporary Debate', *Canadian Journal of Law and Jurisprudence*, Vol. 12, pp. 5-26.

Hamel, G. (1991), 'Competition for Competence and Interpartner Learning within International Strategic Alliances', *Strategic Management Journal*, Vol. 12, pp. 83-112.

Hamel, J. (1990), 'L'économie francophone au Québec à la lumière de la théorie sociologique de la transition', *Sociologie et sociétés*, Vol. 22, pp. 163-90.

Hillman, R. A. (1988), 'The Crisis in Modern Contract Theory', *Texas Law Review*, Vol. 67, pp. 103-36.

Honka, H. (1996), 'Harmonization of Contract Law Through International Trade: A Nordic Perspective', *Tulane European and Civil Law Forum*, Vol. 11, pp. 111-135.

Honnold, J. (1988), 'The Sales Convention in Action – Uniform International Words: Uniform Application?', *Journal of Law and Commerce*, Vol. 8, pp. 207-15.

Honnold, J. O. (1998), 'The Sales Convention: From Idea to Practice', *Journal of Law and Commerce*, Vol. 17, pp. 181-6.

Houle, G. and Hamel, J. (1987), 'Une nouvelle économie politique québécoise francophone', *Cahiers canadiens de sociologie*, Vol. 12, pp. 42-80.

Hunt, A. (1991), 'Marxism, Law, Legal Theory, and Jurisprudence', in P. Fitzpatrick (ed.), *Dangerous Supplements: Resistance and Renewal in Jurisprudence*, Duke University Press, Duke, pp. 12-34.

Huyssen, A. (1984), 'Mapping the Postmodern', *New German Critique*, Vol. 33, pp. 5-27.

Johnson, H. (1996), 'America and the Crisis of Change', *Saint Louis University Law Journal*, Vol. 39, pp. 1143-1162.

Jorde, T. M. and Teece, D. J., 'Innovation, Cooperation, and Antitrust' in T. M. Jorde and D. J. Teece (eds), *Antitrust, Innovation, and Competitiveness*, Oxford University Press, New York, pp. 47-80.

Josserand, L. (1937), 'Vers un ordre juridique nouveau', *Dalloz Chronique*, Vol. 6 pp. 43-46.

Julien, P. A. (1994), 'Pour une définition des PME', in P. A. Julien (ed.), *Les PME. Bilan et perspectives*, Économica, Paris, pp. 21-31.

Julien, P. A. (1994), 'Théorie économiques des PME', in P. A. Julien (ed.), *Les PME. Bilan et perspectives*, Économica, Paris, pp. 41-60.

Julien, P. A. (1995), 'Globalization: Different Types of Small Business Behavior', *Journal of Business Venturing*, Vol. 15, pp. 459-75.

Kahn, P. (1980), 'La Convention de Vienne du 11 avril 1980 sur les contrats de vente internationale de marchandises', *Journal du Droit International*, pp. 951-75.

Kastely, A. H. (1988), 'Unification and Community: A Rhetorical Analysis of the United Nations Sales Convention', *Northwestern Journal of International Law and Business*, Vol. 8, pp. 574-601.

Kennedy, D. (1994), 'Receiving the International', *Connecticut Journal of International Law*, Vol. 10, pp. 1-26.

Kennedy, L. J. (1909), 'The Unification of Law', *Journal of the Society of Comparative Legislation*, Vol. 10, pp. 212-9.

Kerrigan, K. R. (1988), 'Strategic Alliances and Partners Assymetries', *Management International Review*, Vol. 16 , pp. 53-69.

Kessedjan, C. (1995), 'Un exercice de rénovation des sources du droit des contrats du commerce international: les Principes proposés par l'Unidroit', *Revue Critique de Droit International Privé*, Vol. 84, pp. 641-70.

Kleinhans, M. M. and Macdonald, R. A. (1997), 'What is *Critical* Legal Pluralism?', *Canadian Journal of Law and Society*, Vol. 12, pp. 25-46.

Koneru, P. (1976), 'The International Interpretation of the UN Convention on Contracts for the International Sale of Goods: An Approach Based on General Principles', *Minnesota Journal of Global Trade*, Vol. 6, pp. 105-129.

Kreps, D. M. (1990), 'Corporate Culture and Economic Theory', in J. Alt and K. Shepsle (eds), *Perspectives on Positive Political Economy*, Cambridge University Press, Cambridge, pp. 134-69.

Laforest, G. (1995), 'Identité et pluralisme libéral au Québec', in S. Langlois (ed.), *Identité et cultures nationales. L'Amérique française en mutation*, Presses de l'Université Laval, Sainte-Foy, pp. 301-23.

Lalive, P. (1986), 'Ordre public transnational (ou réellement international) et arbitrage international', *Revue de l' arbitrage*, pp. 329-54.

Lavallée, A. and Lafond, C. (1998), 'Les festivals au Québec: entre économie et identité. Le cas d'un festival mondial de folklore', *Loisir et société*, Vol. 21, pp. 213-34.

Lefebvre, G. (1993), 'La bonne foi dans la Convention des Nations Unies sur les contrats de vente internationale de marchandises', *Revue Juridique Thémis*, Vol. 27, pp. 563-79.

Lepart, J. (1997), 'La crise environnementale et les théories de l'équilibre en écologie', in C. Larrère (ed.), *La crise environnementale*, Insitut National de la Recherche Agronomique, Paris, pp. 131-45.

Létourneau, J. (1997), 'Nous autres les Québécois. La voix des manuels d'histoire', L. Turgeon et J. Létourneau (eds), *Les Espaces de l'identité*, Presses de l'Université Laval, Sainte-Foy, pp. 99-123.

Leydet, D. (1997), 'Mondialisation et démocratie: la notion de société civile globale', in F. Crépeau (ed.), *Mondialisation des échanges et fonctions de l'État*, Bruylant, Brussels, pp. 258-75.

Lutz, M. A. (1995), 'Centering Social Economics on Human Dignity', *Review of Social Economy*, Vol. 2, pp. 171-95.

Lyons, B. and Mehta, J. (1997), 'Contracts, Opportunism and Trust: Self-Interest and Social Orientation', *Cambridge Journal of Economics*, Vol. 21, pp. 21-60.

Macaulay, S. (1963), 'Non-Contractual Relations in Business: A Preliminary Study', *American Sociological Review*, Vol. 28, pp. 55-80.

Macaulay, S. (1996), 'Organic Transactions: Contract, Frank Lloyd Wright and the Johnson Building', *Wisconsin Law Review*, Vol. 66, pp. 75-121.

Macdonald, R. A. (1998), 'Metaphors of Multiplicity: Civil Society, Regimes and Legal Pluralism', *Arizona Journal of International and Comparative Law*, Vol. 15, pp. 69-91.

Macleod, C. L. (1994), 'The Market, Preferences, and Equality', *Canadian Journal of Law and Jurisprudence*, Vol. 7, pp. 97-110.

Maclure, J. (1998), 'Authenticités québécoises. Le Québec et la fragmentation contemporaine de l'identité', *Globe. Revue internationale d'études québécoises*, Vol. 1, pp. 9-43.

Macneil, I. R. (1974), 'The Many Futures of Contracts', *Southern California Law Review*, Vol. 47, pp. 691-816.

Macneil, I. R. (1978), 'Contracts: Adjustment of Long-Term Economic Relations Under Classical, Neoclassical, and Relational Contract Law', *Northwestern University Law Review*, Vol. 72, pp. 854-905.

Macneil, I. R. (1983), 'Values in Contract: Internal and External', *Northwestern University Law Review*, Vol. 78, pp. 340-400.

Macneil, I. R. (1985), 'Relational Contract: What We Do and Do Not Know', *Wisconsin Law Review*, Vol. 55, pp. 483-525.

Mapel, D. R. and Nardin, T., 'Convergence and Divergence in International Ethics', in T. Nardin and D. R. Mapel (eds), *Traditions of International Ethics*, Cambridge University Press, Cambridge, pp. 297-323.

Mendes, E. P. (1988), 'The U. N. Sales Convention & U.S.-Canada Transactions: Enticing the World's Largest Trading Bloc to Do Business under a Global Sales Law', *Journal of Law and Commerce*, Vol. 109, pp. 109-30.

Menkel-Meadow, C. (1996), 'The Trouble with the Adversary System in a Post-Modern, Multi-Cultural World', *Journal of the Institute for the Study of Legal Ethics*, Vol. 1, pp. 49-69.

Mestre, J. (1986), 'Obligations et contrats spéciaux', *Revue Trimestrielle de Droit Civil*, Vol. 85, pp. 98-114.

Mischel, K. (1997), 'Webs of Significance: Understanding Economic Activity in its Cultural Context', *Review of Social Economy*, Vol. 54, pp. 67-99.

Monaco, R. (1988), 'Allocution d'ouverture' in Institut international pour l'unification du droit privé (ed.), *Le droit uniforme international dans la pratique*, Oceana, Rome, pp. 3-10.

Moore, G. (1989), 'The Interpretive Turn in Modern Theory: A Turn for the Worse?', *Stanford Law Review*, Vol. 41, pp. 871-957.

Morin, E. (1996) , 'Pour une réforme de la pensée' in *Le Courrier de l'UNESCO*, February, pp. 10-15.

Morris, C. W. (1993), 'What Is This Thing Called Reputation', Working Paper, *Limitation de la rationalité et constitution du collectif*, Colloquim, Cerisy, June 5-12 1993, pp. 9-19.

Mustill, M. (1987), 'The New *Lex Mercatoria*. The First Twenty-five Years', in M. Bos (ed.), *Études Wilberforce*, Oxford U.P., New York, pp. 180-201.

Mustill, M. (1993), 'Keynote Speech' in Albert Jan van den Bergh (ed.) *International Congress for Commercial Arbitration*, Kluwer, Deventer, pp. 23-5.

Nadeau, R. (1994), 'La philosophie des sciences après Kuhn', *Philosophiques*, Vol. 21, pp. 159-73.

Naon, H. G. (1982), 'The UN Convention on Contracts for the International Sale of Goods', in N. Horn and C. M. Schmitthoff (eds), *The Transnational Law of International Commercial Transactions*, Kluwer, Deventer, pp. 89-113.

Nielsen, K. (1998), 'In Defense of Wide Reflective Equilibrium', in D. Odegard (ed.), *Ethics and Justification*, Academic Printing and Publishing, Edmonton, pp. 22-39.

Note. (1993), 'Aspiration and Control: International Legal Rhetoric and the Essentialization of Culture', *Harvard Law Review*, Vol. 106, pp. 723-750.

Nussbaum, M. C. (1998), 'Response: Still Worthy of Praise', *Harvard Law Review*, Vol. 111, pp. 1776-95.

Ohmae, K. (1989), 'The Global Logic of Strategic Alliances', *Harvard Business Review*, Vol. 24, pp. 143-54.

Pannikar, R. (1981), 'Is History the Measure of Man? Three Kairological Moments of Human Consciousness', *The Teilhard Review*, Vol. 16, pp. 39-54.

Pannikar, R. (1977), 'The New Innocence', *Cross Currents*, Vol. 27, pp. 1-10.

Parijs, P. van. (1995), 'La justice entre générations', *Wallonie*, Vol. 41, pp. 7-19.

Paul, J. C. N. (1995), 'The United Nations and the Creation of an International Law of Development', *Harvard International Law Journal*, Vol. 36, pp. 307-88.

Petrella, R. (1989), 'La mondialisation de la technologie et de l'économie: une hypothèse', *Futuribles*, pp. 3-19.

Pieterse, J. N., (1994), 'Globalisation as Hybridisation', *International Sociology*, Vol. 9, pp. 161-75.

Posner, A. (1991), 'Society, Civilization, Mentality: Prolegomena to a Language Policy for Europe', in Coulmas (ed.), *A Language Policy for the European Community*, de Gruyter, Berlin, pp. 124-34.

Postema, G. (1994), 'Implicit Law', *Law & Philosophy*, Vol. 13, pp. 361-87.

Proulx, P. P. (1999), 'L'intégration économique dans les Amériques: quelles stratégies pour tenter d'assurer l'américanité du Québec plutôt que l'américanisation du Québec?', *Politique et sociétés*, Vol. 18, pp. 129-44.

Puchalska-Tych, B. and Salter, M. (1996), 'Comparing Legal Cultures of Eastern Europe: The Need for a Dialectical Analysis', *Legal Studies*, Vol. 16, pp. 157-84.

Randall, K. C. and Norris, J. E. (1993), 'A New Paradigm for International Business Transactions', *Washington University Law Quarterly*, Vol. 71, pp. 599-636.

Rawls, J. (1987), 'The Idea of an Overlapping Consensus', *Oxford Journal of Legal Studies*, Vol. 7, pp. 1-40

Regan Jr., M. C. (1993), 'Reason, Tradition, and Family Law: A Comment on Social Constructionism', *Virginia Law Review*, Vol. 79, pp. 1515-33.

Rhodes, D. J. (1992), 'The United Nations Convention on Contracts for the International Sale of Goods: Encouraging the Use of Uniform International Law', *The Transnational Lawyer*, Vol. 5, pp. 387-399.

Rocher, G. (1998), 'Droits fondamentaux, citoyens minoritaires, citoyens majoritaires', Paper presented at the Colloquium entitled *Droits fondamentaux et citoyenneté – Une citoyenneté fragmentée, limitée, illusoire?*, Onati, May 4-5, pp. 23-41.

Rocque, A. (1988), 'Non-Linear Phenomena', *International Philosophical Quarterly*, Vol. 28, pp. 247-75.

Rosett, A. (1984), 'Critical Reflections on the United Nations Convention on Contracts for the International Sale of Goods', *Ohio State Law Journal*, Vol. 45, pp. 265-305.

Rouland, N. (1994), 'Les fondements anthropologiques des droits de l'Homme', *Revue Générale de Droit*, Vol. 25, pp. 5-47.

Rowlands, I. H. (1997), 'International Fairness and Justice in Addressing Global Climate Change', *Environmental Politics*, Vol. 6, pp. 1-25.

Rucht, D. (1990), 'The Strategies and Action Repertoires of New Movements', in R. Dalton and M. Kuechler, (eds), *Challenging the Political Order*, Oxford University Press, New York, pp. 156-75.

Salbu, S. (1993), 'Parental Coordination and Conflict in International Joint Venture: The Use of Contract to Address Legal, Linguistic and Cultural Concerns', *Case Western Reserve Journal of International Law*, Vol. 43, 221-280.

Salbu, S. (1994), 'True Codes versus Voluntary Codes of Ethics in International Markets: Towards the Preservation of Colloquy in Emerging Global Comunities', *University of Pennsylvania Journal of International Business Law*, Vol. 15, pp. 327-45.

Salbu, S. (1995), 'The Decline of Contract as a Relational Management Form', *Rutgers Law Review*, Vol. 47, pp. 1271-1360.

Samson, C. (1991), 'L'harmonisation du droit de la vente: l'influence de la Convention de Vienne sur l'évolution et l'harmonisation du droit des provinces canadiennes', *Cahiers de Droit*, Vol. 32, pp. 1001-26.

Sax, L. (1978), 'Le petit poisson contre le grand barrage', *Revue Juridique de l'Environnement*, Vol. 5, pp. 368-73.

Scales, A. (1997), 'Disappearing Medusa: The Fate of Feminist Legal Theory?', *Harvard Women's Law Journal*, Vol. 20, pp. 34-56.

Schillaci, C. E. (1987), 'Designing Successful Joint Ventures', *Journal of Business Strategy*, Vol. 8, pp. 59-63.

Schmidt, C. (1997), 'Confiance et rationalité', *Revue d'Économie Politique*, Vol. 107, p. 32.

Scott, A. and Storper, R. (1992), 'Le développement régional reconsidéré', *Espace et Sociétés*, Vol. 66, pp. 7-19.

Seminatore, A. (1995), 'De la crise des fondements au choc des civilisations', *Études Internationales*, Vol. 31, pp. 32-54.

Sen, A. K. (1985), 'Goals, Commitment, and Identity', *Journal of Law, Economics, and Organization*, Vol. 1, pp. 341-55.

Sen, A. K. (1995), 'Culture, Economics and Development', Working Paper, UNESCO, 1995, pp. 1-10.

Sentence CCI 2291 (1976), *Journal du Droit International*, pp. 989-999.

Sentence CCI 2404 (1976), *Journal du Droit International*, pp. 995-1005.

Sentence CCI 2708 (1977), *Journal du Droit International*, pp. 943-955.

Sentence CCI 6281 (1989), *Journal du Droit International*, pp. 1114-1120.

Sève, R. (1988), 'Avant-Propos. La philosophie du droit aujourd'hui'. Archives de philosophie de droit, Vol. 33, pp. 19-22.

Seymour, M. (1998), 'Pour un Québec multiethnique, pluriculturel et multinational', in M. Sarra-Bournet (ed.), *Le pays de tous les Québécois. Diversité culturelle et souveraineté*, VLB Éditeur, Montreal, pp. 219-34.

Smith, J. C. (1993), 'Action Theory and Legal Reasoning', in K. Cooper-Stephenson and E. Gibson (eds), *Tort Theory*, Captus U. P., North York, pp. 104-25.

Snoy, B. (1988), 'Entreprises conjointes et coopération Nord-Sud, expérience de la Banque mondiale' in A. Jacquemin (ed.), *Coopération entre entreprises*, De Boeck, Brussels, pp. 140-54.

Sono, K. (1984), 'UNCITRAL and the Vienna Sales Convention', *International Lawyer*, Vol. 18, pp. 7-15.

Sornarajah, M. (1988), 'Supremacy of the Renegotiation Clause in International Contracts', *Journal of International Arbitration*, Vol. 5, pp. 97-115.

Sousa Santos, B. de (1988), 'Droit: une carte de lecture déformée. Pour une conception post-moderne du droit,' *Droit et société*, Vol. 10, pp. 373-399.

Spanogle, J. A. (1991), 'The Arrival of International Private Law', *George Washington Journal of International Law & Economics*, Vol. 25, pp. 477-522.

Sprigge, T. (1991), 'Are there Intrinsic Values in Nature?', in B. Almond and D. Hill (eds.), *Applied Philosophy: Morals and Metaphysics in Contemporary Debate*, Sage, London, pp. 37-54.

Stephan, P. B. (1999), 'The Futility of Unification and Harmonization in International Commercial Law', *Virginia Journal of International Law*, Vol. 39, pp. 743-97.

Stewart, H. (1995), 'A Critique of Instrumental Reason in Economics', *Economics and Philosophy*, Vol. 11, pp. 57-76.

Sunstein, C. R. (1995), 'Incompletely Theorized Arguments', *Harvard Law Review*, Vol. 108, pp. 1733-72.

Tallon, D. (1994), 'L'inexécution du contrat: pour une autre représentation', *Revue Trimestrielle de Droit Civil*, Vol. 93, pp. 223-38.

Teubner, G. (1988), 'Legal Irritants: Good Faith in British Law or How Unifying Law Ends Up in New Divergences', *Modern Law Review*, Vol. 61, pp. 11-32.

Teubner, G. (1997), 'Breaking Frames: The Global Interplay of Legal and Social Systems', *American Journal of Comparative Law*, Vol. 45, pp. 149-69.

Topco Calasiatic v. *Gouvernement libyen* (1977), *Journal du Droit International*, pp. 350-370.

Trognon, A. (1991), 'L'interaction en général: sujets, groupes, cognitions, représentations sociales', *Connexions*, Vol. 57, pp. 9-23.

Vadcar, C. (1995), 'Relations Nord-Sud: vers un droit international du partenariat?', *Journal du Droit International*, Vol. 122, pp. 599-605.

Valentin, P. (1993), 'Jurisprudence et philosophie du droit', *Revue de la recherche. Droit prospectif*, Vol. 4, pp. 1265-83.

Van Alstine, M. P. (1996), 'Consensus, Dissensus, and Contractual Obligation Through the Prism of Uniform International Sales Law', *Virginia Journal of International Law*, Vol. 37, pp. 1-105.

Van Alstine, M. P. (1998), 'Dynamic Treaty Interpretation', *University of Pennsylvania Law Review*, Vol. 146, pp. 687-793.

Veltz, P. (1990), 'Nouveaux modèles d'organisation de la production et tendances de l'économie territoriale', in G. Benko (ed.), *La dynamique spatiale de l'économie contemporaine*, Éditions de l'espace européen, Paris, pp. 53-72.

Veytia, H. (1995), 'The Requirement of Justice and Equity in Contracts', *Tulane Law Review*, Vol. 69, pp. 1191-207.

Villa, V. (1990), 'Normative Coherence and Epistemological Presuppositions of Justification', in P. Nerhot (ed.), *Law, Interpretation, and Reality: Essays in Hermeneutics and Jurisprudence*, Kluwer, Boston, pp. 431-55.

Wagner, J. M. (1999), 'International Investment, Expropriation and Environmental Protection', *Golden Gate University Law Review*, Vol. 29, pp. 465-538.

Waldron, J. (1989), 'Legislation and Moral Neutrality', in R. Goodin and A. Reeve (eds.), *Liberal Neutrality*, Routledge, London, pp. 79-125.

Wallerstein, I. (1996), 'Social Science and Contemporary Society', *International Sociology*, Vol. 11, pp. 7-29.

Wallerstein, I. (1997), 'Social Sciences and the Quest for a Just Society', *American Journal of Sociology*, Vol. 102, pp. 1241-54.

Wellmer, A. (1996), 'Vérité, contingence et modernité', in J. Poulain (ed.), *De la vérité. Pragmatisme, historicisme et relativisme*, Albin Michel, Paris, pp. 177-95.

Westenberg, J. W. (1990), 'The Quest for Unification', in *Forty Years On: The Evolution of Postwar Private International Law in Europe*, Kluwer, Deventer, pp. 185-200.

Wiener, J. (1999), 'The Transnational Political Economy: A Framework for Analysis',
    online: University   of   Tromso   <http://ananse.irv.uit.no/trade_law...
    or.Analysis.Jarrod.Wiener.UKC.html>.
Williams, J. (1998), 'Is Law an Art or a Science? Comments on Objectivity, Feminism, and
    Power', *American University Journal of Gender, Social Policy and the Law*, Vol. 7, pp.
    373-9.
Williamson, J. G. (1965), 'Regional Inequality and the Process of Natural Development:
    Description of the Pattern', *Economic Development and Cultural Change*, Vol. 13, pp.
    3-17.
Williamson, O. E. (1993), 'Calculativeness, Trust and Economic Organization', *Journal of
    Law and Economics*, Vol. 36, pp. 453-86.
Witt, U. (1998), 'Imagination and Leadership – The Neglected Dimension of an
    Evolutionary Theory of the Firm', *Journal of Economic Behavior and Organization*,
    Vol. 35, pp. 161-75.
Wrengler, W. (1982), 'Les principes généraux du droit en tant que loi du contrat', *Revue
    Critique de Droit International Privé*, Vol. 71, pp. 467-501.
Yamin, F. (1995), 'Biodiversity, Ethics and International Law', *International Affairs*, Vol.
    71, pp. 529-55.
Yelpaala, K. (1993), 'Strategy and Planning in Global Product Distribution – Beyond the
    Distribution Contract', *Law and Policy in International Business*, Vol. 25, pp. 20-100.
Zacher, M. W. and Matthew, R. A. (1995), 'Liberal International Theory: Common Threads,
    Divergent Strands', in C. W. Kegley (ed.), *Controversies in International Relations
    Theory: Realism and the Neoliberal Challenge*, St. Martin's, New York, pp. 107-44.

Newspaper Articles

Bouchard, G. (1999), 'Construire la nation québécoise', *Le Devoir*, 4 September, A9.
Bourque, G. (1999), 'La nation, la société, la démocratie', *Le Devoir*, 3 July, A10.
Delâge, D. (1999), 'Les trois peuples fondateurs du Québec', *Le Devoir*, 24 July, A9.
Denis, J. M. (1995), 'L'ère du mépris', *Le Monde*, 9 December.
Desrosiers, É (1999), 'Une île, une ville est accueilli froidement', *Le Devoir*, 27 May, A1.
Francoeur, L. G. (1999), 'L'Erreur boréale a relancé un débat public', *Le Devoir*, 4 January,
    A2.
Francoeur, L. G. (1999), 'L'avenir de la forêt: la quantité ou la qualité?', *Le Devoir*, 18
    June, C1.
Francoeur, L. G. (1999), 'La forêt boréale est menacée, constate le Sénat', *Le Devoir*, 30
    June 1999, A1.
Jenson, J. (1999), 'De la nation à la citoyenneté', *Le Devoir*, 31 July, A8.
Juteau, D. (1999), 'Le défi de la diversité', *Le Devoir*, 28 August, A9.
Lévesque, K. (1999), 'Une autre superstructure? On est en train de créer un monstre', *Le
    Devoir*, 26 August, A1.
Lévesque, K. (1999), 'Une île, une ville: l'analyse de Harel est contestée', *Le Devoir*, 23
    June, A3.
Taylor, C. (1999), 'De la nation culturelle à la nation politique', *Le Devoir*, 19 June, A10.

Website

International Chamber of Commerce, 'About ICC', online:
<http://www.iccwbo.org/home/intro_icc/introducing_icc.asp>.

Index